AGGREGATE ECONOMICS
and
PUBLIC POLICY

THE IRWIN SERIES IN ECONOMICS

Consulting Editor
LLOYD G. REYNOLDS
Yale University

AGGREGATE ECONOMICS
and
PUBLIC POLICY

BARRY N. SIEGEL, Ph.D.
Associate Dean
College of Liberal Arts, and
Professor of Economics
University of Oregon

Third Edition

1970 *RICHARD D. IRWIN, INC.*
Homewood, Illinois
IRWIN-DORSEY LIMITED, Georgetown, Ontario

THIRD EDITION

First Printing, March, 1970

Library of Congress Catalog Card No. 70–110414

PRINTED IN THE UNITED STATES OF AMERICA

To:
Jetta, Ron, Dan, and Naomi

PREFACE

It is hard to believe that 10 years have passed since the first edition of this book, yet a look in the mirror convinces me that it is true. I do not know that the additional years have brought additional wisdom; however, in this edition I have introduced some major changes. I have simplified the presentation of national income accounting and measurement and reduced from three to one and a half the number of chapters devoted to this subject. In a one quarter or one semester macroeconomics course, an instructor has little time to treat this subject in an elaborate way. He needs only the essentials and they are what I have tried to provide. The two chapters on the consumption function have been completely rewritten and, hopefully, brought up to date by incorporating references to empirical studies and to some of the new consumption function hypotheses. I do not pretend to have given a thorough survey of the vast literature on this topic; nevertheless, the student should be able to move on to this literature with the material provided in the chapters.

The theory of investment, as every teacher of macroeconomic theory knows, is very difficult to teach to junior or senior students. I have never been satisfied with the treatment I gave to this subject in previous editions. In this edition, therefore, I have tried a new tack. I have derived the investment demand schedule from a model which assumes that the investor makes comparisons between the present value of an asset (its demand price) with the cost of acquiring it (its supply price). This approach is, of course, simply an alternative to the one which assumes that the investor compares the marginal efficiency of capital with the rate of interest. Nevertheless, I think it is a more natural way to view the investment decision and, as a result, is easier to understand. Once the investment demand schedule is derived in this manner, it is relatively easy to introduce the alternative view, which I do at the end of the chapter (8).

The final major change is a new concluding chapter discussing the current dispute between the Monetarists and the New Economists. It is my belief that Milton Friedman and his followers have posed a major challenge to orthodox Keynesianism and I felt that a presentation of both his position and the major counterarguments of Keynesians is a fitting climax to a modern text on macroeconomic theory. It may be that a book written from a Keynesian point of view, as is this one, will be seriously out of date 5 or 10 years from now.

The above represent the major changes from the revised edition. I have also made numerous changes and corrections within the other chapters. I have not, however, given in to the temptation to expand the book by including chapters on economic dynamics, especially multiplier-accelerator business cycle models. There is a long chapter on growth; but, essentially, most of the dynamic analysis in this book is confined to verbal descriptions. It is my feeling that, important though they are, multiplier-accelerator models would overly expand the book and make it difficult for the instructor to cover the material in one semester or quarter. The same reasoning underlies my decisions to exclude an otherwise desirable chapter on international problems and to keep the policy chapters brief. I do not expect every instructor to share my beliefs in these matters, but that is the lot of every textbook writer.

Eugene, Oregon
February, 1970

BARRY N. SIEGEL

CONTENTS

Chapter 1

INTRODUCTION TO AGGREGATE ECONOMIC ANALYSIS

Think of the economy as if it were composed of one vast business enterprise, a gigantic household, and a single consolidated government. Imagine also that economic activity is described by the transactions between these entities. The business firm produces and sells a single commodity. In order to produce this commodity, the firm uses labor and other services sold to it by the household. The household uses its income from the sales of these services to buy the produce of the firm. The government also purchases part of the enterprise's production. To do so, it taxes both the household and the firm. If it wishes, the government can use gentler methods: it can borrow from the other two entities or it can even use newly printed money. Either way it can expand its purchases beyond its tax intake. Finally, that part of the enterprise's production which it does not sell to the household and the government it either sells to foreigners or retains for itself. To make their purchases, foreigners either exchange goods with the domestic economy or borrow from it. The business firm finances its retained product by paying the household less than the value household services have produced or by borrowing from the household and using the proceeds to "buy back" some of its own production.

If you now endow the above economy with a huge single bank, a homogeneous bond (or debt instrument), a money supply, a single price for the homogeneous commodity, and a single wage rate for labor (which itself is a homogeneous productive service), you will have an aggregative, or macroeconomic model. After making various behavioral assumptions about the several entities in the model, you will be able to use it to study changes in income, production, employment, the price and wage levels, and the balance of payments of your hypothetical economy. If you are as brave as the common run of economists, you might even use the model to make studies of the real world.

Admittedly, the mental construct of the previous paragraphs is a

1

grand abstraction. The real world economy of the United States contains millions of households and enterprises and thousands of banks and governmental units. These entities deal with a huge assortment of goods and services, each of which carries its own price. Nevertheless, to answer the kinds of questions they ask about the performance of the economy as a whole, economists cannot dwell at the micro level of economic activity. They must use aggregates; otherwise, they will be totally confused.

As an example, consider the following policy problem: In 1964, Congress substantially reduced taxes upon households and the business sector. The main purpose of the reduction was to fulfill President Kennedy's campaign promise to accelerate the growth of the economy. Exactly how the tax cut was to do this is not our concern at the moment. What is important, however, is that Kennedy and his advisors made a diagnosis about the performance of the economy as a whole. Included in this diagnosis was the proposition that the economy was growing at a slower rate than it could if it fully utilized its productive capacity. In order to demonstrate this, the President's Council of Economic Advisors compared a measure of actual aggregate production to a measure of potential aggregate production for the economy. The latter measure was based upon the historical relationship between aggregate employment and production. Given this relationship and its knowledge about aggregate unemployment, the Council was in a position to estimate the output potential for the economy. It found that potential production substantially exceeded actual production.

After finding excess capacity in the economy, the Council proceeded to put this and other information into a macroeconomic model. The information and the model were then used to develop an explanation and cure for the shortfall of production. This policy exercise required the Council to make use of the abstract method of aggregate economics; for, if it had not, the Council would have had to base its judgments upon an exhaustive study of each enterprise in the economy. Even if such a detailed study were possible, it would have yielded little useful information. The Council would simply have had a clutter of information about a vast number of different activities. To weave this information into a meaningful pattern would have required a method of summarizing it, and this would have required the construction of a theoretical basis for summarization. In short, the Council would have been driven to create an aggregative or macroeconomic model. It is only with such a model that comprehensible statements can be made about the workings of the economy as a whole.

Characteristics of Macroeconomic Models

A macroeconomic model is a device for interpreting the collective behavior of groups of economic entities. The purpose of such a device is to picture how these groups interact and to predict the consequences of the interaction. In the model sketched out in the first two paragraphs of this chapter, for example, business firms, consumers, governments, and foreigners were aggregated into separate groups. These groups were then supposed to interact by means of a set of transactions in goods, services, taxes, and loanable funds. The model requires more in the way of assumptions about the behaviors of each of the groups before it can be used to make statements about the consequences of the interactions between the groups. We shall provide these assumptions later in the book; here, we simply note that we construct models for the purpose of explaining a particular set of consequences of group interaction: the way in which income, production, consumer and business demand, and price and wage levels are determined in the economy.

A macroeconomic model never conforms exactly to the economy. It is and is meant to be an approximation to the real world. Grouping people and institutions into common classes implies that economic actors so grouped have common functions and common behaviors. A theoretical system which separates households from business firms, for example, assumes that there is an institutional separation between production and consumption. Even in the United States this is not wholly correct. There is a fringe of subsistence farmers whose economic lives barely touch the money economy. Also, consumers hold capital in the form of houses, automobiles, and other durables. The flow of services produced by this capital is part of the economy's aggregate production, but the services are not actually bought by households with a money transaction. They simply accrue to households as a consequence of household possession of capital goods. Despite these and other examples, macroeconomic models purporting to describe the performance of the American economy almost always provide for a separate business and household sector. The reason is that such a separation is more descriptive of the actual state of affairs than a model which combines the two sectors.

The assumption of common behaviors of entities *within* each group is also a grand simplification. It is usual to assume, for example, that business firms act as if they are perfectly competitive and that they strive to equate marginal costs with the prices of their products in order to maximize profits. This is obviously not true for a large fraction of firms in the economy. The business population of the United States contains many firms possessing monopolistic or oligopolistic powers, and these firms do not equate marginal costs with the prices of their products. Moreover, it is not clear that they even attempt to maximize their profits.

This situation creates several problems for the analyst who wishes to construct an aggregative model. In order to keep things manageable, it is desirable to hold the number of groupings down. If business is split into two sectors, each behaving according to a different principle, the resulting analysis becomes much more complicated, since the number of interactions which must be considered is more than double, assuming that the two business sectors now interact with each other as well as with each of the nonbusiness sectors. Moreover, once having recognized that heterogeneity of the business population justifies two business sectors, it is but a small step to justify the splitting of the sector into three, four, or even more sectors. With each new split the complications grow and the aggregative nature of the model is compromised. Moreover, the application of the model to the real world becomes increasingly difficult, for it becomes necessary to sort out business firms according to the different behaviors assumed in the model.

The same general remarks apply to the other groupings or sectors the analyst may wish to include in his model. The household sector is also heterogeneous. Households may be rich, poor, urban, rural, white, nonwhite, wage earning, salaried, large, small, and so on. Indeed, every household possesses a combination of these characteristics, and households with different combinations may behave in significantly different ways. Similar considerations attach to the government sector, which history has richly endowed with different levels and different forms.

The economist copes with diverse behavior within his groupings by depending upon the stability of average behavior. Thus, although the household sector is composed of various subgroups (distinguished by different income levels, different ages, places of residences, jobs, religions, and so forth), an economist interested in studying the relation between household spending and household income may still lump them all together on the ground that the average spending behavior of the group is likely to show some stability. So long as the structure of the household sector remains relatively unchanged, this assumption will usually work. But, over long stretches of time, significant structural changes usually do take place, and the economist will then be forced to complicate his analysis by taking such changes into account.

One virtue of macroeconomic reasoning is that it permits us to deal with logical pitfalls concerning the relationship of the whole as related to its parts. There are many variants of this problem, but here we mention only a few. A given firm or industry can increase its output by employing more resources; but, if resources are fully employed in the economy more resources can be had in one industry only by drawing down those being used elsewhere. Hence, on net, output for the economy may not change at all. An individual or group of individuals may increase its wealth by saving more, but if its acts of saving reduce the income of other people, the latter may be forced to reduce their saving and wealth accumulation. The result may well be no net change in community wealth accumulation. One individual can increase his spending by acquiring more money, but if the money stock for the economy is fixed, all individuals cannot use this route to expand their outlays. An individual may go into debt, but if all borrowing is internal to the economy, there cannot be a net increase of debt in the economy, because for every debtor there is a creditor. These and other similar relationships form an important part of aggregative economic analysis.

Finally, we note the difference between macroeconomics and microeconomics. Microeconomics is concerned with the behavior of individual firms and industries and with the behavior of individual consumers. It is devoted to an understanding of how firms and households interact to allocate resources and to an understanding of how relative prices are formed. To contrast the two subjects, macroeconomics deals with aggregate output, aggregate employment, average price, and average wage levels, while microeconomics devotes itself to the mix of output, to the mix of employment, to relative prices, and to relative wage payments. This contrast is, of course, a bit too strong. Aggregative analysis does make use of microeconomic theory. For example, it draws upon microeconomic theory for propositions about business and household behavior; but, since macroeconomic theory is interested in statements about the economy as a whole, it does not use these propositions in order to make statements about its individual parts. Macroeconomics, in short, chases a different hare.

The Income Concept

We shall need many concepts in the course of our study, but it is important now to set out a few. We begin with the notion of income. The income of an individual consists of earnings which result from his participation in productive activity. The income of a country is the aggregate of the incomes of the individuals who are residents of the country. They earn their incomes by offering their labor or the services of their property to the productive process.

Note the emphasis upon the link between production and income in this definition. A man may receive money receipts in the form of gifts or transfers from other individuals or from the government, but these receipts are not included as part of income from an aggregative point of view. One man's gain is another man's loss. Unless the transfer of money signifies the exchange of a service, we do not count it as income from a social point of view. Indeed, the earning of income may not even involve a transfer of money. Some people work for payment in kind from others or from themselves (as in the case of subsistence farmers). Households, as noted above, possess all sorts of property the services of which accrue directly to their owners. As a matter of principle, we ought to count such services as part of the community income, but statistical problems prevent us from doing a good job of it. As we shall see, the national income statistics of the United States do capture some of these payments in kind, but by no means all.

Our definition also excludes from income the money a person may realize from a capital gain. A capital gain is the benefit a person receives from the changes in the market price of an asset he holds, such as a stock certificate in a corporation. Since such gains (or losses) are not related to productive activity, they are excluded from our concept of income.

Finally, any reasonable definition of income must account for wear and tear on capital assets. If a portion of a person's assets are used up during the period in which he earns his income, his earnings do not represent a clear gain. Some of the earnings must be devoted to the repair, maintenance, or replacement of assets, or else future earning power will be reduced. Our definition of income must therefore be amended to allow for the expense of maintaining capital.[1]

Income is a "flow" concept. It has a time dimension. A person earns so much per year, per day, per hour, or even per minute. The period of time used for accounting is largely arbitrary. Conceptually, however, it can be extended or reduced according to the needs of the discussion at hand. In macroeconomic discussions, periods of a year or a quarter of a year are typical, mainly because most of the available data are rooted to these periods. The reader should be warned, however, that some theoretical discussions collapse the period to an instant and talk about the rate of income flow at that instant. An analogy is the concept of speed or velocity. The velocity of an automobile is the distance covered

---

1 Logically, a person's outlays in maintaining himself as a worker ought to be treated as an expense. In practice, however, it is extremely difficult and probably impossible to sift out of a man's consumption spending the amount which should be allocated to his maintenance. To do so would imply the existence of some objective standard by which basic needs can be estimated for a large variety of people. Since no acceptable standard exists, social accountants typically avoid making such estimates.

by it over a given period of time. At a particular instant, however, the speedometer of a moving automobile will record a certain velocity. Over an hour, the speed of the car is an average of the velocities of all the instants in the hour. So it is with income. Over a period of time, the income of the period is an average of the rates of income flow of all the instants during the period.

For an individual, money income represents command over goods and services. It is generally assumed by economists that people work, or offer the services of their property, in order to gain such command. This is not altogether true. People may receive direct enjoyment from their work, in which case some of their money income may be a bonus, since they would be willing to offer the same amount of services for less pay. In any event, bonus or not, money income provides people with generalized purchasing power which can be converted into a large variety of goods and services designed to satisfy their wants. Direct psychic income, such as enjoyment of work, does not have this property.

The exercise of money income for purposes of want satisfaction may take place during the same period in which income is earned, but it also may be deferred if people so choose. Deferred gratification of wants is accomplished by saving. Saving is accomplished by the placement of a portion of income into financial assets, such as money, savings deposits, stock certificates, bonds, or by purchasing durable tangible assets, such as a house or an automobile. Generally speaking, except for money, financial assets yield future income in a money form, which is a generalized command over goods and services in the future. Tangible assets yield their returns in kind. In order to convert these services into money the asset must be rented.

When prices of goods and services are changing, money income does not represent an invariant measure of command over goods and services. If prices double, the same money income commands only half the goods and services it did before the doubling of prices. It is therefore common to adjust money income for changes in prices. How this is done we shall discuss later. For now, it suffices to recognize that *real income*—money income adjusted for changes in prices—is the best measure of income considered as command over goods and services.

Production and Income

The previous discussion stressed the link between production and income. Actually, when income and production are properly defined from a social point of view, there should be no difference between the two. Production entails the use of services provided by resource (labor and property) owners for the purpose of creating goods and services. These goods and services have value, and the productive services rendered by resource owners should reflect the values created in the production process.

The meaning of the above comment is best understood with an example. Suppose there are just two firms in a Liliputian economy. The firms are distinct from the household sector, which provides the labor and property used by the firms. The two statements below summarize a year's production activity for the two firms. Each firm received money from sales to the household sector and from sales of raw and semifinished materials to the other firm. In addition, part of each firm's output was devoted to increasing its inventories of finished and semifinished goods. In the parlance of economic accounting, the goods sold to households and the goods added to inventories represent *final goods*, in the sense that they did not enter into the production of goods produced during the year. The raw and semifinished goods sold to the other firm were not "final" in this sense. Instead, along with labor and property services, they were embodied in the goods produced by the other firm during the year. Because of this, such goods are called *intermediate goods.*

How do we calculate the value of production in the economy? One method would be merely to add the total value of Firm A's production to that of Firm B—$125 million plus $90 million equals $215 million.

Firm A Production Statement in Millions of Dollars

Allocations		*Receipts*	
Purchases from Firm B	30	Sales to:	
Wages and salaries	50	Households	95
Interest payments	5	Firm B	20
Depreciation and		Inventory increase	10
capital maintenance	25		
Profit	15		
Total allocations	125	Value of production	125

Firm B Production Statement in Millions of Dollars

Allocations		*Receipts*	
Purchases from Firm A	20	Sales to:	
Wages and salaries	40	Households	55
Interest payments	5	Firm A	30
Depreciation and		Inventory increase	5
capital maintenance	10		
Profit	15		
Total allocations	90	Value of production	90

But, this is surely wrong. For its $125 million of output Firm *A* used $30 million of intermediate goods produced by Firm *B*. Likewise, Firm *B*'s product reflects $20 million worth of goods created by Firm *A*. What we should calculate is the *value added* by each firm to the intermediate products bought from the other firm. Total production for the economy would then be:

Value Added
(in millions of dollars)

Firm *A* .... 125 − 30 = 95
Firm *B* .... 90 − 20 = 70
Economy .... 215 − 50 = 165

Deducting the cost of intermediate goods from the gross value of production gives a correct measure for calculating the economy's output because it avoids counting the same production twice. Actually, we could have arrived at the same figure by counting only the final goods produced during the year. For example, in our hypothetical economy the two firms sold $150 million worth of goods to households and accumulated $15 million in inventories. These figures sum to $165 million, the same figure arrived at by the value added method. This will always be true: *the value of all final goods produced in an economy during the year is always equal to the value added to intermediate goods used in production during the year.*

The next step is to link income with production. Notice that for each firm production entailed various expenses: raw materials purchased from the other firm, wage and salary payments, interest on borrowed money, and depreciation of capital goods used in production. The value of production less these expenses left a certain profit for the year's activity. Now, wage and salary payments, interest, and profits represent income earned in the economy. If we add depreciation of capital to income earned, we get a number equal to the value added by production in the economy:

| | *Payments in Millions of Dollars* | | |
Item	*Firm A*	*Firm B*	*Total*
Wages and salaries	50	40	90
Interest	5	5	10
Depreciation	25	10	35
Profits	15	15	30
Total	95	70	165

One more calculation is necessary to arrive at net income for the community. Recall that we defined net income to be equal to earned income minus the expense necessary to maintain capital. If the two firms had disregarded depreciation of their capital, profits in the economy would have been $65 million rather than $30 million, hence we could have maintained that the value of production and earned income in the economy were identically equal. But, this is bad practice. Since depreciation of capital *is* an expense, we must deduct it from both production and earned income in order to get an honest statement of the value of income and production for the economy. By making such a deduction, we are treating capital used up as if it were an intermediate good, except that it is "bought" from a firm's assets rather than from the current output of other firms. It follows that net income—gross earnings minus depreciation of capital—has an image in a net value added by production figure.[2] In our example, net income and net value added are $130 million.

Wealth and Income

Income and production are concepts which must be kept distinct from another important concept—wealth. Wealth is the *source* of income. It is composed of physical and human assets whose services make it possible to transform raw materials and energy into a flow of production and income. Wealth takes various forms. Nonhuman wealth consists of machines, buildings, land, libraries, roads, and so forth. Human wealth is embodied in men in the form of physical and mental health and, most importantly, knowledge. Both human and nonhuman wealth are indexes of a country's *capacity* to generate income, but they should not be confused with the concept of income itself.

Another important point: wealth is a timeless concept. In this sense it also differs from income. Recall that income is inherently a flow concept, relating earnings to a unit of time. We cannot do this with the notion of wealth. Perhaps a common analogy will help. The amount of water in a lake is, like wealth, a timeless "stock" concept. But a river draining the lake has its flow measured in so many gallons per unit of time. The flow of income, like that of the river, has a time dimension.

---

[2] From a statistical point of view, measurement of gross earned income is more accurate than the measurement of net income. This is because depreciation of capital—physical wear and tear and obsolescence—is extremely difficult to measure. National income statisticians make various estimates of the rate of depreciation of the nation's capital stock, but the degree of accuracy of such estimates is hard to assess.

It is also important to make a distinction between individual and community wealth. An individual counts as wealth all of his financial and tangible assets (as well as his health and skills); but, his financial assets are really claims to physical assets held by someone else. A share of stock, for example, is a claim against the assets of a particular company. It follows that we cannot simply add up individual assets to arrive at total community wealth, since by doing so we would be counting some items twice. The proper procedure for arriving at national wealth is to deduct from the total of individual wealth those items which represent claims—such as stocks and bonds—against wealth held by others.

Consumption, Saving, and Investment

Wealth is the source of income, but it is from income that a community derives its wealth. Consider what happens to the stream of production or income emanating from the community's stock of wealth. Part of that stream, we indicated earlier, usually goes to repair, maintain, or replace the capital which is used up in the process of production. The resulting net income is available for two purposes. It can be embodied in more wealth, or it can be used for the enjoyment of those to whom it accrues. When net income is devoted to the accumulation of wealth, we call the activity *saving*. When it is used for enjoyment, we call the activity *consumption*. Consumption and saving are competing activities, since when net income is consumed a society cannot accumulate wealth.

What forms can saving take? As already indicated, saving for an *individual* represents accumulation of money, savings deposits, stocks, bonds, insurance, and various forms of physical capital. From a social point of view, however, saving makes sense only insofar as it represents the accumulation of physical (or human) capital.[3] Financial assets are not usually considered a source of real income for the community taken as a whole.

This discussion brings up the concept of *investment*. There are many meanings to this term, hence we must be careful to indicate the sense in which it will be used here. By "investment" we shall mean the act

---

[3] Human capital accumulation is rarely measured. For an attempt, however, see T. W. Schultz, "Capital Formation by Education," *Journal of Political Economy,* December, 1960. Note, also, that we are speaking here of a closed economy. If a nation accumulates financial claims against another, it is also accumulating claims against the output of that economy and, hence, is richer.

of acquiring newly produced capital goods. The amount of investment undertaken by a society is simply the value of such goods accumulated during a given period of time. Investment from a social point of view, then, is nothing more than what we have defined as social *saving*. The reason we retain the two terms, however, is that, from an individual point of view, the two terms describe different acts. Individual saving represents the act of "nonconsuming," the purchase of financial or real assets. From a social point of view, however, an individual's purchase of financial assets does not necessarily represent or lead to investment.

Finally, it is also important to distinguish between gross and net investment. *Gross investment* refers to *all* capital outlays, whether they be for maintaining, repairing, or replacing worn-out capital or for adding to the community's stock of wealth. *Net investment* refers only to the part of gross investment which represents wealth accumulation (what we defined as simply investment). The distinction between gross and net investment is important because it reminds us that just because a society is purchasing capital goods it need not be growing richer. For, if a society is not spending enough to cover the capital it is using up, net investment will be *negative:* the society will be impoverishing itself.[4]

Interactions between Households and Business

At this point we need to place some of the concepts discussed previously in a framework which, at least at a simplified level, gives us a view of the overall operation of the economy. The essence of what we want to learn can be captured by a simple model containing only a household sector and business sector. Complications introduced by the presence of government and foreign trade can be introduced later.

Think of an economy in which firms and households are consolidated into two great sectors. Between the business and household sectors there exists two sets of exchanges, as depicted in Figure 1.1. Households sell productive services to business in exchange for money income. Business sells final goods and services to households in exchange for money receipts. The figure is suggestive. It carries with it the implication that, so long as households respend their earned incomes, business will be

---

[4] Actually, this is not altogether true, since part of a community's gross investment outlays are usually devoted to technologically improved capital goods. Such outlays can enhance the community's productive capacity even though they do not actually add to the physical resources embodied in the community's stock of wealth. Under certain conditions, then, it is quite possible for a society to grow richer even though its net investment is negative.

FIGURE 1.1

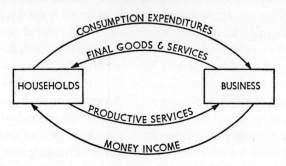

stimulated to provide enough employment to sustain a constant level of household income. Whether or not this happens, of course, depends upon the profitability of production. If business considers its profits satisfactory, it will have incentive to maintain employment and production. If profits are not satisfactory, employment and production (hence household income) will be adjusted to the level at which profits become satisfactory.

Economic theory postulates that employers seek to maximize profits. Suppose that we now envisage a situation in which, after having sustained production at a certain level for some time, firms perceive a chance to raise their profits by expanding output. Our little model shows the consequences of this decision. Extra production entails additional employment of household services. In turn, household income and household expenditures rise. If households respend all of their additional income, all of the additional products will be sold. In short, if households behave themselves by spending all of their earned income, the business sector will have been justified in expanding its output.

We can also conceive of a stimulus to the economy emanating from the household side. Suppose households, drawing on money savings accumulated in the dim past, decide to spend more than their current earnings. If businessmen perceive in this extra demand a chance to increase profits, they will be stimulated to expand output and employment. In the process, consumers will receive extra income which, if they wish, can be used to sustain the new level of consumption and production.

The story of economic activity is obviously much more complicated than the one told by our simple model. Nevertheless, consideration of this ultra simple economy allows us to highlight one important principle: The flow of money income in the economy is largely governed by the flow of spending, and the flow of spending is largely governed by the level of income. Income, so to speak, sustains itself by providing a basis for spending. In the process of spending, households activate the production processes which create the income upon which their expenditures are based. So long as this income-expenditure mechanism functions as described in our simple model, the economic system can sustain any given level of production and employment.

Unfortunately, the income-expenditure mechanism cannot, by itself, explain how the level of production is determined. For one thing, the flow of output in the economy is ultimately limited by the availability of productive services—if you like, the existing stock of physical and human capital—and the efficiency with which these services are used in the production process. The *money* income-expenditure mechanism can propel aggregate *real* income up to this limit, but not beyond. Further advances must await increases in physical capital, the labor force, or improvements in technology.

Another problem is that households may not spend all of their earned income. Instead, they may save part of it in the form of money balances, securities, or deposits in savings institutions. To the extent this happens, the business sector will not experience a demand for goods equivalent in value to what it has produced (recall that value added by production equals income). This means that the business sector must find an additional market for its production; otherwise it will be moved to contract output and employment (hence income).

Fortunately, business itself provides a market for part of final output. It does so in two forms: the purchase of fixed capital goods—plant and equipment—and inventories of finished and semifinished goods to be carried over for future sales. Taken together, these purchases constitute business investment demand. Investment and consumption demand, taken together, constitute total demand for final goods and services in our simple economy. Figure 1.2 replaces Figure 1.1 as a description of the flow of economic activity.

How is the flow of economic activity maintained in this more complex situation? It is clear from the diagram that so long as business investment demand offsets household saving, economic activity can go on at an undiminished pace. Should investment demand fall short of saving, however, *total* demand will fall short of aggregate production, and businessmen will be moved to reduce employment. A contraction of this sort can emanate from an increase in household saving (a decrease in consumption) which is uncompensated for by an increase in business investment demand. It can also result from a decline in invest-

FIGURE 1.2

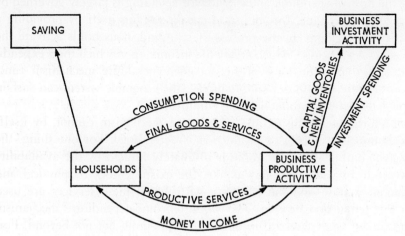

ment demand which is not offset by a decrease in saving (an increase in consumption). By parallel reasoning, we can say that increases in investment spending or reductions in saving stimulate production and income. It appears, then, that a balance between saving and investment demand is a necessary condition for maintaining any particular flow of activity.

As we shall soon see, balance between saving and investment demand is indeed a condition for income maintenance. But it is important to emphasize here that there is no reason to expect such balance to be achieved automatically in the economy. For the most part, saving in the economy is done by a different group and for different reasons than is investment. Households accumulate savings for future consumption, or in order to leave estates for future generations. Business invests to provide a basis for expanding output and profits in the future. In order to assure a balance between saving and investment demand, an efficient capital market is needed to translate the financial savings of households into financial resources for business investment spending. This is the job of financial intermediaries (banks, savings institutions, insurance companies) and stock and bond markets. There is no assurance, however, that the institutions of the capital market can always do their job efficiently and smoothly. Indeed, history argues otherwise. In the real world, therefore, one ought to expect expansion and contractions of economic activity which stem from the lack of balance between investment demand and saving.

Equality between Realized Investment and Saving

At this point there may be some confusion in the reader's mind over the distinction between saving and investment. Earlier, we argued that social saving and social investment are really the same thing—that what it not consumed out of a nation's output must have gone into the accumulation of wealth or investment. In the previous section, however, fluctuations in income and employment were attributed to lack of balance, or equality, between household saving and business investment demand. If social saving and investment are always equal (indeed, identical), how can there be such a lack of balance?

The paradox is rooted in semantics, not logic. The semantic problem lies in the concept of investment. As used in the previous section, investment meant investment *demand,* or *intended* business investment. Intended and realized investment are not the same thing. Intended investment need not equal saving. Realized investment will always equal saving.

Consider the hypothetical information contained in the accounts below for our simple economy. The numbers in the accounts refer to realized magnitudes. Investment (net of depreciation) is equal to saving for the economy, as it should be. Suppose, however, that households had saved $40 billion rather than $30 billion, while business had *tried* to maintain $30 billion of investment (purchases of new capital goods plus new inventories). In this case, as argued above, business would have been producing (and paying out in income) more than it would have been receiving back in demand. For, instead of $100 billion, consumer

Household Sector in Billions of Dollars

Allocations		Receipts	
Consumption	100	Earned income	130
Saving	30		
Total	130	Total	130

Business Sector in Billions of Dollars

Allocations		Receipts	
Payments to households (wages, interest, rent, profits)	130	Sales to consumers	100
		Sales to business [capital goods (net of depreciation)]	20
		Change in inventories	10
Net income	130	Net value of production	130

spending would have been $90 billion. This would have meant that business would have had an *extra* $10 billion of inventories beyond the $10 billion it *desired* to accumulate. *Realized* investment, then, would have been $40 billion, not $30 billion.

A parallel argument for decreases in saving would show that undesired inventory reductions also lead realized investment into a necessary equality with saving. The point is that when we speak of social saving as being identical with investment for the nation, we are speaking of realized magnitudes, not intended ones.

An algebraic formulation of the point may help: Let Y, C, S be income, consumption, and saving,[5] respectively. Let I_r be realized investment, consisting of I_i, intended investment, and I_u, or unintended investment (unintended inventory accumulation). Our previous definitions (verify with the accounts in this section) say that:

$$Y \equiv C + I_r \tag{1}$$
$$Y \equiv C + S \tag{2}$$
$$I_r \equiv I_i + I_u . \tag{3}$$

The equation for identity (1) simply says that all final goods and services produced are sold to households (consumption) and business (investment). The equation for identity (2) says that income (equal to value of final goods produced) is allocated by households to consumption and saving (nonconsumption). Identities (1) and (2) imply that

$$S \equiv I_r \tag{4}$$

But the equation for identity (4) merely says that saving and realized investment are necessarily equal. It does *not* say that $S = I_i$ (that saving and intended investment are equal). This will be true only if $I_u = 0$. As we have seen, this condition is not necessarily true. $S = I_i$ (with $I_u = 0$) is a condition for maintaining a given flow of income, but it is not an accounting identity. $S \equiv I_r$ (with $I_u = 0$ or $\neq 0$) *is* an accounting identity.

Expansion of the Simple Model

An approach to reality complicates the description of economic activity provided by the simple model of the previous sections. The basic nature of the process nevertheless remains the same. Adding a govern-

---

[5] In this analysis, we are assuming that households base their saving decisions on current income and that their realized saving equals their intended saving. If households base their saving plans on previous income, it is quite possible for their realized saving to differ from intended saving, particularly if current income differs from previous income.

ment sector, for example, adds an additional source of production and an additional source of demand for the products of the business sector and for the services of the household sector. Government spending enhances household income either directly (by employing productive services owned by households) or indirectly (by purchasing goods from business, which entails employment of household services). At the same time, of course, government taxes drain away earned income, leaving less for consumption and saving. It follows that the identities (1), (2), and (4) of the previous section are now:

$$Y \equiv C + I_r + G \tag{5}$$
$$Y \equiv C + S + T \tag{6}$$
$$S + T \equiv I_r + G, \tag{7}$$

where G represents government purchases of final goods and services and T represents taxes. The first identity states that production (income) flows into consumer goods, investment goods, and to government. The second, (6), says that income earned in the production process goes to finance consumption, to build savings, and to pay taxes. The result, (7), is that the *sum* of realized investment and government spending equals the *sum* of saving and taxes.

An interesting complication now arises. Suppose that our previous condition for maintaining the flow of income is not realized: e.g., that $S > I_i$. An excess of saving over intended investment in the absence of government implies a positive level of unintended inventory investment, i.e., $I_u > 0$. But, with government present, this may not be true. If government spends more than it taxes (by deficit financing), it can, with proper planning, absorb the production going into undesired inventory accumulation. In doing so, government can prevent a possible decline in production and employment. Similarly, if $S < I_i$ (or $I_u < 0$), government can prevent an expansion of the income stream by taxing in excess of its expenditures. As we shall see, government fiscal operations provide an important weapon for policies designed to stabilize the economy.

We shall not further complicate our model at this point. Enough has been said to provide the reader with a feel for the basic concepts to be used in the balance of the book. Our main purpose will be to expand upon these concepts and to provide a more rigorous statement of the determinants of income, production, prices, and employment. Before we proceed, however, we should pause a moment to discuss the relation between our objective measure of the community's income and the economic welfare of the community. Such a discussion is important because it gives us a chance to assess the meaning and purpose of macroeconomic theory and policy.

Real Income and Psychic Income[6]

A large number of policies advocated by politicians, economists, and others are based upon the assumption that real income is some sort of index to social and individual welfare: an index of psychic income. Otherwise, there would not be much sense to programs for raising the level of employment, for increasing the rate of economic growth, for reducing tariffs, for providing educational opportunities for the poor, for building better roads, and so on. Many governmental programs are designed either to increase aggregate real income or to redistribute it in one way or another. The presumption is that by doing so government influences the level and distribution of welfare in the country.

Unfortunately, we are in deep water here. The problem is to specify some objective standard by which we may judge whether or not government policies which increase or redistribute real income also leave the community better off—raise the aggregate level of psychic income. To be honest, there is no such standard. In the final analysis, we must still depend upon various ethical judgments to determine whether or not the results of a given policy are good or bad. To see why this is so, it is instructive to look briefly at the way in which economists have attempted to solve this problem.

One branch of thought concentrates on the notion of a *cardinal utility function*. This approach assumes that, in principle, it is possible to measure the psychic income, or utility, that a man derives from his real income. The relationship is such that as real income increases psychic income also increases, but at a diminishing rate. The implication is that the marginal utility of income diminishes with increases in real income. With diminishing marginal utility of income, a man derives more additional satisfaction out of an extra dollar if his income is $5,000 a year rather than $10,000 a year.

Provided that we ignore interpersonal self-comparisons (e.g., jealousy), the doctrine of diminishing marginal utility of income justifies all sorts of policies. Suppose, to take an easy case, government launches

―――――――

[6] On the subject of this section, see any of several introductions to Welfare Economics. A good place to begin is E. J. Mishan's, *Welfare Economics, Five Introductory Essays* (New York: Random House, 1964). Mishan's book has an excellent bibliography.

a program the result of which is to increase the real income of at least one person in the community without affecting anyone else. If the rest of the community is not jealous of this one man, we can unambiguously say that the program improves community psychic income. The same can be said of any program which improves any number of individual real incomes without hurting others.

Next, consider a harder case. Suppose that in the process of helping some people the government injures others. Now, even though the policy may lead to a larger aggregate real income, we have the problem of determining whether or not, on net, aggregate utility in the community is improved. This involves comparing the utility lost by those who have been injured against the utility gained by those who have benefited from the policy. Such an assessment, in turn, requires that the authorities be able to measure the marginal utility of real income of the various individuals in the community. Needless to say, the task is beyond human powers. However, it may be possible to retain the approach if we can devise a procedure which avoids the need actually to calculate the marginal utility of income.

One procedure is to assume that all people are equal in their capacities to enjoy real income. If true, this assumption would carry the principle of diminishing marginal utility of income a long way. It would allow us to say, for example, that any policy which moves the community in the direction of income equality also leads to an improvement in aggregate welfare. For, if we give a poor man a dollar and take one away from a rich man, the principle tells us that we are giving the poor man more utility than we are taking from the rich man. It also tells us that we can do this right up to the point where their incomes are equal.

Unfortunately, we assume too much when we assert that people are equal in capacity to enjoy real income. While such may be an expedient political hypothesis, there is no scientific basis to the assertion. Because of this, many economists have abandoned the principle of diminishing marginal utility of income as a scientific guide to economic policy. Instead, they have sought a basis for their judgments in a weaker variant of the utility principle: the *ordinal utility hypothesis*.

Those who hold to the ordinal utility hypothesis agree that there is a positive relationship between real and psychic income. They agree that a man's sense of well being improves (or deteriorates) with every increase or decrease in his real income. They do not agree, however, that it is possible to measure the amount of utility gained or lost with changes in real income. They are only willing to agree to a positive ordering of utility with respect to income. This simply means that more income always allows a man to achieve higher levels of satisfaction, but that meaningful numbers cannot be placed on these levels.

Compared to the notion of cardinal utility, the concept of ordinal utility, is a weak basis for policy. It implies, for example, that since we cannot make objective interpersonal utility comparisons, we cannot judge the aggregate effects of government programs which involve redistributions of individual real incomes. Thus, even though it may raise aggregate real income, if a program involves the reduction of the income of any part of the community, the doctrine says that we cannot assess its overall goodness.

Since it is difficult to think of programs which do not involve at least some income redistributions, the ordinal utility doctrine would seem to be a doctrine of despair. This is not wholly correct. Suppose we know that in the process of increasing aggregate real income we also know that certain individuals will experience losses. If we can devise a method of compensating the losers with some of the gains of the winners, we can then be sure that the community as a whole is better off: If, after compensation, no one has lost any real income, but aggregate real income has increased, it follows that at least some people's positions have been improved.

It is not true, therefore, that the ordinal utility hypothesis is a doctrine of despair. Nevertheless, it is still a very limited basis for policy. For one thing, it cannot be used to justify a policy of income equalization which in any way causes the reduction of any person's real income. Progressive taxation, for example, is ruled out. The doctrine also imposes heavy knowledge requirements upon government. In order to right the wrongs of its policies, government must seek out those who have been injured and properly assess the amount of injury. Since many government programs have complex consequences, this might prove to be an impossible task. Finally, like the doctrine of cardinal utility, the ordinal utility hypothesis ignores the presence of interpersonal self-comparisons. Once we admit that the satisfactions people derive from their incomes are affected by other people's incomes, no statement about the overall welfare effects of government policies is safe.

What is safe? Unfortunately, very little. An objective procedure for forming judgments on the welfare effects of government policies does not seem possible. But, since almost all economic polices have distributional impacts, *some* procedure must be used by those in power. Not surprisingly, the procedure generally is to fall back upon ethical judgments derived from tradition and from perceptions drawn from the political process. Indeed, the political process may be viewed as a method of revealing information on community values. It is more than that, of course, since it is also a process by which power to enforce values is acquired by various interest groups. What emerges as policy is the result of the pull and push of politics. If a community is lucky, policy may reflect generally held notions of what is right and wrong. But if it is not, policy may lead to serious distortions.

In view of the previous comments, how are we to view the relation between aggregate real income and community or social welfare? A safe position is an agnostic position. We can deny our ability to make any statement. This follows from the fact that virtually all changes in aggregate real income carry distributional changes whose effects we cannot accurately trace or assess. However, this position is too conservative. A better statement would be that increases in aggregate real income carry with them *potential* welfare improvements. Whether or not society efficiently uses its new potential is, of course, an open question. Nevertheless, whatever the values one might wish to apply, it still remains that a high level of aggregate real income gives society a better chance of improving social welfare than does a low level. This admittedly conservative position is enough to justify the economist's concern with macroeconomic theories of income and employment.

We now proceed to the more prosaic task of finding out how real income is measured and how it is determined by economic forces.

ADDITIONAL READINGS

See end of chapter 2.

Chapter 2 | NATIONAL INCOME MEASUREMENT

Before undertaking an intensive discussion of macroeconomic theory, we should pause to find out how income for a nation is actually measured. We shall do no more than sketch out the necessary concepts. More comprehensive discussions are available elsewhere.[1] National income accounting is an ancient art, going back at least to William Petty's "political arithmetick" in 17th century England. Today it is practiced all over the world in a variety of forms, although the United Nations has attempted to introduce standardized concepts in order to facilitate international comparisons. Here we shall concentrate on the art as it is practiced in the United States by the U.S. Department of Commerce.[2]

The development of national income accounting in the United States owes much to the work of the National Bureau of Economic Research and of Simon Kuznets,[3] in particular. Mention should also be made of the work of John Maynard Keynes in his *General Theory of Employment, Interest, and Money*.[4] Keynes' General Theory made use of concepts quite congenial to the framework of the national income accounts, thus giving the latter the status of essential raw materials for the purpose of testing the theory and prescribing national policies based upon Keynes' system of thought. The United States now has the most comprehensive set of national income accounts in the world. The accounts

---

[1] A standard textbook is John P. Powelson, *National Income and Flow-of-Funds Analysis* (New York: McGraw-Hill Book Co., 1960). For other references see bibliography at the end of this chapter.

[2] For a history of national income accounting and a survey of the practices of various countries, see Paul Studenski, *The Income of Nations* (New York: New York University Press, 1959).

[3] See Simon Kuznets, *National Income and Its Composition, 1919–1938* (New York: National Bureau of Economic Research, 1941).

[4] Keynes, *General Theory of Employment, Interest, and Money* (New York: Harcourt, Brace, and Co., 1935).

go back to 1929 on an annual basis and to 1939 for quarterly information. These accounts provide analysts with an enormous amount of information on the structure and functioning of the American economy. It is hard to conceive of how modern economic analysis and policymaking could proceed without the information they provide.

Gross National Product

The key concept in measuring output in the United States is gross national product (GNP). We define gross national product as *the total value of final output of goods and services produced by residents of a country during a given period of time.* An analysis of this definition provides a good opportunity to explore some of the major conceptual problems of national income accounting.

What is included and excluded from *final output?* Before answering this question, we note that final output is equivalent to "value added by production." Intermediate goods and services, as in our definition of aggregate production in Chapter 1, are not part of gross national product. Among other things, this means that GNP has a counterpart on the income or allocations side, comprised of a series of charges against the production of goods and services. We also note that both goods and services are included in the definition of final output. This is as it should be. Production is a process by which services are rendered to users. It should make no difference that some of these services are direct rather than embodied in some tangible form and hence indirectly available to users.

There is a problem, however, in deciding what to call final output. It is a convention that anything produced and sold through the market to final users should be included as part of GNP. But, is this enough? If we chose to be purists, we would argue for the inclusion of all activities that satisfy wants. The chores of a housewife, a game of chess, or even an act of religious worship would be counted as part of GNP. Clearly, we cannot be purists. We cannot place an economic value on *all* human activity. This would destroy the usefulness of GNP as a measure of production reflecting the play of economic forces and the use of hired resources, and this, essentially, is what we want.

Unfortunately, concentrating upon production sold through the marketplace leads to some curious results. Under this practice (to use a common example), if a man marries his housekeeper, national production, as measured by GNP, will go down! Similarly, if a man hires a gardener to mow his lawn, instead of doing it himself, GNP will rise.

These and many other possible examples demonstrate that measuring GNP by using the facts of the marketplace gives rise to potentially serious errors. Indeed, this is why one must be careful in using GNP as a way of comparing economies which differ substantially in industrial structure. In our country, for example, clergymen are often paid a salary; hence, their services count in GNP (even though such services may be those of intermediaries!). This is not the case in many underdeveloped countries where religious services are free. Many common personal and household services are commercialized in this country but not in others. The size of the U.S. gross national product relative to that of many other countries reflects the fact that we have commercialized a large part of life.[5]

Actual practice in the United States represents a cross between an all-inclusive "purist" definition and a market oriented definition of final output. The GNP estimates for the United States include some private production which is not marketed and also production occurring within the government sector. For the private sector, for example, statisticians impute value to the rental services of owner-occupied homes and to home-consumed farm production. Since these items are not sold to the people consuming them, prices of similar items in the market are used to make the valuations.

Government production represents a special problem. It is clear that the value added by government business-type enterprises, such as the Bonneville Power Administration and the Tennessee Valley Administration, form part of gross national product. But what of the non-business activities, which comprise the lion's share of the work of government. The practice is to value these activities at factor cost—at the wage and salary cost of providing the services[6]—and to add the resulting valuation to privately produced GNP for the purpose of finding the total for the economy. There is really not much else that can be done, since for most government services there is no private market from which comparable valuations can be made. The only other approach would be to use tax payments as a means of valuing govern-

---

[5] These same remarks apply to comparing the recent GNP of a country with that of its past. The industrial structure of the United States is now very different than it was 50 or 100 years ago.

[6] In the United States, interest paid by government to the private sector is not regarded as part of the factor cost of government production. Instead, it is treated as a transfer payment. The rationale is that most of the interest paid is for debt accumulated during World War II and subsequent wars; hence, it represents government production rendered in the past and not the services of currently owned government capital. Not all countries treat government interest payments in this way.

ment output. The rationale for such a practice would presumably be that taxes represent the value of privately produced goods and services that the public is willing to forgo in order to enjoy the services of government. This position might be tenable if it could be maintained that taxes represent a voluntary sacrifice of income on the part of the public. To some extent this is probably true. Nevertheless, it is also true that much taxation represents *forced* extractions of income from the public; hence this method of valuing government services is also imperfect.

Valuation problems aside, there is still room to argue that government activity does not belong to GNP. Some economists, such as Simon Kuznets, have argued that government is a precondition to economic activity but not the result of that activity itself. In this view, government services aid in the production of goods and services but, like intermediate goods and services, they should not be treated as final output. Indeed, in socialist countries, strangely, ordinary government activities are not treated as part of national income. In the stronghold of capitalism, however, government production is given its place alongside private production as part of the community's output of final goods and services.

Continuing now with other parts of the definition of GNP, note that it is confined to the production of *residents* of the country. This means that U.S. GNP includes production by U.S. residents within the United States' political boundaries and also production undertaken by U.S. residents abroad. On the other hand, home production the income from which accrues to foreigners is not included as part of U.S. gross national product. The GNP estimates for the United States therefore include only production which results in the accrual of income to residents of the United States, regardless of the geographical location of that production.

The definition of GNP refers to a *given period of time.* As indicated in Chapter 1, income is a flow concept, hence it has no meaning unless it refers to a specific period of time. Gross national product estimated on an annual basis, for example, is not the same as gross national product estimated on a quarterly basis. A GNP of $900 billion per year means that the quarterly rate during the year averaged $225 billion. Nevertheless, it is customary to report quarterly estimates of GNP as if they were annual rates. In the first quarter of 1968, for example, the Department of Commerce reported a quarterly GNP of $835 billion. This simply means that if the (implied) quarterly rate of $209 billion were continued for the rest of the year, GNP for the year would have been $835 billion. Quarterly GNP on an annual basis, therefore, is simply the quarterly rate multiplied by four.

A word should be said about prices. For the most part (except for government production) final output is valued at market prices. Hence, the phrase "total value of final output" in the GNP definition means that (government output aside) when all final goods and services are multiplied by their market prices and added together, the result is the private sector contribution to GNP. When government output, valued at its fatcor cost, is added to the private sector's output, the result is GNP. Unfortunately, there is one important problem with this procedure. Prices of goods and services sold by the business sector include a number of so-called indirect business taxes, such as excise taxes, sales taxes, and license fees. Economic theory suggests that businessmen shift a large portion of these taxes to their customers in the form of higher prices. It follows that GNP must be adjusted to take note of this problem. This will be done in what follows.

Finally, it is important to emphasize that we are discussing *gross* national product. This means that we are counting as final output the production necessary to replace the capital goods used up or otherwise destroyed during the period in question. It also means that in order to match the value of the nation's product to the incomes earned as a result of the creation of that product, we will have to make a deduction for capital consumption. This deduction, along with an appropriate correction for indirect business taxes, will bring us to an estimate of national product (or income), which is in line with the concept of net social income discussed in the last chapter.

GROSS NATIONAL PRODUCT AND RELATED MEASURES

There are three ways to measure gross national product: by (1) value added, (2) expenditures, (3) income. Conceptually, with appropriate adjustments all three of these methods should come to the same total. For example, the outlays made by consumers, business, government, and foreigners upon the final output of the economy should exhaust the value added by production in the economy. Again, the incomes earned from production (plus indirect business taxes and capital consumption) should equal value added (or the value of final output). Department of Commerce statisticians, using a variety of data sources, such as business records, tax returns, production indices, government accounts, and balance of payment data, use a combination of these approaches. The necessary equality between the results which should emerge, say, from the income and the value added approaches, allows statisticians to make separate estimates of GNP from each approach. This allows them to check the accuracy and consistency of their estimates.

Gross national product and its related measures are ordinarily summarized and presented in a form similar to Table 2.1. This table displays the sources of GNP, or the set of expenditures on final goods and services originating in the various sectors of the economy (and abroad). The allocations side of the table essentially represents the income concept, with various adjustments for capital consumption, taxes, and statistical errors resulting from the fact that each side of the table represents an independent method of making the GNP estimate. Included on the allocations side are various related measures, the significance of which will emerge from our discussion of the table.

Derivation of National Income

We begin the discussion of Table 2.1 with the allocations side. The first order of business is to derive an estimate of *national income* (Y),

TABLE 2.1

Sources and Allocations of Proceeds from U.S. Gross National Product, 1968
(billions of dollars)

Allocations	1968	Sources	1968
Gross national product (GNP)	865.7	Gross national product (GNP)	865.7
Less: Capital consumption allowances	73.3		
Equals: Net national product (NNP)	792.4	Personal consumption expenditure	536.6
Less: Indirect business taxes	77.9	Gross private domestic investment	126.3
Other adjustments*	.9		
Plus: Subsidies less surplus of government enterprises	.8	Net exports of goods and services	2.5
Equals: National income (Y)	714.4	Government purchases of goods and services	200.3
Less: Corporate profits after taxes and inventory valuation adjustment ..	46.6		
Corporate profits tax	41.3		
Social insurance contributions	47.0		
Plus: Government transfer payments (interest and other)	81.9		
Dividends	23.1		
Business transfer payments	3.4		
Equals: Personal income	687.9		
Less: Personal taxes	97.9		
Equals: Disposable personal income (Yd)	590.0		
Less: Personal consumption expenditure ..	536.6		
Consumer interest payments	14.2		
Personal transfer payments to foreigners	.8		
Equals: Personal saving	38.4		

* Includes business transfer payments and statistical discrepancy.
Source: *Federal Reserve Bulletin*, April, 1969. Department of Commerce estimates.

sometimes referred to as the "factor cost" of aggregate production. By factor cost of production we simply mean the payments for the services of labor, capital, and natural resources used to create the national output. As before, the first step is to deduct capital consumption allowances (depreciation plus accidental damage to capital assets) from gross national product. In the simple economy of the last chapter, this would have been enough to give us an estimate of national income. In the real world, however, there are complications which force us to make additional adjustments; hence, instead of national income, the subtraction of capital consumption allowances from gross national product yields what is commonly called *net national product* (NNP). In 1968, GNP was $865.7 billion. Capital consumption allowances reduced this by $73.3 billion, to yield a NNP of $792.4 billion.

The calculation of national income requires several other adjustments. Recall that in this first step we are trying to estimate the factor cost of aggregate output; that is, the payments made to elicit the productive services used to create the nation's output. The first thing we must do, therefore, is to deduct indirect business taxes, which are assumed by national income accountants to have been shifted forward into the prices of the products sold by the business sector. Next, we deduct a term called "other adjustments." This includes two items: business transfer payments and statistical discrepancy. Business transfer payments include such things as corporate gifts to charitable institutions and bad debts of consumers. When GNP is estimated on the product side, the value of final output reflects the source from which these transfers are made. But, such transfers are not necessary to elicit the productive services used to create final output; hence, in computing national income, business transfer payments must be subtracted from gross national product. The second item—the statistical discrepancy—arises from the fact that GNP is estimated in two ways: from the records of business and other entities to get final output or product and from tax and other records to get income. The difference between the product and the income approach inevitably gives rise to a statistical error or discrepancy. This discrepancy is deducted from GNP before presenting the estimate of Y.

A final adjustment consists of adding government "subsidies less the current surplus of government enterprises." Subsidies paid by government to business and other entities are often necessary to elicit production from them; hence, such subsidies must be considered part of the factor cost of production. The surpluses (or profits) of government enterprises, however, do not represent a factor payment in the ordinary sense, since although government enterprises, such as the Tennessee

Valley Authority, do contribute to the nation's output, the surpluses of such enterprises are not considered as a payment for entrepreneurship. Moreover, many government enterprises sustain a loss because they engage in activities which, in essence, subsidize the private sector. The perennial deficits of the post office, for example, are the result of the fact that services such as third class mail are sold to business below cost, hence represent a subsidy to the business sector.[7]

The steps for computation of national income are now complete. From here on, we shall discuss the derivation of a number of other important items. Before doing so, however, it is important to note exactly what national income means. Using the income approach, instead of the series of deductions and additions from GNP, we could have arrived at essentially the same figure. That is, we could have *added* together the following items: compensation of employees in the private and public sectors, the income of noncorporate business, the rental income of persons (mainly an imputed item), corporate profits (with an inventory valuation adjustment, explained below), and the net interest income of business and individuals.[8] All of these items are recorded on a *before tax basis* in Table 2.2 for 1968. Note that the resulting total is the same as the national income figure embedded in Table 2.1: $714.4 billion.

Personal Income and Disposable Personal Income

We are now interested in how much income accrues to households in the form of spendable income. Note that spendable income is not the same thing as earned income. Aggregate earned income is simply the national income figure. The amount households have available to spend—*disposable personal income*—depends upon (1) how much earned income is retained by corporations; (2) how much is taxed away by various levels of government; and (3) how much is received back by households in the form of transfer payments.[9]

Consider Table 2.1. Before we may calculate *personal income* (pretax disposable personal income), a series of adjustments must be made. The first involves corporate profits. Corporate profits before taxes in-

---

[7] For a more complete discussion of this item, see the *Survey of Current Business, National Income Supplement*, 1954, p. 49.

[8] "Net" because it is interest received minus interest paid.

[9] Transfer payments are income payments made without a corresponding productive service being rendered. Examples are social security payments, unemployment compensation, and welfare payments.

TABLE 2.2

National Income by Distributive Shares, 1967 and 1968*
(billions of dollars)

Distributive Shares	1967	1968	1968 (quarters)			
			I	II	III	IV
National income	654.0	714.4	688.8	707.4	724.1	737.3
Compensation of employees	467.4	513.6	495.1	507.0	519.8	532.3
Wages and salaries	423.5	465.0	448.2	459.0	470.7	482.1
Private	337.3	369.0	355.9	364.5	372.7	382.8
Military	16.2	18.0	17.3	17.6	18.7	18.3
Government civilian	70.0	78.0	75.0	76.8	79.3	80.9
Supplements to wages and salaries	43.9	48.6	47.0	48.0	49.1	50.2
Employer contributions for social insurance	21.8	24.4	23.6	24.1	24.7	25.3
Other labor income	22.1	24.2	23.4	23.9	24.5	25.0
Employer contributions to private pension and welfare funds	18.4	20.1	....	....	....	....
Other	3.7	4.1	....	....	....	....
Proprietors' income	61.9	63.8	63.2	63.6	64.1	64.1
Business and professional	47.2	49.2	48.4	49.2	49.3	49.7
Income of unincorporated enterprises ..	47.5	49.9	....	....	....	....
Inventory valuation adjustment	−.3	−.7	....	....	....	....
Farm	14.7	14.6	14.8	14.3	14.8	14.4
Rental income of persons	20.8	21.2	21.1	21.2	21.2	21.4
Corporate profits and inventory valuation adjustment	79.2	87.9	82.5	88.2	90.6	90.3
Profits before tax	80.3	91.1	87.9	90.7	91.5	94.5
Profits tax liability	33.0	41.3	39.9	41.1	41.4	42.9
Profits after tax	47.3	49.8	47.9	49.7	50.0	51.6
Dividends	21.5	23.1	22.2	22.9	23.6	23.8
Undistributed profits	25.9	26.7	25.7	26.7	26.5	27.8
Inventory valuation adjustment	−1.1	−3.2	−5.3	−2.6	−.9	−4.2
Net interest	24.7	28.0	26.7	27.5	28.4	29.3

* Quarterly data are seasonally adjusted totals at annual rates.
Source: *Survey of Current Business*, July, 1969.

clude essentially two items: corporate net earnings from the productive activity undertaken during the year and a capital gain or loss on inventories. The capital gain or loss on inventories results from the fact that most companies value inventories at the beginning of the accounting period at cost. If, during the year prices have risen (or fallen) part of the profits reported by these companies will reflect what in effect are capital gains (or losses) on beginning inventories. Since such capital gains and losses do not reflect true factor incomes, the reported profit figure for corporations must be reduced (or increased) by the gain (or loss) on inventories so that profits might reflect what is properly earned income. In 1968, the pretax value of corporate profits after the inventory valuation adjustment was $87.9 billion (see Table 2.2).

It is the pretax corporate profits (after inventory valuation adjustment) which one must add to other factor income in order to estimate national income at factor cost (again, see Table 2.2). But in order to estimate personal income, one must take into account a series of subtractions and additions reflected in Table 2.1. First, of course, corporate profits are subject to a tax; this is a drain going to government. Second, individuals and business make contributions to social insurance schemes, such as social security and unemployment compensation programs. Personal income can be computed only after these governmental drains are subtracted from national income. Third, corporations distribute only part of their profits to stockholders, the rest is retained by the companies for various purposes, such as financing additional capital outlays. Finally, households received various transfer payments: some in the form of government transfers (government pensions and unemployment compensations and interest payments)[10] and some in the form of business transfers (already explained). As Table 2.1 shows, these series of adjustments cause personal income to vary from national income by a considerable margin: by $27 billion in 1968.

Personal income in the U.S. national income accounts is the counterpart to what we called household income in the last chapter. Actually this is something of a misnomer. Included in personal income is an item called "proprietors' income." It is not possible to segregate statistically the net income of unincorporated business into the part taken home and the part left in the business. For this reason, all proprietary income is treated as household income. Personal income as defined here also differs from that of the last chapter because it includes transfer incomes. The simple model of the last chapter had no such category; hence all of

---

[10] See footnote 6.

household income in that model represented earned income. When government enters the picture, simple models must go!

Indeed, the presence of government spoils even the personal income concept as a measure of spendable income. Before deriving such a concept it is necessary to subtract taxes on household income—such as income taxes, property taxes, and license fees.[11] Once this is done, we arrive at the concept we are seeking: *disposable personal income.* This concept is of great importance in the analysis of aggregate spending behavior, since a major method of affecting consumer expenditure is via policies which affect disposable income.

Aggregate Expenditures

The sources side of Table 2.1 gives an estimate of gross national product from the "expenditures" point of view. Recall that each category of expenditure refers to expenditure on final product. Table 2.3 provides a more detailed breakdown of the various types of outlay than does Table 2.1. Even more detailed breakdowns are available in the various July numbers of the *Survey of Current Business,* published by the U.S. Department of Commerce.

A bit of explanation is in order for some of the expenditure categories in Tables 2.1 and 2.3:

a) Note, first, that consumer expenditures do not include outlays on residential construction. Such outlays are regarded as capital expenditures—investment—by national income statisticians. This practice raises the logical question of why all consumer purchases of durables are not treated as investment. Logically, a family car, a suit of clothes, or even a can opener is as much of an investment as is a house. There is really no answer to this objection, except to say that a line must be drawn somewhere. The statisticians have simply drawn it at a point that permits them to evade many nasty decisions as to what is and what is not an investment good for the consumer. Those interested in drawing their own lines can do so with the aid of the more detailed data provided by the Department of Commerce in the *Survey of Current Business.*

b) Gross private domestic investment is largely self-explanatory from the tables. The category of *net exports* requires some explanation, es-

---

11 In theory, one might argue that household social insurance contributions should be subtracted here rather than before personal income is calculated. The practice of the Department of Commerce is purely arbitrary in this matter. Actually, when the principal objective is the calculation of disposable personal income, it doesn't make a great deal of difference when these contributions are deducted.

TABLE 2.3

Gross National Expenditure, 1967 and 1968*
(billions of dollars)

Gross National Expenditure	1967	1968	1968 (*quarters*)			
			I	*II*	*III*	*IV*
Gross national product	793.5	865.7	835.3	858.7	876.4	892.5
Personal consumption expenditures	492.3	536.6	520.6	530.3	544.9	550.7
Durable goods	73.0	83.3	79.5	81.8	85.8	86.3
Nondurable goods	215.1	230.6	226.1	228.5	233.3	234.3
Services	204.2	222.8	215.1	220.0	225.8	230.1
Gross private domestic investment	116.0	126.3	119.4	126.6	125.2	133.9
Fixed investment	108.6	119.0	117.7	116.7	118.0	123.4
Nonresidential	83.7	88.8	89.1	86.4	88.1	91.5
Structures	27.9	29.3	29.8	28.3	29.0	30.1
Producers' durable equipment	55.7	59.5	59.4	58.1	59.1	61.4
Residential structures	25.0	30.2	28.6	30.3	29.9	31.9
Nonfarm	24.4	29.6	28.0	29.7	29.4	31.4
Farm	.6	.5	.6	.6	.5	.5
Change in business inventories	7.4	7.3	1.6	9.9	7.2	10.5
Nonfarm	6.8	7.4	1.3	10.3	7.5	10.7
Farm	.6	−.1	.4	−.4	−.3	−.2
Net exports of goods and services	5.2	2.5	1.9	3.4	3.6	1.2
Exports	46.2	50.6	47.7	50.7	53.4	50.6
Imports	41.0	48.1	45.9	47.3	49.7	49.4
Government purchases of goods and services .	180.1	200.3	193.4	198.4	202.5	206.7
Federal	90.7	99.5	96.3	99.0	100.9	101.9
National defense	72.4	78.0	76.1	77.9	78.8	79.3
Other	18.4	21.5	20.1	21.1	22.1	22.5
State and local	89.3	100.7	97.1	99.4	101.7	104.8

* Quarterly data are seasonally adjusted totals at annual rates.
Source: *Survey of Current Business*, July, 1969.

pecially since it was not discussed in the last chapter. Net exports include two items. The first is what national income accountants refer to as *net foreign investment.* The second is an item including net gifts and grants from the government and from households to foreigners (that is, gifts and grants to foreigners minus gifts and grants from foreigners).

Net foreign investment represents the net sales of goods and services by the home economy to foreigners. As such, these net sales generate production and income for residents of the home economy. On the other hand, this production is not consumed at home; rather, it is like domestic investment in that it has a counterpart in domestic saving. This domestic saving represents an increase in net claims on the future production of foreigners. This comes about either because the net sales of goods and services were financed by an increase in domestic holdings of foreign currencies or foreign securities, by a gold inflow from abroad (which is certainly spendable on foreign goods), or by a reduction of foreign holdings of domestic money (or securities). But all exports are not financed in these ways. Some of them are financed by gifts and grants from the government and households of the domestic economy. If we add net gifts and grants to foreigners to the net sales to foreigners (defined as net foreign investment) we will get the concept of net exports as represented by the item on the right hand side of Table 2.1.[12]

It should be noted that while net foreign investment increases gross national product, the part of net exports financed by gifts and grants does not. The latter is balanced by a reduction of domestic consumption and domestic government expenditures. Looked at another way, grants and gifts are international transfers; hence while they do not represent a reduction of gross national product, they do represent a reduction of the availability to domestic entities of goods produced at home.

c) As with gross private investment expenditures, government expenditure includes only outlays on final product and on services, mainly labor, bought from individuals. Payments of interest, social security expenditures, and all other such items are regarded as transfers and are *not* included in the figure given in Table 2.1. It might be argued, of course, that, as with household outlays on residential construction, part of government spending is really investment from a social point of view. This is true for government construction of buildings, roads, parks, and purchases of many equipment items. There is considerable merit to this point, but national income statisticians have chosen not to include government capital expenditures with investment, presumably on the ground

---

[12] A little algebra may clarify. Let $(X - M)$ be net exports. Let X be total sales abroad. Total sales abroad consist of a part financed by foreigners, X_F, and a part financed by gifts and grants from the home economy, X_R. We therefore have:

$$X = X_F + X_R$$
$$(X - M) = (X_F - M) + X_R$$

The term in the parentheses on the right-hand side of the bottom equation is net foreign investment. The second term on the right is equal to net gifts and grants. Together they equal net exports $(X - M)$.

that it does not respond to the same forces (interest rates, for example) as does private investment.

Calculation of National Saving

The complexities introduced by government and the foreign sector do not disturb our basic notion of saving. Saving is still income less consumption. In the present context it is gross national income less consumption, or gross saving. Gross saving includes the following items: personal or household saving, capital consumption allowances for business and retained corporate profits (business saving), and the excess of government taxes over government expenditure. The latter item needs explanation. Taxes withdraw spendable income from the economy. Government expenditures, on the other hand, either transfer back part of that income to the community (as with social security payments and interest payments on government debt) or absorb part of the community's output in the form of government consumption. If taxes, net of government transfer payments, exceed government expenditures on goods and services, it follows that saving in the economy is enhanced; for, if the private sector were given the government's surplus, it might spend part of it. Because all of the surplus accrues to government, it is kept out of private hands and thereby represents in its entirety unconsumed output.

Gross saving and its calculation (for 1968) are shown in Table 2.4. The data have been calculated from Tables 2.1 and 2.2. Notice, that gross private saving, when added to the government surplus or deficit, equals the sum of gross domestic investment and net foreign investment (after allowing for the statistical discrepancy). This is as it should be, since net foreign investment, like domestic investment, represents unconsumed output and has a counterpart in unconsumed gross income, which we have defined as gross saving.

The relationships in Table 2.4 can perhaps be made a bit clearer if we indulge in a little algebra. Ignore the statistical discrepancy, which is the result of measuring GNP independently by the product method and the income method, and define GNP as:

$$\text{GNP} \equiv D + S_b + T + R, \text{ or} \qquad (1)$$
$$\text{GNP} \equiv C + I_d + G + (X - M) . \qquad (2)$$

In the equation for identity (1): D is what households have available to spend out of their disposable income after making interest payments and transfers; S_b is business saving, consisting of capital consumption

TABLE 2.4

Sources and Uses of Gross Saving, 1968
(billions of dollars)

Sources	
Gross private saving	135.1
Personal saving 38.4	
Undistributed corporate profits 76.7	
Corporate inventory valuation adjustment .... −3.2	
Corporate capital consumption allowances 45.9	
Noncorporate capital consumption allowances 27.3	
Government deficit (−)	−6.6
Statistical discrepancy	−2.5

Uses	
Gross investment	126.0
Gross domestic investment 126.3	
Net foreign investment .... −.3	

Source: *Survey of Current Business*, July, 1969, p. 37.

allowances and retained corporate earnings adjusted for changes in the value of inventories; T is government tax intake, net of its transfers back to the public in the form of various social insurance payments and interest; and R is the sum of private and government transfers abroad, or net gifts and grants to foreigners. In the equation for identity (2): C is domestic consumption; I_d is gross domestic investment; G is government spending on final goods and services; and $(X - M)$ is net exports.

Now, substract (2) from (1) and rearrange the terms:

$$(D - C) + S_b + (T - G) \equiv I_d + [(X - M) - R]. \qquad (3)$$

$(D - C)$ is personal saving; $(T - G)$ is government's surplus (or deficit) and $[(X - M) - R]$ is net foreign investment. Hence, in words, the equation for identity (3) says that the sum of personal, business, and government saving is equal to the sum of gross domestic investment and net foreign investment. Except for the statistical discrepancy, this is precisely what the data in Table 2.4 say.[13]

---

[13] Again, the reader is warned that the accounting identity between saving and investment refers to realized magnitudes, not intended or planned magnitudes.

GNP in Current and Constant Dollars

The Commerce Department has calculated GNP and its components back to 1929. Figure 2.1 displays two variants of these calculations: GNP in current dollars and GNP in constant (1958) dollars. Notice that current dollar GNP has risen much more over the period than has the constant dollar measure. This is due to the fact that the growth in

FIGURE 2.1

U.S. Gross National Product, 1929–1968: Current and Constant (1958) Dollars (billions of dollars)

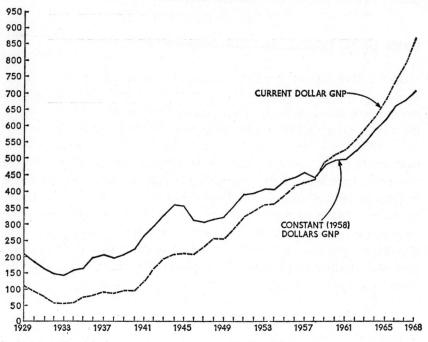

Source: Council of Economic Advisors, *Annual Report*, 1967, and *Federal Reserve Bulletin*, August, 1969.

current dollar GNP reflects two things: (*a*) changes in real output of goods and services, and (*b*) changes in the price level. Constant dollar GNP reflects only changes in output, since it expresses each year's output in terms of 1958 prices. The method by which this is done is discussed in the appendix to this chapter. Both measures of GNP have their uses, but the major interest of economists and public policy makers centers upon constant dollar GNP. Constant dollar GNP is a better measure of the economy's performance in generating real income. It is also more closely connected with variations in the use of productive factors, such as labor and capital. For those interested in measuring changes in the overall productivity, or technical efficiency, of labor and/ or capital inputs in the economy, constant dollar GNP is essential.

It is possible to express other aggregate measures in terms of constant dollars. In the theoretical discussions of the following chapters, most of the time we shall be using constant dollar, or "real" measures. Thus, when we refer to national income, disposable income, investment, consumption, government spending, and so on, we shall usually be referring to their constant dollar magnitudes.

USES OF NATIONAL INCOME ACCOUNTS

The statisticians of the Department of Commerce provide us with an incredibly rich variety of data. This book is not devoted to national income accounting as such, hence we will not actually present all of the ways in which GNP and its components are reported by the government. At the end of this chapter, the reader will find references which will permit him to pursue his interests in this matter. Suffice it to say that, aside from annual and quarterly estimates of the sources and uses of GNP as presented above, the Department of Commerce also provides monthly estimates of personal income. In addition, it provides detailed breakdowns of consumer spending, government spending and taxes, and investment spending. For those interested in the structure of the economy, the statisticians provide us with an annual series on national income by industry of origin. There is also a breakdown of GNP on the basis of the production of goods and the production of services. Regional variations in the economy can be studied with separate estimates of personal income for each state. More recently, income estimates have been made for each *county* in the United States, going back to 1929 for selected years.

There is, then, much material for rather detailed studies on both the structure and performance over time of the American economy. There is also material for studying the relationships between various parts of the economy and its overall performance. We can, for example, study the variation of consumer spending in relation to variations in disposable personal income. We can also study the behavior of business investment spending as it relates both to overall changes in GNP and to other types of spending (together, perhaps, with data on interest rates, profits, and other variables). Another use to which the national income accounts are put is economic forecasting. To be sure, the data in the accounts are not sufficient to provide a basis for forecasting. Nevertheless, when we put the data into a meaningful model of macroeconomic behavior of the kind we shall discuss, they do provide a powerful instrument for peering into the future. Both government and business make extensive use of the national income accounts for this purpose. Indeed, it is difficult to see how policy planning, as it is presently practiced at the national level, can be pursued without the information provided by Department of Commerce statisticians.

APPENDIX: GROSS NATIONAL PRODUCT IN CONSTANT DOLLARS

The Problem

The measurements of GNP to which we have been referring are in the main measurements of the *current dollar* volume of output and expenditure. This means that the increases and decreases in GNP represent increases and decreases in the physical volume of output, changes in the prices of the physical volume of output, or changes in both output and prices. Since the performance of the economy is best measured in terms of the output of goods and services, it is desirable to remove the element of changing prices in the measurement of GNP.

More specifically, our problem is of the following sort: Assume that the economy produces only one good in the quantity q in year a. Suppose also that the price (p) of the good is also known in year a. The total value of production in year a, therefore, is

$GNP_a \equiv p_a q_a$, or, using numbers, $GNP_a \equiv \$1 \times 10$ units of $q \equiv \$10$.

Now, suppose the value of production in the next period, year b, is

$$GNP_b \equiv p_b q_b \equiv \$1.50 \times 12 \text{ units of } q \equiv \$18 .$$

The value of GNP_b is $8 more than the value of GNP_a; but, as can be seen, only part of this value increase is represented by an increase in ouput.

One way of eliminating the influence of the price change upon the measure of changes in real output is to divide GNP of each year by the ratio of prices in that year to prices in the base year. Choosing year a as the base year, we get the following:

$$\frac{GNP_b}{\dfrac{p_b}{p_a}} \equiv \frac{p_b q_b}{\dfrac{p_b}{p_a}} \equiv p_a q_b \equiv \$12 .$$

The result of the calculation is that output in year b is measured in terms of the price of the good in year a. If the same type of calculation were used for years c, d, e, and so on, a series of measurements of GNP in constant dollars would be the result. The term "constant dollars" refers to the fact that output in each year is being measured in terms of the price of the good in the base period, year a. Of course, any year in the series might be used as the base period.

The problem of measuring GNP in constant prices is considerably more difficult when a large number of goods is involved. To do the job correctly, each and every one of the thousands of goods and services which enters into the GNP calculation would have to be valued at base year prices, and then the value of the quantities would have to be added to one another. The calculation would be as follows for all goods:

$$GNP_b \text{ (in prices of year } a) \equiv p_{1a}q_{1b} + p_{2a}q_{2b} + p_{3a}q_{3b} + \ldots + p_{na}q_{nb}$$

$$\equiv \sum_{i=1}^{n} p_{ia}q_{ib} .$$

GNP in year b, in terms of the prices of year a, therefore, is the result of summing the products of the year a price of each (ith) good and the quantity of that good produced in year b.

It is impossible, as a practical matter, to use this method of estimating GNP in constant dollars: even if the data were available, the cost of collecting it would be prohibitive. GNP in constant dollars must therefore be estimated by dividing (deflating) the current value of GNP for each year by a *price index* (not the actual price ratios for each good) having its base in the year chosen as the base.

Index Numbers of Price and Quantity

While this is not the place for a full-blown discussion of index numbers of price and quantity, a brief discussion of them is necessary at this point. Consider the following expression:

$$PI_a \equiv \frac{\Sigma p_b q_a}{\Sigma p_a q_a},$$

where PI_a is the symbol for a price index based in year a. $\Sigma p_b q_a$ is the total value of GNP in year a, valued in prices of year b, and $\Sigma p_a q_a$ is the total value of GNP in year a, valued in the prices of year a. The ratio of the two values for GNP may show a difference, or it may not; that is,

$$PI_a \text{ may } \gtreqless 1 .$$

If the ratio shows that a difference exists, the reason is that at least one of the p's has changed; the q's, it will be noticed, are the same in both numerator and denominator of PI_a. This is why PI_a may be regarded as a price index. Moreover, because of its ratio form, PI_a measures price changes relative to year a; it does not measure absolute changes in prices.

Another feature of PI_a is worth noting: if any particular q is large relative to others in the base period, and if its price changes, the index will reflect a greater change than if the good had been a smaller part of the total aggregate of goods produced in the base year. Similarly, if a particular q is a small part of total production in the base period, changes in the associated price will cause PI_a to change less than if the q had been larger. The q's, therefore, act as *weights* for their associated prices: the larger any given q relative to others in the base period, the more influential is a change in its associated price upon PI_a.

The choice of the base period for weights in the index is completely arbitrary. We could just as easily have chosen year b as the base period. If we had done so, the index would have read as follows:

$$PI_b \equiv \frac{\Sigma p_b q_b}{\Sigma p_a q_b} .$$

The difference between PI_b and PI_a is that the former's quantity weights, the q's, are derived from the physical composition of goods in year b.

PI_a and PI_b answer two quite different, equally valid, questions. PI_a answers the question of the relative cost of the basket of goods in year a as between the two years. PI_b gives the relative difference in cost between the two years of the basket of goods produced in year b. Since each index answers a different question, it will not be surprising if they give different answers.

To make this clear, consider the following example in which GNP in each year is made up of only three goods:

Good No.	p_a	q_a	p_b	q_b
1	$1.00	10	$1.10	11
2	.50	20	.60	20
3	.30	50	.30	60

$$PI_a \equiv \frac{\Sigma p_b q_a}{\Sigma p_a q_a} \equiv \frac{\$11.00 + 12.00 + 15.00}{\$10.00 + 10.00 + 15.00} \equiv \frac{\$38}{\$35} \equiv 1.086$$

$$PI_b \equiv \frac{\Sigma p_b q_b}{\Sigma p_a q_b} \equiv \frac{\$12.10 + 12.00 + 18.00}{\$11.00 + 10.00 + 18.00} \equiv \frac{\$42.10}{\$39.00} \equiv 1.077$$

$$PI_a \times 100 \equiv 108.6$$
$$PI_b \times 100 \equiv 107.7 \;.$$

PI_a shows an 8.6 percent increase in the price level of the three goods and PI_b shows an increase of 7.7 percent. The reason for the difference lies in the fact that the first and second goods, the higher priced ones, constitute a smaller proportion of total production in year b than they do in year a.

Index numbers of quantity, as well as price, may also be developed. An index with weights based in year a would read:

$$QI_a \equiv \frac{\Sigma p_a q_b}{\Sigma p_a q_a} \;.$$

An index of quantity with weights in year b would read:

$$QI_b \equiv \frac{\Sigma p_b q_b}{\Sigma p_b q_a} \;.$$

In both QI_a and QI_b, the p's are fixed and the q's vary. They are therefore both indexes of quantity, showing the relative increase in output over time. QI_a uses prices in year a as weights and QI_b uses prices in year b as weights. Both indexes will show a relative change in GNP in constant dollars when at least one of the q's in year b is different than in year a.

Since each index is defined with different weights, each will produce different and equally valid answers. Using the data of the previous example, for instance, we get the following values for each index:

$$QI_a \equiv \frac{\Sigma p_a q_b}{\Sigma p_a q_a} \equiv \frac{\$11 + 10 + 18}{\$10 + 10 + 15} \equiv \frac{\$39}{\$35} \equiv 1.114$$

$$QI_b \equiv \frac{\Sigma p_b q_b}{\Sigma p_b q_a} \equiv \frac{\$12.10 + 12 + 18}{\$11 + 12 + 15} \equiv \frac{\$42.10}{\$38.00} \equiv 1.108$$

$$QI_a \times 100 \equiv 111.4$$
$$QI_b \times 100 \equiv 110.8 .$$

QI_a is greater, by a small amount, than QI_b, due to differences in the price weights; but both indexes register an increase in the quantity of output from year a to year b. Both are valid measures of the relative change in real GNP because both are concerned with the change in terms of constant prices. It just happens that each uses a different year for price weights.

It should be apparent that if significant changes in the price weights occur, QI_a will diverge significantly in value from QI_b. When this happens, neither of the indexes is adequately taking into account the actual relative importance of the various q's. Thus if years a and b are separated by 20 years of history, during which time relative prices have significantly changed, QI_a and QI_b will be significantly different, and neither of them will reflect the proper relative importance of goods for both years. Added to this difficulty is the fact that new goods are entering into production and old goods are dropping out. Moreover, quality improvements in old goods are constantly taking place. Over long periods of time, therefore, comparisons of output by use of a quantity index have only limited, and imprecise, meaning. The extent to which any particular index has lost its validity is measured by the difference between QI_a and QI_b. When the difference is too great, a new index should be constructed for subsequent years.

Deriving Constant Dollar Gross National Product

When the dollar value of GNP for any year is divided by a price index, the result is as follows (using b as the current year and a as the base year):

$$\frac{GNP_b}{PI_a} \equiv \Sigma p_b q_b \div \frac{\Sigma p_b q_a}{\Sigma p_a q_a} \text{, or} \tag{1}$$

$$\frac{GNP_b}{PI_a} \equiv \Sigma p_b q_b \times \frac{\Sigma p_a q_a}{\Sigma p_b q_a} \text{, or} \tag{2}$$

$$\frac{GNP_b}{PI_a} \equiv \frac{\Sigma p_b q_b}{\Sigma p_b q_a} \times \Sigma p_a q_a \text{, or} \tag{3}$$

$$\frac{GNP_b}{PI_a} \equiv QI_b \times GNP_a . \tag{4}$$

Thus constant dollar GNP for year b is really GNP for the base year "inflated" by a quantity index using year b's prices as weights. This is not exactly what we would like to have—since a true constant dollar GNP would value each year's output in terms of base year prices. Nevertheless, the U.S. Department of Commerce estimates constant dollar GNP by using index numbers of the PI_a type. However, it does not compile an overall price index as implied in the equations for identities (1)–(4). Instead, it breaks GNP into various components— e.g., consumption, investment, government production—and, for each component, it compiles a price index.[1] The various subcomponents of current dollar GNP are "deflated" by their own price indexes, and the resulting constant dollar components are then added together to get a total constant dollar estimate for GNP. As we shall see in the next chapter, constant dollar GNP is currently being expressed in terms of 1958 prices.[2]

ADDITIONAL READINGS FOR CHAPTERS 1 AND 2

EDEY, H. C. and PEACOCK, A. T. *National Income and Social Accounting.* London: Hutchison's University Library, 1954.

KUZNETS, SIMON. *Economic Change.* New York: W. W. Norton Co., 1953, chap. 6, 7, 8.

KUZNETS, SIMON. *National Income: A Summary of Findings.* New York, 1946.

NATIONAL BUREAU OF ECONOMIC RESEARCH. *A Critique of the United States Income and Product Accounts.* Studies in Income and Wealth, Vol. 22. Princeton, N.J., 1958.

RUGGLES, R. and RUGGLES, N. D. *National Income Accounts and Income Analysis.* New York, 1965.

U.S. DEPT. OF COMMERCE. *National Income, 1954 Ed.* (supplement to the

---

[1] Actually, the broad components mentioned here are broken down into many more subgroups by the Commerce Department.

[2] The reader may have seen reference to a price index called "the implicit GNP deflator." This index is computed by dividing current dollar GNP for any year, by the constant dollar total (derived by the method indicated in the text) for the same year. The index is "implicit" because it is not computed directly.

Survey of Current Business). Washington D.C., 1954.

————. *U.S. Income and Output,* 1958.

————. *Survey of Current Business,* August, 1965. Contains revised estimates of national income and product accounts for the U.S., 1929–64, together with an explanation for the sources of revision and changes in some of the concepts used.

Chapter 3

CLASSICAL MACROECONOMICS

Aggregate economics takes on to itself several "grand themes." It seeks to explain the forces determining the level and growth of national income and to elucidate the relationships between the level and growth of income and the level of employment and unemployment. A third major theme is the value of money, or the problems of inflation and deflation.

Historically, economists have varied their emphases on these problems. Prior to the publication of John Maynard Keynes' *General Theory of Employment, Interest, and Money* (1936), macroeconomic theory concentrated upon two principal themes: economic growth and the value of money. Instability of production and employment were recognized as problems, but most economists thought that capitalism contained recuperative powers sufficient to prevent prolonged, if not severe, depressions. The Great Depression of the 1930's was a blow to the practitioners of what we now loosely call "the classical theory." Nevertheless, that theory held the minds of its adherents, and, as so often is the case, it took a theory which could better explain the plain facts of experience to free men's minds from the doctrines of the past. In the rest of the book we will be concentrating upon the newer approach. However, in order to be fair to the older theory, and in order to show how the new has evolved from the old, we shall spend this chapter upon a discussion of classical macroeconomic theory.

Modern interpretations of classical macroeconomic theory[1] have exposed a basically simple set of ideas. However, when these ideas are in-

---

[1] There are now many expositions, of which those of J. R. Hicks, "Mr. Keynes and the 'Classics'," *Econometrica*, April, 1937, reprinted in *Readings in the Theory of Income Distribution* (Philadelphia: Blakiston, 1946 [now a Richard D. Irwin, Inc., publication]), and Franco Modigliani, "Liquidity Preference and the Theory of Interest and Money," *Econometrica*, 1944, reprinted in *Readings in Monetary Theory* (Blakiston, 1951 [also now an Irwin book]) are two of the best earlier ones. A textbook exposition more detailed than the one here is in Gardiner Ackley, *Macroeconomic Theory* (New York: Macmillan, 1961), Part 2.

tegrated they form a self-contained system of analysis which has considerable power. Classical economic reasoning sought to explain no less than the following: (*a*) the aggregate level of employment, (*b*) the average real wage, (*c*) the economy's output level, (*d*) the pace of capital formation, (*e*) the rate of interest, (*f*) the economy's price level and average money wage rate.

The Production Function

Graph 3.1 displays a *production function.* Production function, a fundamental concept in both new and older theory, refers to the relationship between an input, or a set of inputs, and the output of a pro-

GRAPH 3.1

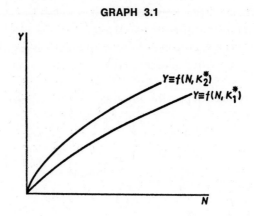

ducing unit. Each production function in Graph 3.1 plots a very simple relationship between labor input (N) and output (Y).[2] The relationship is drawn so as to display certain properties. First, of course, is the positive association of the two variables. Increases in inputs are generally expected to produce increases in outputs. Second, increases in a particular kind of input will generally be accompanied by increases in output which are proportionately less than the increase in the amount of the input applied. This will be true particularly in those cases where the specialized input is increasing more rapidly than other inputs. The student will recognize this as nothing more than a statement of the law of variable proportions, or, if all inputs other than the one under consideration are not changed, the law of diminishing returns.

---

[2] In this chapter, Y is the symbol for real or constant dollar national income or product, not national product in current prices.

Ideally, both inputs and outputs would be measured in homogeneous units. N, for example, would refer to manhours of labor with equal efficiency on a given task. Y would refer to amounts of a uniform commodity or service. While such ideals can be approached in applying the concept of a production function to an individual firm or industry, we have to be satisfied with less precision when applying the notion to an economy. In the latter case we must be content with some sort of production index, or constant dollar value added figure (which Y represents), to represent output, and the labor input must be reduced to a properly weighted index of manhours.[3]

The most bothersome part of applying the production function idea to aggregative behavior is the assumption, implicit in the use of any weighted index, that both the input mix and the output mix do not vary substantially when output expands and contracts. This is patently not true, but the hope is that the errors arising from the use of this assumption are not too great. In any event, we shall be using such an assumption in what follows, and the student is hereby warned of the pitfalls of such a usage.

If we wish, we may depict the production function symbolically:

$$Y \equiv f\,(N, K^*)\,, \tag{1}$$

where K^* reminds us that variable labor inputs are being combined with a constant stock of capital. Technology is also presumed to remain the same. If either technological conditions or capital input is altered, we must write or draw a different production function. $Y \equiv f\,(N, K^*_2)$ for example, indicates that more capital equipment is being used at all levels of employment than in $Y \equiv f\,(N, K^*_1)$. This is shown in Graph 3.1 as an upward shift of the production function. A similar shift could result from technological improvement, even if capital input remained unchanged.

The Demand for Labor

The production function drawn in Graph 3.1 indicates an increase in labor requirements for output expansion. Just how much labor employers actually use is not indicated. To determine this we need a theory

---

[3] This is now being done by researchers at the National Bureau of Economic Research. In a recent book, *Productivity Trends in the United States* (Princeton University Press for the National Bureau of Economic Research, 1961), John Kendrick used a man-hour index for the economy in which manhours were weighted by rates of pay, under the assumption that higher rates of pay reflect more efficient units of labor input.

of labor demand. Fortunately, the production function, along with the ordinary assumption of profit maximization for the firm, helps to define a demand function for labor. The law of diminishing returns tells us that, as more units of labor are combined with given amounts of other inputs, further applications of labor yield fewer additions to output. That is to say, the marginal product of labor (MPN), the added output per added unit of labor (i.e., $\Delta Y/\Delta N$), declines as the labor input is increased. Conversely, as labor is withdrawn from production, the marginal product of labor rises.

Now consider the decision of an employer when he seeks to increase both his use of labor and production. If he is guided by the rule of profit maximization, he will continue to add labor inputs so long as the additional manhours yield more revenue than it costs to hire the additional labor. More formally, if MPN is the marginal product of labor, P the price of the product, and W the money wage rate, the employer will hire additional manhours so long as

$$MPN \cdot P > W, \text{ or} \tag{2}$$
$$MPN > W/P. \tag{2a}$$

The employer will *stop* adding labor when

$$MPN \cdot P = W, \text{ or} \tag{3}$$
$$MPN = W/P. \tag{3a}$$

for then further additions to the labor force will be unprofitable.[4]

Equation (3) expresses the equilibrium labor demand condition for the employer. When expressed in the form of equation (3a), the condition stipulates that the marginal product of labor must equal the *product wage,* or the money wage corrected by the price of the product being produced and sold by the employer. Actually, this condition is really no more than the familiar marginal-cost-equals-marginal-revenue rule for a competitive firm. For, if W represents the additional cost of the extra output, and MPN represents the additional output, equation (3) could be altered to read:

$$W/MPN \equiv \text{marginal cost} = P.$$

How do we derive a demand function for labor from the rule expressed in equation (3), or in (3a)? The answer is that if we confront

---

[4] Let $MPN = 3$, $P = \$2$, and $W = \$3$ per hour. Under these conditions it would pay to use additional manhours, for $3 \times \$2 > \$3$. The $3 profit on marginal additions to labor would be eliminated, however, if continued expansion of labor input brought the MPN down to 3/2 [$(3/2) \times \$2 = \$3$]. While it would pay an employer to go this far, it would not pay him to go farther, for then the MPN would dip under 3/2 and he would incur losses on the extra manhours.

an employer with consecutively lower product wages, his urge to increase profits will cause him to hire additional workers until the MPN falls by enough to come into equality with the lower wages. Conversely, an increase in W/P will cause an employer to lay off workers. The reduction in manhours will lower output and raise the MPN until it comes back into equality with the (now higher) W/P.

In this way, we can state that the demand for labor (D_n) is an inverse function of the product wage:

$$D_n \equiv f_1 (W/P, K^*) \tag{4}$$

The K^* in the equation serves to remind us that the capital stock, with which the units of labor are being combined, is fixed. So too is the technology of the firm. Graph 3.2 also portrays the labor demand function.

The above reasoning can be applied to the economy, as well as to the firm, provided we are willing to make do with the assumption of a competitive economy,[5] and to tolerate the error introduced by aggregation. In this event, however, W should stand for the average money wage in the economy and P should represent the economy's price level. Since prices of consumer goods ordinarily fluctuate along with other prices, W/P can now be considered the average *real wage rate* (the money wage rate corrected for changes in purchasing power) rather than the product wage.

GRAPH 3.2

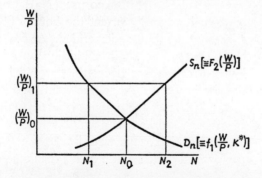

---

[5] If imperfect competition is assumed, equations (3) and (3a) are no longer applicable, since employers must now equate the marginal revenue product of labor with the money wage. That is, marginal revenue *times* the marginal physical product of labor must equal the money wage in equilibrium. Since marginal revenue equals $P(1 - 1/e)$, where e is the elasticity of demand for a firm's product, the equilibrium condition becomes $P(1 - 1/e) \cdot MPN = W$, instead of the expression in equation (3). Since the analysis is not particularly improved with assumptions of imperfect competition, we shall continue to use pure competition as a model in the text.

The Supply of Labor

A classical labor supply function is positively sloped as sketched in Graph 3.2; it may be symbolized by

$$S_n \equiv f_2\left(W/P\right). \tag{5}$$

This function assumes a distaste for work, so that more manhours can be drawn from the labor force only if higher real wages are offered. Each point on the function may be interpreted in two ways: either as the minimum real wage which must be paid to elicit the indicated number of manhours, or as the maximum number of manhours which workers will offer at the given real wage. By definition, any real wage and manhour combination on the curve represents *full employment*, since at the given real wage workers will not be willing to offer more labor.

Equilibrium in the Labor Market

We said above that unless the economy's labor input is somehow determined it would not be possible to determine the economy's level of real output. We are now in the position to determine the level of labor input, at least for the classical system. Graph 3.2 indicates that N_0 is the equilibrium level of employment, at the equilibrium real wage $(W/P)_0$. This can be demonstrated by assuming a real wage either above or below $(W/P)_0$. At $(W/P)_1$, workers would be offering more manhours (N_2) than employers would be willing to use (N_1). Competition for jobs would bring the real wage down, cut the hours of work offered, and increase the amount of hours demanded. A real wage below $(W/P)_0$ (not shown) would result in a bidding up of wages, since employers would seek to buy more hours than would be available at that real wage. The rise in the real wage rate would reduce the amount of hours demanded and increase the amount offered. Only at $(W/P)_0$ would the desires of both workers and employers be the same; the amount of work offered at that wage would exactly equal the amount demanded and employment would settle at N_0 manhours.

The Equilibrium Level of Employment and Output

The simple relationships indicated above gave classical theorists the answers to three tremendously important questions: What determines the level of employment? The real wage rate? The level of output? As shown in Graph 3.3, these are really three interrelated questions. Competition among employers for workers and among workers for jobs set both the real wage and the level of employment at $(W/P)_0$[6] and N_0, respectively. With N_0 set, it is possible to determine the level of output in the economy, as at Y_0 in Graph 3.3. Note that since the equilibrium employment level falls on the supply curve of labor, N_0 and Y_0 represent *full-employment* magnitudes.

GRAPH 3.3

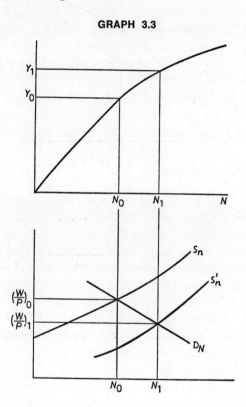

Changes in employment, real wages, and production in the classical model evidently come from only three sources: Changes in the availability of labor, capital accumulation or decumulation, and technological change. Population change, for example, would presumably shift S_n to the right (S_n' in Graph 3.3); reduce equilibrium real wages [to $(W/P)_1$], because of worker competition for jobs; and increase equi-

---

[6] Notice that the money wage, W, is irrelevant. Given an appropriate price level, either a very high or a very low money wage can be an equilibrium wage. It is the ratio W/P that counts.

librium employment (to N_1) and production (to Y_1), as employers find it cheaper to produce more.

Technological improvement and increased capital input raise employment, production, and real wages. As shown in Graph 3.4, for

GRAPH 3.4

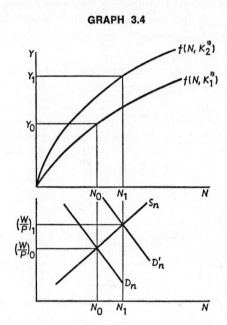

example, increased capital shifts the production function upwards [to $f_1 (N, K^*_2)$], increasing the output possible with any given amount of labor input. The marginal productivity of labor is also increased, making it profitable for employers to acquire more manhours at any given real wage. Thus D_n shifts to the right (to D_n'), raising both employment (to N_1) and the real wage [to $(W/P)_1$]. Output consequently also increases (to Y_1).

Capital Formation: Investment

Competition in the labor market sets the equilibrium level of employment. This employment level, in turn, sets the level of production in the economy. The division of production between consumption goods and investment goods, however, depends upon competition between those who wish to buy these two types of goods. This competition also determines how resources are ultimately allocated between the two major areas of production.

Businessmen wishing to purchase additional capital goods can resort to three sources of funds: (a) their own internal saving, (b) financial institutions, and (c) consumers. In each case, funds for the purchase of investment goods will cost something to acquire. Borrowing from financial institutions or consumers involves an explicit interest cost. Use of internal funds entails an implicit cost in the sense of either foregone consumption by the businessman or the interest earnings which he may earn by lending rather than spending.

Investment spending must therefore justify itself, in that the rate of return expected from the acquisition of new capital goods must either exceed or at least equal the interest cost of the funds used. The less (more) expensive are these funds, of course, the more (less) businessmen will invest.[7] Graph 3.5 sketches out this relationship between

GRAPH 3.5

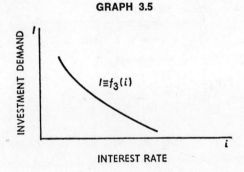

business demand for investment goods (I) and the interest rate (i). The relationship can also be depicted in symbolic terms as

$$I \equiv f_3 (i) \tag{6}$$

where an *inverse* relationship between i and I is understood.

Capital Formation: Saving

Capital goods are produced with resources which might otherwise be used to produce consumer goods. Consumers must therefore be induced to reduce consumption spending in order to release resources for capital goods construction. In the classical theory, the principal device for inducing a reduction of consumption is an increase in interest rates.[8]

---

[7] We shall return to this subject in detail in Chapters 8 and 9.

[8] Notice the use of the word *induce*. Forced reductions in consumption through taxes and other devices are always possible. However, classical theory dealt with a market economy, in which activity is governed by inducements of one sort or another.

While we shall deal with this subject again in Chapter 7, a brief examination of the relationship between consumption (or saving) and the interest rate is relevant here.

The interest rate denotes a rate of exchange between future and present goods. The higher the rate of interest, the less expensive will be future goods relative to present goods. Given their tastes for present as opposed to future consumption, consumers will try to get the most from their incomes. A rise in interest rates will cause a substitution of future consumption for present consumption. Hence the amount of current income spent on present consumption (C) should also decrease with a rise in interest rates, that is:

$$C \equiv f_4\,(i)\,, \qquad\qquad (7)$$

where C is inversely related to i.

This relationship is also depicted in Graph 3.6(b). Notice the graph is drawn so that at i_1 consumption equals aggregate income which,

GRAPH 3.6

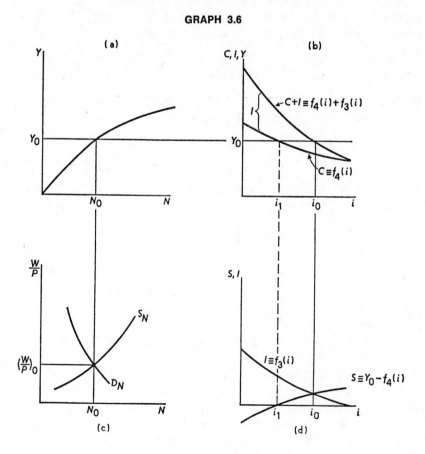

remember, is equal to aggregate production, Y. Below i_1, future goods become so expensive for consumers that they actually reduce them by eating into their accumulated wealth (which is the only meaning one can attach to a condition where consumption exceeds production).

The obverse side of reduced consumption, increased saving, is shown on Graph 3.6(d). Subtract consumption from income to get saving (S):

$$Y_0 - C \equiv S, \text{ or} \tag{8}$$
$$Y_0 - f_4(i) \equiv S. \tag{8a}$$

The saving function in Graph 3.6(d) is constructed by deducting each point on the C-curve from Y_0, the latter being given by the labor market and the production function.

The Equilibrium Rate of Capital Formation

The investment demand function is reproduced in Graph 3.6(d) and superimposed on consumption demand in 3.6(b). Adding the two expenditure streams gives total expenditure as a function of the interest rate:

$$C + I \equiv f_4(i) + f_3(i). \tag{9}$$

If the demand for goods, both consumer and new capital goods, is to equal production in the economy, then

$$Y_0 = C + I, \text{ or} \tag{10}$$
$$Y_0 = f_4(i) + f_3(i) \tag{10a}$$

are equilibrium conditions for the economy. And, since $S \equiv Y_0 - f_4(i)$, we have:

$$S = I, \text{ or} \tag{11}$$
$$Y_0 - f_4(i) = f_3(i). \tag{11a}$$

Equation (11) states that saving equals investment. This is a familiar enough statement; however, since both saving and investment are related to the interest rate, we must interpret equation (11) as pertaining to *intended* saving and investment. The interest rate is then the price variable which equates the resources businessmen want to use for capital goods with the resources consumers want to "sell," or at least not buy for purposes of present consumption.

If the interest rate is too low, consumers and business taken together will want to buy more than is available. Graph 3.6(b) shows this: $C + I > Y_0$ at all interest rates *below* i_0. If $C + I < Y_0$, such as at all interest rates above i_0, combined demand will fall short of production. At i_0, $C + I = Y_0$.

If $C + I > Y_0$, the economy will have inflationary pressure; if $C + I < Y_0$ deflationary pressure will ensue. What keeps the economy on an even keel in the classical system? Evidently, it is a flexible interest rate, and a flexible interest rate depends on the existence of a market whereby exchanges between savers and businessmen can be effected. In other words, there must be a capital market. The structure and operations of capital markets is a complex subject. Here we can only sketch out the essentials of such a market:

First, we can remove from consideration internal business saving used to finance investment; transfer of such saving to investment is not mediated by a capital market. Unspent business income plus consumer saving, however, is available to borrowers in the market, either directly through the purchase of securities, or indirectly through financial institutions which use customer funds to purchase securities. It is through these securities that borrowers attempt to elicit saving: higher interest rates encourage more direct purchases of securities (more saving) and allow financial intermediaries to offer depositors higher rates. Hence, the saving function in Graph 3.6(d) can be interpreted as a demand schedule for securities.

Similarly, the investment demand schedule in the same graph can be interpreted as a supply of securities: the lower (higher) the rate of interest, the larger (smaller) will be the volume of securities issued by businessmen. Equilibrium then must mean that the interest rate is such that new securities being supplied match the demand for such securities. Behind this statement stands the statement that resources demanded by businessmen match, at the equilibrium rate of interest, the resources being released by lack of consumer demand. If the security markets are competitive, the interest rate need have no trouble equilibrating aggregate demand with the level of production in the economy.[9]

General Equilibrium in the Classical Model

The power of the classical model should now be evident. Competition in the labor market determines a level of employment and real wages. Moreover, the equilibrium level of employment and output are

---

[9] It is important to note that classical theory denied money hoarding as an economically rational method of consumer saving. Since money yields no explicit return, most classical theorists assumed that, except for transaction purposes, consumers would not hold or add to money balances.

full employment quantities. The capital market, on the other hand, sets both the equilibrium interest rate and the pace of capital formation. The latter, when added to consumption spending, is just enough to clear the market of all goods being produced. *In other words, in the classical system demand is never chronically deficient: Interest rate adjustments always ensure an adequate level of demand.*

To illustrate this, consider Graph 3.7. An increase in the supply of

GRAPH 3.7

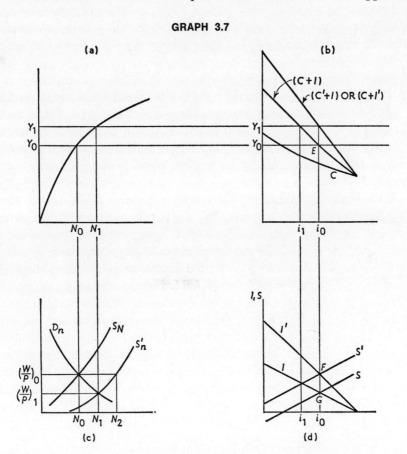

labor from S_n to S_n' reduces the real wage from $(W/P)_0$ to $(W/P)_1$. The lower real wage encourages employers to expand employment from N_0 to N_1. (If lack of competition in the labor market prevents a fall in the real wage, the increase in labor supply simply produces unemployment, equal to $N_2 - N_0$.) N_1 manhours, given the existing capital stock and state of technology, results in output expanding from Y_0 to Y_1.

Now, the crucial point: Output, Y_1, exceeds the old level of demand, i_0E. A general glut of goods can be prevented only if demand increases and/or output falls. The latter route courts disaster—unemployment. The former route prevents disaster.

How may demand increase? First, of course, the consumption schedule may rise. This is shown in Graph 3.7(b) by a shift of total demand from $(C + I)$ to $(C' + I)$. For consumption to rise, however, there must be a reason, and classical theory gave no argument linking a shift in consumption demand with expanded production. Remember this, for such a relationship is a key element in the Keynesian departure from classical theory.

Next, demand may rise because of a shift in the investment function to I', so that aggregate demand $(C + I')$, absorbs the higher output level. Notice that such an occurrence implicitly assumes a simultaneous increase in the saving function to S': Since the consumption demand schedule has remained unchanged, output must now exceed consumption at each interest rate by an amount equal to the increase in production.

The simultaneous increases in investment demand and saving serve to keep the interest rate stable at i_0 and to assure maintenance of the new full employment level of production. Unfortunately, again, there is nothing in the classical theoretical lexicon to promote a rise in investment demand sufficient to match the increased output level. Indeed, there is nothing in the theories of J. M. Keynes to ensure such a rise either. It is only in the modern offshoots of Keynesian theory, i.e., in the work of Roy Harrod, that such a relationship is postulated. Chapter 14 discusses Harrod's theories.

In the absence of an upward shift in consumption or investment demand, the full burden of adjustment of aggregate demand to the increased output level is thrown upon the interest rate. Graph 3.7(b) shows a surplus of supply over demand (Y_1 *minus* E) at i_0. Graph 3.7(d) indicates that the surplus expresses itself in the form of an excess of intended saving over intended investment (F *minus* G). The latter gap should show up in the capital market as an excess demand for new securities.

If the capital market is in good working order, the excess demand for securities should drive the interest rate down: competition among savers for securities should cause some buyers to undercut others, thus forcing the interest rate down. As the interest rate falls, however, investment spending should rise, increasing the supply of securities. The increased supply of securities, combined with the decreased demand of those savers who drop out of the bidding, should ultimately close the gap and stabilize the interest rate at i_1.

Note the beneficial effects of the capital market mechanism. The drop in the interest rate secures the new output level by increasing the amount of goods demanded for both consumption and investment purposes. Indeed, the increase is sufficient to close the gap between aggregate demand and supply.

Say's Law of Markets

A properly functioning capital market is evidently very important to classical theory. Interest rate adjustments determine the division of output between consumer and producer goods. They also promote an adequate level of demand. Indeed, in this latter role, interest rate adjustments ensure that lack of demand provides no barrier to the attainment or maintenance of full employment. If the labor market is working properly—if competition between workers and employers settle real wages and employment at equilibrium levels—interest rate adjustments always ensure adequate demand. Should investment demand falter, interest will decline and consumption spending will increase. Should saving rise, the interest rate will fall and investment spending will increase. Prolonged deficiency of demand is impossible.

A similar logic is behind the doctrine of an early French economist, J. B. Say. Say argued that under competitive capitalism, a chronic glut of goods is impossible: production is undertaken for the purpose of acquiring goods from someone else. If the income earned in the process of production is not spent on consumer goods, it will be spent on capital goods. If some goods are produced which people do not want, price declines drive them out of the market. Excess saving is impossible; for the act of saving is committed only by entrepreneurs, who simultaneously invest what they save. (The capital market adjustment of saving to investment is a bit more modern.) From all this it follows that a general and prolonged deficiency of demand is not possible; for supply, in effect, creates its own demand. Such is *Say's Law of Markets*.

Confronted with the facts of the Great Depression and with a theory which said that such an event is impossible, J. M. Keynes and some other economists concluded that the theory was wrong. But where? In the logic of the model? No, the logic was right. In the assumptions? The trouble had to be there!

In the *General Theory*, Keynes mounted an attack on classical theory at several points. He insisted that Say's Law of Markets is invalid, primarily because the classical economists overlooked the importance of the hoarding of money. If an act of saving includes the possibility of additions to money hoards, savers might not compete for securities and the classical interest rate mechanism might not work. Put diagramatically, as in Graph 3.8(b and d), the interest rate might stick at i_1, generating a deficiency of demand. As we shall see, Keynes argued that such a state of affairs would lead entrepreneurs to reduce production (to Y_1). The reduction in output and income would lead to a fall in employment (to N_1) and a reduction in saving (to S'). Indeed, to get ahead of our story a bit, it is the reduction in saving which finally leads to a new equilibrium. As shown in Graph 3.8, the new equilibrium at the sticky interest rate, i_1, is one characterized by underemployment.[10]

Notice that the underemployment equilibrium implies a disequilibrium real wage rate. $(W/P)_1$ in Graph 3.8(c) is such that under the assumptions of classical employment theory, workers should be competing for jobs thereby lowering both the money and real wage rates. Assume that such a competition lowers the real wage rate to $(W/P)_0$. Employment and output should then rise to N_0 and Y_0. But the sticky rate of interest will generate another surplus of aggregate supply over aggregate demand. This surplus should generate a decline in the price level. The decline in prices, assuming a temporarily sticky money wage, will raise real wages back to $(W/P)_1$. Hence, despite an initially flexible money wage, the sticky interest rate prevents anything more than a temporary return to full employment. *So long as this situation persists,*

---

[10] Another possibility is that even if the interest mechanism does work, a negative interest rate might be needed. In the diagram, $C + I < Y_0$ at all positive rates of interest. This implies that, if Y_0 is a full-employment level of output, it will not be achieved unless the interest rate turns negative, a very unlikely state of affairs. Hence, production will fall to Y_1, the saving function will shift to S' and the interest rate will rise to zero. It follows that even at a (unlikely) zero rate of interest, equilibrium might be an underemployment variety.

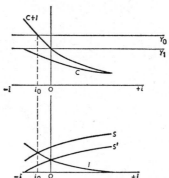

GRAPH 3.8

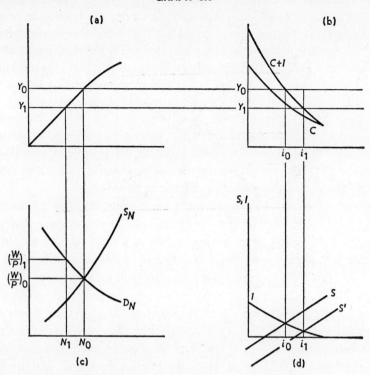

even a fully flexible wage and price level will prevent a return to sustained full employment.[11]

Keynes had one more fundamental criticism of classical theory. Suppose the labor market does not function as indicated above. Suppose workers stipulate for a money wage rather than a real wage. Under conditions of collective bargaining, such a hypothesis is not necessarily unwarranted. Moreover, as Keynes pointed out, wage bargains set money wages, not real wage rates. Individual or collective agreements have no way of setting general price levels. Hence, real wages for individual unions are determined by the bargain over money wages plus whatever the price level turns out to be.

Suppose the bargaining process sets a money wage at W^*. The supply curve of labor is then $(W^*/P_1) Z S_n$ in Graph 3.9. A money wage below W^* will result in a complete withdrawal of labor. A money wage in excess of W^*, on the other hand, will increase labor offered (on the

---

[11] Post-Keynesian writers have disputed this conclusion. More on this later.

GRAPH 3.9

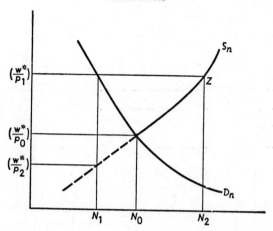

S_n function), since workers will obviously react positively to an *increase* in real wages. Keynes argued that workers would not resist a cut in real wages if the cut comes about from an increase in prices. Hence a rise of employment to N_0 can be achieved if the price level rises to P_0 $(P_2 > P_0 > P_1$ in Graph 3.9).

Does this make sense? While it is true that such an argument assumes a "money illusion" on the part of workers (that workers think real wages are affected only by money wages), in Keynes' day the argument made some sense. Today, large numbers of workers are covered by wage contracts whereby money wage rates are adjusted for cost-of-living changes. Hence, Keynes' assumption is probably no longer as well founded today as it was in his day.[12]

But, the argument made some sense in another way. The supply curve S_n (including the dotted portion) indicates the minimum real wage workers are willing to accept at given levels of employment. If N_1 is the employment level, W^*/P_2 is the minimum real wage acceptable to *employed* workers. W^*/P_1 is a real wage which exceeds this minimum. If unions or prevailing norms keep the money wage at W^*, there is no reason to expect employed workers to withhold their labor in the event of a fall in the real wage induced by rising prices. Only if prices rise beyond P_0 (say to P_2), will employed workers begin to withdraw from the labor market. But at such a real wage level an excess demand for labor will occur and money wages will be driven up.

---

[12] Nevertheless, these agreements have not yet faced the problem of survival under conditions of general deflation.

Such reasoning led Keynes to conclude that the classical explanation of the labor market is defective. Sticky wage rates, combined with a labor supply function of the sort postulated in Graph 3.9 [(W^*/P_1) $Z\,S_n$], could keep the labor force in a state of what Keynes called "involuntary unemployment" (equal to N_2 *minus* N_1 in Graph 3.9).

Keynes further concluded that full employment would be reached only through an increase in aggregate demand. For such an increase would allow employers to raise prices (reduce real wages) by enough to employ the appropriate amount of labor (N_0 in Graph 3.9). The rise in prices, according to Keynes, would come about because expanded production induces rising marginal costs.

Hence, Keynes had two principal criticisms of classical theory: (*a*) that Say's Law might not work, and (*b*) that even if Say's Law does work, the labor market might fail to give employment expansion.[13] Both situations, according to Keynes, can be cleared up by the expansion of demand. As a result, most of Keynes' analysis bore upon the problem of demand, an emphasis we also shall give in the coming chapters.

Classical Theory of Prices

The capstone to classical analysis was its theory of price levels. Most students are well aware of the quantity theory of money, or its expression in the equation of exchange. We shall give only a short exposition of the theory here in order to indicate the place it had in the classical scheme.

Let M be the stock of money. If people spend their dollars at the rate of V times per year, total expenditure per year will be $M \times V$. It is a truism that expenditure equals sales. If the value of sales per year is $P \times Y$, it follows that

$$MV = PY \text{ or} \qquad (12)$$
$$P = MV/Y . \qquad (12a)$$

Equation (12) is the familiar equation of exchange. Classical theorists assumed that V is more or less constant, fixed by the frequency of income receipts and expenditures, the rapidity of transportation and communications, habits regarding the use of credit, etc. M can be assumed

---

13 Assume Say's Law does work, but that sticky money wages prevent the labor market from functioning. In Graph 3.8 employment might settle at N_1, with the real wage at $(W/P)_1$. This produces an output level of Y_1, with a saving function at S'. Equilibrium in the capital market gives i_1, hence saving equals investment and $Y = C + I$. The capital market has done its job; however, short of an increase in demand, employment will not increase unless wage rates fall.

to be either under the control of the authorities or (in earlier days) fixed by the stock of gold or silver. Y, of course, depends upon competition in the labor market and the production function. Hence, the price level is fully determined, provided M, V, and Y are given.

Equation (12a) indicates this dependency of P on the other three elements of the equation of exchange. Causation runs from M, V, or Y to P, and only rarely the other way. Graph 3.10 also indicates the place of money and prices in the classical theory.

Graph 3.10(c) pictures the equation of exchange. $M V$ is a rectangular hyperbola, indicating that a constant M and V generate a volume of money expenditure that can be split up among an infinite number of combinations of P and Y. However, since Y_0 is given by the labor market and the production function, P_0 becomes the equilibrium price level.

A rise in M to M', or an increase in V to V' will shift the expenditure function to the right, raising prices to the level P_1.

Knowing P_0 now allows us to estimate the money wage level in the

GRAPH 3.10

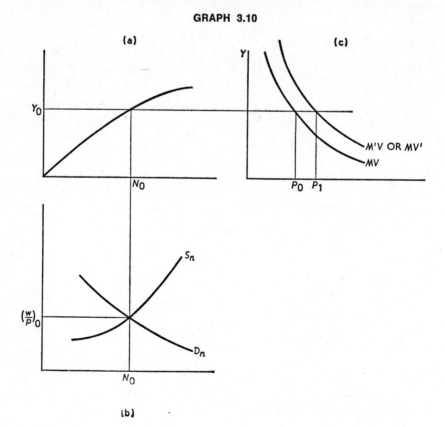

classical system. For if $(W/P)_0$ is the real wage in equilibrium, then $W_0/P_0 \equiv (W/P)_0$ and

$$(W/P)_0 \cdot P_0 \equiv W_0. \tag{13}$$

W_0 is the equilibrium money wage rate.

The classical theory of prices was extremely mechanical. Essentially, it involved tacking equation (12) on to the rest of the system. Since the other equations stand or fall without (12), the latter becomes something of a "fifth wheel." We shall in Chapters 10, 11, and 12 return to a more sophisticated view of the role of money and prices, where these variables are better integrated into the system.

ADDITIONAL READINGS FOR CHAPTER 3

(See footnote 1 in this chapter.)

KLEIN, L. R. *The Keynesian Revolution.* New York: Macmillan Co., 1949, chaps. 1–3.

Chapter 4 | AN EXPENDITURE MODEL OF NATIONAL INCOME

In the classical theory, the level of real national income, or output, was unrelated to the level of expenditure. Competition in the labor market produced full employment. The full employment quantity of labor was combined with the existing capital stock and technology to produce the (full employment) level of output. This level of output was absorbed by consumers and investors, with adjustments in the interest rate providing the necessary mechanism to bring demand into equality with the existing level of production.

Keynes, as we have seen, broke with this tradition in at least two ways: He postulated a rigid money wage and the possible existence of interest rates which are unresponsive to gaps between saving and investment.

The consequences of Keynes' break with traditional assumptions are many. We shall explore them at length later in the book. For now, we need only concentrate on the fact that Keynes' rigid money wage assumption destroyed the classical theory of output. For, if workers are willing to accept a whole range of employment offers at the going money wage, a whole range of real income levels becomes possible, even with a fixed capital stock and an unchanging technology. This range of potential output extends below and up to the full employment level.

The Keynesian system, then, recognizes two states or conditions for the economy. The first state is one in which the labor force is not fully employed. Under this condition, the aggregate level of real income or output is determined by what Keynes called the level of effective demand, or the combined level of real consumption, investment, government, and net foreign outlays. The second state is characterized by a fully employed labor force. Here, effective demand is not the main determinant of aggregate output. Instead, as with the classical system, real national income depends on the size of the labor force, the stock of

68

capital, and the "state of the arts," or technology. Our job in this and the next several chapters will be to examine the first situation. We shall first analyze the way in which effective demand affects the level of real income and employment. After that, we shall examine the forces affecting the various components of effective demand. As we shall see, these forces are partly independent and partly dependent on the level of real income itself. What will emerge is a picture of the economy characterized by a high degree of interaction between its various parts.

METHOD OF ATTACK

Our method of attack will be to begin with a simple hypothetical economy, complicating it as we proceed. The main outlines of the simple economy are (1) an absence of government spending and net exports, (2) which implies that consumption and domestic investment spending are the only relevant expenditure flows. (3) We shall also exclude corporations from the analysis, so that all income accrues to the household sector, which does all the saving. (4) Note that we are dealing with *real, or constant dollar national income,* not nominal, or current dollar GNP. All investment and saving are therefore net of depreciation and the price level is assumed to be fixed. These assumptions will be gradually relaxed as we proceed.

Another important comment: we shall be using, until further notice, a method of analysis called *comparative statics.* The meaning of this can perhaps best be shown by use of an analogy. Suppose that we can define the forces which, at any point in time, operate to produce an equilibrium position for a rocking chair; that is, the forces which place the chair at rest. We know that if the chair is nudged it will come back to rest in the old equilibrium position. However, if a weight is added to one side of the rockers, the position of equilibrium for the chair will change: it will come to rest at a different position. An engineer or mathematician should be able to describe the comparative forces which lead to the two positions of equilibrium. Of course, in essence the nature of the forces are the same; their magnitude and direction, however, have changed. The analyst should be able to tell us, by proper measurements, exactly what it was in the magnitude and direction of forces that produced the one position of rest as opposed to the other.

We want to do the same thing with national income. We want to be able to describe the forces which lead national income to alternative levels of equilibrium. Not that we ever expect income to be in equilibrium: the forces which might produce such positions of rest are constantly changing in magnitude and direction. This does not mean that national income is not being affected by them. It is, and it is only a simplifying device to assume that the forces produce equilibria. With this in mind, therefore, we shall proceed to inquire into the forces which produce one equilibrium level of income as opposed to another and, as the word *statics* implies, we shall be temporarily unconcerned with the problem of time.

The Circular Flow of Income and Expenditure, Again

Let us give specific content to the problem. Suppose that national income (Y) is set at a certain value, say $200 billion. If this level of income is not to change, certain conditions must be met. The sum of consumption (C) and net domestic investment (I) expenditures must neither exceed nor fall short of this level of income. If it did, national income would be different from the $200 billion figure. Let us see why: Suppose that consumption and investment spending were $190 and $20 billion respectively. If Y were $200 billion, businessmen would be producing a level of output less than the total level of spending on that output; their receipts, in the aggregate, would be $10 billion greater than the factor cost of output. Since production would be less than the total value of sales, businessmen would meet the added demand out of inventories, then hire additional workers, increase production, and pay out more incomes. National income rises under such conditions; it continues to rise until final output and spending come into equality. Under conditions where consumption and investment are less than current output, say $190 billion as opposed to $200 billion of output, national income cannot be maintained: business receives less than the factor cost of production, inventories pile up, and workers must be laid off.

The requirement for an equilibrium level of income and output, then, is that consumption and intended investment spending add up to the current level of output; i.e., that

$$C + I = Y .^1 \tag{1}$$

Since consumption equals national income minus saving out of current income $(C \equiv Y - S)$, the substitution of $(Y - S)$ for C makes the equilibrium condition:

---

[1] Note the implicit requirement here that the real wage shall not exceed or fall short of the marginal product of labor. Also implicit is the Keynesian assumption that workers are receiving a real wage which at least equals their minimum acceptable real wage at the existing level of employment. See Chapter 3.

$$Y = (Y - S) + I, \text{ or} \tag{2}$$
$$S = I,$$

or that people in the economy shall save the same amount that they and others intend to invest.

The level of final expenditure will be inconsistent with the level of income in two circumstances: (1) If $C + I > Y$, then, since $C \equiv (Y - S)$, $(Y - S) + I > Y$ and $I > S$. Because total demand is greater than total output, investment will exceed what people plan to save, the equilibrium condition will not be met and national income will tend to rise. (2) If consumption-plus-investment spending is less than the level of final output, if $C + I < Y$, $(Y - S) + I < Y$, and $I < S$. National income under these circumstances will tend to fall.

A simple diagram (Fig. 4.1) emphasizes these important results.

FIGURE 4.1

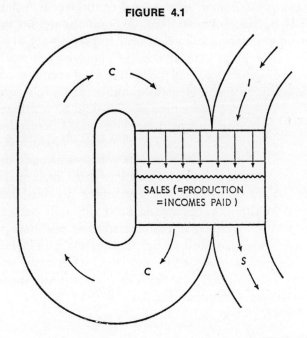

The figure depicts a certain flow of consumption and investment spending pouring into firms, which, in turn, are stimulated to ·produce an equivalent level of output. An equal level of income, Y, is, in turn allocated to the factors of production that produce the final output of goods and services. Part of this income re-enters the spending stream in the form of consumption spending, and part of it leaks out in the form of current saving. If the inflowing stream of investment spending matches the saving leakage, output and income will not rise or fall. If the incoming stream of investment is greater than the saving leakage, national income will tend to rise as workers are hired and paid to replace and add to the depleted inventories. If the stream of investment spending is less than the outflow of saving, income will contract.

It is apparent that the I and S streams can become unmatched under a variety of conditions. If income recipients decide to save more (consume less), while investors do not change their expenditure, the income stream will contract as the increased saving leakage prevents firms from recovering in sales the total amount of factor costs they have incurred in production. On the other hand, a decrease in the rate of saving (increase in consumption) will expand the income stream, because firms are receiving back more than the current value of final output. Increases and decreases in the rate of investment spending, saving remaining the same, will also tend to increase and decrease the size of the income stream.

A SIMPLE EXPENDITURE MODEL

In order to explain how national income is determined, then, we must isolate the influence of consumer and investor spending upon the level of final output. Let us begin as simply as possible and assume that the level of investment is given; that is, no matter what happens, businessmen will spend only a certain annual amount upon capital goods, say I^*, or \$10 billion.[2]

Let us also make some reasonable assumption about the behavior of consumer spending. We know that most people tend to increase their consumption spending when their incomes rise and to reduce it when their incomes fall. It is also reasonable to assume, however, that when income falls to zero consumption does not also drop to zero: people have to live, even if they are forced to draw upon their past savings or to borrow. Consumption spending will tend to be positive, even if income is zero.

If these statements are acceptable descriptions of consumer behavior, we may depict such spending as being related to national income as in Graph 4.1, the C-line. At zero income consumption is positive, indicating that people in the economy are dissaving as a whole and that the capital

---

[2] At present, we are ignoring the effect of the interest rate on both investment and saving. Keynesian theory, as we shall see, considers both.

GRAPH 4.1

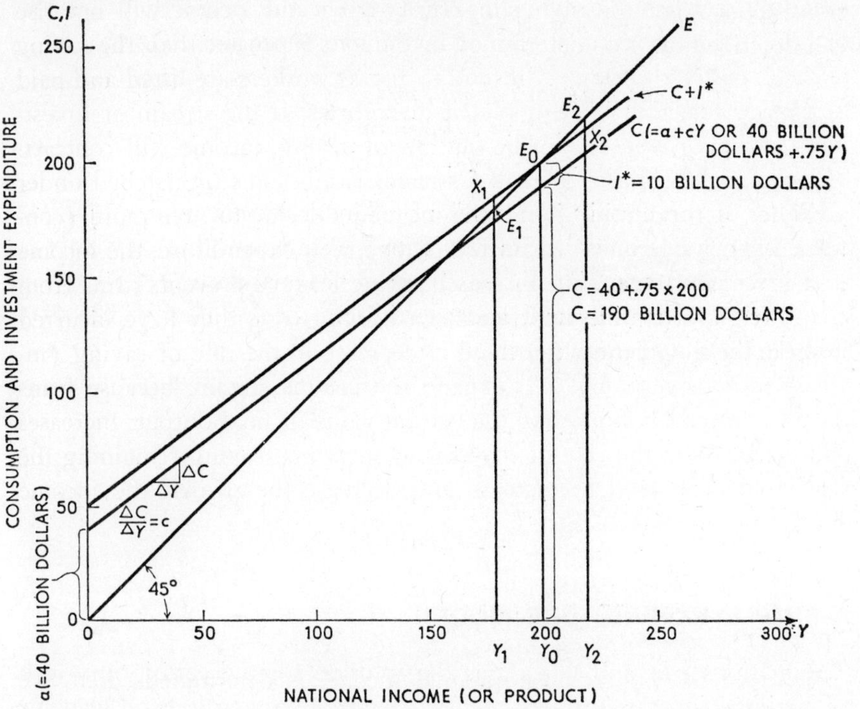
C,I
250
200
150
100
50
0
CONSUMPTION AND INVESTMENT EXPENDITURE
a(=40 BILLION DOLLARS)
E
C+I*
C(=a+cY OR 40 BILLION DOLLARS +.75Y)
I*=10 BILLION DOLLARS
C=40+.75×200
C=190 BILLION DOLLARS
E2
X2
E0
X1
E1
ΔC
ΔY
ΔC/ΔY=c
45°
0
50
100
150
200
250
300 Y
Y1 Y0 Y2
NATIONAL INCOME (OR PRODUCT)

stock is being depleted at the rate of this dissaving (since $S = I$, $-S = -I$). At higher levels of income, consumer spending can increase. The rate by which consumption rises per unit increase in national income is measured by the slope of the *C*-line. This rate is called the *marginal propensity to consume* (the MPC). Expressed symbolically, the MPC $\equiv \Delta C/\Delta Y = c$, where ΔC is the change in consumption and ΔY is the change in national income. Since we have drawn a straight *C*-line in Graph 4.1, $\Delta C/\Delta Y$ is a constant, *c*. This is tantamount to assuming that, regardless of the level of income, the rate of change in consumption spending per added or subtracted unit of national income will be the same. While this may not be correct in general, the assumption is a useful simplifying proposition which can always be relaxed in further analysis.

The equation for the *C*-line takes the form of an equation of a straight line. Call *a* the intercept (i.e., the amount the community will spend on consumption if national income is zero), and *c* the slope of the line (the MPC). The dependency of *C* on *Y* can therefore be described by the expression: $C = a + cY$. Now, gathering our assumptions about I and C, and giving I^*, a, and c the indicated values, we can describe how Y is determined by the two expenditure flows:

Assumptions about I and C
$$I = I^* = \$10 \text{ billion}$$
$$C = a + cY_\bullet = \$40 \text{ billion} + .75Y.$$

What is the equilibrium level of national income under these assumed expenditure flows? Starting with the statement that consumption and investment spending $(C + I)$ equal national income (Y), when the latter is in equilibrium, and substituting the assumed nature of C and I in the statement, we get:

$$Y = C + I \tag{1}$$
$$Y = (a + cY) + I^*, \text{ or} \tag{3}$$
$$Y = a/(1 - c) + I^*/(1 - c) \tag{4}^3$$

$$Y = C + I \tag{1}$$
$$Y = 40 + .75Y + 10 \tag{3a}$$
$$Y = 40/(1 - .75) + 10/(1 - .75) \tag{4a}$$
$$= \$200 \text{ billion.}$$

Equations (4) and (4a) give the solution for the equilibrium level of national income implied in the assumptions regarding the behavior of consumption and investment spending. Does the level of income derived satisfy the $I = S$ condition of equilibrium?

GRAPH 4.2

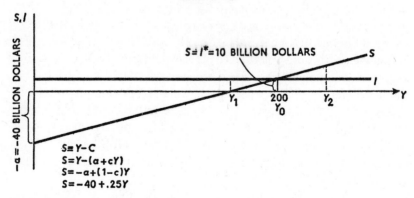

----

[3] (4) is derived from (3) as follows:
$$Y = a + cY + I^*$$
$$Y - cY = Y(1 - c) = a + I^*,$$
$$Y = a/(1 - c) + I^*/(1 - c).$$

$$I^* = 10$$
$$S \equiv (Y - C), \text{ from } Y \equiv C + S.$$

Substituting $(40 + .75Y)$ for C and 200 for Y, we get

$$S = 200 - (40 + .75 \times 200)$$
$$S = 200 - 40 - 150$$
$$S = 10.$$

Since $S = 10$ and $I^* = 10$, the condition is satisfied.

The forces affecting the size of national income are also shown in Graph 4.1. If national income is in equilibrium, not tending to change, output of final goods and services will be exactly absorbed by the sum of investment and consumption spending. Line OE in Graph 4.1 shows the alternative levels of national income (output) which could be sustained by alternative levels of expenditure. Since the sum of investment and consumption spending must equal the value of income at these alternative equilibrium levels of income, line OE intersects the Y axis of the graph at O (at a 45° angle). The horizontal distance from O to any point on Y, say Y_1, will be equaled by the vertical distance to OE from that point, say Y_1E_1. In Graph 4.1 we might say that supply, represented by OY_1, equals demand, depicted by Y_1E_1, at the equilibrium level of national income, OY_1.

We can argue that an excess of demand over supply $(C + I > Y)$ would drive national income up, because current output would be over-absorbed by current demand. Conversely, a deficiency of demand $(C + I < Y)$ would produce a contraction in income. In Graph 4.1 line C (from $C = a + cY$) represents consumer demand at various levels of income. If to consumer demand we add a constant amount of investment demand (I^*), the result is a total demand line, labeled "$C + I^*$" in the diagram. It is plain from the diagram that, at the level of final output of goods and services OY_1, total demand (Y_1X_1) exceeds total supply by an amount E_1X_1, OY_1 being equal to Y_1E_1. Income and output should therefore tend to rise. At income level OY_2 ($=Y_2E_2$), total expenditure is insufficient to absorb total production of final goods and services, and national income should tend to contract. The level of income will not tend to change from the annual rate of OY_0, however, because at this level final output ($\$200$ billion) is just being absorbed by total spending ($C + I^*$, or $\$190 + \$10$ billion).

It is easy to see from the graph that the equilibrium level of national income satisfies the condition that saving equals investment. Investment, on Graph 4.1, is measured by the vertical distance from line C to line $C + I^*$. Saving $(Y - C)$, the vertical distance from line C to line

OE, varies with the alternative levels of income. Plotting *I** and *S*, so derived, yields Graph 4.2. From this diagram it is apparent that investment is greater than saving out of current income to the left of Y_0, and that it is less than saving to the right of Y_0. At Y_0 investment is just equal to what people are saving, and national income is in equilibrium. In terms of our former argument, national income is in equilibrium because the rate at which investment funds are pouring into the economy is just counterbalanced by the rate at which saving is leaking out of it.

The Nature of the Equilibrium Position

There are several things to note about the equilibrium level of national income. First, under the assumptions made, there is one and only one level of national income possible. This follows from the fact that investment is fixed at *I**, or $10 billion. Moreover, even though consumption is not fixed at a given rate of annual expenditure, but varies with the level of income, there is only one level of income, and one level of consumption, which will satisfy the condition of income equilibrium. These levels of consumption and income must be such that $S (\equiv Y - C)$ will equal the postulated level of I (I^*). This is demonstrated by the final form of the equilibrium statement (derived from $C + I = Y$), after inserting the assumed values of consumption and investment into the equilibrium equation: "$Y = a/(1 - c) + I^*/(1 - c)$" is a statement which asserts one and only one value for Y, because *a*, *c*, and *I** are *all constants*.

But, what happens if investment is allowed to vary? The first thing is that Y loses its uniqueness; for, now that a variety of investment levels are possible, a variety of income levels are possible. Graph 4.3 shows the alternative levels of Y which are associated with alternative levels of I. At $C + I_{-1}$, where investment is zero, income will settle at Y_{-1}, or $160 billion; at $C + I_0$ and $C + I_1$, where investment is $10 and $20 billion respectively, national income settles at Y_0 ($200 billion) and Y_1 ($240 billion).

Y, in fact, is related in a linear fashion to I. For every $10 billion increase in I, Y increases by $40 billion. This flows from the definition of the equilibrium statement of Y in equation (4), after substituting the variable I for the constant I^*:

$$Y = a/(1 - c) + I/(1 - c), \text{ or}$$
$$Y = 40/(1 - .75) + I/(1 - .75), \text{ or}$$
$$Y = 160 + 4I.$$

GRAPH 4.3

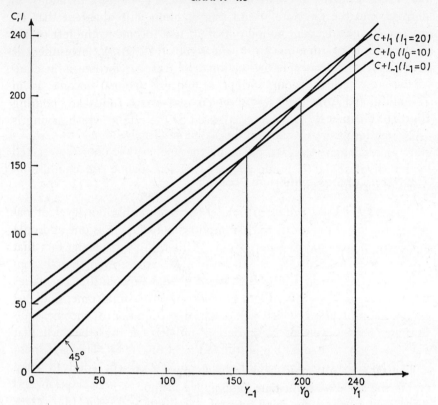

Stated in its numerical form on the right, the linear dependency of Y upon I is clear: for every unit change in I, Y increases by four times. It is a simple matter to draw a graph of the relationship between Y and I. If I is zero, Y is \$160 billion. Thereafter, Y increases by four units for every unit change in I. Graph 4.4 shows this relationship: The line on the graph depicts the locus of alternative national income equilibria under alternative rates of investment spending, given the constants a and c.

How is it that national income increases by more than the increase in investment? The answer is that the increase in income, induced by the increase in investment, itself induces an increase in consumption spending which, in turn, increases national income further. The increases in income, however, are more rapid than the increases in consumption, so that saving also increases. When income has increased enough to cause saving to come into equality with the new level of investment, no further rise in income will take place. For, at this point, the saving leakage will again balance the investment expenditure being injected into the circular flow of income and output.[4] The characteristics of the new level of national income are: (*a*) income has increased by a multiple of four times the increase in investment spending; (*b*) three fourths of the rise in national income and expenditure is taken up by the increase in consumption (on Graph 4.4, ΔC, or $C_1 - C_0$); and (*c*) additional investment spending (ΔI, or $I_1 - I_0$) absorbs the other fourth of the increase in Y.

No matter where we start on the Y-line in Graph 4.4, $\Delta Y = 4\Delta I$. To show this, compare any two points on the line, say the ones represented by coordinates (I_0, Y_0) and (I_1, Y_1). Then, define the equilibrium levels of income Y_0 and Y_1:

$$Y_1 = a/(1-c) + I_1/(1-c) \tag{5}$$
$$Y_0 = a/(1-c) + I_0/(1-c) . \tag{6}$$

Subtracting (6) from (5), in order to get ΔY, gives us

$$Y_1 - Y_0 = (I_1 - I_0)/(1-c), \text{ or}$$
$$\Delta Y = \Delta I/(1-c) = \Delta I[1/(1-c)] . \tag{7}$$

Since $c = .75$,

$$\Delta Y = 4\Delta I .$$

The same result could have been obtained from the graph by computing the slope of the Y-line. The above method, however, shows the constituent parts of the coefficient of ΔI, commonly called the *multiplier*. The size of the multiplier is dependent upon the value of c (the marginal propensity to consume, or the MPC). The larger c the larger is the multiplier; and vice versa. The reason should be clear: if the increase in income induces large increases in consumption, the increase in consumption will, in turn, cause income to grow rapidly. The total increase in income will be large, and saving, now a smaller proportion of increases in income, will come into equality with the higher level of investment only at levels of income which are higher. Small increases in income would simply not induce enough additional saving to create an equilibrium.

To make this clear, suppose we examine two extreme cases. At one extreme, assume that the MPC $= 0$. Hence, an increase in investment

---

[4] This is a Keynesian innovation. He made income, not the interest rate, the principal determinant of consumption and saving. In the classical system, an increase in investment raises the interest rate and saving. With Keynes, increases in investment raise income, and the latter raises saving in accordance with the MPC. In other words, for Keynes, adjustments in Y equilibrate S and I. In the classical system, the interest rate does the job.

GRAPH 4.4

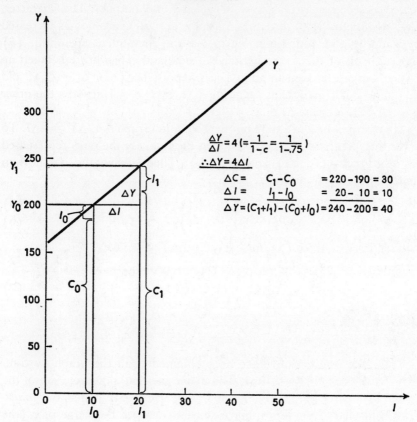

$$\frac{\Delta Y}{\Delta I} = 4 \left(= \frac{1}{1-c} = \frac{1}{1-.75}\right)$$

$$\therefore \Delta Y = 4\Delta I$$

$\Delta C = \quad C_1 - C_0 \quad = 220 - 190 = 30$

$\Delta I = \quad I_1 - I_0 \quad = 20 - 10 = 10$

$\Delta Y = (C_1 + I_1) - (C_0 + I_0) = 240 - 200 = 40$

will induce a change in income; but, because $c = 0$, there is no induced increase in consumption. This being the case, the whole increase in income is saved, and no rise of income beyond the initial increase caused by the increase in investment takes place. Inserting the value 0 in equation (7) shows that the change in income will not go beyond the amount of the increased investment when the marginal propensity to consume is zero. At the other extreme, assume the MPC to be unity. In this case, every increase in Y induced by changes in investment will be matched by an increase in consumption spending. Saving will never increase by enough (it will not increase at all) to come into equality with the new level of investment spending. National income will continue to rise indefinitely: it will, so to speak, explode.[5]

---

[5] That is, income will "explode" to the full employment limit. Further increases in income can only be in terms of price level inflation.

It should be apparent that the closer c is to zero, the smaller will be the increase in national income induced by any given change in investment spending. It is also plain that, as c approaches 1, the changes in national income induced by increased investment spending approach infinity. Indeed, we might say that the stability condition for national income is that c is equal to or greater than zero, and less than unity: i.e., that $0 \leqq c < 1$. Otherwise, changes in investment would cause national income to either expand indefinitely or, if investment declines, to drop to zero.

In the case of a decline in investment spending, income will also decline, and the extent of the decrease will again depend upon the value of the MPC. If the multiplier is 4, because c is .75, a decrease in the rate of investment spending of $10 billion will cause a decline of $40 billion in national income. The decline of Y will halt at $40 billion because, by this time, saving will have declined by enough to come into equality with the new and lower level of investment spending. For this to happen, the marginal propensity to consume has to be less than unity or equal to or greater than zero. If it were not, saving would not decline with the decline in income; the leakage out of the income stream in the form of saving would always be greater than the reinjections from investment spending, and the stream would dry up to nothing. Again, for income to reach a lower and stable level of equilibrium, above zero, the MPC must be at least zero or less than 1.

The Multiplier

In the previous section we made use of what we earlier called "comparative statics" in order to derive the multiplier. That is, we simply subtracted the equation defining equilibrium Y_0 from the equation defining equilibrium Y_1. The difference was the term $\Delta I[1/(1 - c)]$, the second element of which we called the multiplier. Since the precise meaning of the multiplier may not be obvious from this derivation, it will pay to approach its derivation somewhat more dynamically.

We start with the observation that increases in investment spending, when met by increases in final output on the part of businessmen, have the effect of putting into the hands of earners an amount of income equal to the increase in investment itself. But the process does not stop there. Income recipients now have more to spend. If they spend a fraction c of their additional income, the initial increase in production (income) resulting from the rise in investment spending will be joined by a further increase equal to c times the rise in investment: That is, $\Delta Y =$

$\Delta I + c\Delta I$. This further increase, which is new consumption spending, will also form the basis for additional spending, since in order to meet the increase in consumption employers will have to put on more hands. Having earned $c\Delta I$, these new hands will consume $c(c\Delta I)$, if their marginal propensity to consume is the same as the first group. This new consumption will, in its own turn, swell national income and production and form a basis for additional consumption spending. In short, the *total* change in national income resulting from a change in investment will equal the initial change in investment itself plus a series of terms reflecting the induced increases in consumption spending. Each induced increase in consumption will, itself, induce further increases in income. The series will be as in equation (8):

$$\Delta Y = \Delta I + c\Delta I + c^2\Delta I + \ldots \ldots + c^n\Delta I, \text{ or} \tag{8}$$
$$\Delta Y = \Delta I(1 + c + c^2 + \ldots \ldots + c^n), \text{ or} \tag{9}$$
$$\Delta Y = \Delta I [1/(1-c)]. \tag{10}$$

It is evident that if n (the number of periods during which income is expanding) is very large, the total increase in national income will eventually approach some limit. The reason is that the marginal propensity to consume, c, is less than unity; hence, each succeeding term finds ΔI multiplied by a smaller value. This means that the successive increases in consumption spending continue to fall off until they virtually approach zero. Equation (10), derived from equation (8)[6], shows that the limit to ΔY is the change in investment times the very same multiplier we derived above.

We have derived the multiplier from a dynamic statement of the impact of new investment upon the level of income. Since the derivation was a bit abstract, it will be helpful to expand upon it with a numerical example: Assume an initial level of income of $200 billion, $190 of which is consumption and $10 of which is investment spending. Assume, also, that any dollar increase in national income causes consumers to increase

---

[6] Define the term in the parentheses of (9) as K:
$$K = 1 + c + c^2 + \ldots \ldots + c^n, \text{ where } o < c < 1 \tag{i}$$
Multiply both sides of the previous equation by c:
$$cK = c + c^2 + \ldots \ldots + c^n + c^{n+1}. \tag{ii}$$
Subtract the second equation from the first to get
$$K - cK = 1 - c^{n+1}, \quad \text{or}$$
$$K = \frac{1 - c^{n+1}}{1 - c}. \tag{iii}$$
Because $o < c < 1$ and n is very large,
$$\lim_{n \to \infty} K = \frac{1}{1-c}. \tag{iv}$$

their spending by 75 cents. In other words, the MPC, or c, is .75. Now, let the annual rate of investment spending rise to $20 billion. $C + I$ is now greater than $200 billion because investment has risen by $10 billion (stage 2 of table below). At this point, supply is less than demand, because the old equilibrium level of national income ($200 billion), which measures the supply of goods at factor prices, is less than the new flow of expenditure (= $210 billion). Inventories of businessmen are reduced by $10 billion and additional labor must be hired to replace them and to take care of the new level of demand. But, by hiring workers and other factors of production business pays them income, and this added income (= $10 billion) measures the new level of national income (stage 3). Seventy-five percent of this added income is used by its recipients for consumption, and in the new stage (3) total expenditure $(C + I)$ still exceeds total output by $7.5 billion; inventories are therefore again reduced. Stage 4 begins with a national income of $217.5 billion, after additional productive factors are hired; but, since expenditure is now $223.1 billion $(C + I = 203.1 + 20)$, income rises again. The process continues until $C + I = Y$, or, as in the example, income has risen over the stage 1 equilibrium level by $40 billion.

Stage	Y	C	I	Change in Inventories
1	200	190	10	0
2	200	190	20	−10
3	210	197.5	20	−7.5
4	217.5	203.1	20	−5.6
5	223.1	207.3	20	−4.2
6	227.3	210.6	20	−3.3
7	230.6	....	..	...
	....	....	..	...
	....	....	..	...
End	240.0	220.0	20	0

Notice, we could have gotten the same answer by applying the rule $\Delta Y = \Delta I[1/(1 - c)]$; for, since the marginal propensity to consume in the example is .75 and ΔI is $10 billion, $\Delta Y = 10[1/(1 - .75)]$ or $40 billion.

The system also works in *reverse;* that is, if investment drops by $10 billion, income will drop by $40 billion, i.e., $\Delta Y = [1/(1 - .75)] \cdot (-10) = -$40 billion.

For the change in income to be permanent, the change in the rate of investment expenditure must also be permanent. In order to see this, consider the following example, which assumes an MPC of .75 and a rise in stage 2 of investment by $10 billion. In stage 3, investment falls back to its old level, so that the change in investment is not permanent.

Stage	Y	C	I	Change in Inventories
1	200	190	10	0
2	200	190	20	−10
3 ....'......	210	197.5	10	+2.5
4	207.5	195.7	10	+1.8
5	205.7	194.3	10	+1.4
6	204.3	....	..	...
....	....	....	..	...
....	....	....	..	...
End	200	190	10	0

At first, income rises to $210 billion, as before; but, although consumption in stage 3 is $197.5 billion, the drop in investment back to its initial level of $10 billion lowers total expenditure and income to $207.5 billion. This lowers consumption spending even further, which results in an additional fall in income, the final settling point of which is the old equilibrium level of $200 billion.

Notice the role played by inventory investment in the example. Assuming that businessmen always want to adjust inventories to sales, we see that the initial inventory depletion of $10 billion in stage 2 forces them to increase output in stage 3 by $10 billion. Although this results in an additional $10 billion of income, and $7.5 billion of new consumption spending, the drop in investment spending to its old $10 billion level forces them to invest $2.5 billion in excess inventories. The result is that they lay off workers and reduce output to the annual rate of $207.5 billion. But the decline in national income causes consumption spending to drop to $195.7 billion, and, despite the layoffs, $1.8 billion of excess inventories are produced in stage 4. This forces further layoffs, further declines in income and consumption spending. The process continues until the excess inventories are worked off.

A moral can be drawn from this analysis: excess inventories ordinarily induce businessmen to reduce employment, output, and income payments. But, if *all* employers are reducing output and employment, consumption spending will also drop, leaving businessmen with continued overinvestment in inventories. Since the process of inventory liquidation is somewhat self-defeating, it may be a long and painful one for the economy, painful enough to cause a serious decline in income and employment.

Usefulness of the Multiplier Analysis

The multiplier tells us by how much a given change in spending will induce a change in income. For the change in income to be exactly the amount predicted by the multiplier, the marginal propensity to consume must be predictable; that is, the slope of the consumption line must be known and must not be subject to change. As we shall see, this sort of knowledge is not available and, in fact, the MPC is subject to unpredictable short-term changes. Nevertheless, the theory of the multiplier is useful as a partial explanation for the often-observed fact that income changes in the economy are cumulative, seeming to feed upon themselves during booms and slumps.

A more important qualification of the theory, however, is that cumulative movements of national income result from forces other than successive rounds of new consumption spending. Investment changes, for example, might also be linked to changes in national income. This being the case, the cumulative movements of income will often be greater than those predicted by the simple multiplier alone.

We shall return to these considerations later, but it should be pointed out here that, although the multiplier is not a complete apparatus for explaining the magnitude of income changes, it is an important *part* of the apparatus which must ultimately be used. The theory should not be tossed out just because it cannot explain everything; it should be supplemented.

Saving Equals Investment, Again

In our discussion we have frequently emphasized the distinction between intended, or planned, saving and investment on the one hand, and realized saving and investment on the other. In the realized sense of the terms, saving and investment are always equal (in an economy with no government or foreign trade), while in the other sense of the terms, we can say that national income changes as a result of differences between the two magnitudes. It is important to have a clear notion of the distinctions between these categories of saving and investment. A numerical example may help: assume the MPC to be .5, and start with an equilibrium level of income at $200 billion.

Stage	(1) Y	(2) C	(3) I (In-tended)	(4) I (Unin-tended) = ΔInven-tories	(5) I (Real-ized) = (3) + (4)	(6) S (Real-ized and Planned)
1	200	190	10	0	10	10
2	200	190	20	−10	10	10
3	210	195	20	−5	15	15
4	215	197.5	20	−2.5	17.5	17.5
5	217.5	....	..	...	...	...
....	....	....	..	...	...	...
....	....	....	..	...	...	...
End	220	200	20	0	20	20

In stage 1, national income is in equilibrium at $200 billion; businessmen are investing $10 billion; households are saving $10 billion and they are consuming $190 billion a year. In stage 2, however, investment spending rises to the intended rate of $20 billion. Since production has not yet increased, incomes do not change and households still plan $10 billion of saving. Because of this, inventories are depleted and businessmen thereby *dis*invest $10 billion. As a result, only $10 billion of investment [col. (5)] is realized by the whole business community, and this is equal to saving. By stage 3, income has risen to $210 billion, causing households to increase their saving by $5 billion; but, because consumption spending has also risen by $5 billion, businessmen are forced to decrease their inventories (to disinvest) by a like amount. Adding this disinvestment to the $20 billion of intended investment spending gives a total of $15 billion of realized investment, which equals realized saving. The process continues until no additional inventory disinvestment takes place and intended investment is equal to intended, or planned saving.

It should be apparent that realized saving and investment are always equal, the latter being compounded of both intended and unintended investment, just as we indicated in Chapter 1. When a difference appears between intended investment and saving, as in stage 2, the result is unintended investment (or disinvestment, as the case may be). This motivates businessmen to change their outputs. If unintended investment is negative, as in the example, businessmen will expand output; if it is positive, then unanticipated inventories will have been "bought" and businessmen will be moved to reduce employment and output until the unintended investment is wiped out. The student is invited to try the foregoing example under the assumption of a *decline* in intended investment spending.

ADDITIONAL READINGS

See end of Chapter 5.

Chapter 5 : EXPANSION OF THE SIMPLE MODEL

So far we have been working with a simplified expenditure model for determining the level of national income. It is now time to bring in the activities first of the government and later of the foreign trade sector of the economy. While this will add some complications to the determination of national income, we will still be operating at a fairly simple level: we will still be forgoing an analysis of the determinants of the main expenditure flows. Changes in national income will bear a simple relationship to *postulated* changes in investment, government spending and taxing, and net foreign investment. The forces influencing these expenditures will be studied later in the book.

ADDING GOVERNMENT ACTIVITY—THE NEW VARIABLES

In the last chapter we were concerned with the determination of national income (Y), without the influence of government activities. Inclusion of these activities, however, requires that we use the concept of net national product (or income: NNP, or NNY), because, as will be remembered, only part of the tax intake of the government—corporate and personal income taxes and social security taxes—are included in the definition of national income. Since the government also collects indirect taxes, we must use the net national product concept. Instead of the cumbersome symbol, NNP, we shall use a new one, Y_n, in the following analysis. Items such as business transfer payments, subsidies, and the statistical discrepancy will be assumed not to exist. Their exclusion will only negligibly affect the analysis.

Government spending, as we have seen, is an important part of total expenditure on final goods and services. We shall symbolize such spending with the letter G. G, it should be emphasized, includes only government expenditure upon final goods and services; it does not include transfer payments made by the government to other sectors of the econ-

87

omy. In addition, it will be remembered that "government" is broadly interpreted to include all levels—federal, state, and local. G includes the spending of all of these units of government.

The other side of the government's budget, the tax side, requires special treatment. If we assume that government's budget is balanced (that it contains neither a surplus or deficit) we can express it by the equation,

$$G + TR_g = T_x,$$

where TR_g represents government transfer payments and T_x represents all tax revenues. Assuming that government nontax revenue is zero, and it is usually negligible, this equation expresses the necessary relation between government expenditures and receipts, when the budget is balanced.

Now suppose we bring TR_g over to the right side of the equation; the relation then becomes:

$$G = T_x - TR_g.$$

In this form, transfer payments appear as a negative tax, as indeed they are, for they put money back into the hands of income receivers, enlarging their disposable income. The right-hand side of the relation, taking into account TR_g, then shows government's net tax receipts. We shall identify these net receipts by the symbol T $(\equiv T_x - TR_g)$. The budget relation is thereby reduced to the simple form of

$$G = T.$$

It will be remembered that one important variant of the income concept is disposable income, Y_d. Disposable income is that which accrues to households after indirect business taxes, social security taxes, corporate retaining earnings, and corporate taxes are deducted from net national product and after government transfer payments to households are added. We shall still temporarily exclude corporations from the analysis, so that disposable income may be defined as follows:

$$Y_d \equiv Y_n - (T_x - TR_g), \text{ or}$$
$$Y_d \equiv Y_n - T, \text{ since } T \equiv T_x - TR_g.$$

It is plain that disposable income is strongly influenced by both the size of net national product and the amount of net taxes collected by the government. Given T_x, the amount of taxes the government is collecting, Y_d is the larger (smaller) the larger (smaller) is net national product or government transfer payments. Given Y_n and TR_g, Y_d is greater (smaller) the smaller (greater) is the size of the tax intake.

Disposable income is a key variable in the system of income determination. Since households utilize the income they receive to save and consume, and since the size of net national income is partly dependent upon the level of consumer spending, variations in disposable income cause variations in the size of net national product.

To summarize, the new variables we shall be dealing with are:

Y_n, net national income or product, or NNP;
G, government spending on final output;
T, net taxes collected by government $(\equiv T_x - TR_g)$; and
Y_d, disposable income $(\equiv Y_n - T)$.

THE EQUILIBRIUM LEVEL OF NET NATIONAL PRODUCT

Once we add government spending to the model of income determination, the equilibrium statement takes on the following form:

$$Y_n = C + I + G. \tag{1}$$

We know, of course, that consumption spending plus taxes paid and personal saving add up to net national income, because corporations do not exist in the model we are using and net national income cannot be disposed of in any other way. Expressed symbolically, then, we can say that $Y_n \equiv C + S + T$ and that

$$C \equiv Y_n - S - T. \tag{2}$$

Substituting the right side of (2) into (1), for C, we get

$$Y_n = (Y_n - S - T) + I + G, \text{ or}$$
$$S + T = I + G. \tag{3}$$

The equation in form (1) states that demand, the sum of the three expenditure flows, C, I, and G, equals supply,[1] or the current flow of production, as measured by net national product (Y_n), when net national product is in equilibrium. If demand is greater than supply, that

---

[1] It is important to reiterate the meaning of the equilibrium condition of "demand equals supply." *Demand* refers to the planned outlays of consumers, government, and businessmen. Both consumers and government are assumed here to realize their planned outlays. Businessmen, however, may find their realized investments, particularly in inventories, different than what they had planned. In this event, they will take action either to increase or decrease production. Only if planned and realized investment expenditures by businessmen are the same will net national product be in equilibrium.

is, if $C + I + G > Y_n$, Y_n will tend to rise; and vice versa if $C + I + G < Y_n$.

The condition of equilibrium is restated in equation (3), which asserts that expenditures being planned and generated by investors and governments must equal the income being taken out of the spending stream by saving and taxes. If $I + G > S + T$, more money is being injected into the income stream than is being removed from it by saving and taxes. This is possible if government and/or business borrow additional money created by the banking system or spend money accrued from past saving or tax receipts. Income will rise until $S + T$ rises into equality with $I + G$. The opposite happens if $I + G < S + T$.

Notice that the only condition for equilibrium is that the *sum* of S and T shall equal the *sum* of I and G. The separate conditions, $S = I$ and $T = G$, while being sufficient for equilibrium, are not necessary for it. For example, if $I > S$, equilibrium can still be obtained if $G < T$ by the same amount. This is shown by converting equation (3) into the following form: $I - S = T - G$. If we assume that I is 10 and that S is 5, G may be 5 and T may be 10, and equilibrium will be obtained:

$$I - S = T - G, \text{ or } 10 - 5 = 10 - 5.$$

How is the equilibrium level of net national product determined when government spending and taxing are included in the model? As we shall see, the process is much the same as before, except that it is slightly more complicated.

As before, our answer must be couched in terms of how the various expenditure flows combine to influence the level of net national product. Continuing with our earlier method, we shall assume I to be fixed at I^*, or $10 billion. The same assumption can be (more legitimately) made for G, since Congress and the Administration can determine it. Government spending will be assumed to be fixed at G^*, or $10 billion. Consumption spending cannot be so treated. It is known to vary with the level of disposable income, and the latter varies, in our model, with both the level of income and the level of net taxes. We must therefore write the consumption-income relation with the expression $C = a + cY_d$, where $Y_d \equiv (Y_n - T)$.

Net taxes should not be thought of as a constant. They also fluctuate with the level of net national income. The reason is that they are composed of two elements, revenues and transfer payments, each of which varies with the level of aggregate production and income. Revenues, of course, are positively linked with aggregate income through sales taxes and through income and payroll taxes. Transfer payments, on the other hand, have components which vary inversely with aggregate income. As income rises it is accompanied by a rise in employment. This operates to reduce the payment of unemployment contributions. Also, to the extent that the rise in employment opportunities delays retirement decisions, there should also be a retardation of the increase of pension payments. A drop in aggregate income, on the other hand, tends to stimulate transfer payments because of the accompanying increase in unemployment compensation payments and rate of retirements. Taken together, then, revenues and transfers both operate in a manner which promote a positive association of net taxes with aggregate income.

Let us approximate the association between net taxes and net national income with a linear equation, $T = b + tY_n$. The constant b in this equation represents net taxes which *do not* vary with net national income. Examples of such items are property taxes, various nontax revenue items such as business and automobile license fees and various transfer items, such as welfare payments to the disabled poor and the aged and pension payments to permanently retired persons. The coefficient of Y_n, t, indicates the rate at which net taxes change with changes in net national income. It is often called the *marginal propensity to tax* and is symbolized by the ratio of the change in net taxes to the change in net national income: $t = \Delta T / \Delta Y_n$. It follows that any change in Y_n causes T to change by $t\Delta Y_n$.

Gathering together our assumptions and giving values to I^*, G^*, a, b, c, and t of $10, $10, $40, $1, .75, and .1 respectively, we have

$$I = I^* = \$10$$
$$G = G^* = \$10$$
$$T = b + tY_n = 1 + .1Y_n$$
$$C = a + cY_d = 40 + .75Y_d$$
$$Y_d \equiv Y_n - T = Y_n - (b + tY_n)$$
$$= Y_n - tY_n - b = (1 - t)\, Y_n - b = .9Y_n - 1$$

Substituting these values into the equilibrium condition (1) we have

$$Y_n = C + I + G \tag{1}$$
$$Y_n = a + cY_d + I^* + G^*$$
$$Y_n = a + c[Y_n - (b + tY_n)] + I^* + G^*$$
$$Y_n = a + cY_n - cb - ctY_n + I^* + G^*$$
$$Y_n = \frac{a - cb + I^* + G^*}{1 - c + ct} \tag{4}$$
$$Y_n = C + I + G$$
$$Y_n = 40 + .75Y_d + 10 + 10$$

$$Y_n = 60 + .75 \,(.9Y_n - 1)$$
$$Y_n = 60 + .675Y_n - .75$$
$$Y_n = \frac{59.25}{.325}$$
$$Y_n = \$182.4 \text{ billion.}$$

The addition of government spending and taxing makes considerable difference to the level of income. To see why, let us compare our results in equation (4) to those of the previous chapter, where G and T did not exist. It will be remembered that the equilibrium level of income attained in the simple economy, before disturbance, was $200 billion. This can be derived from (4): if G^*, b, and t are zero, (4) reads

$$Y_n = \frac{a + I^*}{1 - c} = \frac{40 + 10}{1 - .75} = \$200 \text{ billion.}$$

Now, let us first look at G^* to see what difference adding government expenditure to the system makes. Assume b and t are still zero. Equation (4), with the addition of a positive value for G^* reads

$$Y_n = \frac{a + I^* + G^*}{1 - c} = \frac{40 + 10 + 10}{1 - .75} = \$240 \text{ billion.}$$

The injection of $10 billion of government spending acted like an injection of new investment, since it brought Y_n up to $240 billion. But, what happens when we add the leakage of taxes to the system? Let b and t assume their given values and we have the completed system, reduced back to a level of income of $182.4 billion.

If the addition of the tax constants to (4) reduced income by more than G^* increased it, it is apparent that in our numerical example T is greater than G, and that, since $Y_n = \$182.4$ billion is an *equilibrium* value of income, investment spending is in excess of saving. Let us see if this is so:

$$Y_n = \$182.4 \text{ billion.}$$

Since $C + S \equiv Y_d$,

$$S \equiv Y_d - C = Y_d - (a + cY_d)$$

or

$$S = -a + (1 - c) \, Y_d .$$

But, using the full description of Y_d, we get

$$S = -a + (1 - c)\,[(1 - t)\,Y_n - b]$$
$$S = -40 + (.25)\,(.9 \times 182.4 - 1)$$
$$S = \$.8\ \text{billion}.$$

To get T, we simply apply the rule

$$T = b + tY_n$$
$$T = 1 + .1 \times 182.4$$
$$T = \$19.2\ \text{billion}.$$

$S + T = \$20$ billion, the same total as $I^* + G^*$. However, I^* exceeds S by \$9.2 billion, as it must if T exceeds G^* by the same amount.

The effect upon the level of income of G^* and T also can be shown graphically. If we first assume that no taxes are being collected by the government—i.e., that b and t are both zero, the level of income will settle at \$240 billion, as shown in Graph 5.1, where $C + (I^* + G^*)$, the line of aggregate demand, crosses the 45° line at $Y_n = 240$.

Now, notice what happens when b and t assume their values, \$1 billion and .1. The consumption line is depressed to a level, for each value of Y_n, described by the dotted line, C_t. I^* and G^* are added to this new

GRAPH 5.1

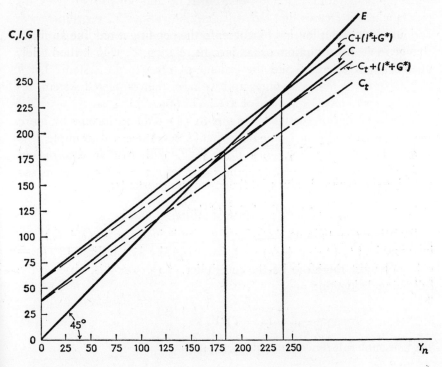

line, and the total demand line, $C_t + (I^* + G^*)$, is also lower than the former total demand line. Equilibrium income is therefore at a lower level—$182.4 billion.

It is plain that taxes depress net national income. The reason is that, although government spending adds $10 million to the circular flow, taxation forces a leakage of income from the system. Money which is taxed away by the government cannot be spent by consumers, and the total level of demand is thereby adversely affected. It should also be clear that government is under no compulsion to spend all it receives in taxes. In our example, government is running a budgetary surplus of $9.2 billion. In another, it may just as well spend $9.2 billion *more* than it receives. Of course, if it did, the total demand line would be higher and net national income would also be higher.

Changes in the Equilibrium Level of Income

The above equilibrium of Y_n at $182.4 billion was unique, because I^*, G^*, and the lowercase letter constants were fixed—see equation (4). However, if we allow I and/or G to vary, Y_n will also vary. Imagine the dotted total demand line to shift up and down. As it does, the points where it crosses line OE will describe various Y_n coordinates, or various equilibrium levels of income. In the absence of any fundamental change in the consumption- or tax-income relation, Y_n will depend solely upon changes in I and G: i.e.,

$$Y_n = \frac{a - cb + (I + G)}{1 - c + ct} \text{ , or}$$

$$Y_n = \frac{a - cb}{1 - c + ct} + \frac{(I + G)}{1 - c + ct} \text{ ,} \tag{5}$$

or, using the assumed values for the lowercase constants:

$$Y_n = 120.7 + 3.1 \ (I + G). \tag{6}$$

Equation (5) tells us that, for every unit increase in $(I + G)$, Y_n increases by $[1/(1 - c + ct)]$, or, from (6), by $3.1 billion. $[1/(1 - c + ct)]$ must therefore be the multiplier. To prove this, observe the following deduction:

$$Y_n = \frac{a - cb}{1 - c + ct} + \frac{(I + G)}{1 - c + ct} \tag{5}$$
$$\text{(the initial level of income)}$$

$$Y_n + \Delta Y_n = \frac{a - cb}{1 - c + ct} + \frac{(I + G) + \Delta(I + G)}{1 - c + ct} \qquad (7)$$

(the new level of income)

Deducting (5) from (7), we get the change in Y_n, or

$$\Delta Y_n = \frac{\Delta(I + G)}{1 - c + ct} = \left(\frac{1}{1 - c + ct}\right) \Delta(I + G). \qquad (8)$$

(8) says that the change in net national income equals the change in investment and/or government spending multiplied by the factor $[1/(1 - c + ct)]$, i.e., multiplied by the multiplier.

If (8) is divided on both sides by $\Delta(I + G)$, the result is

$$\frac{\Delta Y_n}{\Delta(I + G)} = \frac{1}{1 - c + ct}. \qquad (9)$$

This is also shown on Graph 5.2 as the slope of the Y_n-line. This line has been drawn from equation (5), or, with numbers, from (6). It expresses the dependency of Y_n upon $(I + G)$, and its slope measures the

GRAPH 5.2

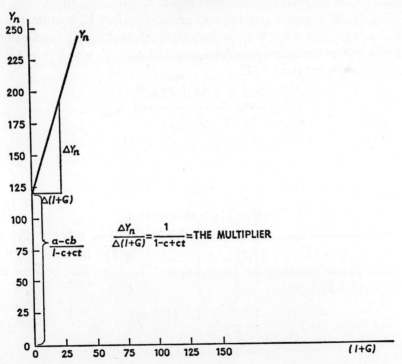

change in income induced by changes in investment and/or government spending. The slope of the line, measured by dividing changes in Y_n by changes in $(I + G)$, is also a measure of the size of the multiplier.

Notice that the multiplier is smaller when taxes are put into the system than when they are not. In the situation where taxes are absent, the multiplier reads "$1/(1 - c)$" (or, using $c = .75$, 4). The multiplier in the situation where taxes are present, as in (9), reads "$1/(1 - c + ct)$" (equal to 3.1).

Given the assumed numerical values for c and t, then, any increase in G and/or I would have to be almost one third greater to reach the same level of income that would prevail in the no-tax $(t = 0)$ situation. The reason, of course, is that when additions of income are subject to taxes, households receive less. Consequently they cannot increase their consumption outlays by as much as they would have had their new incomes not been subject to taxation. As a result, total demand grows by less, and national income also grows by less.

Another way of looking at this, again, is to regard taxes, like saving, as a leakage out of the expenditure stream. Any given increase in investment and/or government spending will run up against larger changes in the leakage out of the income stream when taxes are collected than when they are not. National income will therefore settle at a lower value in the tax situation than it would in the no-tax situation. In the latter situation, each round of increased expenditure is larger because taxes are not reducing the ability of income recipients to spend additions to their incomes. The *sum* of the increases in expenditure is therefore larger than if taxes had reduced the spending ability of households.

Tables 5.1 and 5.2 also show how changes in income are slowed and reduced by the drag imposed upon consumption by taxes. Both tables assume a rise in G (stage 2) of $10 billion and a marginal propensity to consume of .75. In Table 5.1, the tax model, the marginal propensity

TABLE 5.1

Changes in Income—Tax Model

Stage	Y_n	Y_d	C	I	G	Change in Inventories
1	200	180	175	25	0	5
2	200	180	175	25	10	−10
3	210	189	181.75	25	10	−6.75
4	216.75	195.08	186.33	25	10	−4.58
5	221.33	.....	.....	..	..	....
....	.....	.....	.....	..	..	....
Last	231.0	207.0	196.0	25	10	0

to tax, t, is assumed to be .1, and Y_d is equal to $Y_n - T$. Both tables begin with a Y_n of $200 billion.

Income rises faster and farther in Table 5.2 than in Table 5.1 because no tax slows it. The reason is not hard to find: in Table 5.1, because of the drag of taxation, consumption rises by only $21 billion, as opposed to Table 5.2, where, because of the absence of taxes, it rises

TABLE 5.2

Changes in Income—No-Tax Model

Stage	Y_n	C	I	G	Change in Inventories
1	200	190	10	0	0
2	200	190	10	10	−10
3	210	197.5	10	10	−7.5
4	217.5	203.1	10	10	−5.6
5	223.1	....	..	..	...
....	....	....	..	..	...
Last	240	220	10	10	0

by $30 billion. This difference of $9 billion explains the difference between the total change in Y_n in the two cases.

Fiscal Policy and the Level of Income

Equation (5) indicates that government spending and tax policies have important effects upon the level of aggregate income. Because of this, it has become commonplace for governments to use their fiscal powers to achieve aggregative economic goals. Thus, if it is desired to iron out fluctuations in national income and employment which arise out of fluctuations in (say) private investment spending a government can do so by manipulating its spending and taxing powers separately or in some sort of combination. However, just because aggregative goals can be achieved through a variety of techniques, it does not follow that all techniques are equally powerful or equally desirable. Each technique has its own power, its own implications for the government's deficit, and its own implications for the distribution of national product between the public and private sectors.

To fix ideas, let us start with a simple case in which net taxes are imposed in a lump sum form. In this case the marginal propensity to tax is zero and, instead of reading $[1/(1-c+ct)]$, the multiplier reads $[1/(1-c)]$. It also follows that we can replace the constant b

in equation (5) with T, since taxes are not now a variable related to Y_n. Thus changed, equation (5) now reads:

$$Y_n = \frac{a - cT}{1 - c} + \frac{(I + G)}{I - c} . \qquad (10)$$

With (10) we can make an initial investigation into the relative power of different fiscal techniques. First, let us try to increase Y_n with a change in government spending:

$$Y_n + \Delta Y_n = \frac{a - cT}{1 - c} + \frac{(I + G + \Delta G)}{1 - c} . \qquad (10a)$$

Subtracting (10) from (10a) we get:

$$\Delta Y_n = \frac{\Delta G}{(1 - c)} . \qquad (11)$$

Notice that a change in government spending has exactly the same impact upon Y_n as would an equal change in private investment spending. Also notice, however, that in this simple case (with $t = 0$), the government's deficit increases dollar for dollar with the increase in its spending. But, perhaps a more important implication for some people, the stimulus to the economy has been bought at the expense of an enlarged share of government in aggregate output. This price is often regarded as undesirable, hence many people would rather try to use tax cuts as a substitute for increases in government spending as a way to expand the economy. Consider, therefore, the effects of a tax cut on Y_n. Beginning with (10), we get:

$$Y_n + \Delta Y_n = \frac{a - c(T + \Delta T)}{I + c} + \frac{I + G}{I + c} . \qquad (12)$$

Subtracting (10) from (12):

$$\Delta Y_n = \Delta T \left(\frac{-c}{1 - c} \right) . \qquad (13)$$

Equation (13) shows that a tax cut (i.e., a negative ΔT) is *weaker* than an equivalent increase in government spending in terms of its impact on aggregate income. This is because a tax cut does not initially increase expenditure by its full amount. Although disposable income is increased by ΔT, the household sector will spend only $c\Delta T$, since it may be expected to save part of its gain. It follows that $c\Delta T$ is the amount we multiply by the multiplier, $[1/(1-c)]$. As (13) shows, this is equivalent to stating a new multiplier—$[-c/(1-c)]$—for tax changes. Hence, if $c=.75$ the absolute value of the tax multiplier is 3, compared to a government expenditure multiplier of 4. A \$5 billion tax cut will generate a deficit equivalent to a \$5 billion increase in government spending, but will increase aggregate income by only \$15 billion, as compared to \$20 billion with an increase in spending.

A possible virtue of tax cuts is that they allow fiscal policy to increase aggregate income without increasing government's share of income. As we have seen, however, they are weak relative to spending increases. If it is desired to achieve a certain target increase in income with tax cuts, the government's deficit will have to increase by more than it would if only expenditures were used. This is the price of using tax cuts to avoid expansion of government's share of aggregate income.

What are the implications of using equal increases in government spending and taxes as a device for stimulating the economy? This technique will avoid an increase in the deficit. It will not avoid an enlargement of government's absorption of income. Surprisingly, however, it will increase income. Let the government impose an equal change in G and T. The change in income will then be the sum of the positive impact of ΔG and the negative impact of ΔT.

$$\Delta Y_n = \frac{\Delta G}{1-c} - \frac{c\Delta T}{1-c},$$

or, since $\Delta G = \Delta T$,

$$\Delta Y_n = \Delta G \left(\frac{1}{1-c} - \frac{c}{1-c} \right)$$

$$\Delta Y_n = \Delta G \left(\frac{1-c}{1-c} \right)$$

$$\Delta Y_n = \Delta G (1)$$

A balanced increase in G and T therefore expands income by the increase in government spending. The *balanced budget multiplier* is unity. This theorem depends on the assumption that tax increases do not affect other than household expenditures and that tax cuts are evenly spread amongst people whose average MPC is c. But, even if these assumptions do not hold in practice, the basic truth of the balanced budget theorem remains: changes in government spending, even when fully offset by taxes, are not neutral.

It does not follow that a balanced budget increase in G is the best way to achieve income targets. To revert to our previous example $(c = .75)$, if it is desired to raise Y_n by $20 billion, to do so with a balanced budget increase in government spending would require a $20 billion increase in G! Moreover, *none of the increase in aggregate income would go to the private sector.* It would all be absorbed by government. This does not mean that the government would not use the increase in income in ways beneficial to the public. It does mean, however, that those who would insist upon balanced budgets as an accompaniment to fiscal policy must be prepared to accept substantial variations in government's share of aggregate income.

To summarize our findings thus far: If we wish to use fiscal policy as a device for achieving a *given* increase in aggregate income, we can do so by three major methods: (1) increasing G, (2) decreasing T, or (3) increasing G and T by the same amount. Method (1) involves a smaller deficit than method (2), but it increases the share of government in aggregate income. Method (3) does not create a deficit, but it gives government the whole increase in income. Moreover, for any desired increase in income, method (3) implies a much larger expansion in government spending than does method (1). If it is desired to moderate the growth of government, the price of using fiscal policy as a device for stimulating the economy is an increase in the government's deficit [i.e., methods (1) and (2) individually or in combination].

How are these conclusions altered if the marginal propensity to tax is positive? We know, of course, that in this case the absolute value of the expenditure multiplier is smaller than when the marginal propensity to tax is zero—$[1/(1 - c + ct)] < [1/(1 - c)]$. This means that to achieve a given expansion of income, the increase in government spending must be larger than before; however, it does not mean that the government's *deficit* must be larger. Consider our previous example, where desired $\Delta Y_n = \$20$ billion, $c = .75$, and $t = .1$. Using equation (9), we find:

$$\Delta Y_n = \frac{1}{1 - c + ct} \Delta G \qquad \Delta T = t\Delta Y_n$$

$$\$20 = \frac{1}{.325} \Delta G \qquad \Delta T = .1 \times \$20$$

$$\Delta G = \$6.5 \qquad \Delta T = \$2$$

The required ΔG is $6.5 billion, but the $20 billion income growth also induces an increase in taxes of $2 billion. As a result, the *deficit* increases by only $4.5 billion. The conclusion, then, is that the presence of an income-responsive tax system weakens the impact on income of government spending; but it reduces the impact of spending on the deficit. Moreover, if government wishes to promote a *given* expansion of income through increases in spending, a positive marginal propensity to tax promotes a relatively larger increase in the share of aggregate income going to government, since the required ΔG is larger than when $t = 0$.

Our conclusion respecting the weakness of tax cuts relative to changes in government spending is not altered. The tax multiplier is now $[-c/(1 - c + ct)]$; hence, to attain a given change in Y_n we still require a larger increase in the deficit. This is true despite the fact that part of the tax cut is restored by income expansion. Consider, first, the consequences for the deficit of an attempt to raise Y_n by $20 billion with a tax cut that leaves t unchanged, but which lowers the intercept, b, in the tax function (i.e., in $T = b + tY_n$).

$$\Delta Y_n = \frac{-c\Delta b}{1 - c + ct} \qquad \Delta T = \Delta b + t\Delta Y_n$$

$$\$20 = \frac{-.75}{.325}\,\Delta b \qquad \Delta T = -8.67 + .1 \times 20$$

$$\Delta b = -\$8.67 \qquad \Delta T = -6.67$$

It is clear that a reduction of taxes through a change in b increases the government's deficit by more than would a change in government spending designed to achieve the same $20 billion increase in Y_n. Suppose, however, that it is desired to increase Y_n through a cut in t. Here the situation is a bit more complicated, since a change in t alters the multiplier. The appropriate tax multiplier is:[2]

---

[2] (14) is derived as follows: Let the level of income after a change in t be [using equation (5)]

$$Y_n + \Delta Y_n = \frac{(a - cb + I + G)}{1 - c + c(t + \Delta t)}.$$

The level of income *before* the change in t was

$$Y_n = \frac{(a - cb + I + G)}{1 - c + ct}.$$

Subtracting the second equation from the first and dividing through by Δt gives (14) in the text.

$$\frac{\Delta Y_n}{\Delta t} = \frac{-cY_n}{1 - c + c(t + \Delta t)}. \tag{14}$$

Notice that this multiplier requires that we know the initial level of Y_n. Since we are seeking an appropriate change in the *marginal propensity to tax,* in order to find the necessary *amount of taxes* to cut out of the initial income level, we must know that income level. Assume Y_n to be $800 billion. It follows that the cut in t required to get a $20 billion ΔY_n is given by:

$$\Delta Y_n = \frac{-c(-\Delta t) \, Y_n}{1 - c + c(t - \Delta t)}$$

$$\$20 = \frac{.75 \times 800\Delta t}{1 - .75 + .75(.1 - \Delta t)}$$

$$\Delta t \sim .01 \, .$$

A cut in t of .01 implies an initial deficit (on an $800 billion income base) of $8 billion. The ultimate deficit, however, is smaller, since the rise in income promotes a partial recovery of revenue:

$$T + \Delta T = b + (t - \Delta t)(Y + \Delta Y_n); \tag{15}$$

hence, subtracting

$$T = b + tY_n$$

from (15), we get

$$\Delta T = -\Delta t Y_n + t\Delta Y_n - \Delta t \Delta Y_n$$
$$\Delta T = -.01 \times 800 + .1 \times 20 - .01 \times 20$$
$$\Delta T = -6.2 \, .$$

The $6.2 billion increase in the deficit is clearly larger than the $4.5 billion deficit generated by our earlier example of an increase in G. Though the precise deficit generated by a cut in t will vary with the initial level of income, the same conclusion is generally valid: For any *given target* ΔY_n, a tax cut will generate a larger deficit than will the required increase in government spending. We have shown this to be true for the two types of tax change possible in our model.

At this point, a warning: While within the confines of our model it may be true that the government expenditure multiplier is both stronger and less conducive to deficits than are tax cuts, the same may not be true in the real world. Since tax cuts increase the rewards from ownership of caiptal, they contain a potential for increasing private investment spending. Government spending, on the other hand, may at times be devoted to projects which compete with private business and which discourage private investment. Hence, before we apply various fiscal theorems from multiplier theory to the real world, we must take into account the potential impacts of fiscal changes on private investment. A complete analysis could easily lead to conclusions opposite to those reached in this section.

NET EXPORTS AND THE LEVEL OF INCOME

In order to complete the model of income determination, it is now necessary to add the influence of exports and imports. To isolate these variables it will be convenient to exclude government spending and taxing from the model. We shall bring them back later in a final statement of the expenditure model, in which all sectors of the economy will be present.

Goods and services sold to foreigners create income for workers, employers, and other groups in the economy. This income, in addition to that generated internally, is spent on domestic and foreign goods, and it is also saved. Imports and saving are leakages from the income stream; investment and exports are injections into the stream. If saving plus imports is greater than investment plus exports, the leakages from the income stream will be greater than the injections into it, and national income will fall; vice versa if the leakages are less than investment and exports. It follows that the equilibrium condition for income is

$$S + M = I + X,$$

where M represents imports and X stands for exports.

If net exports are represented by $(X - M)$, the equilibrium condition could have been derived from the income-expenditure equilibrium statement:

$$C + I + (X - M) = Y, \tag{16}$$

or, since $Y \equiv C + S$,

$$I + X = S + M. \tag{17}$$

If $I + X > S + M$, income will tend to rise. If $I + X < S + M$, income will tend to fall.

The Import Function

Imports of goods and services fluctuate with national income. They do so because as national income rises or falls households buy more or less foreign goods, just as they do with domestically produced goods. In addition, some domestic production depends upon imported raw and semifinished materials; hence, as domestic production fluctuates imports of these materials are likely to fluctuate in the same general direction. We can therefore postulate an import function which relates imported goods and services to national income. As before, we shall keep things simple by assuming the function to be linear: $M = d + mY$. The d-constant gives the amount of imports which are independent of income. The m-constant tells us the rate at which imports increase with income. The import function is depicted on Graph 5.3. The slope of the function (m) is often called the *marginal propensity to import* (MPM), a use of language parallel to that describing the slopes of the consumption and tax functions.

GRAPH 5.3

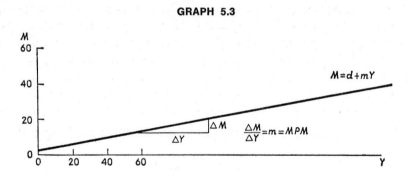

Actually, "propensity to imports" is a little misleading. To be sure, people may have a taste for foreign goods which they exercise as income grows; nevertheless, purchases of foreign goods are also influenced by a number of other factors. The import function may shift about if these other factors change. For example, an increase in the price of home goods and services relative to foreign substitutes will shift the import function up. A decrease in the relative price of home goods will shift the function down. Such changes in relative prices can originate either at home or abroad. A rise in the relative prices of domestic goods can emerge from a domestic inflation or a foreign deflation. It can also come about if domestic prices are inflating more rapidly than foreign prices. Changes in exchange rates also affect relative prices. When the British devalued their currency by 14 percent in 1968, the prices of British goods in terms of U.S. dollars automatically fell. Other things remaining the same, the demand for British goods in the United States should have increased; the import function should have shifted up. The import function is also subject to changes due to changes in competition. Domestic producers may successfully overcome foreign competition in some product lines (e.g., compact automobiles), or they may lose out in other product lines. In the final analysis, then, the import function is the product of a host of forces ranging from technology to various competitive factors and, as such, is subject to substantial shifts. In the short run, a number of these forces are likely to be relatively unimportant, in the sense that their effects upon the *aggregate* of imports take hold only gradually. But some forces, inflation for example, are capable of affecting the whole range of goods and services simultaneously and, as a result, can lead to sharp shifts in the import function.

The Equilibrium Level of Income with Imports and Exports

The procedure for determining the equilibrium level of income is the same as before. We start with the income-expenditure equilibrium statement:

$$C + I + (X - M) = Y. \tag{16}$$

Next, write down the statements for all of the expenditure flows:

$$C = a + cY \text{ } (Y = Y_d \text{ here because } T = 0) \tag{18}$$
$$I = I^* = 10 \tag{19}$$
$$X = X^* = 10 \tag{20}$$
$$M = d + mY \tag{21}$$
$$= 1 + .1Y.$$

Inserting the equations for the expenditure flows into (16), we get:

$$Y = C + I + (X - M), \text{ or}$$
$$Y = (a + cY) + I^* + X^* - (d + mY)$$
$$Y = a + cY + I^* + X^* - d - mY$$
$$Y - cY + mY = a - d + I^* + X^*$$
$$Y(1 - c + m) = a - d + (I^* + X^*)$$
$$Y = \frac{a - d}{1 - c + m} + \frac{I^* + X^*}{1 - c + m}, \text{ or} \tag{22}$$

$$Y = C + I + (X - M), \text{ or}$$
$$Y = 40 + .75Y + 10 + 10 - (1 + .1Y)$$
$$Y = 40 + .75Y + 10 + 10 - 1 - .1Y$$
$$Y - .75Y + .1Y = 59$$
$$Y (1 - .75 + .1) = 59$$
$$Y = 168.6 .$$

Equation (22) provides the solution to the level of income. Since the right-hand side of (22) contains only constants, the solution is unique; no other value than that indicated (168.6) is permissible under the assumed value of the expenditure flows so long as we are only considering the *equilibrium* level of income.

Does the equilibrium level of income we have derived satisfy the condition that $S + M = I + X$? That is, will the inflow of investment and exports and the leakage of saving and imports be such that the circular flow of income and expenditure will stabilize at 168.6? In order to solve this problem it is necessary to calculate S and M; I^* and X^* are given at 10 each and need not be calculated.

$$S = -a + (1 - c) Y \qquad\qquad M = d + mY$$
$$S = -40 + .25 \times 168.6 \qquad M = 1 + .1 \times 168.6$$
$$S = 2.1 \qquad\qquad\qquad M = 17.9$$
$$S + M = 2.1 + 17.9 = I^* + X^* = 10 + 10 .$$

The equilibrium condition is fulfilled.

The system for determining the equilibrium level of national income with exports and imports added can also be shown graphically. Graph 5.4 is an adaptation of the simple saving-investment diagram given by Graph 4.2 in the last chapter. It combines imports with saving and

GRAPH 5.4

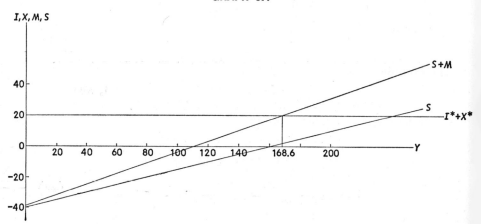

exports with investment. It shows quite clearly that an equilibrium level of income is attained at a point where income has reached a level such that the combined saving-imports leakage is just equal to the combined investment-exports injection into the income stream. If income should happen to wander away from its equilibrium level, it would be driven back to that level by market forces, in a manner analogous to that discussed in the last chapter.

There is an extremely important point to note here. We have proved that the equilibrium condition for national income is satisfied by our solution to the level of income. However, from a monetary point of view, this equilibrium might not be maintained. In our example, exports are smaller than imports. If the country does not have large foreign exchange reserves, and if it cannot borrow from abroad, this level of income certainly cannot be maintained, or perhaps even be reached; for an unfavorable balance of trade drains foreign exchange from a country. The problem can be resolved only if domestic saving is increased and imports are decreased, until the latter come into equality with, or exceed, exports. Failing this, the country will find itself in a foreign exchange bind: it will be unable to import goods from abroad, domestic prices will rise, exports will fall off as foreign buyers turn to other, lower priced markets, and national income will fall.

Nevertheless, many countries are frequently faced with such problems, with exports insufficient to cover a high level of imports and with investment too high relative to the current level of saving. Underdeveloped economies in the process of developing, where emphasis is upon high rates of investment and where heavy dependence upon imports is traditional, are faced with chronic foreign exchange problems. The only cure, which at the same time does not damage the level of economic activity, is to gather more domestic saving and to pare down imports to the bare minimums needed to continue growth.

The Multiplier

The multiplier for this particular national income model can be easily derived from equation (22):

$$Y = \frac{a - d}{1 - c + m} + \frac{I^* + X^*}{1 - c + m} \text{, the initial level of income.} \quad (22)$$

$$Y + \Delta Y = \frac{a - d}{1 - c + m} + \frac{(I^* + X^*) + \Delta(I + X)}{1 - c + m} \text{, the new level of income.} \quad (23)$$

Subtracting (22) from (23) gives us the change in income, ΔY:

$$\Delta Y = \left(\frac{1}{1 - c + m}\right) \Delta(I + X), \text{ where } \left(\frac{1}{1 - c + m}\right) \text{ is the multiplier.} \tag{24}$$

Notice that the multiplier is smaller than it would be if the marginal propensity to import did not exist, i.e., if $m = 0$. The reason is that as income grows the leakage out of the circular flow grows more rapidly than if added imports did not occur. This means that the total leakage of saving and imports reaches the level of injections from investment and exports at a level of income lower than it would without added imports. If imports were not increasing, a higher level of income would have to be reached before the leakage would be sufficiently large to stabilize the circular flow of income and expenditure.

A General Expenditure Model

We can now put together the pieces of this chapter. A general expenditure model emerges from a statement of the equilibrium condition that the sum of expenditure flows must equal (net) national product. This statement, redefined in terms of the variables affecting each expenditure flow, yields a multiplier model for the determination of aggregate income. We begin by listing the appropriate relationships as follows:

$$C + I + G + (X - M) = Y_n \tag{25}$$
(equilibrium condition)
$$C = a + cY_d \tag{26}$$
(consumption function)
$$Y_d \equiv (Y_n - T) \tag{27}$$
(definition of disposable income)
$$T = b + tYn \tag{28}$$
([net] tax function)
$$M = d + mY_n \tag{29}$$
(import function)
$$I = I* \tag{30}$$
(investment [given])
$$G = G* \tag{31}$$
(government spending [given])
$$X = X* \tag{32}$$
(exports [given])

The whole system of equations (25) *through* (32) *is our expenditure model.* The system contains eight variables—C, I, G, X, M, Y_n, Y_d and T—and eight independent equations. It is therefore a self-contained system capable of giving a solution for any of the eight variables. Notice, however, that there are two types of variables within the system. I, G, and X are *given*. This means that we do not need the other equations of the system to find their values. The other five variables— C, M, T, Y_n, and Y_d—are not given: each is defined in terms of other variables within the system. When a variable is "given" (that is, not defined in terms of other variables in a system), it is customary to refer to it as an *exogenous variable*. A variable determined within the system is commonly called an *endogenous variable*. Whether or not a variable is endogenous or exogenous depends on the size of the system; that is, it depends upon the behavioral activity the system encompasses. For example, we have labeled investment as an exogenous variable. Actually, investment spending is influenced by the level of income and financial variables such as interest rates. Had we recognized these influences in our model it would have been necessary to substitute a new equation—say, $I = I^* + gY_n - hi$—for equation (30). Had we done so, investment would have been an endogenous variable. As such, its value would have depended upon other variables in the system. Moreover, because the rate of interest influences investment in the substitute equation, it would have been necessary to add an equation(s) to the system in order to explain how the rate of interest is determined.

We shall be complicating our model in the above fashion later in the book. For the present, however, it is important to note that when we solve for some endogenous variable—Y_n, for example—we can do so in terms of the exogenous variables and the "structural" relations of the model as they are defined by the constants in each of the equations describing the behavior of the endogenous variables. When we do so, we obtain what economists often call a *reduced form* of the system. Equations containing the multiplier, such as (4) in Chapter 4, and (22) in this chapter, are reduced forms for determining national income with the simplified national income models discussed above. In this section we conclude the chapter by developing a reduced form equation for the fuller national income model given by equations (25) to (32).

Substitute I^*, G^*, and X^* for I, G, and X in equation (25). The latter now reads:

$$C + I^* + G^* + (X^* - M) = Y_n . \qquad (25a)$$

In place of C, substitute (28) into (27) and (27) into (26). (25a) now reads:

$$a + c(Y_n - b - tY_n) + I^* + G^* + (X^* - M) = Y_n . \text{ (25b)}$$

In place of M, substitute (29) into (25b), which now reads:

$$a + c Y_n - cb - ct Y_n + I^* + G^* + X^* - d - mY_n = Y_n . \tag{25c}$$

Solve (25c) for Y_n and we have the reduced form solution for net national income:

$$Y_n = \frac{a - cb - d}{1 - c + ct + m} + \frac{I^* + G^* + X^*}{1 - c + ct + m} . \tag{33}$$

Notice that Y_n, an endogenous variable, is defined in terms of the three exogenous variables—I, G, and X—and the constants of the equations expressing the behavior of the endogenous variables.

The multiplier for the generalized expenditure model is $[1/(1 - c + ct + m)]$. It is smaller than the previous multipliers because the full model contains all of the leakages from the income stream that we have discussed in this chapter. Using $c = .75$, $t = .1$, and $m = .1$, the multiplier is 2.35, instead of the multiplier derived from the model which assumed $t = m = 0$.

We have frequently asserted that additional injections of investment, government spending, or exports will cause aggregate income to rise until enough additional leakages are generated to offset the additional injections. Our full multiplier model can be used to demonstrate this point. Let $(I + G + X) \equiv E$. From (33) it follows that

$$\Delta Y_n = \left(\frac{1}{1 - c(1 - t) + m} \right) \Delta E . \tag{34}$$

Notice that the form of the denominator of the multiplier is slightly changed: $(1 - t)$ is the change in disposable income per dollar change in net national income, or $\Delta Y_d / \Delta Y_n$; and $c(1 - t)$ is the fraction of additional net national income consumed. It follows that $[1 - c(1 - t)]$ is the fraction of additional net national income *not consumed;* that is, it is the fraction saved and taxed. The following development proves this point.

$$(1 - t) = \frac{\Delta Y_n - t\Delta Y_n}{\Delta Y_n} = \frac{\Delta Y_d}{\Delta Y_n}$$

hence

$$c(1-t) = \frac{\Delta C}{\Delta Y_d} \cdot \frac{\Delta Y_d}{\Delta Y_n} = \frac{\Delta C}{\Delta Y_n} \, .$$

$$1 - c(1-t) = \frac{\Delta Y_n - \Delta C}{\Delta Y_n}$$

and since

$$\Delta Y_n - \Delta C = \Delta S + \Delta T,$$

we conclude that

$$1 - c(1-t) = \frac{\Delta S}{\Delta Y_n} + \frac{\Delta T}{\Delta Y_n} \, .$$

To complete the argument, we note that $m = \Delta M / \Delta Y_n$. The multiplier equation therefore reads

$$\Delta Y_n = \left(\frac{1}{\dfrac{\Delta S}{\Delta Y_n} + \dfrac{\Delta T}{\Delta Y_n} + \dfrac{\Delta M}{\Delta Y_n}} \right) \Delta E . \tag{35}$$

Multiplying both sides of (35) by the denominator of the fraction we get

$$\Delta S + \Delta T + \Delta M = \Delta E = \Delta I + \Delta G + \Delta X . \tag{36}$$

Equation (36) expresses the point we set out to prove—that national income reaches a new equilibrium when the sum of the additional leakages from the income stream comes into equality with the additional expenditure injections into the income stream from investors, government, or foreigners.

We have now completed our discussion of the basic expenditure model. We refrain from complicating it further because to do so would take us too far afield without particularly adding to our understanding of the way in which variations in exogenous expenditures affect the level of aggregate income. It is now more important to give an intensive discussion of the individual components of the model set forth in this chapter. In the next four chapters we give detailed attention to the determinants of consumption and investment spending. After that, we shall complete the building of the national income model by bringing in monetary considerations.

ADDITIONAL READINGS FOR CHAPTERS 4 AND 5

On the General Expenditure Model

SAMUELSON, PAUL. "The Simple Mathematics of Income Determination," in *Income, Employment, and Public Policy*. New York: W. W. Norton Co., 1948.

The Multiplier, General

HABERLER, GOTTFRIED. "Mr. Keynes' Theory of the 'Multiplier': A Methodological Criticism." *Zeitschrift fur Nationalokonomie*, 1936. Reprinted in *Readings in Business Cycle Theory*. Philadelphia: Blakiston Co., 1944.

KEYNES, J. M. *The General Theory of Employment, Interest, and Money*. New York: Harcourt, Brace, and Co., 1936, chap. 10.

MACHLUP, FRITZ. "Period Analysis and Multiplier Theory," *Quarterly Journal of Economics*, 1939. Reprinted in *Readings in Business Cycle Theory*. Philadelphia; Blakiston Co., 1944.

Foreign Trade Multiplier

MACHLUP, FRITZ. *International Trade and the National Income Multiplier*. Philadelphia: Blakiston Co., 1943.

Fiscal Multiplier Models

MUSGRAVE, RICHARD. *The Theory of Public Finance*. New York: McGraw-hill Book Co., 1959, chap. 18.

Chapter 6   CONSUMPTION (I)

In this and the next chapter, we shall be reviewing the consumption-income relation. This relation is normally called the *consumption function* in the literature of macroeconomics and we shall henceforth use this designation. The models of chapters 4 and 5 indicate the importance of the consumption function. Not only is consumption a large component of aggregate income (in recent years it has been about 62 percent of GNP), but the stability of the multiplier depends heavily upon the stability of the consumption function. If the constants in the consumption function—a and c in $C = a + cY_d$—jump about in an unpredictable fashion, both the level and changes in the level of national income become unpredictable. Policy makers will not be able to forecast national income from forecasts of investment and government spending.

In the first decade following the publication of Keynes' *General Theory,* economists thought they had discovered a stable consumption function. Keynes had stated the notion as a fundamental law: "The fundamental psychological law, upon which we are entitled to depend with great confidence both a priori from our knowledge of human nature and from detailed facts of experience, is that men are disposed as a rule and on the average, to increase their consumption as their income increases, but not by as much as their income."[1] However, Keynes did not necessarily believe that consumption was a stable function of income in the short run: "For a man's habitual standard of life usually has first claim on his income, and he is apt to save the difference which he discovers between his actual income and the expense of his habitual standard . . . . Thus a rising income will often be accompanied by increased saving, and a falling income by decreased saving, on a greater scale at first than subsequently."[2] Thus Keynes hypothesized that the short

---

[1] Keynes, *General Theory of Employment Interest and Money,* p. 96.
[2] *Ibid.,* p. 97.

period, or cyclical, marginal propensity to consume (MPC) is smaller than the long period MPC, primarily because it takes time for people to adjust their consumption standards to new income levels. When the first comprehensive national income accounts became available in 1942, it became possible to put Keynes' ideas to test. Using annual estimates of consumption and disposable income for the years 1929 to 1941, economists found a very good statistical fit between the two variables. Moreover, there was no evidence of short-run variations in the MPC, as Keynes had predicted. It was widely believed that a stable consumption function had been found.[3]

The consumption function based upon prewar data was widely used by economists during the war as a basis for predicting what would happen to the economy once the war was over. The profession was almost unanimous in predicting a serious depression. Needless to say, they were wrong. The reason: the consumption function appeared to lead a life of its own. For some reason, the prewar relationship did not hold in the postwar period; the function had shifted up. Since that time, economists have come to understand that the consumption behavior of the public is no simple matter.

Indeed, understanding the consumption function has for the last three decades been a major research interest of economists. Since Keynes' original statement of the hypothesis, increasingly sophisticated studies have been made. These studies have taken so many different directions that it is not possible to review them all here. At the end of the next chapter, the reader will find a set of references which will lead him rather deeply into the literature if he desires to pursue the subject. In this book we shall try only to summarize some of the main trends of thought. Before doing so, however, we must review a few technical matters.

Definition of Consumption and Income

Keynes, and most economists after him, defined the consumption function in real terms. That is, instead of relating current dollar consumption to current dollar income, real consumption and real income are related. The reason is that consumers are not thought to suffer from a "money illusion." If they did, a doubling of all prices and wages would lead them to increase their consumption, even though their real incomes remain unchanged. This does not seem logical, since, if consumers are content with their real consumption before the price change,

---

[3] For a discussion of this evidence, see Gardiner Ackley, *Macroeconomic Theory* (New York: The Macmillan Co., 1961), pp. 224–27.

there is no reason, real income not having changed, for them to change their consumption after the price change. Admittedly, some consumers might suffer from money illusion. Nevertheless, most economists have preferred to frame their studies in terms of real or constant dollar consumption and income.

A second problem relates to what ought to be included in the consumption function. When we speak of consumption in our income determination models we are, of course, speaking of consumption *expenditures*. We are not speaking of the enjoyment of the implicit stream of services from consumer owned capital. Since much of this capital has been accumulated over the years, enjoyment of its services is not highly correlated with current income. On the other hand, many analysts treat the purchase of consumer durables in the same way they treat the purchase of nondurables: as current consumption. In recent years, however, there has been a tendency for researchers to segregate consumption spending into spending on durables and spending on nondurables, treating the former as investment decisions on the part of households and the latter as consumption proper. We should expect nondurable consumption expenditures to be more closely related to income than expenditures on durables. In contrast, we should expect expenditures on durables to be more sensitive to credit conditions than expenditures on nondurables.

The proper concept of income is also an issue. Our expenditure models have used *current disposable income* as the most influential variable affecting consumption. As the quotation of Keynes implies, current income may not be the most meaningful income concept to use. People do not necessarily allow their consumption outlays to fluctuate just because their current incomes fluctuate. They may base their consumption decisions on what they expect their average incomes to be over several periods of time. Some analysts even argue that it is the *lifetime* income prospects of consumers which determine most of their current consumption behavior. Another possibility is that consumption depends upon the joint action of current and *past* income, since the latter might be influential in setting consumption standards. We shall explore these arguments more fully below.

Aggregate and Cross-Sectional Consumption Functions

Another important distinction is the one between *aggregate* and *cross-sectional* consumption functions. Aggregate consumption functions trace the reaction of consumption spending of the whole household sector to changes in the disposable income of the sector taken as a whole. In effect, the sector is treated as if it were a single behavioral entity responding to changes in its income. The theoretical consumption function used in the last two chapters is an aggregate consumption function. What might be called historical aggregate consumption functions are also commonly used in the literature. The functions are derived from statistical procedures which regress time series of consumption outlays against time series of income. These functions are used to test various hypotheses about the consumption function and will be referred to below.

Cross-sectional consumption functions relate the expenditures of various individuals or households to the income of these individuals or households *for a given period of time.* Thus, households in a particular year might be classified on the basis of their incomes in order to observe their consumption outlays. The average consumption of households in each income class yields a point on the cross-sectional consumption function. The collection of such points, each associated with a different income level, forms the locus of the whole cross-sectional function.

Cross-sectional consumption functions have been derived a number of times from various budget studies and have played an important role in the evolution of consumption function theory. We shall take note of these studies below. Here it is mainly important to note that the shape of the aggregate consumption function and that of the cross-sectional function need not be the same. An aggregate time-series consumption function traces out *aggregate consumption-income relations over time for all households taken together.* A cross-sectional function records the *differences between average household consumption levels as they relate to differences in their income levels for a particular period of time.*

Though aggregate and cross-sectional consumption functions are conceptually distinct, they are related. The relationship is best discussed in terms of a commonly used concept, the *average propensity to consume* (the APC). The APC is a designation for the proportion of income consumed. It is C/Y, as distinct from $\Delta C/\Delta Y$, which defines the MPC, or the marginal propensity to consume. Together, the APC and the MPC specify most of what we wish to know about any particular consumption function.

In any year, the aggregate average propensity to consume of all households taken together is a weighted average of the APCs of households in each income class. Typically, the average propensity to consume of upper income people is smaller than that of lower income people. At issue is whether or not we should expect the aggregate propensity to consume of all households taken together to decrease as income increases over time, just as it does cross-sectionally for a given period of time. The answer is ultimately an empirical one, which we shall address below. Here it suffices to point out that the answer depends upon how people in each income group respond to increases in their income over time and upon what happens to the distribution of income over time. Suppose aggregate income doubles over time without changes in the distribution of income between lower and upper income groups. In this case, there will be a uniform shift of low-income households into income classes which were occupied by high-income groups in the earlier years. If each group adopts the consumption behavior of the *absolute income class* into which it is drawn, the aggregate APC will fall with the increase in aggregate income.[4] In contrast, if the consumption behavior of households depends upon their *relative* income positions, it does not matter that their absolute incomes change, since shifting to a higher level of income will not change their propensity to consume. In this case, a doubling of all incomes will leave the aggregate APC unchanged, even though it may still be true that the cross-sectional consumption function displays a falling APC with increases in household income.[5]

Finally, it is also clear that if the distribution of income shifts along with changes in the level of aggregate income, the aggregate propensity to consume might be further affected. The direction of the effect, however, is not obvious, since it depends upon whether absolute or relative income controls spending behavior. If relative income controls, shifts in the distribution of income might be accompanied by changes in consumption behavior. James Duesenberry, for example, has argued that much household consumption spending depends upon relative income and is motivated by emulation: by attempts of lower income households to emulate the consumption standards of higher income households.

---

4 This follows from the fact that the aggregate propensity to consume is a weighted average of the APC in each income class and that the latter declines as we move higher up the income class scale. Thus a household earning $5,000 a year before the income change might consume 90 percent of its income. In the same year, a $10,000 household may be consuming 80 percent of its income. Since a $10,000 income counts twice as much as a $5,000 income, the aggregate APC is 83 1/3 percent [= 90(1/3) + 80(2/3)]. After incomes double, the households earn $10,000 and $20,000, respectively. If the consumption proportion for the higher income household is now 70 percent, and if the lower income household now consumes at the rate previously held by the higher income household, the aggregate propensity to consume will fall to 73 1/3 percent [= 80(1/3) + 70(2/3)].

5 Using the numbers of footnote 4, the statement that consumption behavior depends on *relative* income positions means that the proportion of income consumed by the two households will remain at 90 and 80 percent even after the incomes of the two households have doubled. In the second year, this means that the aggregate APC remains at 83 1/3 percent.

Such attempts would lead lower income people to consume greater proportions of their disposable income than higher income people. A change in the distribution of income in the direction of more equality would therefore have two effects. The first effect would be to reduce the income and consumption of high-income groups. The second effect (following from the first) would be a reduction of the emulation pressure on lower income groups and a possible *reduction* of the proportion of their income which they consume. If Duesenberry is correct, therefore, a shift in the distribution of income in the direction of equality might actually cause a decrease in the aggregate propensity to consume. By parallel reasoning, an increase in income inequality between households might generate additional emulation pressure and lead to an *increase* in the aggregate propensity to consume. An important implication of Duesenberry's theory is that if aggregate income growth is not accompanied by changes in the distribution of income, the aggregate average propensity to consume will not change, despite the fact that cross-sectional studies in each year might continue to show that the proportion of income consumed declines with increases in household income.[6]

Shape of the Consumption Function

Throughout the history of consumption analysis economists have speculated about the form of the consumption function. Three of the most prominent types are given in Graph 6.1. The first, in Graph 6.1(a) shows a linear function with a zero intercept. This function displays a constant marginal and average propensity to consume. Moreover, the MPC and the APC are equal to each other and to the c-constant in

GRAPH 6.1

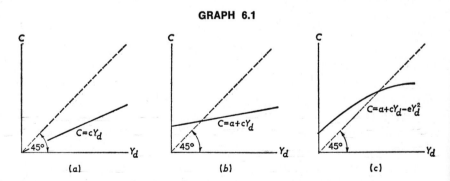

---

[6] Duesenberry's main work on this subject is in his *Income, Saving, and the Theory of Consumer Behavior* (Cambridge: Harvard University Press, 1947).

the equation: $\Delta C/\Delta Y_a = C/Y_a = c$. The function in Graph 6.1(b) is the type used earlier in this book. It possesses a constant MPC $(\Delta C/\Delta Y_a = c)$; but, since the intercept, a, is positive, the APC declines with increases in income: $C/Y_a = a/Y_a + c$. In the third function— Graph 6.1(c)—both the average and the marginal propensities to consume are variable. In fact, they both decline with increases in income. The decline in the MPC can be seen in the decreasing slope of the function as income increases (or in the first derivative of the equation of the function: $dC/dY_a = c - 2eY_a$). The decline in the APC can be shown by dividing both sides of the equation by Y_a: $C/Y_a = a/Y_a + c - eY_a$. As Y_a increases, C/Y_a decreases.

The differences between the three functions displayed in Graph 6.1 have important implications for the performance of the economy. If, as a great many economists believe, fluctuations of income and employment are mainly caused by wide fluctuations in investment and government spending, then consumption functions of the types indicated in Graphs 6.1(b) and 6.1(c) should (if they are stable) help to moderate booms and slumps. The reason is that as income rises, these functions indicate decreasing average propensities to consume. A decreasing average propensity to consume means an increasing average propensity to save. An increasing propensity to save means that investment and government spending have a relatively larger leakage from the income stream with which to contend. Hence, to sustain a rapid percentage rate of increase of income during a boom, investment and government spending must continue to accelerate. If they cannot, the boom will taper off. In the opposite direction, a slump will also be moderated if the functions of Graphs 6.1(b) and 6.1(c) exist, because as income falls the average propensity to save decreases.

The function in Graph 6.1(a) does not imply a moderating influence over the cycle from the side of consumption and saving, since it implies that saving is a constant proportion of income. But if the true function for the economy is of this type, rather than the other two, then the economy might find it easier to sustain its growth in the long run. The reason is that investment and government spending need not continue to grow as a percentage of total spending, as implied by the functions in Graphs 6.1(b) and 6.1(c). To achieve this sustained growth, of course, the economy must find a way to avoid wide fluctuations in investment and government spending, since such fluctuations might cause short-run disturbances severe enough to spoil the long-run growth potential of the economy. Unfortunately, a consumption function with a constant average propensity to consume (and save) tends to make an economy more prone to severe short-run disturbances than a consumption function with a variable propensity to consume.

Conflicting Evidence on the Function of the Consumption Function

Most of the hypotheses about the shape of the consumption function start with Keynes. Earlier, we quoted his opinion that the short-run marginal propensity to consume is probably less than the long-run marginal propensity to consume; hence, he obviously believed it appropriate to distinguish between two types of consumption functions—one for the short run and one for the long run. In addition, he believed that the short-run consumption function has a positive intercept, as in Graph 6.1(b) or 6.1(c): "a decline in income due to a decline in employment, if it goes far, may cause consumption to exceed income . . . ."[7] The implication is that for periods over the cycle Keynes believed that the average propensity to consume varies, decreasing during the boom and increasing during the slump.

For the long run, Keynes hypothesized a falling average propensity to consume:

> But, apart from short-period *changes* in the level of income, it is also obvious that a higher absolute level of income will tend, as a rule, to widen the gap between income and consumption. For the satisfaction of the immediate primary needs of a man and his family is usually a stronger motive than the motives towards accumulation, which only acquire effective sway when a margin of comfort has been attained. These reasons will lead, as a rule, to a greater *proportion* of income being saved as real income increases.[8]

This hypothesis rules out Graph 6.1(a) as a description of the long-run consumption function. However, it does not rule out a curved function going through the origin, or functions like those in Graphs 6.1(b) or 6.1(c).

Keynes did not work out a theory connecting the short-run and long-run consumptions functions. Nor did he adduce much evidence for his views. To be fair to him, however, when he wrote his book there wasn't much evidence to be had. Now our statistical resources are much better developed; hence, it has become possible to test out and elaborate Keynes' ideas.

What does the evidence show? First, Keynes' hunch that the average

---

[7] Keynes, *op. cit.*, p. 98. It is hard to say whether Keynes believed the consumption function to be linear or curved, as in Graph 6.1(c).

[8] *Ibid.*, p. 97.

propensity to consume fluctuates over the cycle seems to be true, at least for the United States. In the pre-World War II period, for example, the APC rose steadily from .927 in 1929 (a peak year) to 1.007 in 1933. Saving at the bottom of the Great Depression was actually negative! From 1933 to 1937 (another peak year), the APC fell to .934, only to rise again during the severe relapse of 1938 to .976. After 1938, the ratio fell again to a value of .935 in 1940, the year before the United States entered the War. During World War II, consumption was severely depressed due to rationing and the unavailability of goods; the APC fell to a low of .740 in 1944. Since World War II, the pattern of cyclical change in the APC has been less pronounced than in the prewar period. Nevertheless, if one removes durables from consumer spending, the pattern is similar.[9]

What about the evidence concerning the long run? Keynes' hypothesis was that as society becomes richer, the average propensity to consume should fall. Economists have tried to test this hypothesis in two ways. The first is by pressing back as far in time as the data will carry them and by computing consumption-income ratios for enough years to average out cyclical movements in the APC. The second approach has been to examine cross-sectional consumption functions in the hope that consumption behavior revealed by these functions might shed light upon the aggregate historical consumption function.

The first major time-series study of the long-run consumption function was that of Simon Kuznets,[10] who examined the evidence for the period 1869–1929. Kuznets, using overlapping decade averages of consumption and national income, found that the average propensity to consume did not decrease during the period; instead it showed a relative constancy, varying between .84 and .89 and averaging about .86. In a later study, Raymond Goldsmith verified Kuznets' basic results for the period 1896–1949; the APC out of personal income during this period averaged about .88.[11] Hence, Keynes' hypothesis of a decreasing propensity to consume has not been confirmed by historical studies. Indeed, if anything, the data show a slight upward drift in the proportion of income consumed. L. R. Klein and R. F. Kosobud fit a trend equation

---

[9] Data in the paragraph are computed from Dept. of Commerce estimates of consumption and personal disposable income. The statement for the postwar period is based upon data given by Michael K. Evans in *Macroeconomic Activity* (New York: Harper and Row, 1969), p. 17.

[10] Kuznets, *Uses of National Income in Peace and War* (New York: National Bureau of Economic Research, 1942).

[11] Goldsmith, *A Study of Saving in the United States,* Vol. 1 (Princeton: Princeton University Press for the National Bureau of Economic Research, 1955), p. 22.

to the C/Y ratio for U.S. data and found that it had a slight average rise of 0.129 percent per year.[12] It follows that of the three functions displayed above, Graph 6.1(a) most closely describes the long-run consumption function for the United States as estimated from aggregate time-series data, although it is also probably true that this function is slowly twisting to the left as the years progress.

As indicated earlier, cross-sectional studies show strikingly different results. The U.S. Bureau of Labor Statistics conducted family budget studies for the periods 1935–36 and 1941.[13] In each survey it found that (1) at low-income levels saving tends to be negative; (2) the average propensity to consume falls with increases in income; and (3) the marginal propensity to consume falls with increases in household incomes. The results have been confirmed several times in later studies;[14] they imply a consumption function of the type displayed in Graph 6.1(c) and, as such, are in sharp conflict with the results of the time-series studies of the consumption-income ratio.

The great task of consumption function studies in the last 30 years has been to rationalize the statistical observations discussed in the previous paragraphs. More particularly, the problems have been to (1) reconcile theoretically the short- and long-run behavior of consumption, and (2) reconcile the findings of the historical time-series studies with those of the cross-sectional budget studies. In pursuit of this goal, economists have worked with several hypotheses. In the balance of this chapter we shall examine these hypotheses in turn. In the literature they have come to be called: (*a*) the *absolute income hypothesis;* (*b*) the *relative income hypothesis;* and (*c*) the *permanent income hypothesis.*

The Absolute Income Hypothesis

If absolute income is the basis for consumption decisions and if the cross-sectional consumption function shows a decrease in the average propensity to consume as family income rises, then the aggregate average propensity to consume should also show a decline as aggregate income over time increases. Kuznets' and Goldsmith's evidence, however, show the contrary. Does this mean that we can rule out absolute

---

[12] Klein and Kosobud, "Some Econometrics of Growth: Great Ratios of Economics," *Quarterly Journal of Economics,* May, 1961, p. 177.

[13] U.S. Dept. of Labor, Bureau of Labor Statistics, *Bulletins 642–49.*

[14] For example, see I. Friend and S. Schor, "Who Saves," *Review of Economics and Statistics,* May, 1959.

income as the appropriate variable for explaining consumption? Not necessarily. There are two reasons for this. The first is that income is not the sole variable affecting consumption spending. The second is that over the long period encompassed by the Kuznets and Goldsmith studies, changes have taken place in the distribution of income. It follows that the consumption-income relation over this period could have been profoundly affected by the operation of other variables or by changes in the distribution of income.

A strong candidate for influencing the propensity to consume is household wealth. The motive for saving is, of course, the accumulation of wealth. After a household has accumulated a sufficient amount of wealth, its desire to save may wane. In a study reported in the early postwar period, James Tobin concluded that absolute income determines the consumption-income ratio, but that the existence of asset accumulations by households tends to depress the propensity to save. His explanation of the long-term constancy of the average propensity to save was that the asset accumulations over the years by households tended to offset the effect of higher levels of income which, in the absence of increasing household wealth, would have led to increases in the propensity to save. Tobin was not sure, however, that the effect of wealth was strong enough to offset completely the influence of higher absolute incomes on consumption.[15] Tobin's hypothesis has been thrown into doubt by more recent work. Michael K. Evans, in a recent article, tested the proposition that wealth is an important variable in the consumption function.[16] His results were mixed. For the postwar period, 1947–62, he found that the ratio of wealth to income was not a statistically significant part of the consumption function. For the 1929–62 period, however, he did find it to be significant. Since the postwar study was based upon quarterly data, and the 1929–62 study upon annual data, the latter might seem to be a better test of the long-run effects of wealth on consumption.

The distribution of income seems to have been moving in the direction of more equality. In 1929, the bottom 40 percent of U.S. families received 12.6 percent of total family personal income (after federal taxes), while the 5 percent of the families at the top of the income scale received 29.5 percent of family income. In 1962, 33 years later, the share of the bottom 40 percent of the families had risen to 16.4 percent

15 See Tobin, "Relative Income, Absolute Income, and Saving," in *Money, Trade, and Economic Growth* (New York: The Macmillan Co., 1951).

16 Evans, "The Importance of Wealth in the Consumption Function," *Journal of Political Economy,* August, 1967, Part I.

of income—perceptible, but not much of a change. The share of the top 5 percent, however, fell to 17.7 percent of total family income—perceptible and a large change. Most of the loss in position for the top 5 percent families was picked up by families ranking between the 40th and 80th percentile in income. Their share of total family personal income (after federal taxes) rose from 33.4 percent in 1929 to 39.9 percent in 1962.[17] Lack of comparable data prevents us from saying whether or not these distributional changes are an extension of a long-term trend from before 1929; but, if they are, it is quite possible that the long-term propensity to consume has been affected by them. The absolute income hypothesis, of course, would predict an upward shift in the consumption function from these changes in the distribution of income. But, whether or not the changes have been sufficient to produce enough of a shift to result in long-run constancy of the APC is hard to say.

Relative Income Hypothesis

The relative income hypothesis has received considerable attention as a means of reconciling the conflicting evidence on consumption. As stated before, this hypothesis is mainly connected with James Duesenberry, who was one of the first economists to give it a substantial test. There are two aspects to this hypothesis. The first, as we have already seen, is that the average propensity to consume for a family is determined by emulation; hence it is the relative position, not the absolute position, on the income scale which determines a family's consumption behavior. We have also seen that this hypothesis implies constancy of the aggregate APC if the distribution of family income remains constant over time, even though aggregate income may be increasing. A narrowing of the distribution, as has occurred since 1929, should, according to Duesenberry, have resulted in a decrease in the consumption-income ratio, which has not occurred. This is not necessarily inconsistent with Duesenberry's hypothesis. As in the case of the absolute income hypothesis, changes in the distribution of income might have been too slight to produce profound effects on the aggregate ratio of consumption to income. Moreover, even if the effect of changes in the distribution of income have had the effect of decreasing the ratio of consumption to income, other factors may have been operating to increase it.

---

[17] These data are from Edward C. Budd, ed., *Inequality and Poverty* (New York: W. W. Norton & Co., 1967), p. xvi.

Among these possible factors are (1) the increasing urbanization of the U.S. population (farmers have higher saving ratios than do city dwellers; (2) the increasing proportion of the population who are old and retired (who save less than do younger people; (3) a relative decline in income from self-employment and proprietorship;[18] (4) possible changes in saving attitudes due to the increased stability of the U.S. economy since the 1930's.

We hasten to add that these same factors might be enlisted to supplement the absolute income hypothesis as a basis for explaining the secular behavior of the propensity to consume. The interpretation here would be that had these structural changes in population, occupations, and income distribution not taken place, the aggregate average propensity to consume would have fallen. So far, there is not sufficient grounds for discriminating between the absolute and relative income hypotheses as a basis for explaining the historical long-term consumption function.

The second part of Duesenberry's hypothesis is designed to reconcile the short-run aggregate consumption function with the long-run function. Recall that the short-run function looks like Graph 6.1(b), while the long-run function looks like Graph 6.1(a). The absolute income hypothesis would connect up the two by superimposing an upward drifting short-run function upon a long-run function, in the manner indicated on Graph 6.2. The drift of the short-run function (from C_s' to C_s''') would be caused by the trend factors mentioned above. During any short-run period, however, trend factors are less important, and the propensity to consume is dominated by short-run variations in income. Average income over the cycle, however, determines average consumption over the cycle. Points like 1, 2, 3 are such averages, and their locus over time traces out the long-run consumption function, C_l.

Duesenberry's relative income hypothesis provides a much more explicit theory of the interaction between long- and short-run consump-

---

[18] Entrepreneurial income receivers save a much larger fraction of their income than do others. Two studies, one by the Bureau of Labor Statistics and the Wharton School of Finance (University of Pennsylvania) and another by L. R. Klein and J. Margolis have obtained entrepreneurial saving ratios that are 3 times as high as the general average in their samples. The studies are reported on by I. Friend and I. B. Kravis, "Entrepreneurial Income, Saving, and Investment," *American Economic Review,* June, 1957. Friend and Kravis argue (p. 270) that "entrepreneurs" (farmers, professional men, small businessmen, etc.) account for most personal saving—70 to 80 percent—despite the fact that in their study the group had only 31 percent total disposable income. For the country as a whole, incidentally, business and professional income as a percent of total family income fell from 18.1 percent in 1929 to an average of 11.0 percent in 1960–65. See Selma Goldsmith, "Changes in the Size Distribution of Income," in Edward C. Budd, *op. cit.,* p. 70.

GRAPH 6.2

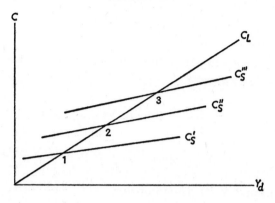

tion behavior. The relative income hypothesis is built on the theory that people emulate their neighbors and that, at the same time, they strive constantly toward a higher standard of living. An implication of such striving is that once people have attained a higher standard of living they are reluctant to give it up. *Consumption standards, in other words, are irreversible over time.* Once having achieved a peak income, as at a cyclical peak, people will seek to maintain the consumption associated with that peak income.

Working with this kind of reasoning, Duesenberry hypothesized that the aggregate consumption-income ratio is a function of the ratio of current income to the highest income level previously achieved:

$$\frac{C}{Y_d} = a - b\,\frac{Y_d}{Y_d{}^*}, \tag{1}$$

where Y_d is current aggregate disposable personal income and $Y_d{}^*$ is the previous peak of aggregate disposable personal income.

The hypothesis of equation (1) provides a link between the short- and long-run consumption function which, at the same time, reconciles empirical findings respecting these two functions. The equation clearly provides for a C/Y_d ratio which fluctuates over the cycle. When $Y_d < Y_d{}^*$, the ratio rises; vice versa when $Y_d > Y_d{}^*$. Over the long period, however, steady growth in income will produce constancy in the ratio of consumption to income. Let the average rate of growth in income be g per unit of time. Each year's income will then be equal to income in the previous year (under steady growth, each $t - 1$ year is a previous "peak") times $(1 + g)$: i.e., $Y_{dt} = Y_{dt-1}(1 + g)$. From this, it follows that for any year t,

$$\frac{C_t}{Y_{dt}} = a - b\,(1 + g) = \text{a constant,} \tag{2}$$

as required by the theory.

Let us put some numerical flesh on these bones. Duesenberry estimated equation (1) to be:[19]

$$\frac{C_t}{Y_{dt}} = 1.20 - .25\,\frac{Y_{dt}}{Y_d*}. \tag{3}$$

If we use this equation we can estimate that APC and MPC for both the short and long run. Assume that the cyclical fluctuation of Y_d is 10 percent around Y_d*. The short-run APC will then vary between 0.925 and 0.975:

$$\frac{C_t}{Y_{dt}} = 1.20 - .25 \times .90 = 0.975, \text{ and}$$

$$\frac{C_t}{Y_{dt}} = 1.20 - .25 \times 1.10 = 0.925\,.$$

The short-run MPC also depends upon the ratio Y_d/Y_d*—

$$\frac{\Delta C_t}{\Delta Y_{dt}} = 1.20 - 2 \times .25\,\frac{Y_{dt}}{Y*_{dt-1}}\,;$$

hence, if the ratio fluctuates between .90 and 1.10, the MPC will also vary, rising during slumps (to .75) and falling during booms (to .65). Notice that the short-run MPC is much smaller than the short-run APC.

For the long-run, Duesenberry's consumption function gives equality between the MPC and the APC, as it should if both are constant. Assume that income grows at an average rate of 3 percent a year, which is roughly true of U.S. experience. The long-run average and marginal propensities to consume are then 0.94:

$$\frac{C_t}{Y_{dt}} = 1.20 - .25 \times 1.03 \cong 0.94\,.$$

_____

[19] Duesenberry, *op. cit.*, p. 90. Actually Duesenberry estimated $\dfrac{S_t}{Y_{dt}}$. His years were 1929–40. His equation holds up very well. Myron Ross reports an estimate by one of his graduate students, Jay Fishman, using quarterly data for 1945 to 1966. Fishman obtained a value of 1.2 for *a* and −0.27 for *b*. See Ross, *Income: Analysis and Policy* (2nd ed.; New York: McGraw-Hill, 1969).

Duesenberry's hypothesis appears to fit the data fairly well, particularly for the years since 1929;[20] nevertheless dissatisfaction with its conceptual base and some of its predictive shortcomings have led economists to propose other ways of reconciling the empirical findings. Prominent among these proposals is Milton Friedman's permanent income hypothesis.

The Permanent Income Hypothesis

To economists of an orthodox or classical persuasion, connecting the propensities to consume and save with either current or recent past income is somewhat superficial. For the classical writers, the average propensity to save depended mainly upon the rate of interest. They postulated that people generally prefer present to future consumption, and that to overcome this preference they must be offered a reward in the form of interest. They did not necessarily believe that people would save nothing if not offered interest; however, they did believe that the propensity to save would be relatively small without it.

The classical theory was considerably enriched by a prominent American writer, Irving Fisher.[21] Fisher accepted the argument that people prefer present to future consumption. However, he also believed that the propensity to consume is strongly influenced by income. As do some modern writers, he believed that the propensity to consume falls with increases in income. More importantly, however, he also believed that *expected income,* particularly as regards its *time shape* and *variability,* is a significant determinant of consumption behavior. Picture a man viewing his prospective lifetime income. If he expects (with certainty) a rising income stream over the future, it is likely that he will consume more of his present income than if he expects a declining income stream. The reason is that his future will be more amply provided for than his present, hence he can afford to indulge his preference for present goods without seriously affecting future consumption. An expectation of a falling income stream, on the other hand, will lead to a smaller propensity

---

[20] Kuznets' long-run APC averaged about .86, but he used net national product instead of disposable personal income (estimates of which did not exist for pre-1929 years). He also used a concept for saving which included corporate as well as personal saving; hence his APC was bound to be much lower than the one appropriate for Deusenberry's study.

[21] See, especially, Fisher, *Theory of Interest* (New York: Augustus M. Kelly, 1961, reprint of original, 1930), chap. 4, 5.

to consume out of present income, because satisfying the desire for present consumption competes less heavily with the desire to maintain consumption standards in the future. This aspect of Fisher's theory is supported by recent empirical research, which has found that young families (who have expectations of rising income) consume more than do middle-aged families (whose retirement incomes are expected to be low relative to current incomes) .

Fisher believed that uncertainty about future income also diminishes the propensity to consume out of present income. A man who is uncertain about the future is likely to worry about his chances of maintaining future consumption, hence he is likely to save more now in order to protect it. Again, evidence of modern research supports Fisher. Farmers and nonfarm entrepreneurs have more variable incomes than do wage earners, and (as discussed above) their propensities to save out of current income are much higher.

In an important book, Milton Friedman[22] has put forth a theory of consumption which in some ways is reminiscent of Fisher's theory. Friedman argues that in any year a man's consumption is mainly determined by his *permanent income.* Permanent income, for any year, is not what statisticians ordinarily measure. *Measured income* is the actual receipts a man acquires during the year. Permanent income, on the other hand is a representation of the average income a man *expects* to receive over his lifetime. Friedman's definition of permanent income is not precise, but what he seems to have in mind is something of the following sort: In any given year a man will possess a given amount of wealth. Part of that wealth will be his "human capital," which is the source of his power to earn future income from the use of his brain and brawn. Another part of his wealth will be nonhuman capital—financial assets and durable physical assets, such as his house, a car, and so on. The average expected return on this conglomerate of wealth forms what Friedman calls permanent income.

Clearly, there is no reason why permanent income and measured income should be the same in any given year. Over his lifetime, a man may expect his *average* measured income to equal his permanent income; but, current measured income is subject to cyclical and random changes and it may be above or below permanent income. Friedman calls the difference between current measured income and permanent

---

[22] Friedman, *A Theory of the Consumption Function* (Princeton, N.J.: Princeton University Press for the National Bureau of Economic Research, 1957).

income *transitory income.* From its definition, it is clear that transitory income may be positive or negative; its average, over a man's lifetime, is zero.

Corresponding to these three concepts of income, Friedman proposes three concepts of consumption: permanent consumption, measured consumption, and transitory consumption. He hypothesized that most measured consumption is really permanent consumption, in the sense that the major controlling factor on consumption is permanent income, not measured income. This means that even though measured income may fluctuate from year to year, consumption spending will be relatively stable, because it depends mainly upon permanent income. An implication of this hypothesis is that transitory consumption (the difference between measured and permanent consumption) is not related to transitory income.

Put more formally, Friedman's theory of consumption is as follows:

$$C_p = kY_p \tag{4}$$
$$C_m \cong C_p, \tag{5}$$

and

$$C_{tr} \neq f(Y_{tr}). \tag{6}$$

The letters *m, p,* and *tr* mean measured, permanent, and transitory, respectively. Equation (4) states that permanent consumption is some fraction or proportion, *k,* of permanent income. Equation (5) argues that measured consumption will approximate permanent consumption; hence, expression (6), which states that transitory income will not be related to transitory income. It might be noted that Friedman does not believe that *k* in equation (4) is necessarily constant over time; rather, he thinks it subject to change due to changes in interest rates, the ratio of human to nonhuman wealth, and tastes. Nevertheless, the hypotheses embodied in his theory do have fairly strong implications. Since over the long run one should expect measured income to be approximately equal to permanent income, one should also expect the long-run marginal propensity to consume to equal the long-run average propensity to consume and to be relatively constant, as implied in equation (4). Over the cycle, however, one should expect the measured average propensity to consume to fall during booms and to rise during slumps. This follows from the hypothesized lack of correlation between transitory consumption and transitory income: When, during booms, measured income rises above permanent income, Friedman's expectation is that most of the resulting transitory income will be saved; vice versa when slumps cause measured income to fall below permanent income.

Friedman's theory is roughly in accord with the Kuznets-Goldsmith data on the long-run consumption-income relation and with studies showing short-run variability in the consumption-current income ratio. It might also be noted that there is much evidence from cross-sectional data to support his hypothesis. For example, farm families and nonfarm self-employed families have relatively low marginal propensities to consume; moreover, these families have relatively large positive saving-income ratios when their incomes are high and relatively large negative saving ratios when their incomes are low, which is consistent with the fact that these families also have relatively variable incomes with high transitory components in any year.[23] This same phenomenon may also explain the consistent findings of the various budget studies which, recall, tend to produce consumption functions shaped like the one in Graph 6.1(c). If the upper end of the income scale is dominated by families possessing large amounts of positive transitory income, while the lower end is dominated by families with negative transitory income, budget studies would tend to trace out cross-sectional consumption functions with positive intercepts and with marginal propensities to consume smaller than average propensities to consume.

Unfortunately, evidence is not all in favor of the permanent income hypothesis. In an attempt to test the zero propensity to consume out of transitory income, Bodkin[24] found that veterans who received large unexpected dividends early in 1950 from their National Service Life Insurance consumed a higher proportion of their windfall income than their ordinary income. (In another study of windfall income, however, Kreinin[25] discovered a low MPC to consume out of restitution payments made by Germany to former citizens in Israel). This and other negative evidence might possibly be rationalized by adherents of the permanent income hypothesis, but the same can be said concerning other major consumption function hypotheses. However, whether correct or not, the permanent income hypothesis is a major contribution to research and thought, particularly as concerns its emphasis on the importance of wealth and long-term expectations in affecting consumer behavior. Moreover, in stressing the notion of transitory income, the hypothesis

---

[23] Kravis and Friend, *op. cit.*, p. 275.

[24] R. Bodkin, "Windfall Income and Consumption," in I. Friend and R. Jones, eds., *Proceedings of the Conference on Consumption and Saving*, Vol. 2 (Philadelphia, 1960).

[25] M. Kreinin, "Windfall Income and Consumption," *American Economic Review*, June, 1961.

has helped to focus research on income variability as a major source for varying patterns of behavior.[26]

Concluding Comments

We have not developed all the possible approaches to explaining observed consumption behavior respecting income and wealth. In particular, we have not gone beyond Duesenberry in discussing the influence of past income (or consumption) on current consumption. Nor have we adequately explored the role of consumer wealth as it affects their current behavior. Actually, these variables are intimately related to the ones already discussed. It would extend this discussion too much to go into their possible effects.[27] Hopefully, however, the reader has by this time become aware of the complexities which have beset economists in their attempts to discover an empirically relevant consumption function. Unfortunately, however, the theoretical work described in this chapter concerns only the consumption-income (and wealth) relation. This relation, whatever it may be, is possibly subject to a set of other variables which might influence its stability. In the next chapter, we discuss some of these variables.

ADDITIONAL READINGS

Most of the following items have been mentioned already in the footnotes of this chapter but are repeated here to give emphasis to their usefulness as good introductions to the vast literature on the consumption function.

ACKLEY, GARDNER. *Macroeconomic Theory*. New York: The MacMillan Co., 1961, chaps. 10, 11, 12.
EVANS, MICHAEL K. *Macroeconomic Activity*. New York: Harper and Row, 1969, chaps. 2, 3.

---

[26] For a review of positive and negative findings on the permanent income hypothesis, see R. Ferber, "Research on Household Behavior," *American Economic Review*, March, 1962, pp. 25–32. Also, see the favorable discussion in M. Evans, *Macroeconomic Activity, op. cit.*, chap. 2, 3. F. Modigliani and A. Ando in "The Life Cycle Hypothesis of Saving: Aggregate Implications and Tests," *American Economic Review*, March, 1963, have developed and tested a theory close to that of Friedman's. They do not, as does Friedman, lump income from labor and income from nonhuman wealth together. Instead, they consider the lifetime resources available to an individual at any moment of time to be his current labor income, the present value of his future income from labor, and his net (nonhuman) worth. Consumption in their theory is considered a separate function of each of these components of available resources, with the individual allocating his income in such a manner as to maximize his utility over his lifetime. See M. Evans, *op. cit.*, for a good discussion of the Ando-Modigliani theory.

[27] The reader is referred to Evans, *ibid.*, for a detailed discussion of these variables.

FERBER, ROBERT. "Research on Household Behavior," *American Economic Review,* March, 1962.

KRAVIS, I. and FRIEND, I. "Entrepreneurial Income, Saving, and Investment," *American Economic Review,* June, 1957.

SUITS, DANIEL. "The Determinants of Consumer Expenditure: A Review of Present Knowledge," in Commission on Money and Credit, *Impacts of Monetary Policy.* Englewood Cliffs: Prentice-Hall, 1963.

Chapter 7

CONSUMPTION (II)

In this chapter we discuss the impact of variables other than income (however defined) upon consumption. In the previous chapter we had occasion to comment upon some of these variables, such as wealth and income distribution, and the occupation, age, and location of the consuming unit. In this discussion we shall expand upon the list of nonincome variables. We first take up the effects of a group of monetary factors—prices, interest rates, liquid assets, and credit. This will be followed by an examination of some demographic variables and of a set of other factors, such as attitudes and tastes.

Prices

In discussing the influences of prices upon consumption behavior it is important to distinguish between the *price level, the expected price level,* and *relative prices.* As indicated, most theories of consumption behavior relate real consumption spending to real income on the ground that rational consumers faced with equiproportionate changes in the prices they pay for goods and the prices they receive for their services will not change their previous decisions to apportion income between consumption and saving. These theories assume that rational consumers do not operate under a "money illusion"—the feeling that they are richer just because their money (but not real) incomes have increased. Not all consumers are necessarily rational, of course, and it is quite possible for some actually to increase their real consumption in response to an increase in the price level, particularly in the short run before they realize that increases in their money incomes are also being accompanied by an increase in prices. Nevertheless, if higher prices persist, consumers should eventually realize that the real value of their saving has declined and, as a result, they will have a strong incentive to reduce their real consumption back to previous levels. So far, economists have not been able to uncover much evidence respecting the operation of a money illusion.

Whether or not price levels are important as an influence upon the propensity to consume, *expected* price levels can have important effects. If for some reason consumers become generally convinced that the near future promises rapid increases in prices, they are likely to buy now what they think will be more expensive in the future. Conversely, a generally held expectation of price declines will lead consumers to hold off consumption for the future. These remarks are most appropriate for purchases of consumer durables, but under conditions of rapid inflation or deflation the same speculative mentality may also apply to various categories of nondurables, such as clothing, storable foods, repairs, and so forth. At this writing (June, 1969) the United States is undergoing a rapid inflation. The price increases in beef have been particularly rapid in the last few months. The author is hastening to fill his home freezer with beef in order to avoid the possibility of paying more in the near future. Since he is digging into his savings to do so, his propensity to consume has suddenly increased. At times, the speculative phenomenon is noticeable in the data. Immediately after the outbreak of the Korean War in June, 1950, the saving-disposable income ratio was cut in half. This was partly due to the expectation of absolute shortages (people were still remembering rationing during World War II), but it was probably also due to the very rapid increase in prices which followed the outbreak of war.

If changes in price levels are accompanied by changes in relative prices, there may be further effects on the propensity to consume. The decreased demand for goods and services which are becoming relatively more expensive may not exactly offset the increased demand for goods which are becoming relatively less expensive. Unfortunately, there is as yet no empirical evidence to shed light on this issue.

The price effects discussed in the previous paragraphs are direct effects. Prices, working through some other variables, may also have some indirect effects upon consumption. First, under a progressive tax system, increases in the money value of incomes lead to an increase in the tax burden upon real income. The resulting decrease in disposable real income may cause a decline in the level of consumption, though the *ratio* of consumption to disposable income may not be affected.

Second, an increase in prices will cause a decline in the real value of that portion of its wealth which the household sector keeps in the form of liquid assets. By liquid assets, we mean money and financial assets which are fixed in money value. The latter include commercial bank time deposits, deposits and shares in saving institutions, government securities, and bonds issued by nonfinancial business firms. The household sector typically holds more liquid assets than it owes in the form of debt. On net, therefore, it is a creditor and, as such, its position deteriorates when prices rise and improves when prices fall. The deterioration in the position of the household sector during periods of inflation may well lead it to decrease its consumption. But, if rising prices lead to widespread expectations of further inflation, the household sector may actually spend more on consumption for fear that in the near future its liquid assets will be worth even less. We shall discuss some of the empirical findings on this question later.

Finally, we must note the fact that variations in relative prices might have effects upon the distribution of income and, through the distribution of income, effects upon the aggregate propensity to consume. During inflations, for example, prices may outrun wage rates and lead to a shift in the distribution of income in the favor of profit receivers. Since profit receivers tend to save more than wage earners, the aggregate propensity to consume should tend to shift down.

The Influence of Interest Rates

Modern economists rarely assign an important role to interest rates as a possible influence upon the aggregate consumption-income relation. If this were a book written in the tradition of some 40 years ago, our discussions would have featured interest as the main influence upon saving. The typical orthodox view of the saving process is illustrated by Graph 7.1 (a). Given the level of income, it was thought that the rate of saving in the community would increase (and that the level of consumption spending would correspondingly decrease) as the interest rate assumed higher and higher values. At certain low levels of interest (below i_0), however, it was thought that individuals would tend to borrow, because such interest rates would not be high enough to give them a return on lending sufficient to offset the dissatisfaction entailed in giving up present consumption.

The saving-interest relation described by Graph 7.1 (a) is not the only possible one. Stability and time shape of expected income, size and age of family, position on the income scale, and other things strongly affect the propensity to consume. Graph 7.1 (a), for example, would seem to apply to spending units expecting stable, or rising, levels of income. Those expecting rising incomes would be willing to borrow in the

GRAPH 7.1

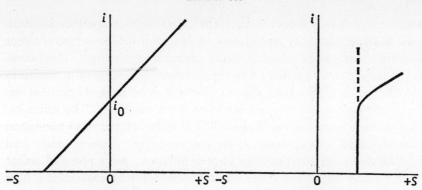

Neoclassical Relation; or Families Expecting Stable or Rising Incomes
(a)

A Given Sum Dedicated to Insurance; Retirement Premiums; or the Very Rich
(d)

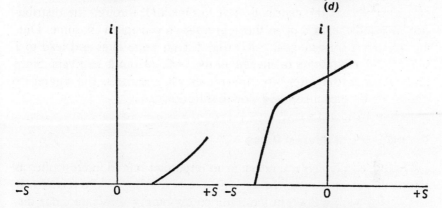

Families Expecting Falling Incomes
(b)

Young Family Expecting Rising Income, but Wanting Durables
(e)

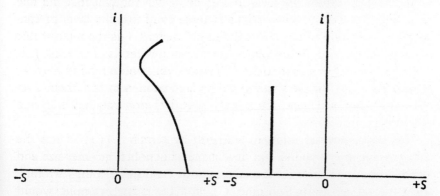

People Wanting to Build an Estate of a Given Size
(c)

Old People in Retirement and Leaving No Estate; or, the Very Poor
(f)

present and could be enticed into lending (saving) only at higher rates of interest. Spending units expecting stable levels of income would have a similar shaped function, but would probably require lower rates of interest before they would be willing to borrow. The interest-saving relation would, in this event, be below the one depicted on Graph 7.1(a).

In other situations, the saving-interest function might be quite different. Families expecting future income to be smaller than present income would be stimulated to save out of current income, even if the interest rate were zero. Positive interest rates, of course, might stimulate them to save even more (see Graph 7.1(b)). Regardless of the income expectations of families, however, other motives influence saving. Suppose a family wants to accumulate an estate of a given size for its heirs. In this event, saving might occur at zero interest; but, as the interest rate assumes higher values, it becomes easier to achieve the desired bequest, and the rate of saving out of current income might fall off, only to be increased again at fairly high levels of interest [Graph 7.1(c)]. Graph 7.1(d) depicts two possible situations. It may represent a middle-income spending unit that devotes a certain fixed amount per period of time to life insurance or retirement premiums. Only fairly high interest rates would induce it to save more. On the other hand, as the dotted vertical extension of the saving line indicates, this may be a very rich family which saves simply because it has more money than it can spend, and it would save this much regardless of the level of interest rates.

Graph 7.1(e) shows the case of a young family with expectations of higher future income, but, because of current needs, must build up its stock of durables (and children). It may take very high interest rates to reduce the borrowing of this family and induce it to lend. As a final example, Graph 7.1(f) indicates a family in which the head has retired and which is living on its past savings with no thought of the future. Indeed, since saving is necessarily a forward-looking act, it will not take place if there is nothing to look forward to. Another possibility for Graph 7.1(f) is that it represents the behavior of a poor family which must, so long as lenders are willing, live by borrowing. In this case, dissaving is very little, if at all, connected with the interest rate.

The effect of interest upon the aggregate personal saving rate, therefore, is not very predictable. It depends upon the predominance of one type of saver or another in the total of all groups in the household sector. It is possible for saving to be negative at certain rates of interest, say below i_0, if groups (a), (e), and (f) are dominant. On the other hand, the behavior of all groups, taken together at various rates of interest, may produce a constant level of positive saving. For these reasons, we shall not argue for a very strong relation between the rate of saving and interest, at least insofar as we are considering the aggregate level of personal saving. This is not, of course, to eschew the importance of interest rates in other dimensions of the economy. Business saving (as distinct from personal saving), credit conditions, investment policies, and international money movements are still very much affected by the cost of borrowing and the return to lending. Nevertheless, it still remains that economists have had a very difficult time isolating a convincing relationship between aggregate personal saving and interest rates.

Liquid Assets

According to a recent survey of consumption function literature, "the role of liquid assets in the consumption function has not yet been discovered."[1] This statement does not mean that economists have not thought about the role of liquid assets, nor that they have not made empirical studies of the role. Indeed, they have done both—extensively. In the early postwar years, in particular, intensive interest centered upon liquid assets. One reason for this was the poor postwar forecasts of consumption spending, which were based upon simple notions of the consumption function. A number of economists believed that the bad forecasts resulted from a lack of consideration of the very large accumulation of liquid assets (in the form of money, saving bonds, and so on) which consumers were forced to make during the wartime years of price control and rationing. Another reason for this interest was an extensive reconsideration of the foundations of macroeconomic theory in which wealth as well as income was being given an important role in determining expenditure. Wealth includes liquid assets, and the real value of liquid assets fluctuates not only with variations in their nominal amounts but also with variations in the price level. Economists who have followed this line of thought do not argue that real liquid assets are necessarily on a par with (say) income as a determinant of consump-

---

[1] Daniel Suits, "The Determinants of Consumer Expenditure: A Review of Present Knowledge," in Commission on Money and Credit, *Impacts of Monetary Policy* (Englewood Cliffs, N.J.: Prentice-Hall, 1963), p. 411. For a review of the literature emphasizing liquid assets see Don Patinkin, *Money, Interest and Prices* (2d ed.; New York: Harper and Row, 1965), note M.

tion. Neverthelesss, they do argue that such assets do have a significant effect, and at times this effect might become very important.

One reason for uncertainty over the role of liquid assets in consumption is the conflicting nature of the evidence. A number of aggregate consumption function studies have included liquid assets as one of several variables affecting consumption. Many of these studies have shown positive correlation between consumption and liquid assets variously defined. Yet, certain perplexities remain. Several studies seem to show that consumption in the postwar period has been much more responsive to variations in liquid assets than consumption in the prewar period.[2] This conclusion has, however, been disputed by Patinkin.[3] Another problem is the proper level of aggregation for consumption. Suits[4] has shown that if consumption is broken down into expenditures upon automobiles, other durables, nondurables, and services, the effect of liquid asset variations varies with the category of expenditures. He found that consumer outlays upon automobiles (in particular) and other durables have been quite sensitive to variations in liquid assets. The sensitivity of these items was most pronounced for the postwar period; but, Suits found the behavior of nondurables and services to be quite strange. In the postwar period both were sensitive to liquid asset variations; in prewar, however, neither category responded to liquid asset changes.

Recent work by Evans[5] has put liquid assets into further doubt. Using data defining consumption both inclusive and exclusive of durables purchases and for the span of years 1946–64, Evans showed (1) that the ratio of consumption to disposable income was high during the years 1947–49 but has since fluctuated around lower levels and (2) that the ratio of liquid assets to income was also high in the years 1947–49, but since 1961 it has *exceeded* its values in the early postwar years. These data are hardly consistent with the hypothesis that liquid assets are a strategic component of the consumption function. Evans attributed the high postwar consumption-income ratio to a different factor. He pointed out that the postwar inflation reduced real disposable income below its wartime levels; hence, if people base their consumption either upon

---

[2] See, for example, A. Zellner, "The Short Run Consumption Function," *Econometrica*, Vol. 25 (1957), pp. 552–67.

[3] *Op. cit.*, pp. 54–5. Patinkin argues that different data and the different methods of investigation of the various studies make the conclusion uncertain.

[4] *Op. cit.*, pp. 32–5.

[5] Michael K. Evans, *Macroeconomic Activity* (New York: Harper & Row, 1969), pp. 41–4.

previous peak, or "permanent" disposable income, one would have expected them to consume higher proportions of their income during the periods of abnormally low income in the postwar years, which they did.

Unfortunately, Evans' conclusions are also open to question. There is a difference between voluntary (or *desired*) and involuntary (or *undesired*) asset accumulations. One would not expect consumers to increase their consumption in the face of desired accumulations of liquid assets, since undertaking the latter may well involve reducing the former. But, if consumers find themselves with "forced" or undesired accumulations, one would expect them to increase their outlays. The high liquid asset ratios in the early postwar years were, to some extent, forced upon them. The same is not true of the later years. Hence, it is still possible to interpret the high ratios of consumption to income in those years as a reaction to (undesired) holdings of liquid assets. It is also possible to interpret the subsequent fall of the consumption ratio to more normal levels as a response by consumers to the fact that they had worked off their excess liquidity.[6]

Cross-sectional studies also show ambiguous results. In a study by L. Klein (reported by Suits[7]), a significant negative correlation was found between fraction of income saved and the ratio of liquid assets to income. Nevertheless, the behavior of different groups in the study was quite different. The negative relationship between saving and liquid assets was much stronger for spending units who experienced a decline in income than those who experienced an increase. This and other studies imply a buffer role for liquid assets—i.e., their use as a device for evening out consumption despite fluctuations in income. If true, such a finding is disturbing to those who would make consumption depend upon liquid asset accumulations. As Suits points out, it is not possible to speak of an "effect" on consumption of liquid balances that are deliberately accumulated to be spent when needed. As he says, "One might as well hold Christmas clubs responsible for the December retail boom."[8] The problem for those who would make liquid assets a strategic variable in the consumption function is to isolate them as a true independent variable. As indicated earlier, this requires a method for discriminating between desired and undesired real liquid asset holdings.

---

[6] According to Evans, the ratio of liquid assets to income fell from 0.71 in 1947 to 0.62 in 1950. At the same time, the ratio of total consumption to income fell from 0.972 to 0.939. A good deal of the shrinkage in the liquid asset ratio was due to inflation. From 1946 to 1950, the consumer price index rose from 68.0 to 83.8 (1957–59 = 100).

[7] *Op. cit.,* p. 42.

[8] *Op. cit.,* p. 43.

Consumption Spending and Consumer Credit

Consumer credit is extensively used in the United States, mainly to purchase automobiles and other consumer durables. Most consumer credit takes the form of installment credit. For the end of 1968, the *Federal Reserve Bulletin* (April, 1969, table A52) recorded total consumer debt to be $113.2 billion, or 20 percent of disposable personal income. (The figure for 1939 was $7.2 billion, or 10 percent of disposable income.) Installment credit in 1968 made up 80 percent of total consumer debt (mortgage debt is not included). Approximately 35 percent of installment credit was for automobiles; the rest was for other durables, repairs and home modernization loans, and nondurables outlays.

The principal question for us is whether or not the presence of installment credit affects the consumption function; that is, does it affect the propensity to consume? One approach to this question has been through the so-called burden theory. According to this theory, the availability of credit does not permanently alter consumption but merely evens it out over time. At the beginning of an upswing, households are supposed to expand their purchases of durables based upon installment credit; hence, the ratio of debt to income rises. A rise in debt binds borrowers to future repayments; therefore, when a downturn in economic activity takes place consumers will find themselves obligated to honor their debts out of smaller disposable incomes. The burden of debt is therefore postulated to be the cause of a reduction in the propensity to consume, since in order to continue repayments during the slump households will have to reduce their consumption. Presumably, consumer spending on both durables and nondurables will be affected. Presumably, also, the reduction in durables purchases and continuing repayments reduces consumer debt and puts them in a position to acquire more durables and more debt when the revival in business activity occurs.

The burden theory assumes that the household sector has some maximum debt/income ratio beyond which it is not willing to go. This limit is what is supposed to trigger the downturn in consumer spending sometime during the boom. If such a limit exists, economists have had a difficult time finding it. Since 1945, the ratio of installment credit to disposable personal income has grown from 2.5 percent to 14.2 percent in 1968. This growth has been rather steady, despite some minor fluctuations. Indeed, during some recession years the ratio has actually risen. In

1949, for example, it rose to 4.3 percent from 3.5 percent in 1948. The ratio also increased during the 1954 recession. This does not mean that a limit to the debt/income ratio does not exist. Obviously, consumers cannot be expected to reach a point where most of their incomes are going into installment payments. The lesson of the data in this paragraph is simply that whatever the limit may be, it has not yet been reached in the United States.[9]

So far we have only argued that the burden of installment credit does not seem to have been an important deterrent to spending on consumer durables. This does not mean, of course, that such expenditures are not unstable over the cycle. As a matter of fact, they are. But, this instability is not necessarily due to the burden of installment credit. Automobiles and other durables purchases are cyclical because they can easily be postponed during recessions. Fluctuations in durables purchases would take place even if consumer credit were not available. There also have been times when the availability of installment credit has probably heightened instability of durables spending,[10] but it would be wide of the mark to say that all such instability is due to credit.

A second theory stresses the long-run influence of credit upon the consumption of durables. This theory—called the "replacement theory" by M. K. Evans[11]—says that installment credit makes the acquisition of durables easier for households and that, once having enjoyed the services of these goods, households are reluctant to give them up. An implication of this theory is that, contrary to the arguments of the burden theory, households will not refrain from extending debt during slumps if they must replace durables which were purchased earlier and which have worn out.

The replacement theory does not necessarily imply long-run effects upon the propensity to consume. Clearly, if debt rises during both boom and slump, repayments can come from reduced consumption of nondurables as well as from reductions in forms of saving other than debt repayments. Moreover, as a definitional matter, it is probably more logical to call household investments in durables saving rather than con-

---

[9] A. Enthoven, in "The Growth of Installment Credit and the Future of Prosperity," *American Economic Review*, December, 1957, put the limit at about 19 percent. He deduced this limit from a model which makes the equilibrium debt/income ratio depend upon the rate of growth in income. The higher the rate of growth, the higher the equilibrium ratio. The reason for this is that high rates of income growth reduce the burden of repayments on debt which was contracted for during earlier periods when income was lower.

[10] A famous example is the spurt in automobile purchases in 1955 following a sudden increase in credit availability.

[11] *Op. cit.,* p. 454. Also, see Suits, *op. cit.,* p. 44.

sumption. Indeed, there is evidence to the effect that durables and saving are substitutes. Michael K. Evans, using data for the years 1949–64, found a negative correlation between the durables purchases/income ratio and the saving/income ratio.[12] Hence, if one wishes to include outlays on durables as consumption, it might be argued that the availability of installment credit increases the propensity to consume. With a narrower definition of consumption, however, it is not clear that credit availability has this effect.

There is other evidence to support the replacement theory. Janet Fisher[13] in a study of consumers who used cash and consumers who used credit to buy a particular durable, found that consumers who already were in debt, or who had used installment credit in the past 10 years, were much more likely to use credit than those who were not in debt or who had not used debt in the past 10 years. Other cross-sectional studies have given similar results. The implication is that use of credit is habit forming. Is anyone surprised?

We now turn to the effects of *credit terms.* Credit terms refers to interest and other finance charges connected with a consumer loan, down payments as a percentage of the loan, and the length of the loan. Consumers are often held to be mainly interested in the size of their monthly payments rather than in the level of interest rates and other finance charges they pay. Since most studies on the effects of credit terms have been conducted for periods without wide fluctuations in interest rates on consumer loans, it is not possible to answer this question. In any event, the size of the monthly payments is potentially quite important and will vary directly with interest and finance charges; it will also vary—inversely—with the length of the loan and with the required down payment as a percentage of the loan.

Most writers hypothesize that the demand for consumer *credit* varies directly with the length of the loan, inversely with interest and finance charges, and inversely with down payment requirements. Whether or not credit terms similarly affect the demand for consumer *goods* is another question. Households faced with harsher terms have the option of using up liquid assets or reducing consumption of nondurables. Hence, though there may be significant correlation between the demand for credit and credit terms, there may be little or no correlation between the demand for goods and credit terms.

---

12 *Op. cit.,* pp. 177–79.

13 Fisher, "Consumer Durable Goods Expenditures, with Major Emphasis on the Role of Assets, Credit, and Intentions," *Journal of the American Statistical Association,* September, 1963, referred to in Evans, *op. cit.*

The evidence on the effects of credit terms is mixed. A. Kisselgoff[14] found that credit terms and the demand for *credit* are related, but he was not able to find a significant relationship between credit terms and the demand for consumer goods in general. The latter result has been supported by studies of the relationship between aggregate outlays on durables other than automobiles, but two studies, one by Daniel Suits and another by Evans and Kisselgoff[15] have found that automobile demand is significantly affected. The latter authors found automobile demand to be particularly sensitive to changes in down payment requirements and length of loans. This is especially interesting in that it is precisely these terms which were controlled by the Federal Reserve Board under Regulation W during World War II and the Korean War. Evans and Kisselgoff argue that such controls can have sizeable effects on automobile demand.

Demographic Effects

Young families (aged 18–24) usually save very little. The same is true of retired people, many of whom actually dissave. The bulk of household saving is done by people in age groups in between, mostly to prepare for retirement, but partly to leave bequests. It also appears to be true that large families have a higher propensity to consume than small families. Changes in a country's demographic structure, therefore, can have important effects upon its aggregate propensity to consume. These are usually long-run effects and they are clearly related to the way in which a country's population grows. Historically, population growth in most Western countries has been achieved by a fall in the death rate followed, after a lag, by a decline in the fertility rate. In the United States, these two effects have been heavily supplemented by immigration, though in recent decades the latter has not been an important factor. Declines in the death rate and immigration tend to increase the size of the preretirement age groups, while a fall in the fertility rate is connected with a fall in average family size. Hence, population growth in the United States has probably favored saving, in which case the propensity to consume has probably been smaller than it would have been had population grown more slowly.

---

[14] Kisselgoff, *Factors Affecting the Demand for Consumer Installment Credit* (New York: National Bureau of Economic Research, Technical Paper No. 7, 1952).

[15] Suits, "The Demand for New Automobiles in the United States, 1929–56," *Review of Economics and Statistics,* 40 (1958), pp. 273–80. M. K. Evans and A. Kisselgoff, "Demand for Consumer Installment Credit and Its Effects on Consumption," *The Brookings Model: Some Further Results* (Chicago: Rand McNally, 1968).

The dissimilarities between the saving propensities of pre- and post-retirement people have another interesting implication. Since retired people do not participate in production, an increase in income per head will accrue mostly to preretirement age groups. It follows that a rise in per capita income favors an increase in the aggregate propensity to save. If the population and income of a country were stationary, and if people saved only enough to provide for the balance of their life after retirement, the aggregate propensity to save would be zero. Growth in aggregate income from population growth or from an increase in per capita income would therefore cause the ratio of saving to income to rise. F. Modigliani and R. Brumberg[16] argue that the saving ratio is proportional to the rate of growth in aggregate income. If true, a *given* rate of growth in aggregate income will produce a constant propensity to save, and the propensity to save will be independent of how this rate of growth is compounded of changes in population and changes in per capita income, so long as both change steadily. Modigliani and Brumberg found that, under certain simplifying assumptions, a 1 percent growth rate of aggregate income produces a 3 to 4 percent ratio of saving to income. A 3.5 percent rate of income growth—roughly the U.S. historical average—therefore implies a propensity to save of 10.5 to 14 percent.

The Modigliani-Brumberg theory, labeled the *rate-of-growth hypothesis* by Farrel, is an interesting contribution to consumption function theory. If correct, it also would appear to be an important supplement to standard growth theory. The latter argues that saving is a principal source of income growth. The rate-of-growth hypothesis turns this proposition around. It does not, however, necessarily imply that the standard theory is incorrect. It merely says that if saving leads to a certain rate of growth in aggregate income, the latter, in turn, will produce the saving necessary to sustain itself. An economy must save to grow, but it must also grow to save. Unfortunately, to acquire all the benefits of this powerful mechanism for maintaining growth, an economy must not be allowed to fluctuate. No industrial economy has been able to avoid fluctuations in income and employment.

---

[16] Modigliani and Brumberg, "Utility Analysis and Aggregate Consumption Functions: An Attempt at Integration," unpublished. Referred to by M. J. Farrel, "The New Theories of the Consumption Function," *Economic Journal,* December, 1959, reprinted in R. A. Gordon and Lawrence Klein, eds., *Readings in Business Cycles* (Homewood, Ill.: Richard D. Irwin, Inc., 1965). See, also A. Ando and F. Modigliani, "The 'Life Cycle' Hypothesis of Saving: Aggregate Implications and Tests," *American Economic Review,* March, 1963, reprinted in Gordon & Klein, *ibid.*

Attitudes and Tastes

The standard formulation of the consumption function treats consumption and saving as primarily passive responses to income. Moreover, it treats income as a variable which is out of the control of the consumer. Both of these propositions have been attacked, particularly as they bear upon the short-run behavior of consumers. In a high-employment economy, in which consumers possess large holdings of assets and which also provides ample credit facilities for the purchase of durables and other items, households have considerable discretion to vary the timing of their purchases. The link between consumption and income, in other words, may be relatively weak. In place of income, psychological attitudes may dominate consumption decisions.

George Katona, of the University of Michigan, has been the major proponent of the importance of psychological attitudes in consumption.[17] Using an index of consumer attitudes compiled by the Survey Research Center of the University of Michigan, Katona and his colleagues have been able to show that attitudes are at least, if not more, important than income in explaining fluctuations in spending on consumer durables.[18] That attitudes can have an important influence upon spending is not denied by most economists. What can be disputed, however, is that attitudes represent a source of spending variation which is independent of income or other economic variables. Evans, for example, reports that inclusion of the unemployment rate in a study of automobile demand greatly reduces the significance of attitudes as a separate independent variable. Other studies on both auto and nonauto durables spending have produced similar results.[19]

The question of consumer control over income is a more serious threat to the theory of the consumption function. In a high-employment economy, such as the United States has enjoyed in most of the years since World War II, many households have opportunities to increase their incomes if they find good reason to do so. Thus, a family that wants to buy a new car or washing machine, send its children to college, or take a trip to Europe may find its father an extra job, or the mother may go

---

[17] See Katona, *The Powerful Consumer* (New York: McGraw Hill, 1960).

[18] See references to this work in Suits' survey, *op. cit.,* pp. 18–19. By "attitudes" is meant responses of a panel to general questions about the respondents' opinions on future economic conditions.

[19] See Evans, *Macroeconomic Activity,* pp. 164–68. The great automobile boom in 1955 seems to be an exception.

to work to supplement the father's income. In cases such as these, and they are quite frequent, it is difficult to maintain that consumption is a function of income. The true relationship may be the other way around; or more properly, the link between consumption and income may be a reflection of a more fundamental choice between goods and leisure. To be sure, this argument has less merit during serious recessions, and even in times of high employment households may only to a limited extent be able to exercise their tastes for goods over their tastes for leisure. Nevertheless, the presence of this phenomenon should warn us that the one-way causation between consumption and income expressed in most formulations of the consumption function is probably too simple.[20]

Final Remarks

The consumption function literature is rich, diversified, confusing, and, unfortunately inconclusive. The various theories of the consumption function discussed in the last chapter all have their deficiencies in explaining consumption behavior, and the effects upon consumption of variables other than income, however defined, are not yet completely understood. Perhaps it is absurd to believe that a complex aggregate like total consumption spending can ever be understood. Some students of the subject argue that research ought to be undertaken at a highly disaggregated level. If we aim for precision this is probably true. Nevertheless, this approach also has its drawbacks, since with too much disaggregation we may lose the forest for the trees. High-speed electronic computers allow us to build detailed models, but the computer is yet to be constructed which will allow us to disaggregate to a fine degree. In the meantime, we must make do with simpler and less satisfactory models of consumption spending. In the balance of this book we shall follow this course. Our concern is with relatively simple models of macroeconomic activity, and the consumption function we use must be tailored to fit that concern. Hence, even though we admit it to be somewhat tarnished, in the following chapters we still make use of the Keynesian absolute income hypothesis.

---

[20] Suits, *op. cit.,* pp. 21–23, has an interesting discussion of the problem noted here. As he points out, it could have serious implications for standard multiplier analysis. For example, multiplier analysis teaches us that a tax cut should increase consumption spending, since it increases disposable personal income. However, if households are working extra hours in order to maintain certain consumption standards, the tax cut may give them the means to reduce their work effort and maintain their consumption. In this event, the multiplier effect of the tax cut would be completely blunted.

ADDITIONAL READINGS

See the end of Chapter 7. Also useful are:

EVANS, M. K. *Macroeconomic Activity.* New York: Harper and Row, 1969, chap. 6.

FARREL, M. J. "The New Theories of the Consumption Function," *Economic Journal,* December, 1959. Reprinted in R. A. Gordon and L. Klein, *Readings in Business Cycles.* Homewood, Ill.: Richard D. Irwin, Inc., 1965.

MCCRACKEN, P.; MAO, J. C. T.; FRICKE, C. V. *Consumer Installment Credit and Public Policy.* Ann Arbor: University of Michigan, Bureau of Business Research, 1965.

Chapter 8 : THE FORMAL THEORY OF INVESTMENT

The sum of the expenditure flows determines the level of national income. The last two chapters dwelt upon the determinants of consumption spending. Although quantitatively less important than consumption, investment often plays a crucial role in determining the level of economic activity. Historically, many fluctuations in income and employment have been set off by fluctuations in investment spending, and the speed and character of economic growth have been intimately related to the volume of capital formation, which investment spending determines.

The Theory of Investment

Businessmen buy capital goods because they expect them to be profitable. This is true whether the capital goods are new or old, or whether they are to be used to replace worn-out assets or to increase the total capital stock of the firm (net investment).[1] The discussion which follows will be based upon this assumption; if motives other than (maximum) profitability enter into the investment decision, as they almost always do, the analysis must be qualified to that extent. However, such qualifications will not be too serious if profit is the *principal* motive for investment.

Another warning: we shall not be speaking of the purchase of already existing capital goods. It is true that businessmen may satisfy their objectives equally well by buying already existing assets or by purchasing newly produced goods. Purchases of old assets, however, do not represent investment spending for the economy as a whole; what counts as investment spending for the buyer is disinvestment for the

---

[1] The discussion which follows is confined to net investment spending. The general principles also apply to replacement investment, but the latter's special problems will not be specifically discussed.

seller: the two acts cancel each other. We are interested in investment spending for the economy as a whole because the purchase of newly produced goods gives rise to current income and employment and creates a basis for future increases in income and employment.

The purchase of a capital asset is an act of faith. It is based upon the businessman's belief that after taking into account the financial and other costs of making the investment, the future returns from the asset will leave him with a profit. Put in somewhat different language, a businessman must believe that a capital asset is worth more than it costs before he will agree to buy it. It behooves us, therefore, to begin our formal analysis of the investment decision with a discussion of the way in which a businessman places a value upon a capital asset. We shall follow this with a discussion of the factors which affect the cost of new asset acquisitions. This will put us in the position of studying the way in which the interplay between value and cost determines the level of investment spending for the individual firm and for the economy.

The Present Value of an Investment

In Chapter 1 we said that capital assets are valued because they are sources of income. A person holds an asset because during its lifetime it will yield him a series of returns. The forms of these returns may be in money or in kind (as in the case of a home), but for present purposes we shall concentrate upon the monetary form. At any moment of time the value, or price, which a businessman attaches to a capital item he holds depends upon the monetary returns he expects from the asset. The monetary returns must be sufficient to recover the cost of the asset during its lifetime. It must also be net of any other expenses associated with the use of the asset. (Thus, a businessman investing in a lathe expects the return from the lathe to cover its depreciation and to yield net receipts over and above labor and raw material costs involved in using it.) Since the value of an asset depends on its lifetime returns (net of costs) a businessman will place a higher or lower value upon the asset should he expect an increase or decrease in returns over the life of the asset.

We are interested in the value of an asset *now*, hence we are interested in its *present value*. We shall use the letter V as a symbol for present value. The return from the use of the asset, net of operating costs but inclusive of its depreciation, shall be assumed to come in the form of an annual series R_1, R_2, ..., R_n, where R_1 is the return after one year of operation, and R_2 is the return (separate from R_1) after the second year of operation, and R_n is the return (separate from R_1 through R_{n-1}) after the nth or last year of the life of the asset. This is a simplification, since assets really yield their returns continuously; but, the assumption that they do so at the end of each year simplifies exposition without sacrificing basic principles. Our problem is to relate the present value of an asset to the series of annual returns expected from it.

If the year in which an asset yields its return did not matter, our problem would be simple. Unfortunately, time matters. The value *today* of a $1,000 *a year from now* is not a $1,000. If we invest $952.38 today in a one-year bond at 5 percent interest, we shall have $1,000 a year from now. If we invest at a 7 percent rate of interest, we can get the $1,000 with a present outlay of only $934.58. Money today and money in the future are not equivalent. Future money is *worth less* than present money, and for that reason its present value is less than its face amount. At 5 percent, the present value of $1,000 one year from now is $952.38 because that is the sum which, if invested now at 5 percent, will give us $1,000 one year hence. A $1,000 10 years from now is worth even less today. Its present value at 5 percent is $613.91, because the latter sum, left for 10 years at 5 percent, will accumulate to $1,000. Thus the present value of a future sum of money depends upon both the rate of interest a person can acquire and the date at which the future money will appear.

The present value of a sum of future money is computed by *discounting* the future sum at an appropriate rate of interest. Consider a one-year investment whose return, R_1, at the end of one year is $1,050. If we invest a sum of money, V, or $1,000 at the beginning of the year at a rate of interest, i, or 5 percent,[2] then

$$V(1+i) = R_1 = \$1,000(1+.05) = \$1,050. \qquad (1)$$

Equation (1) gives the general relation between V, R_1, and i. It tells us that if we accumulate V at a rate of interest of i we shall get R_1 after one year. Now, assume we know only the value of R_1 and the rate of interest, i, and that we wish to find the present value, or V, of R_1. We simply reverse the process of accumulation and *discount* R_1 at the rate of interest. To do so, we divide both sides of (1) by $(1+i)$:

---

[2] We shall follow the practice of referring to the rate of interest as a percentage in the text but in its decimal form in the equations. Thus, "5 percent" is .05 in the equations.

$$V = \frac{R_1}{(1+i)} = \$1{,}000 = \frac{\$1{,}050}{(1+.05)} \,. \tag{2}$$

V, then, is the discounted value of R_1. The value of any future sum of money discounted back to the present is also its present value. From equation (2), it is also clear that V depends upon the interest rate used to discount R_1. A lower interest rate increases V; a higher rate decreases V.

Now, suppose a businessman makes an investment whose yield, R_2 ($\$1{,}050$), will appear only *after two years.* What is the discounted present value of his investment? To find out, first accumulate an (unknown) V for two years at interest rate i (5 percent):

$$V(1+i) = A \tag{3}$$
$$A(1+i) = V(1+i)^2 = R_2 \,. \tag{4}$$

Dividing (4) by $(1+i)^2$ gives us V, or the discounted present value of R_2:

$$V = \frac{R_2}{(1+i)^2} = \frac{\$1{,}050}{(1.05)^2} = \$952.38, \tag{5}$$

which is less than the present value of the same sum of money one year into the future. This illustrates that the longer we must wait for future money, the less will be its present value. Not a surprising result!

How do we determine the present value of an investment which yields its returns over a number of future years in a series $R_1, R_2, \ldots, R_n$? The answer is that we sum the separately discounted returns. Thus, let V_1 be the discounted present value of R_1, V_2 the discounted present value of R_2, etc. Hence,

$$V = V_1 + V_2 + \ldots + V_n, \text{ and}$$

$$V = \frac{R_1}{(1+i)} + \frac{R_2}{(1+i)^2} + \ldots + \frac{R_n}{(1+i)^n} \,. \tag{6}$$

To get a feel for what (6) means, consider an investment with three years of life whose expected returns are discounted at 5 percent:

1) Let $R_1 = \$100$, $R_2 = \$200$, $R_3 = \$300$

2) Therefore:

$$V_1 = \frac{\$100}{(1+.05)} = \$\ 95.24$$

$$V_2 = \frac{\$200}{(1+.05)^2} = \$181.46$$

$$V_3 = \frac{\$300}{(1+.05)^3} = \$259.14$$

3) V, the present value of the asset is equal to $V_1 + V_2 + V_3$, or

$$V = 95.24 + 181.46 + 259.14 = \$525.84.$$

Now, reverse the values for R_1 and R_3:

4) Let $R_1 = 300$, $R_2 = 200$, $R_3 = 100$

5) Therefore:

$$V_1 = \frac{\$300}{(1+.05)} = \$285.72$$

$$V_2 = \frac{\$200}{(1+.05)^2} = \$181.46$$

$$V_3 = \frac{\$100}{(1+.05)^3} = \$ \ 86.38$$

6) V, the sum of V_1, V_2, and V_3, is now $553.56.

In both examples, the series R_1, R_2, and R_3 add to the same total: $600. However, the present value of the first series is smaller than that of the second. Why? The answer is that the *earlier* the returns the *higher* is the sum of their present values. Though two investments may yield exactly the same returns over equal lifetimes, the one which delays its returns the most has the least present value. This result is a natural consequence of the more general proposition that, from today's standpoint, future money is less valuable than present money.

To summarize, the present value of an asset is calculated by summing the discounted expected returns of the asset for each year of its life, where each return is discounted back to the present. The present value of the asset thus depends upon (1) the size of each expected return, R_1, R_2, ..., R_n; (2) the time shape of the expected series of returns; and (3) the interest rate used to discount the series. It is higher for assets yielding larger and earlier returns, and it will respond positively to lower interest rates. Lower and late returns, or a higher interest rate, will reduce an asset's present value.

Supply Price of a Capital Asset

The present value of a capital asset is sometimes called its *demand price*. This term is highly descriptive of what is involved in a rational investment decision. A businessman will not pay more than the present value of a capital good, since if he did he would be passing up the opportunity to purchase for less money a bond yielding the same interest rate he used to discount the prospective returns from the capital asset. The present value of a capital good, or its demand price, is therefore the *maximum price* a businessman should pay for the good.

The actual cost to the businessman of a new capital asset is its *supply price*. A particular asset's supply price is not something determined by the businessman. Rather, it is determined by its cost of production. Keynes, who coined the term, defined it as "the price which would just induce a manufacturer newly to produce an additional unit of such assets."[3] Keynes' definition is clearly geared to an investment decision entailing newly produced capital goods. This is as it should be, since his concern was with investment decisions leading to the production of new goods and the expansion of employment. We shall follow Keynes in this regard. However, we shall add the *acquisition cost* of an asset as part of the definition of its supply price. The total cost of an asset to the investor includes not only the price he must pay the manufacturer, but also the extra costs he incurs within his own organization for planning and for putting the asset into place.

Finally, another important point: Keynes' definition implies that the supply price of an asset is related to its marginal cost of production. If so, the more of it a manufacturer produces during a given period the higher must be the price which would just induce him to produce an additional unit, provided, of course, that his firm is operating under conditions of increasing marginal costs. We might argue that the acquisition costs of assets also rise with increased purchases per period. The reason is that larger investments entail more planning and more shuffling about of firms' operations to make room for the new assets. These activities could easily cause marginal acquisition costs to rise.

Demand Price, Supply Price, and the Investment Decision

We have defined the demand price as the *maximum price a businessman should pay* for a capital asset. The *minimum price he can pay* is its

---

[3] Keynes, *General Theory*, p. 135.

supply price. Hence, we can frame the investment decision in terms of a comparison between an asset's demand and supply prices. If the demand price for a new capital good exceeds its supply price, a rational business-man will purchase it, because the good's present value—its *worth*—exceeds its cost. If the demand price for an asset is less than its supply price, a rational investor will not buy it, because the asset is worth less than it costs.

This formula seems simple enough. Nevertheless, it is a bit too sim-ple, since it appears to assume that a businessman has a firm notion of the stream of returns to be yielded by the asset during its life. As we all know, there is a great deal of uncertainty attached to such notions; hence, such an assumption is not likely to be correct. Nevertheless, deci-sions must be made one way or another. This being the case, we must assume that an investor in a capital asset has already taken into account the uncertainty he feels about its prospective yield. The investor's de-mand price for the asset, therefore, can be presumed to incorporate a "discount" for risk. Our formula for rational decision making must be understood as a comparison between the present value of an asset, cor-rected for risk, and its supply price. It follows that an investment deci-sion which seems rational under one set of risk conditions might be irrational under another set of risk conditions.

The Equilibrium Level of Investment

If the demand price (corrected for risk) of a new capital asset ex-ceeds its supply price, we have said that a rational investor will go ahead with its purchase; but, once having made this decision, he will face another. Suppose there are still profitable opportunities available. How far should he go? How far should he extend his planned investment expenditures? The answer is that so long as he can borrow at the rate of interest used to compute the present value or demand price of his investments, he should continue to invest until the demand price for the last asset bought is equal to or falls below its supply price. Once this happens, there is no incentive to increase further the level of investment spending; that is, *when investment has proceeded to the point where the demand price for the marginal new asset is equal to its supply price, investment is at an equilibrium level.*

We have not proved, of course, that there is such a thing as an equilibrium level of investment. What is to prevent an individual busi-nessman from believing it possible to profitably spend an infinite amount on new assets? After all, it is the beliefs of businessmen which count in determining the decision to invest, not the objective facts of the situation. If a businessman misinterprets those facts he may be led to investing a very large sum of money in basically unprofitable ventures. This happens every day in capitalist economies. Nevertheless, we must assume that most businessmen are not irrational. We must assume they inform themselves about investment opportunities before they commit themselves to new ventures. To argue otherwise would be to insist that men are not held accountable for their actions, that punishments are not visited upon those who act unwisely, and that society has unlimited resources to put at the disposal of men who wish to put those resources into schemes for the future.

What are the facts which influence businessmen to limit their pace of investment? Before we answer this we must recall the distinction between investment (a flow) and capital (a stock). Investment is the act of acquiring capital. Capital is the stock of assets possessed by those who desire the productive services of the assets. Businessmen who invest do so because they are dissatisfied with their stock of capital assets. Consider the position of a firm which has $1 million worth of assets and desires to increase its capital to $1.5 million. In order to do so it must invest $0.5 million; but, the *pace* at which the firm acquires the new assets is another matter. If the firm attains its desired capital stock in one year, we can say that the firm is investing at an annual rate of $0.5 million. However, if the firm speeds its rate of acquisition by accomplishing the desired expansion in six months, we must revise our statement to say that it is investing at a rate of $1 million per year. A two year investment plan, on the other hand, would change the rate of investment to a $0.25 million per year. The point is that the investment is a flow and, as with all flows, it must be specified in terms of some time rate.

We are now in a position to assess the reasons why individual businessmen may wish to limit the pace of their investment. There are two sets of reasons. The first has to do with the effect upon the demand price for marginal assets of an increased rate of investment. The second has to do with the way in which an increase in the rate of investment might affect the supply price of assets. The first set of reasons can be understood as follows: When a businessman plans to increase his stock of capital assets to a certain level, he is not necessarily sure that the level he desires is correct. He is uncertain for two reasons. The market may not be able to sustain the higher level of productive capacity in his firm and his competitors may also be undertaking expansions of their own. Hence, if he accomplishes his goal too rapidly he might find himself with a capital stock which is too large for maximum profitability. It is therefore best to assume that the businessman proceeds with increasing caution as he contemplates higher levels of spending.

Cautious behavior should reflect itself in an increasing "risk discount" for marginal assets as the level of investment contemplated by the firm increases. That is, we should expect the firm to regard the returns from marginal assets to be more uncertain the faster it invests. Uncertainty of returns from marginal assets would lead the firm to reduce the present value of marginal assets as investment is increased. Hence, if we graphically depict the relationship between the demand price for marginal assets and the rate of investment spending, the graph should show the demand price falling with increased investment. This is done in Graph 8.1 with the curve labeled "$V_{i=5\%}$."

GRAPH 8.1

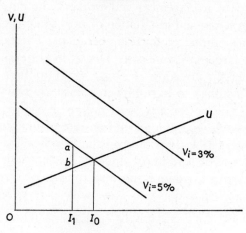

V = present value or demand price
U = supply price
I = net investment

The graph also shows that the demand price depends upon the rate of interest used to compute it. A reduction in the rate of interest increases the present value of an asset regardless of how much a firm has already invested. This would be reflected in the graph by a higher V curve for a lower interest rate. A higher interest rate would lower the V curve.

Businessmen may also limit their pace of investment because the supply price for marginal assets increases as the rate of investment is increased. This is a bit more difficult to justify in the case of an individual businessman than is the argument for a declining demand price. It is difficult to see why a businessman should expect to influence the cost of the capital goods he buys. After all, an individual firm is only one of many purchasing assets from capital goods producers. In most cases, individual firms form only a small part of the capital goods market. In addition, if they find their purchases cause the prices of the capital goods they buy to rise; they can always switch to other producers. Therefore, if supply price refers only to the *production cost* of new capital assets, we should not generally expect individual businessmen to anticipate a rising supply price of assets as they increase their rates of investment. Nevertheless, we have argued for the inclusion of acquisition costs in the concept of supply price. The case for anticipating increasing marginal acquisition costs is stronger than the case for anticipating increasing marginal production costs because the *activity* of investment costs the firm something. Investment activity involves the time and energy of management and workers, the employing of extra hands for construction and installation of new equipment, and a disruption of the firm's normal production operations. The faster the pace of investment, the larger are these costs. Hence, in our earlier example, we would expect a firm investing at a rate of $1 million per year ($0.5 million in six months) to have higher acquisition costs than investing at a rate of $0.5 million per year ($0.5 million in one year). By the same reasoning, we would expect a $4 million rate of investment ($0.5 million in three months) to impose upon the firm heavier costs than a $1 million annual rate of investment. Indeed, it is not unreasonable to expect acquisition costs to go up faster than the rate of investment. Should this happen marginal acquisition costs will increase and, along with the increase of these costs, the supply price of marginal assets should also rise.

Graph 8.1 shows that the supply price (U) of new capital assets increases with increased investment. This reflects the assumptions made in the last section that marginal production costs and marginal acquisition costs for new assets rise with increases in the amounts being produced and bought per period of time. Improved conditions in the capital goods producing industries, or improvements in the abilities of firms to plan for or absorb new assets can shift the U-curve down and to the right. Nevertheless, for any given period of time these conditions and abilities are not likely to change much; hence, we can regard the U-curve as being essentially stable for short-run periods.

We are now in a position to show that, under given conditions, there will be an *equilibrium rate of investment* for a firm. Assume the rate of

interest is 5 percent (thus fixing the V-curve) and that a firm is con-
templating a level of investment spending I_1 (Graph 8.1). At that level
of investment, the demand price for an additional unit of capital will
exceed its supply price by an amount ab. The firm will clearly have an
incentive to increase its investment spending. How far will it go? If it
goes beyond I_0, it will find that the supply price of the marginal investment exceeds its demand price, hence the value of the marginal asset
will fall short of its cost. This is going too far. It follows that the firm
will stop adding to its investment spending when the supply price is
just covered by the present value of the last asset bought. This is at I_0;
hence, I_0 must be the equilibrium level of investment spending for the
firm.

Our description of the forces determining the equilibrium level of investment spending is, of course, highly stylized. For one thing, we have
assumed the V-curve to be a smoothly falling or continuous function.
In practice, this is not likely to be true for an individual firm. Instead,
the V-curves for individual firms are more likely to be step-shaped, since
investment in new assets is not continuous, but takes place in lumps.
For another thing, the present value of the marginal unit of capital is
not likely to be very precise in the mind of the person making the investment decision for the firm. Nevertheless, if we are interested in
broad principles, the process described in the graph is reasonably accurate. In place of a precise equilibrium point, the reader may prefer to
think of investment spending as approximating a level like I_0.

The Investment Demand Schedule: Derivation

We are now in a position to derive an investment demand schedule
for the firm and for the economy. An investment demand schedule
shows the alternative amounts of investment which a firm, or the economy, will undertake at various interest rates. To keep things clear,
recall that we are still speaking of net investment. When we refer to
"the" interest rate we are assuming that all businessmen are facing a
common rate. This is not true in practice, since the economy is characterized by a whole set of interest rates. These rates vary a good deal
between different sets of borrowers and lenders, and to some degree the
rates will also depend upon the terms of the loans. In this discussion we
are abstracting from this complex of rates and assuming that they can
be represented by a single rate, which is not too much of a departure

from reality, since most interest rates move up and down together. Use of a representative interest rate allows us to interpret the investment demand schedule as one which is applicable to the whole economy.

Consider Graph 8.2: The horizontal axis is drawn both to the left

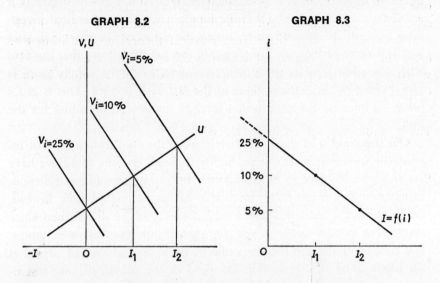

GRAPH 8.2   **GRAPH 8.3**

and to the right of the zero point in order to depict both negative and positive net investment. This is done in order to recognize that businessmen may at times find it unprofitable even to maintain their existing stock of capital assets, much less increase it. The curve depicting the supply price—the U-curve—is drawn into the negative quadrant because, though businessmen might be allowing some of their assets to wear out without replacement, they might still be replacing others, in which case they must pay an amount equal to replacement costs to the asset manufacturers. The various V-curves represent the demand price, or present value schedules under different interest rate assumptions. Each intersection with the U-curve represents a different equilibrium rate of investment spending. Hence, when the interest rate is (say) 25 percent, equilibrium net investment will be zero. Lower rates of interest (10 or 5 percent) will raise the equilibrium rate investment, while rates of interest above 25 percent will depress net investment into the negative range. If we imagine the whole range of interest rates possible under 25 percent, we can imagine the V-curve drifting to the right, tracing out alternative equilibrium levels of positive net investment spending. Hence, if we plot equilibrium investment against the interest rate, we derive a schedule like the one shown in Graph 8.3. The dashed extension of the schedule indicates negative net investment for interest rates above 25 percent.

The investment demand schedule depicted in Graph 8.3 is the same one we discussed in Chapter 3, particularly if we think of it as aggregate schedule, or the summation of all individual investment decisions. Modern theory differs very little from classical theory in visualizing the basis for rational investment behavior. Nevertheless, the manner in which we have constructed the investment demand schedule in this chapter allows us to analyze it in some detail.

The Investment Demand Schedule: Slope

Consider the meaning of the *slope* of the investment demand schedule. If changes in investment spending are viewed as responses to changes in the interest rate, then the slope of the function measures the degree of response. A function with a steep slope—I' in Graph 8.4—

GRAPH 8.4

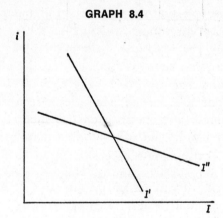

indicates a low degree of responsiveness, while I'' indicates a high degree of responsiveness. What are the factors which affect the slope of the investment demand curve?

There are two: (1) the steepness of the supply price function and (2) the sensitivity of the present value functions to changes in the interest rate. Beginning with the first, imagine for Graph 8.2 a U-function which is *steeper* than the one shown. This would mean that as the interest rate falls each V-curve would intersect the U-function to the left of the points shown on the graph. Thus, $V_{i=10\%}$ would cross the steeper function at a point to the left of I_1, and the same would be true for all other V-functions. Hence, for each interest rate there would be a lower rate of investment spending, which translates into a *steeper* investment demand function.

The slope of the U-function (the supply price schedule) clearly depends upon the cost conditions in the industries manufacturing capital assets and upon the acquisition costs in the firms buying the new assets. Generally speaking, the more durable the assets and/or the more complicated they are, the steeper we should expect the function to be, because durability and complexity should tend to produce sharply rising marginal production and acquisition costs. Unless we know the *mix* of asset demand for the economy, therefore, we cannot say very much more about the steepness of the aggregate U-function. Nevertheless, the economic rationale for its influence on the interest-responsiveness of investment spending should be clearly understood. A drop in interest rates increases the demand price for investment goods. If marginal increases in the production and acquisition of new investment goods lead to sharp increases in their supply prices, the reduction of interest rates will not significantly increase investment spending in the economy. However enthusiastic low interest rates may make businessmen for new capital goods, that enthusiasm may be considerably dampened by the costs of the goods they wish to acquire.

The sensitivity of the demand price, or present value function to changes in the interest rate depends upon (a) how long the asset is expected to yield its returns and (b) the time shape of the prospective series of returns. Both of these propositions can be illustrated with a simple example: Suppose we compare the sensitivity of the present values of two assets—A and B—to changes in the rate of interest. Let the interest rate initially be 5 percent and let both assets have an initial present value of \$952.38; but, let asset A have only one year of life, yielding a total return of \$1,000, and asset B have two years of life, yielding nothing in its first year, but giving its owner \$1,050 at the end of the second year.[4] Asset A is therefore not only more short lived than asset B, but, if we wish to compare the two assets over the same two years in terms of the time shape of returns, asset A gives a declining series, while asset B gives a rising series of returns. The information is summarized in the following table.

---

[4] In present value terms, \$1,050 at the end of two years is equal to \$1,000 at the end of one year.

		Stream of Returns		
Asset	Life	After 1st Year	After 2d Year	Present Value at Beginning of 1st Year
A	1 year	$1,000	0	$V_A = \$952.38 = \dfrac{\$1,000}{1.05} + \dfrac{0}{(1.05)^2}$
B	2 years	0	$1,050	$V_B = \$952.38 = \dfrac{0}{1.05} + \dfrac{\$1050}{(1.05)^2}$

We must now show that V_B, which is the present value of the asset having the longer life and the rising series of returns, is more sensitive to changes in the interest rate than is V_A. The following table shows this for interest rates above and below 5 percent. At 6 percent, V_B falls to $934.50, while V_A falls by less, to $943.40. An interest rate of 4 percent promotes a larger increase in V_B than in V_A: to $970.79, as opposed to $961.54.

**Present Values for Assets A and B at
Various Interest Rates**

Interest Rate	V_A	V_B
4%	$961.54	$970.79
5	952.38	952.38
6	943.40	934.50

Though our example is very simple, it does demonstrate that assets which are durable and/or which produce their yields in a rising series of returns have demand prices, or present values, which are more responsive to given changes in interest rates than short-lived and/or early yielding assets. Translated into Graph 8.2, this means that the V-function shifts less with changes in interest rates when the assets are of type A rather than type B. Not surprisingly, this produces steeper investment demand schedules when the mix of spending favors assets of type A.

In summary, the steepness of the economy's investment demand schedule depends upon the mix of the capital assets desired by businessmen. If the mix of investment favors assets whose production and acquisition conditions favor steeply rising supply prices, or whose expected life is short, with the bulk of the yield coming early, the investment demand function for the economy will be steep, reflecting relative insensitivity of investment to changes in the interest rate. The demand for investment will be more sensitive to interest rate changes as the mix favors assets with gently rising marginal production and acquisition costs, or assets with long lives and yields which come later.[5]

The Investment Demand Schedule: Position

The derivation of the investment demand schedule also indicates the sorts of influences which fix its position. We shall discuss these influences more in the next chapter, but for now we merely note that the schedule will shift up or down with changes in the expectations of businessmen and with changes in the production and acquisition costs of the capital assets.

Since the demand price for an asset is strongly influenced by the expectations businessmen have of the series of returns over the life of the asset, a rise in the expected series of returns will increase the demand price, while a decline in the series will decrease the demand price. This would be reflected in Graphs 8.1 or 8.2 by shifts in the V-curves for given interest rates. Thus, each V-curve in Graph 8.2 will shift to the right with an increase in expected yields, even though the shifted curves will still retain the same interest rate subscripts. A decrease in expected yields will shift each of the curves to the left. In shifting, the curves will cross the U-curve at higher or lower levels of investment, depending upon whether they have shifted to the right or the left. These new equilibrium levels of investment spending can be indicated by investment demand functions which stand to the right or to the left of the one shown in Graph 8.3 (but they are not actually drawn in the diagram).

---

[5] The argument of this paragraph is neatly summarized by the following. Let the interest-responsiveness of investment be measured by dI/di, the inverse of the slope of the investment demand function of Graph 8.3 or Graph 8.4. The rate of change in supply price per unit increase of investment is dU/dI and the sensitivity of the demand price to changes in the interest rate is measured by dV/di. It follows that

$$\frac{dI}{di} = \frac{dI}{dU}\frac{dU}{dV}\frac{dV}{di}$$

or, since in equilibrium $dU = dV$ and $dU/dV = 1$, the equation becomes:

$$\frac{dI}{di} = \frac{dV}{di} \bigg/ \frac{dU}{dI}.$$

Thus, the interest-responsiveness of investment varies positively with the interest-responsiveness of the demand price and negatively with the sensitivity of the supply price to changes in the rate of investment spending.

It is also important to note that our discussion implies that the mix of investment depends partly upon the *level* of interest rate. Low rates encourage long-lived and late-yielding projects, while high rates encourage the opposite.

Examination of Graphs 8.2 and 8.3 will make it clear that changes in the supply price function also shift the investment demand function. For example, cost saving innovations in the industries producing capital assets, or improvements leading to reductions in acquisition costs in the firms acquiring the assets, shift the U-curve to the right. Provided that the V-curves are not vertical, the rightward shift in the supply price curve promotes increases in investment spending even though interest rates remain the same. These increases in investment spending translate to the investment demand function in Graph 8.3 as a shift to the right. By similar reasoning, leftward movement in the supply price curve causes a leftward shift of the investment demand function.

Dynamics of Capital Formation

Discussion of the factors which fix the position of the investment demand schedule brings to the fore the dynamic effects of capital formation. Recall the distinction between *stock and flow* economic variables. The purpose of net investment spending is to change the stock of capital goods being used by businessmen. Net investment spending is a flow: it is the *rate,* per unit of time, at which the stock of capital is being changed. If an economy possesses $1 trillion worth of capital, net investment spending of $50 million per year will raise the stock of capital to $1.05 trillion after one year, $1.10 trillion after two years, and so on. If net investment spending is zero, the capital stock will stabilize at $1 trillion. If net investment is negative, the capital stock will decline.

We have already seen that net investment spending is governed by comparisons between the demand prices and supply prices of new assets. This same set of comparisons governs the rate at which the whole capital stock of a country grows. We must now ask whether or not the growth of the capital stock itself has any effects upon the rate of investment spending. That is, does the fact that net investment spending is adding to the capital stock react back upon the incentive to invest?

A clear answer to this question is best approached with a prior discussion of what economists call an equilibrium or optimum capital stock. At any point in time, an individual firm will possess a certain amount of capital assets. The services of these assets will be combined with other factors of production to carry out the production and sales plans of the firm. The question at hand is whether or not the firm is satisfied with its existing stock of assets. "Satisfaction" means that the firm's owner or manager believes that any attempt to increase or decrease the firm's asset holdings would lower profits. Dissatisfaction implies that the firm's profits would benefit from a change in its asset holdings. When a firm is satisfied with the stock of capital it holds, we shall call that stock an equilibrium or optimum stock of capital.

An optimum stock of capital does not mean that a firm's holdings are completely static. As assets are used they wear out and require replacement. All that we require in our definition is that the process of depreciation and replacement shall not lead to a reduction or increase in the stock of capital in the firm's hands. Beyond this, if we wish to apply the notion of an optimum stock of capital to the whole economy, we can imagine a situation in which some firms are adding to their asset holdings, while others are allowing them to decline. So long as these additions and subtractions to the economy's holdings are balanced, and so long as firms are decreasing and increasing their holdings at the rates they desire, we can think of the resulting constant economywide capital stock as being an equilibrium or optimum stock.

Directing our attention to the level of the firm again, we can look at its equilibrium or optimum stock of holdings in a slightly different way. We earlier argued that the demand for new or additional assets by a firm is determined by a comparison between the demand and supply prices of new assets. A firm should evaluate its existing asset holdings in the same way. If the present value of existing holdings exceeds replacement costs, the firm has an incentive to add to them. If the present value of existing assets falls short of replacement costs, the firm will not wish to replace depreciating assets and it will allow its capital stock to decrease.

Our discussion implies that an equilibrium or optimum stock of capital assets is such that the present value of one more (one less) unit is smaller (larger) than its supply price. In such a situation, a firm has no incentive either to add to or to subtract from its existing holdings. Such a situation is depicted on Graph 8.5, where the V-curve for an interest rate of 3 percent intersects the U-curve at an investment rate of zero. The same situation is portrayed on Graph 8.6, which shows zero investment spending at an interest rate of 3 percent for the investment demand schedule labeled I_a. The derivation of other points on I_a is not shown in the graphs, but the reader can do it for himself by imagining the V_a curve to shift up and to the right with reductions of the interest rate below 3 percent. Though the present value (at $i = 3$ percent) of the returns on the existing capital stock is not enough to encourage further investment, a decrease in the rate of interest increases the present value of the same returns and, as a consequence, encourages investment.

GRAPH 8.5

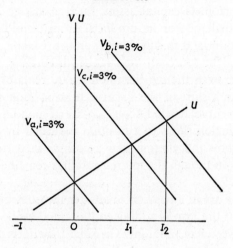

GRAPH 8.6

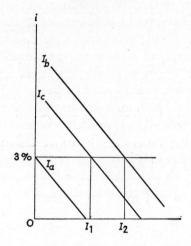

Investment, of course, rises only to the point where the new present value curve crosses the supply price curve. I_a in Graph 8.6 is derived by imagining a whole series of interest rates below 3 percent. Each interest rate discounts the same returns implicit in the curve labeled V_a.

If the interest rate remains fixed at 3 percent, it is clear that while the function I_a prevails, net investment will be zero and the firm's assets will stabilize at an equilibrium level. Suppose, now, a change occurs in the firm's operating conditions which also increases the returns the firm expects from ts capital assets. Such a change can come from increases in the demand for its products, from technological developments which encourage it to substitute capital for labor, and from other factors. Whatever the source of the change, the present value of capital assets should rise, even though the interest rate remains fixed at 3 percent. This implies a shift of the V-curve to a position such as the one indicated by the curve labeled $V_{b,\, i\,=\,3\%}$. Correspondingly, the investment demand function shifts to a position indicated by the one labeled I_b. Both graphs show that there is now a positive incentive to invest—at the rate of I_2—even though the interest rate has remained unchanged at 3 percent.

At long last we are in a position to answer the question posed earlier. Does the fact that the firm is adding to its capital stock affect its desire to continue an investment program? Consider the effects of adding to the firm's assets at a rate indicated by I_2. The capital stock is no longer static, since the firm desires it to grow. However, if the conditions which first shifted the investment demand function to I_b continue to prevail, the addition of new assets to the firm's holdings will allow it gradually to achieve a new optimum level of holdings. As it approaches this level, the returns from continued investment should fall; as they fall, the present value function, and with it the investment schedule, should shift to the left (e.g., to the positions subscripted with c). Eventually, the firm's new optimum level of asset holdings will be achieved and the investment demand function, together with the present value function, will return to the levels indicated by the subscript a. Investment, at this point, will cease.

The lesson of the previous paragraph is that investment undermines itself. The lesson is a correct one, of course, only if the marginal productivity of the firm's capital stock declines with its increase. There are many who would dispute this assumption on the ground that, for an individual firm at any rate, there is no reason why the marginal productivity of capital should fall. In adding to its capital stock a firm can also add to the other factors of production it uses. Hence, unless the firm faces diminishing returns to *scale,* there is no reason why it should face diminishing marginal productivity of capital.

There are two answers to this line of argument. The first is that many firms do face scale diseconomies which would cause the marginal productivity of its capital stock to decline. The second is that when the argument is applied to the whole business sector, it is quite possible for the capital stock to grow more rapidly than other factors of production, especially labor. When this happens, labor costs will be driven up as firms compete for workers to man their expanded operations. The rise in labor costs, in turn, pinches the profitability of capital assets and depresses the marginal productivity of capital. In short, even though individual firms may not experience a decline in the marginal product of capital if *they alone are expanding, a combined expansion* of all firms can produce this result.

Even for the aggregate level, of course, it is quite possible for the capital stock to expand at a rate equal to or less than the rate of growth in the labor supply. In this event, investment spending can be maintained without serious effects upon the marginal productivity of capital. In a modern economy, however, the aggregate investment demand schedule is generally buoyed up by technological advances which enhance the productivity of capital. Hence, even if the capital stock is growing more rapidly than the labor force, diminishing marginal productivity is continually offset by technological innovations. Indeed, as we shall see in Chapter 14, the principal source of economic growth in the United States appears to be technological change.

The Marginal Efficiency of Capital

We are essentially finished with the formal derivation of the investment demand function. At this point, however, it is necessary to translate that derivation into a language which is more commonly used by economists and which appears more frequently in the literature. Here we have used the equality of demand price and supply price as a condition for investment equilibrium. We adopted this language because it seems natural; that is, it seems natural to imagine a businessman comparing the worth of an additional asset to its cost. The more common treatment, however, is to imagine a businessman comparing the *marginal efficiency of capital with the interest rate* in order to make his investment decision. In what follows, we shall derive the investment demand schedule with this alternative language. The results will be identical with those given previously; but, because of its more common usage, we shall retain the new language in the balance of the book.

We first define the *marginal efficiency of capital,* which will be identified with the acronym "MEC."[6] Keynes defined the MEC as "being equal to that rate of discount which would make the present value

---

[6] To confuse matters a bit more, many writers have recently used the label *marginal efficiency of investment* (MEI) instead of the MEC label. Here, we shall stick to the MEC label in deference to Keynes, who originated the concept.

of the series of annuities given by the returns expected from the capital asset during its life just equal to its supply price."[7] Let us give this definition symbolic content, using U for the supply price of the asset.

$$U = \frac{R_1}{(1+r)} + \frac{R_2}{(1+r)^2} + \ldots + \frac{R_n}{(1+r)^n}. \qquad (7)$$

This formula should look familiar, since it has the same form as the one in equation (6) of this chapter. The latter equation, however, was used to determine the present value of an asset from a known series of returns and a *known interest rate*. In equation (7) the problem is to determine the rate of discount, r, from a known supply price and a known series of returns.

The mechanical problem of finding r is not too difficult. Since an investor will have the series $R_1, R_2, \ldots, R_n$ fixed in his mind, and since he will also have a good idea of the supply price from the price quoted to him by the asset manufacturer and from estimates of its acquisition cost, he need only experiment with different values of r in the equation. Once he has found an r which brings the right-hand side into equality with the left-hand side, he will have found the marginal efficiency of that particular asset.

The semantic content of the MEC concept can be understood if we reverse the discounting process and imagine the following kind of experiment: Suppose an investor wishes to purchase an asset whose supply price is $1,000. If, after one year, he expects to recover the cost of the asset plus $100, he will estimate the *rate of return* on the asset at 10 percent. This same 10 percent, of course, is also the rate of discount which would make the present value of $1,100 one year hence equal to $1,000, which is the supply price of the asset. In other words, the MEC is 10 percent. From our experiment, it can be seen that the MEC is really the rate of return over the cost of the asset. Some writers refer to it as the "internal rate of return on an asset." But, whatever we call it, the MEC is nothing more than an expression, in terms of a discount rate, of the profitability of a capital asset. When the asset has a life extending beyond one year, as indicated in the definition of equation (7), the MEC is the average discount rate applicable to the whole series of expected returns.

It is very important to distinguish between the MEC and the rate of interest. The rate of interest for an individual investor is the cost of borrowing or the return from lending. The MEC is the return from in-

---

[7] *General Theory*, p. 135.

vesting in new physical assets. It is this distinction which led Keynes to pose the investment decision in terms of a comparison between the interest rate and the MEC; for, it is clear that if the marginal efficiency of a new capital asset is greater than the interest rate an investor must pay to borrow or that he might receive as a lender, he has an incentive to go ahead with his investment. If the MEC is lower than the interest rate, the investor will refrain from purchasing the new asset.

The marginal efficiency of capital should vary with the level of investment for the reasons similar to those discussed earlier in this chapter. As the investment program of a firm expands, it should encounter a declining yield and an increasing supply price on marginal asset acquisitions. As equation (7) indicates, a declining yield and a rising supply price act to depress the rate of discount—the MEC—used to discount the series of returns in order to bring them into equality with the supply price of the marginal new asset.

Thus it is that investment for a firm ceases, or is in equilibrium, when the MEC comes into equality with the interest rate. If we assume such behavior for all firms in the economy, and if we assume that they all face a common interest rate (as we did earlier), we can imagine this same equilibrium condition for the economy as a whole. Somewhere in the economy, there will be a project or projects whose MEC(s) just equal(s) the interest rate. Projects whose MECs fall below the rate of interest will not be undertaken. It follows that under given conditions, further investment will come about only with a decline in the rate of interest. By postulating various interest rates, therefore, we can derive an investment demand schedule. As we shall momentarily prove, this is exactly the same schedule derived earlier from a comparison of the demand price with the supply price of capital assets. We merely note here that because of the method of derivation described in this paragraph the investment demand schedule is often called the *marginal efficiency of capital schedule*. Other authors refer to it as the *marginal efficiency of investment schedule*. Unfortunately, there is as yet no settled usage.

We have restated the investment equilibrium condition as equality between the MEC and the interest rate, or

$$r = i. \tag{8}$$

Earlier, we gave an alternative statement of the equilibrium condition as equality between the demand price and supply price of the marginal asset, or

$$V = U. \tag{9}$$

It is simple to prove that the equilibrium conditions (8) and (9) are not separate conditions, but are simply separate expressions of the same equilibrium condition. To do so, substitute from equations (6) and (7) to rewrite (9):

$$\frac{R_1}{(1+i)} + \frac{R_2}{(1+i)^2} \cdots + \frac{R_n}{(1+i)^n} = \frac{R_1}{(1+r)}$$

$$+ \frac{R_2}{(1+r)^2} + \ldots + \frac{R_n}{(1+r)^n}. \tag{10}$$

Since the same series of expected returns appear on both sides of (10), there must be an equality between r and i, which is precisely what the equilibrium condition expressed in equation (8) shows. It follows that (8) and (9) are merely alternative ways of stating the same investment equilibrium condition. It also follows that the investment demand schedule we derived from condition (8) is the same one we derived from condition (9). All of the properties we assigned to that schedule therefore also apply to the one derived in this section.

The material in this chapter provides a framework for discussing the factors affecting investment demand. While the theory was developed in the context of business decision making, there is no reason why, in its essentials, the same sort of reasoning cannot be applied to household decisions regarding durable goods expenditures, particularly housing. The reader is invited to make such an application. In the meantime, we should try to give more life to the formal theory. The next chapter considers in more detail the role of expectations, technological change, financial conditions, and several other matters as they relate to investment spending in the economy.

ADDITIONAL READINGS

CLOWER, R. W. "An Investigation into the Dynamics of Investment," *American Economic Review*, March, 1954.

DAVIDSON, P. "A Keynesian View of the Relationship between Accumulation, Money, and Money Wage Rate," *Economic Journal*, June, 1969.

FELLNER, W. *Trends and Cycles in Economic Activity*. New York: Henry Holt and Co., 1956, chap. 8.

KEYNES, J. M. *The General Theory of Employment, Interest, and Money*. New York: Harcourt Brace, 1936, chap. 11.

LERNER, A. *Economics of Control.* New York: The Macmillan Co., 1944, chap. 25.

—————. "On the Marginal Product of Capital and the Marginal Efficiency of Investment," *Journal of Political Economy,* February, 1953.

WITTE, J. G., JR. "The Microfoundations of the Social Investment Function," *Journal of Political Economy,* October, 1963.

Chapter 9

ADDITIONAL ELEMENTS
IN THE THEORY
OF INVESTMENT

The theory of investment presented in Chapter 8 is only the beginning of what a complete theory ought to be. A more complete analysis should start with the factors influencing the expectations of businessmen regarding the future stream of returns resulting from added capital equipment. Some attention must then be paid to the process of innovation and technical change and the impact of population movements and other variables. Institutional influences, such as the structure of product markets and government activities, also shape the stream of investment, while the structure and practices of money and capital markets often determine whether investment shall have its finance. Finally, the general level of economic activity and the rate of growth of national income add their effects, making the analysis of investment a very complicated process.

Expectations and Investment

Businessmen and economists like to stress the role expectations play in business investment decisions. Indeed, some think expectations so important that they have based theories of the business cycle on the psychology of businessmen. In these theories, waves of optimism determine booms and waves of pessimism cause depressions. While it cannot be denied that business psychology plays an important role in *accentuating* boom and bust, there is room for more than a little suspicion in a theory which leads to the policy conclusion that pep-talks can lead us out of depressions. A more realistic view is that business psychology is based upon objective factors, and that subjective evaluation of those factors gives rise to optimism and pessimism.

Guesses about the future are normally based upon current and past events. When a businessman decides to invest, or not to invest, in a new capital facility, he is betting that his guess about the future will be right. Decisions to invest or not to invest result from interpretations of the data available to businessmen at the time of the decision. The data upon which these interpretations are based are enormously varied, and the weight given to individual facts, real or supposed, differs among different businessmen. Nevertheless, it is reasonable to suppose that the profitability of a certain line of investment will be the first thing looked at, and that the businessman carefully examines the factors contributing to that profitability.

The information contained in the books, reflecting both past and current developments in the demand for his output, costs, and taxes, is a good starting place for the study of profitability. Beyond this information are the facts of the growth of a firm's industry, population growth, the availability and cost of new technology, the level and rate of growth of national income, guesses about the availability and future prices of labor and raw materials, the supply price of capital, etc. There are also the opinions of journalists, government officials (who are always optimistic, unless they are members of the party out of power), fellow businessmen, and professional pundits. All this information, in whole or in part, perfectly or imperfectly, must be absorbed and evaluated before the decision to invest can be made. One point seems clear: guesses about the future, and decisions based upon them, result from the extrapolation of past and current events and information into the future. It is difficult to see how expectations can otherwise be formed.

Expectations of future events are rarely held with certainty. Extrapolations, after all, are leaps into the unknown, and no clear set of probabilities can be assigned to predicted events. For this reason, many students of business behavior have been led to emphasize entrepreneurial attitudes toward risk taking as a key element in investment decisions. Speculations along this line have led to several interesting conclusions. One is that favorable events will have less of an impact upon business investment than will unfavorable events; that is, optimism will breed less of an increase in investment than a similar degree of pessimism will breed a decline. The reason for this is simple: larger profits do not threaten the life of the firm; losses do. Capital commitments in times of slump impose a burden on business liquidity, and a firm must remain liquid in order to keep its credit standing and to pay its current bills. It is understandable if some firms show a special aversion to new investment during slack times.

Another conclusion is that firms have an interest in eliminating uncertainty. This can be done by individual firms with attempts to gain monopolistic positions, or by groups of firms via agreements about prices and market sharing. Logically, such agreements can lead to further agreements on sharing new productive capacity through the assignment of investment quotas, either formally or informally. Needless to say, such anticompetitive activity can impose a drag upon the increase of the nation's capital stock and upon technological change. Defenders of these agreements, however, point to the stabilizing results of such agreements, arguing that they help eliminate overinvestment and hence help keep the economy on an even keel.

In any event, the argument that uncertainty breeds instability in investment demand is modified by the nature of the key industries in the American economy. Most of these industries are dominated by large-scale corporations which are not seriously threatened by minor business contractions. Indeed, it would probably take a relatively long and heavy contraction in business activity before these institutions become concerned about their liquidity. Taking the behavior of these firms along with that of smaller firms, it would seem that a considerable amount of short-term stability of investment demand exists in the *economy,* insofar as the effect of uncertainty is concerned.

Government and Private Investment

Since government in the modern economy looms so large, it is not surprising that private investment activity should be strongly influenced by what government does. Indeed, given the size of the modern local and federal budgets, given the myriad policies affecting business practice, and given the special help programs government has instituted for various parts of the economy, government *cannot help* affecting private investment activity.

The influence of government activity can be interpreted through its effects upon the marginal efficiency of capital. Take, first, government spending: this has both direct and indirect effects. Government orders for goods, especially on a continuing basis, raise the marginal efficiency of capital and stimulate private investment demand. The force of this influence can be readily appreciated when the growth of the aircraft industry is considered. Without orders for military aircraft, the capital plant of that industry would hardly be what it is today.

The indirect effects of government spending upon private investment are less generally appreciated, but nevertheless are substantial. A new multipurpose dam, for example, opens new land to improvement, lowers the cost of power to industrial users, and reduces the hazard of flood. New or improved roads widen markets and reduce the costs of transportation. Educational expenditures increase the skills and efficiency of the labor force. The name given these indirect effects by economists is "external economies." They are external because they result from influences outside the firm and the private economy. They are economies because they lower the costs of production. Because they do the latter, the marginal efficiency of capital is raised and investment is encouraged.

Many businessmen, and some economists, like to stress the unfavorable indirect effects of government spending, especially when the latter involves items such as power. Public power opponents have argued, at times, that government spending in this direction has discouraged private power interests from building new facilities, either because it was feared that competing government facilities would be built, or because outright socialization and confiscation of the industry would take place. The truth of this particular argument is hard to verify; however, in view of the kinds of things government purchases, and the kinds of activities it ordinarily undertakes, the net indirect deterrent provided by government spending must be small. Moreover, although the political climate of the New Deal period may have provided some basis for the argument, the recent atmosphere provides little material for such a charge. Indeed, if the activities of the Atomic Energy Commission are any measure, it would seem that the emphasis should be put the other way: AEC-sponsored research has been put at the disposal of private industry.

Taxes influence the marginal efficiency of capital in several ways. Sales and excise taxes, to the extent they cannot be shifted, are absorbed by the firm and lower the expected revenue from investment. Payroll and property taxes increase the costs of production, and corporate income taxes reduce the net return from investment.

Investment spending can therefore be encouraged or discouraged by changes in tax policies. During periods of economic contraction one often hears proposals for tax relief for business, and government sometimes responds. Immediately after World War II, partly in response to the fear of a reconversion depression, excess-profits taxes, levied upon corporations during the war as an anti-inflationary device, were removed. In recent years, business firms have been allowed to write off their capital more rapidly in order to encourage them to invest more. Other countries make even more use of tax incentives for investment. Mexico, for example, exempts certain firms from taxes for specified periods of time if they will invest in industries deemed important for the national interest. Indeed, use of taxes as a growth-stimulating device

has a long history, even in this country. The protective tariff, first proposed by Alexander Hamilton in his celebrated *Report on the Subject
of Manufactures* (1791) was designed to encourage the growth of
industry.

Government also uses special programs, not directly related to its
budgetary activities, to encourage or discourage investment activity. In
the field of construction, for example, the Federal Housing Administration guarantees mortgage loans to individuals, and the Veterans
Administration does the same thing for veterans. In another area, the
Small Business Administration grants loans to businesses that cannot get capital elsewhere. In the field of agriculture, investment has
been stimulated by a number of government programs, some designed
to ease credit to farmers and some designed to improve techniques of
production. Indeed, it is difficult to think of an important area in the
economy in which the government, through one program or another,
has not encouraged investment.

INVESTMENT FINANCE

In the last chapter, the discussion of investment activity assumed
that funds were freely available to investors at the going rate of interest. This argument must now be qualified in several ways: First, there
is no single rate of interest at which funds are available to all firms.
There are a number of different interest rates at which firms borrow.
Normally, the longer the term of the loan, the higher will be the interest rate charged to the firm. In addition, lenders will charge higher
rates to firms they consider less creditworthy. Actually, both of these
situations boil down to charging higher interest in order to cover lender's risk: Long-term loans involve greater risks than do short-term loans,
because the borrower has a longer time in which to default on a loan,
and because the lender is giving up the opportunity to take advantage
of high-interest, short-term loans which may present themselves before
the long-term loan reaches its maturity.

An important second qualification is the phenomenon of credit
rationing. When money is tight banks are not able to lend to everyone
who comes to them for credit. While the theoretical reaction may be
for them to raise interest rates in such situations, recent studies have
shown that this is only one of a variety of methods banks use to
discourage borrowers. To be sure, interest rates are usually raised somewhat in such situations, but the rise in rates might not directly appear

on the loan contracts negotiated: banks might still give loans at the old rates while requiring borrowers to maintain a portion of the loan on deposit as "compensating balances." This widespread practice has the effect of increasing the *effective* interest rates borrowers must pay. Banks are often reluctant to increase rates substantially to regular and valued customers. At the same time, they are also reluctant to cut them off from credit; hence, it is common during tight money periods to observe banks rationing credit by the simple expedient of refusing loans to marginal or new and less valued customers, or by imposing terms upon them which are so onerous as to cause them to withdraw their loan applications. Thus, even though this latter group of borrowers may be willing to pay the interest rates currently being charged by the banks, the money is simply not available to them.

While credit rationing is a qualification to the analysis of the last chapter, the argument is not changed very much. The only amendment is that a mechanism other than interest changes may impinge on the money markets to cut back the amount of investment activity. Graph 9.1 shows that either a rise in interest or the rationing of credit can cause the same cutback in investment activity; either a rise in interest from i_0 to i_1 or rationing of credit to the level of investment of I_1 can produce a limiting of investment to I_1.

Another qualification to the analysis of the last chapter involves sources of investment funds other than those available in the money

GRAPH 9.1

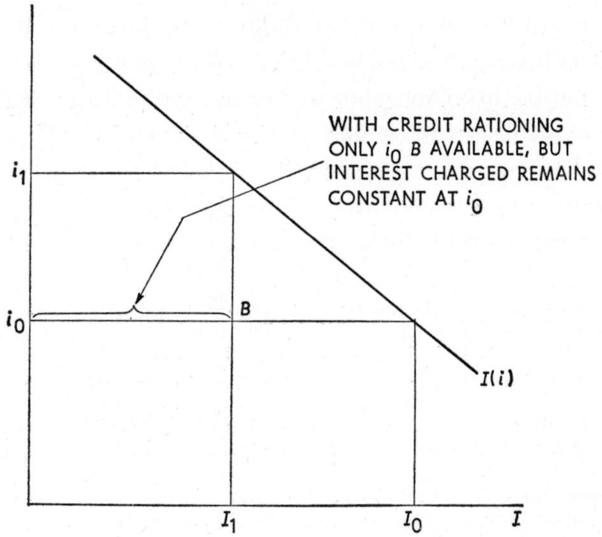

WITH CREDIT RATIONING ONLY i_0 B AVAILABLE, BUT INTEREST CHARGED REMAINS CONSTANT AT i_0

markets. There are three such sources: the two internal (to the firm) ones of depreciation allowances and retained earnings, and the outside capital markets. It should not be supposed that internal funds are freely available to the firm. Depreciation allowances and retained earnings bear the cost of foregone opportunities to use such funds elsewhere than within the firm itself. This cost is at least the yield on government bonds. Moreover, increased use of retained earnings for investment purposes is subject to rising (imputed) costs. The higher the ratio of retained earnings to dividends paid to stockholders, the lower, other things equal, becomes the value of the stock. An excessive use of retained earnings may, in fact, cause enough grumbling among stockholders to threaten management's control over the firm. Nevertheless, many corporations are so solidly in the hands of management that a considerable amount of the cost of finance may be safely shifted to stockholders without fear of successful revolt. This is what makes the corporate device such a superior fund-raising institution. Proprietorships and partnerships are so constituted that the pain of saving is directly felt by the firm's owners, and they are less prone than are stockholders to give up the present enjoyment of income, if only because they have no guardians.

The sale of new equities may also encounter implicit costs. If the market does not believe that the proceeds of the new stock issue can be invested at a yield equal to the ratio of average expected earnings to the issue price, the price of the new issue will fall. Other things remaining equal, the greater the new stock issue the larger will be the fall in the stock price. This fall in the price of newly issued stock is akin to interest, because it means that the company must commit itself to a higher earnings-price ratio, the more dollars it seeks from investors. Investors, in offering less for the additional stock issues, are reacting to their "lenders risk," which demands a higher premium the less sure is the return on the new issue of stock.[1]

---

[1] The analysis in this and the previous paragraph owes much to James Duesenberry in his book, *Business Cycles and Economic Growth* (New York: McGraw-Hill Book Co., Inc., 1958), p. 91. It is well to note that the costs of finance which are shifted to stockholders may not be felt, even by them. In the first place, the burden of saving can hardly be felt by people who never had the income (dividends) to save in the first place. Secondly, the fall in stock values resulting from an increasing use of retained earnings or from new issues may be obscured by rising prices in the stock market as a whole. This does not mean that a "burden" does not exist; for purchase of new capital facilities involves, for the community, some foregone consumption. Fortunately, modern capital markets and the corporate institution diffuse saving so thoroughly throughout the community that most people do not realize that they are actually saving.

GROWTH FACTORS

American economic growth has been characterized by innovations in productive activity, population growth, and the filling-up of a geographical vacuum, especially in the West. Population growth is an especially important stimulant to investment activity. New consumption-goods industries and homes are needed to service added population; a growing labor force is required to service these new industries. Labor force growth also helps to offset the diminishing returns to capital which might occur if capital formation proceeds too rapidly or if laborsaving innovations fail to materialize.

Nevertheless, despite America's growing population, fed until 1920 both by heavy immigration and by natural increase, the country cannot be characterized as one having a labor surplus. Evidence of this is the continued rise in per capital real income. Since this rise has been accompanied by increasing wages, it may be fairly asked why investment has not been discouraged. The answer, in large measure, is technical change. Technical change leads to the reductions in production costs which offset wage increases and keep the marginal efficiency of capital high. Without the reductions in costs brought about by railroads, electric power, more efficient equipment, etc., the American economy would have stagnated long ago. We shall discuss this point more thoroughly in Chapter 14.

Another stimulant to investment in the past was the geographical frontier of the West. The conquest of the frontier required enormous outlays for railroads and other communications; funds for building cities and farms; and new productive capacity in the East for the purpose of servicing the growing Western markets. The West, in turn, added the further stimulus of cheap food and raw materials for the consumption of Eastern labor and industry. While it is true that public grants, especially to railroad builders and to farmers (in the form of free land), helped the investment process, it is nevertheless also true that the frontier, during the 19th century, provided this country with one grand private investment opportunity. To a certain extent, this is still true, for the West continues to grow more rapidly than other parts of the country.

The Great Depression of the 1930's lasted a long time. When recovery from the trough in 1933 proved to be weak, and especially when the relapse of 1938 occurred, some economists began to talk about the "mature" U.S. economy, about relatively permanent stagnation in which a slow rate of economic growth, not sufficient to produce full employment, would probably characterize American capitalism. As a buttress to their arguments, the protagonists of the "stagnation thesis" pointed to a slowing down of population growth, to the end of the frontier, and, what may seem surprising to the present generation, to a reduced rate of technical innovation. These events, they believed, signaled a drying up of the incentive to invest, a permanent reduction in the marginal efficiency of capital.

The stagnation thesis was a favorite theme of a widely known and respected economist, Alvin Hansen.[2] Through his influence, the doctrine gained a large number of adherents and continued to affect the thinking of many economists even in the postwar years. The current generation of economists no longer appears to be seriously infected with the stagnation virus, principally because the performance of the economy since World War II has been basically strong, despite a period of slow growth from 1957 to 1962. Indeed, the highly respected Simon Kuznets, summing up the evidence on capital formation trends in the United States,[3] has argued that far from stagnating due to deficient investment, the American economy may run into trouble because it cannot generate enough saving to finance the burgeoning investment opportunities which seem to have been the outgrowth of its rapidly advancing technology, its continued population growth, and its high rate of urbanization. To be sure, much of America's potential saving is being absorbed by a very high level of government activity, particularly in the military sphere; hence, the stagnationists might still have an effective rebuttal to the Kuznets' argument. A true test of the stagnation argument cannot be conducted for an economy in which government activity remains so important. Until the time when (if ever) government activity declines in relative importance, therefore, both the stagnationists and their opponents can continue with their beliefs without fear of being contradicted by the facts.

INTEREST AND INVESTMENT, AGAIN

Another qualification of the theory of investment is now in order: We argued, in the last chapter, that businessmen tend to invest up to the point where the marginal efficiency of capital of the last unit of

---

[2] A good source for Hansen's view is "Economic Progress and Declining Population," American Economic Association, *Readings in Business Cycle Theory* (Philadelphia: Blakiston, 1944).

[3] Kuznets, *Capital Formation in the American Economy, Its Formation and Financing* (Princeton, N.J.: Princeton University Press, for the National Bureau of Economic Research, 1961).

investment equals the interest rate. To some extent, we have already qualified the analysis by observing that capital rationing and the imputed costs of using internal funds or new stock issues will prevent this equality from being realized. A further amendment, in some ways more serious, must be made. It may well be that the investment schedule is not sensitive to the rate of interest, that variations in interest, within a relatively wide range, may not produce significant changes in investment.

Before presenting the argument as to why investment may not be sensitive to interest rate movements, let us see why such insensitivity is important. Consider the two investment demand functions in Graph 9.2: I' and I''. Suppose that I_f represents the full-employment level of

GRAPH 9.2

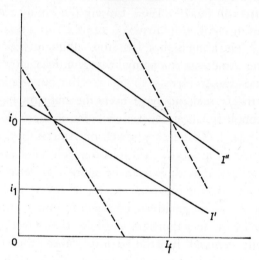

investment at a level of interest i_0. If the investment demand schedule falls to I' from I'', the interest rate must fall to i_1 in order to reestablish the full-employment level of investment I_f. With I-functions as elastic as I' and I'', this is not difficult. Recovery may take place simply by having the Federal Reserve System reduce interest rates by pumping more money into the economy. Suppose, however, that the I-functions are not so elastic, that the dotted lines on Graph 9.2 represent their true shapes. Then, no matter how far the interest rate falls, recovery back to I_f is not possible. In this situation, action by the Federal Reserve, no matter how liberal, will be of no avail. The only way I_f may be reestablished is through a rightward shift of the investment demand schedule, and such shifts result from factors affecting the marginal efficiency capital schedule, not the interest rate.

A number of studies have shown that businessmen do not take interest rates into account in their investment decisions as much as has been traditionally believed by economists. Rather, factors such as the level of unused plant capacity, the growth of markets, the cost and availability of labor, new techniques of production, and the availability of funds seem to play a greater role. Aside from the availability of funds, all of these factors relate to the position of the investment demand schedule, not to its slope. The slope of the schedule is determined by the rate of fall of the MEC as investment is extended, *other things being equal.*

Actually, the sensitivity of investment demand to changes in interest rates is a matter of much dispute amongst economists. Econometric studies have given conflicting answers, and various surveys of business sentiment have given ambiguous results.[4] Rather than review these studies, however, let us use the formal theory advanced in the last chapter to comment on the problem.

Recall that the formal theory of investment makes the slope of the investment demand function depend upon the slope of the supply price of capital function and upon the sensitivity to changes in the interest rate of the present value or demand price for new assets. A steep supply price curve or insensitivity of present value to interest rate changes will cause the investment demand function to be steep. Conversely, a flat supply price function or sensitivity of present value to the interest rate will flatten the investment demand schedule. It follows that the aggregate investment demand function depends upon the mix of assets sought by businessmen, since it is this mix which determines whether or not supply price effects or present value effects will dominate the slope of the aggregate investment demand curve.

More concretely, suppose that the mix of investment spending in the economy leans in the direction of short-lived investments, such as investments in inventories and fast-depreciating equipment. From this it would follow that present values would lean to the interest-insensitive side, resulting in a relatively steep or interest-insensitive aggregate investment demand function. A mix of investment favoring long-lived, or

---

[4] For a discussion of these surveys, see W. H. White, "Interest Inelasticity of Investment Demand: The Case From Business Attitude Surveys Re-examined," *American Economic Review,* September, 1956.

durable projects would favor a flat aggregate investment demand function—one in which investment spending is sensitive to interest rate changes. These conclusions follow from the proposition developed in the last chapter that the interest sensitivity of present values depends upon the durability of capital assets, with the sensitivity varying directly the degree of durability of the assets.

The effects of durability, however, are likely to be offset by the supply conditions in capital goods industries. Short-lived assets such as inventories and fast-depreciating equipment are often produced in industries having relatively flat marginal cost curves. Highly durable capital—such as buildings, roads, dams, turbines, etc.—are generally produced under conditions of rising marginal production costs. Marginal acquisition costs also rise rapidly for such goods. It follows that interest-insensitive present values for nondurables are likely to be offset by relatively flat supply price functions, while sensitive present values for durables are likely to be offset by steep supply price functions. The sensitivity of aggregate investment demand to interest rate changes, therefore, is less affected by the durability mix of investment spending than we might have first supposed.

Nevertheless, the argument does help us to speculate somewhat more on the shape of the aggregate investment demand function. At very high interest rates the demand for highly durable goods is likely to be low. Correspondingly, the industries producing these goods are likely to be in a slack condition. Declines in interest rates which lead to increases in the demand price for durables are not likely to be met by sharp increases in their supply prices. Hence at high interest rates—say above 7 or 8 percent—investment demand for durables is likely to be quite sensitive to changes in the interest rate. As the interest rate falls, however, demand for capital goods is likely to be met by more sharply rising costs in the capital goods industries. The aggregate investment demand schedule is therefore likely to become steeper for durables at lower interest rates.

Similar arguments can be made for nondurables, except that production conditions in industries producing them are not likely to lead to sharply rising marginal costs as rapidly as it happens in durables industries. The steepening of the aggregate investment demand function at lower interest rates is therefore likely to be less than if durables alone were counted in the aggregate. It follows that the aggregate investment demand function—from high to low interest rates—probably has a shape something like Graph 9.3 with an interest-sensitive portion at high rates and an interest-insensitive portion at low rates.

GRAPH 9.3

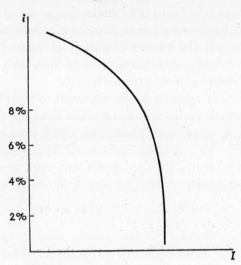

INVESTMENT AND THE INCOME LEVEL

One of the main arguments in this book has been that consumption spending is highly dependent upon the level of household (disposable) income. Disposable income, on the other hand, is closely related to the level of national income. When national income rises, consumption spending rises as a result of the rise in household income associated with the rise in national income. Because consumers have more to spend, they spend more. Can we argue the same for business spending? When national income rises, profits increase, and a base for increased investment spending is created at the same time. Indeed, businessmen may have plans on the shelf which can be translated into investment spending only when the profits available from increases in national income are realized. In this event, national income can be put alongside the interest rate as a determinant of the level of investment spending.

Investment spending which is related to the level of national income may be labeled *level-induced investment*. Level-induced investment causes national income to grow faster and farther than it would if such investment were absent. Suppose, for example, that national income begins to grow as a result of an increase in government spending. Without level-induced investment, the final settling point of national income would be dictated by the induced increases in consumer spending. The total change in national income would equal the increment in government spending plus the increase in consumer spending. However, if level-induced investment occurs, the final settling point of national income would include a change in investment, as well as the changes in government and consumer spending. The total change in national income would be greater than before.

The multiplier is affected by the inclusion of level-induced investment in the analysis of income change. Consider the determination of national income in the simple system. The equilibrium condition for the system is that the sum of consumption and investment spending shall equal the flow of output of final goods and services as measured by national income; that is,

$$C + I = Y, \text{ or, since } C = a + cY, \tag{1}$$
$$a + cY + I = Y. \tag{2}$$

The argument of this section breaks down the I of equation (2) into a part that is influenced by a comparison of the MEC with the interest rate (call it I_i) and a part influenced by the level of national income (call it I_y). Total investment can therefore be symbolized by

$$I = I_i + I_y. \tag{3}$$

For simplicity, let us assume that I_y represents some constant proportion of national income; that is,

$$I_y = uY, \tag{4}$$

where u is the given proportion. Now, substituting (4) into (3) and (3) into (2), we get

$$a + cY + I_i + uY = Y, \text{ or}$$
$$Y = a/(1 - c - u) + I_i/(1 - c - u). \tag{5}$$

From equation (5) it is easy to see that a change of investment due, say, to a lowering of the interest rate would give a change in the income level equal to the change in investment multiplied by $1/(1 - c - u)$. That is to say,

$$\Delta Y = (\Delta I_i) \, 1/(1 - c - u). \tag{6}$$

The multiplier is therefore $1/(1 - c - u)$. Notice how it differs from the multiplier derived from the simple system earlier in the book. That multiplier, $1/(1 - c)$, had a smaller value because u was assumed to be zero. Changes in national income were smaller than they would have been had level-induced investment been included in the system.

Graph 9.4 further illustrates this result. Suppose that equilibrium income initially settles at Y_0 (at a point, for convenience, where total investment is zero). Now, assume that a shift in the investment demand schedule brings about an increase in investment spending by an amount indicated by the difference between the $C + I_i$-line and line C. Without level-induced investment, the new equilibrium level of income would be Y_1. The addition of level-induced investment (indicated by the difference between $C + I$ and $C + I_i$) yields an equilibrium level of income at Y_2, a level greater than Y_1. The reason for this is not hard to find. At equilibrium income Y_1, saving is S_1E_1. However, with level-induced investment added, this saving rate is exceeded by total investment spending, the excess being E_1X_1. National income must therefore rise to Y_2, where the excess of investment over saving will be wiped out.

The slope of line C (and $C + I_i$) is given by the marginal propensity

GRAPH 9.4

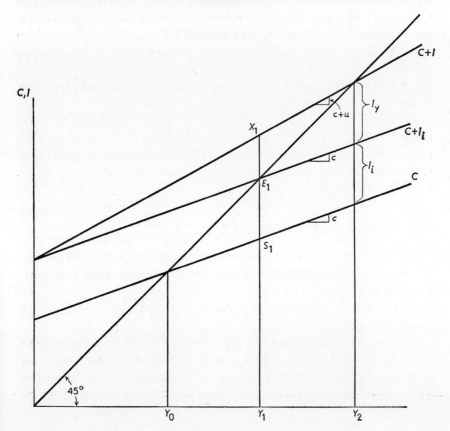

to consume. The slope of line $C + I$ includes both the marginal propensity to consume and the additional investment per unit added income [the u in equation (4)]. It is evident that line $C + I$ cannot have a slope greater than the 45° helping-line; if it did, the level of expenditure would constantly exceed the level of output and national income would be required to grow indefinitely. Since the slope of the 45° line is 1, then, the stability condition for national income is that the slope of line $C + I$ shall be less than 1 (that $1 - c - u > 0$) which is tantamount to saying that the marginal propensity to save ($= 1 - c$) shall be greater than u. That this condition is required can be seen easily from equation (6). If $1 - c \leqq u$, the multiplier is undefined or negative. Only if $1 - c > u$ can the multiplier be said to have a meaningful value: one that will produce positive and finite changes in national income.

Before leaving this topic, it is well to point out that level-induced investment is probably not as closely related to income as is consumption spending. Its value probably tends to change over the business cycle. At depression levels of national income business profits are likely to be quite low, and u, as a result, is probably near zero. As income begins to recover, however, profits will also grow and u should assume a positive and significant value. As the recovery gathers wind, it may in fact exceed $(1 - c)$ for a while. As can be seen from the multiplier, a rising u will make national income rise at an accelerated rate. However, as the boom proceeds, further increases in u are unlikely. Indeed, because u initially rises as a result of the activation of investment plans made possible by rising profits in the recovery stage, it probably falls once those plans have been realized. During the contraction stage in the business cycle, u will again fall to very low values, bringing with it a fall in the multiplier.

THE ACCELERATION PRINCIPLE

Fluctuations in national income are normally accompanied by even wider relative fluctuations in private investment spending. Graph 9.5 shows that this has been true of the American economy for virtually every contraction in business activity, as well as for peacetime periods of boom, since 1929.

It is important to explain this phenomenon; for, if investment spending is so unstable, it is an obvious source of trouble for the economy. Indeed, many economists believe that the instability of investment spending is the prime source of boom and slump in the American economy.

GRAPH 9.5

Gross National Product and Gross Domestic Investment, 1929–1968*
(1929 = 100)

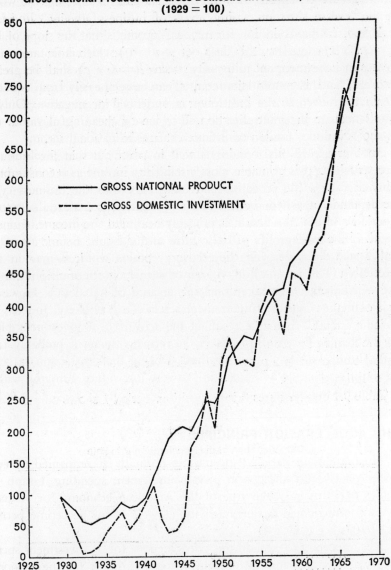

* Source: Economic Report of the President, 1969.

We have already discussed some of the reasons for the instability of investment. When the economy begins to slump, and when pessimistic expectations develop in such an atmosphere, businessmen are likely to cut back their spending. Such actions breed further declines in national income, more pessimism, and more reductions in investment spending. In the reverse situation, rising levels of business activity can breed optimism, increases in investment, and further increases in national income. Yet, somehow, this does not seem to be the whole story. Decreases in investment spending often occur *before* a general slump has occurred, and increases, similarly, often develop prior to recovery. Again, the movements of investment and national income often develop simultaneously in either direction. In none of these situations is the psychological explanation of investment instability adequate.

Another explanation for investment instability lies in the *acceleration principle*. This principle roots instability of investment in the durability of capital and its technical relation to production. Suppose that the demand for a hypothetical firm's production is a steady $100,000 a period and that the firm has adjusted its capital facilities to that demand. If the average life of the capital owned by the firm is 10 years, and if each dollar of production during a period requires three dollars invested in facilities, the firm will own $300,000 worth of capital goods, and will have a periodic replacement demand of $30,000 for the purpose of maintaining the required ratio between capital equipment and periodic output. Under these assumed conditions, a change in demand for the firm's product will cause the firm to change its expenditures on capital equipment in a proportion which far exceeds the change in output of finished goods.

Table 9.1 demonstrates this proposition. Period 1 shows output hold-

TABLE 9.1

Demonstration of the Acceleration Principle

Period	Output ($1,000)	Required Capital ($1,000)	Replacement Investment ($1,000)	Required Spending on New Capital ($1,000)	Total Investment ($1,000)
1	100	300	30	0	30
2	105	315	30	15	45
3	115	345	30	30	60
4	120	360	30	15	45
5	115	345	30	−15	15
6	115	345	30	0	30

ing steady at $100,000. Under the assumed conditions, the firm's only demand for new capital goods is for the purpose of replacing the depreciating capital equipment—$30,000. In period 2, however, the demand for the firm's finished product grows to $105,000. Because it cannot service this increase in demand with its old capital stock of $300,000, the firm increases its investment to $315,000, making its total outlay on capital goods $45,000 during period 2. A 5 percent increase in demand has caused a 50 percent increase in investment!

The increase in capital equipment is not enough, however; for in period 3 demand for the firm's product grows to $115,000. In order to meet the capital needs of the new demand level, the firm increases its outlay on capital to $60,000 ($30,000 for replacement of depreciated equipment and $30,000 for additional equipment). An interesting aspect of period 3 is that, although the relative growth in output is greater than it was in the previous period, the relative growth in investment spending by the firm is less than in period 2. Even with the rate of growth in output still in the acceleration stage, growth in investment spending is already slowing down. This situation becomes even more pronounced in period 4. Here the firm's output, while continuing to grow in absolute terms, has slowed markedly in relative terms. Its spending on capital goods has not only slowed, it has actually dropped, despite the continued rise in output. Pessimism, interestingly enough, has played no role in the decline of investment spending.

The events of period 5 emphasize that the fall in investment, which, in addition to reflecting the earlier reduced growth in output, also reflects the effect of an absolute drop in production. The fall in production has made some of the firm's capital stock redundant, so that, even though $30,000 of the original capital stock is still depreciating and needs replacement, the excess of new capital, $15,000, causes the firm to reduce its outlays on capital goods to $15,000. Period 6 shows what happens when a fall in output is halted: since the redundant capital stock was eliminated in period 5, investment now rises back to its initial value of $30,000, an amount equal to the replacement demand for the initial capital stock. This rise in investment spending due to a halt in the fall of output is symmetrical to the situation in which a cessation of an increase in output will cause a fall in investment spending. In the latter case, the deficiency of capital is eliminated and investment in new equipment stops, leaving only replacement demand.

The foregoing example of the operation of the acceleration principle can easily be amended to show how changes in demand would affect investment in inventory spending by business and housing investment by households. This shall not be done here, but it should be apparent that similar effects, less pronounced in the case of inventory purchases and more pronounced in the case of housing expenditures, would be had.

The acceleration principle complements the multiplier process in explaining the pattern of business fluctuations in industrial capitalistic economies like the United States. Both ideas are consistent with the fact that changes in national income and employment are cumulative and self-reinforcing, a pattern which is characteristic of the American and other industrial economies. But, equally, if not more, important, the acceleration principle, in its marriage with the multiplier analysis, helps us to understand why cumulative increases and decreases in income and employment come to an end, reversing themselves in the process. Imagine an increase in government spending after a period of equilibrium in national income. The increased spending will induce changes in national income which, in turn, will induce further increases in consumer spending. A rise in the stream of consumer spending, in turn, will put pressure upon the consumption-goods industries to increase output. If the increased output of goods requires expansions of the capital stock of producers, they will increase their investment outlays. Now, in addition to the boost given it by increased consumer spending, national income is further stimulated by an increase in the stream of investment spending. The result is further increases in consumer spending, additional pressure on consumption goods production, more investment, and so on.

The crucial point is this: if the combined values of the marginal propensity to consume and the accelerator (the amount of additional capital required for each additional unit of production) are high, the cumulative increase in national income will be explosive—national income will be pushed into the region of continuous inflation because the amount of investment induced by every increase in production will be such as always to exceed the new saving generated by increases in national income. On the other hand, smaller values of the accelerator and the MPC will produce *fluctuations* in national income. This is because the increases in consumption spending during the expansionary process will become progressively weaker, resulting in a slowing of the increase in national income. As we have seen, a reduction in the rate of change in output will act to depress investment even before output reaches a peak. Once this happens, the process will go into reverse, with national income being dragged down by induced decreases in consumption and investment spending. But, as with the rise in national income, the multiplier-acceleration process may cause a reversal of the cumulative movement. As the induced decreases in consumption become smaller, the decline in national income will slow, and, because of this, total investment spending will begin to rise *before* national income reaches the bottom of the cumulative decline. Depending upon the relative values of the multiplier and accelerator, the fluctuations will continue indefinitely, settle down to a new equilibrium level, or continue around a rising trend. What actually happens is not important at this moment. The main thing is to recognize that, inherent in the very processes of change in a capitalist economy, is the possibility of self-generating fluctuations of national income and employment.[5]

A word of warning is appropriate here. The acceleration principle, even though it has explanatory value in the field of business-cycle analysis, is as yet an unconfirmed hypothesis, despite some fairly elaborate attempts to demonstrate its validity.[6] That it has not been confirmed should not be surprising. The mechanical model of Table 9.1 contains a number of assumptions which, if not realized in fact, will seriously impair the precision with which the acceleration effect works. First, the model assumed that businessmen were working with plant and equipment which were fully utilized before the process began. This assumption will rarely be realized in fact, especially for the economy as a whole.[7] A further assumption was that each increase in demand for finished goods is regarded as permanent by entrepreneurs. Businessmen may prefer to press their equipment at an overcapacity rate of use until they are sure that the increase in demand is permanent enough to justify additional capital facilities. Moreover, if demand has been increasing for a period, they may even anticipate future increases by buying enough equipment to satisfy future as well as current output. A final assumption was that the technical capital-output relation was constant, that the new equipment designed to provide additional productive capacity, as well as to replace the depreciated facilities, was the

---

[5] The classic article about the multiplier-accelerator cycle mechanism was written by Paul Samuelson, "Interactions Between the Multiplier Analysis and the Principle of Acceleration," *Review of Economics and Statistics,* Vol. XXI, No. 2 (May, 1939), pp. 75–78, reprinted in *Readings in Business Cycle Theory* (New York: Blakiston Co., Inc., 1944), pp. 261–69.

[6] See J. Tinbergen, "Statistical Evidence on the Acceleration Principle," *Economica,* Vol. V (n.s.) (May, 1938), pp. 164–76; S. Kuznets, "Relation Between Capital Goods and Finished Products in the Business Cycle," *Economic Essays in Honor of Wesley Mitchell* (New York: Columbia University Press, 1934), pp. 211–67.

[7] A number of recent studies have been made of the acceleration principle with excess capacity taken into account. See, for example, Alice Bourneuf, "Manufacturing Investment, Excess Capacity, and the Rate of Growth of Output," *American Economic Review,* September, 1964.

same as the old. Actually, many businessmen use different and technologically superior equipment in their expansions and replacements. There is no certainty that the capital output ratio which was good for past production will also be good for future production. Besides technical changes in the quality of capital assets and in the organization of production, there are also changes in the costs of labor and other production inputs. Moreover, when we consider the relationship between aggregate production and the aggregate capital stock, we can see that changes in the aggregate capital output ratio can come about through changes in the mix of output and from the birth of new products as well as the death of old ones.

Because the assumptions underlying the acceleration principle model are never true in fact, a neat statistical confirmation of the principle should not be expected. Nevertheless, it is hard to imagine that the notion does not have *some* validity for the explanation of investment spending. That businessmen should base part of their investment spending upon changes in output is almost self-evident. What the previous discussion should teach us, however, is that the actual operation of the acceleration principle in the economy can be muted by many forces, some of which act to alter the capital output ratio and spoil the neat relation between changes in output and investment. In addition, we have seen that business expectations and the presence or absence of excess production capacity can also limit the operation of the principle. Together with the rest of the factors which might affect investment spending (such as tax changes, interest rates, and other financial conditions), it is not to be expected that we can explain all fluctuations in business investment in the economy with the idea of acceleration. Few economists have actually advanced this proposition. Nevertheless, most would probably agree that the idea, at least in a loose form, is a valuable addition to our stock of concepts about the way the economy works.

Concluding Comment

Recent refinements in econometric techniques, high-speed computers, and availability of new data have all conspired to permit economists to engage in a number of empirical studies designed to test the theories of investment behavior sketched out in this and the last chapter. Inevitably, the theories have undergone a number of refinements in the process. Unfortunately, this literature is too large to summarize here. Unfortunately, also, the present state of knowledge is not yet sufficiently settled to allow us to report firm conclusions. In the bibliography at the end of this chapter, there appears a list of items which should allow the student to enter this vast and fascinating literature. He should be warned, however, that before he can adequately comprehend it, his mathematical and statistical tools will need considerable sharpening.

ADDITIONAL READINGS

DUESENBERRY, J.   *Business Cycles and Economic Growth.* New York: McGraw-Hill Book Co., Inc., 1958.

EISNER, R., and STROTZ, R.   "Determinants of Business Investment," *Impacts of Monetary Policy.* Commission on Money and Credit. Englewood Cliffs, N.J.: Prentice-Hall, Inc., 1963. This useful article contains a very extensive bibliography.

EISNER, R.   "A Permanent Income Theory for Investment," *American Economic Review,* June, 1967. An empirical study which stresses the relation between past changes in output and expectations as an influence upon investment spending.

HICKMAN, B. G.   *Investment Demand and U.S. Economic Growth.* Washington, D.C.: Brookings Institution, 1965.

JORGENSON, D.   "Capital Theory and Investment Behavior," *American Economic Review,* May, 1963. Presents a "neoclassical" theory of investment based upon a model of optimal capital accumulation, with some tests of the hypothesis.

MATHEWS, R. C. O.   *The Business Cycle.* Chicago: University of Chicago Press, 1962. A good introduction to business cycle models based upon multiplier-accelerator mechanisms.

MEYER, J. R., and KUH, E.   *The Investment Decision.* Cambridge, Mass.: Harvard University Press, 1957. A major study of the variety of potential influences upon investment spending.

Chapter 10 | THE GENERAL THEORY OF AGGREGATE DEMAND

National income is made up of sales of final goods and services to consumers, investors, government, and the rest of the world. The money expenditures of these four sectors comprise the aggregate demand for final output in the economy. In Chapters 4–9, we developed the analysis of aggregate demand in some detail, first by showing how the various expenditure streams combine to produce a given level of national income and, second, by considering at length the determinants of the two major private spending streams, consumption and investment. A direct analysis of government spending has not been made for the reason that this spending stream is primarily determined from without (exogenous to) the adjustment mechanism of the economy. Government spending and taxation are political variables and, although official policies respecting them are often in the nature of responses to happenings in the economy, the responses are not dependable enough for the economist to include them as an integral part of his theory. We shall also exclude a detailed discussion of net exports, not because this variable doesn't respond to fluctuations in income and employment, but because in the American economy it is far less important than the other spending streams. Were this book directed toward readers in countries heavily dependent upon foreign trade, we would devote considerable space to the topic.

Our analysis of aggregate demand still lacks completeness, for we have yet to discuss the determinants of the interest rate. This is important because entrepreneurial comparisons of the marginal efficiency of capital with the interest rate help to determine the level of investment demand in the economy. Moreover, since the interest rate (or rates, of which *the rate* in this discussion is representative) is not determined from without the economy, but arises internally from its workings, we cannot set it aside.

Our first task, therefore, is to discuss the forces relevant to the determination of the interest rate. We shall find that the discussion leads back to the determination of aggregate demand and national income.

THE THEORY OF INTEREST

The Keynesian versus the Classical Approach

Recall from Chapter 3 that classical theory centers the explanation of interest in the capital market. Saving and investment interactions reflect in the market for new securities, which determines the rate of interest. For Keynes, however, saving and investment interactions determine the level of income. The classicals assumed that competition in the labor market determines the level of income and employment. Hence, they believed that the interest rate operates mainly to determine the allocation of resources between investment and consumption goods. Keynes thought that the level of income and employment depends mainly upon the level of aggregate demand; he therefore gave the interest rate a crucial role to play in determining the income level. Having done this, he had to construct a new theory of interest, designed to fit the role he assigned to that variable. In what follows, we shall describe the Keynesian interest theory, with amendments made by more recent theorists.

THE DEMAND FOR MONEY

Instead of focusing upon the volume of saving as a determinant of the interest rate, Keynes concentrated attention upon the *forms* in which savings are held. At any moment in time there exists an accumulation of assets, both real and financial, which represent the embodiment of *past saving*. Fresh saving can be looked at as a sum of money, waiting to be placed in one or another of the variety of forms available, including money itself. Now if savers, e.g., corporations, place their funds directly in capital goods, neither the interest rate nor the level of income is affected. Such an act represents a simultaneous and equal reduction in both the supply and demand for securities, and the reduction in consumption demand represented by the saving is immediately offset by the purchase of investment goods. New saving which is not placed directly in capital goods must seek some kind of financial form and be held along with past saving embodied in similar form.

There is a large variety of financial assets available to wealth owners. At one end is money itself, devoid of interest yield and free of default risk. Ninety-one-day U.S. Treasury bills and other federal obligations provide default-free investments with interest yields. Side by Side with federal instruments are a profusion of state, local, and private securities, with various maturities and degrees of risk.

While a study of the markets for financial instruments is interesting, we shall not probe this subject here. Instead, we shall confine our attention to the competition between money, on the one hand, and all variable-priced securities on the other. In the course of our discussion, however, we should not forget that the various financial instruments compete against one another as well as against money for wealth holders' favor.

Why do people hold money? Keynes gave four reasons:[1]

1. The *income motive*—cash is necessary to bridge the gap between the receipt of income and its disbursement. Presumably, the larger the level of income and the longer the interval between receipt and expenditure, the more will be the money people demand for this purpose.
2. The *business motive*—businessmen need money to bridge the gap between the time of incurring business costs and the time of receiving sales proceeds. The strength of money demanded for this purpose should depend upon the value of current output (income) and the degree of business integration (how many independent suppliers businessmen buy from).
3. The *precautionary motive*—the need to provide for sudden contingencies. Such contingencies include the chance to make an advantageous purchase, or the need to pay out a sum in case of emergency.
4. The *speculative motive*—explained below.

Motives (1) through (3) are ordinarily lumped together as *transactions motives,* and the money so demanded is labeled L_1. We should expect L_1 to be positively related to the level of national income, as shown in Graph 10.1.

However, as Keynes was quick to point out, the relationship between L_1 and Y is not necessarily stable. Indeed, a moment's reflection raises the interesting question as to why people must bridge the payments interval by holding barren money. If an alternative asset yielding a return is available, why is it that people hold money instead? The answer is that people hold money instead of other assets when the returns on

---

[1] Keynes, *General Theory,* chap. 15.

GRAPH 10.1

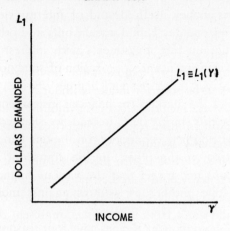

other assets fall short of the costs of transferring into and out of those assets.

Let us expand on this statement. Assume there are fixed value assets such as time and saving deposits, credit union shares, or saving and loan shares available to holders of cash balances. Since interest on these assets is paid at fairly long intervals, there would not be much point in holding them as opposed to money for transaction purposes, at least for most people. Assume now that L_1 holders have available to them very short-term commercial paper, or even treasury instruments. Since there is a fairly good market for such instruments, and since they fluctuate little in price, L_1 holders might be tempted to invest in them. However, even if there were no price fluctuations in these instruments, brokers' charges for both moving into and moving out of the securities may provide a barrier to their purchase. The interest yield must be enough to exceed this cost. When short-term interest rates are low, there is not much incentive to switch out of cash. However, when these rates are high, people can economize on cash by reducing their L_1 holdings relative to other short-term assets. Hence, we should expect curve OA to drift down a bit when short-term interest rates rise, particularly to high levels.[2]

---

[2] It should also be noted that both the frequency and size of transactions influence the choice between L_1 and short-term assets. Frequent and small transactions encourage large L_1 holdings, mainly because brokerage fees have a fixed element, independent of the size and number of transactions. Hence small and frequent switches into and out of securities are likely to raise the costs of such transactions above the interest return from the securities. See James Tobin, "The Interest-Elasticity of Transactions Demand for Cash," *Review of Economics and Statistics*, August, 1956.

Once the transactions motive is satisfied, people might wish to hold funds in a variety of forms, that is, in portfolios which include a variety of investments. The composition of portfolios would presumably vary from person to person, reflecting their preferences as between types of assets. Influencing these preferences is the liquidity of assets, or ease with which they can be sold for money without loss; the rate of return expected from assets, including both the interest return and possible capital gains arising from increases in the prices of assets; and the risk that the party originally issuing the security might default. Since money is default free, and since it is also the most liquid of all assets, some people will undoubtedly hold it in their portfolios. However, such holdings are not free. The interest lost by not holding other assets, plus the possible capital gains from those assets, represent the costs of holding money.

Presumably, the amount of money people wish to hold in the portfolios will vary with the cost of holding money. The higher the cost, the less money people will desire; conversely, lower cost should cause people to shift into money and out of other securities. Hence it is possible to draw a schedule (Graph 10.2) relating the amount of money people wish to hold to the cost of holding it, as represented by the interest rate.

GRAPH 10.2

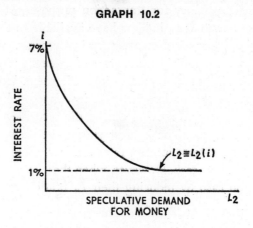

The schedule in Graph 10.2 reflects what Keynes called the *speculative demand for money,* which we shall symbolize as L_2. The term "speculative" is used because of the following explanation of the shape of the schedule. At any moment of time, asset holders have different opinions concerning the future course of interest rates. Some people are "bearish," believing that interest rates in the near future are going to rise or, what is the same thing, that security prices are going to fall. Others are "bullish," believing in a fall in interest rates and a rise in security prices. Some opinion may even exist that interest rates will continue unchanged.

Now, the "bears" have an obvious interest in holding money rather than securities, while the "bulls" have the opposite incentive. Indeed, the more certain are the bears that security prices are going to fall, the more they want to hold their assets in money form, for the liquidity of those assets represents an important factor influencing the demand for them.

So far, we have not actually related the amounts of L_2 demanded to alternative interest rates. To do this, we must relate the degree of bearishness to the level of interest. Keynes did this by supposing that at any moment market opinion considers a certain range of interest rates as being normal. Opinion as to what are the highest and lowest points in this range varies. The range, for example, may be between 1 and 7 percent. At 1 percent, no one in the market may believe that interest rates can fall further. Indeed, everyone may be bearish and wish to hold all of his liquid assets in the form of money. For this reason, the elasticity of the L_2 schedule at low rates of interest may be very great, perhaps extending to infinity at the floor (1 percent in the example).

At 2 percent, some of the bears will drop out and perhaps become bulls. At 3, 4, 5, and 6 percent, fewer and fewer bears remain and more and more bulls are created. Finally, at 7 percent, the bulls completely dominate the field: all of the bears will have retired. Virtually all asset holders will now believe that the interest rate is "too high" and that it will come down. Since a falling interest rate implies rising security prices, asset holders should want to hold a minimum of cash and a maximum of securities in their portfolios.

The flat portion of the L_2 function at 1 percent implies, as we have said, that everyone wishes to hold his assets in money. It also implies that any increases in the money stock will be completely absorbed in money itself—that is, hoarded. For this reason, the flat portion of the curve is often referred to as a *liquidity trap*. The existence of this trap, however, is questioned by many economists.

The whole speculative demand schedule may shift up or down, depending upon market opinion as to the "normal" range of interest rates. For example, if the public begins to believe that the Federal Reserve System is going to engage in tight money policies in the future, the range may shift from 1–7 percent to 3–8 percent. Conversely, a belief that credit in the future is going to be less tight may lead to a downward shift of the schedule.

Tobin's Theory of Money Demand

An important objection to the theory of speculative demand given here is that the classification of the market into "bulls" and "bears" does not allow for portfolio diversification. A bull, for example, would never wish to hold money, while a bear would never wish to hold securities. This is because both groups have definite notions of the future course of interest rates.

James Tobin, in an important article,[3] has made use of the notion of risk in his explanation of the interest elasticity of the demand for money. As he shows, people can vary their asset holdings in a way which gives varying combinations of risk and return. If only money is held, both risk and return on assets will be zero. If only securities are held, both return and risk will be maximized. Risk is measured by the expected stability in value of the securities purchased. An unfavorable decline in prices can wipe out interest income, and more.

Tobin would argue that most people are risk averters, willing to accept lower return in exchange for less risk. The way people do this is to diversify their assets between money and securities. Diversification, however, does not mean fixed holdings. If interest rates increase, people may find it advantageous to reduce money holdings and increase their security holdings, since the extra risk is compensated for by higher earnings. Conversely, a lower interest return should increase the demand for money and reduce the demand for securities.

As can readily be seen, a world dominated by risk averters would lead to a negatively sloped L_2 demand for money, as shown in Graph 10.2. Tobin's theory also has the virtue of explaining the obvious fact that asset owners diversify their holdings. Indeed, in Tobin's model it is mainly "risk lovers" who do not. These people attach a positive utility to risk; hence they tend always to hold securities, rather than money, even at very high interest rates. Needless to say, if these people dominated the asset markets we could not draw a well-behaved L_2 function for money, such as in Graph 10.2.

---

[3] Liquidity Preference as Behavior Towards Risk," *Review of Economic Studies*, February, 1958.

EQUILIBRIUM IN THE MONEY MARKET

The demand for money is evidently jointly determined by the level of transactions and interest rates. If we assume that the transactions vary in proportion to the level of national income, we may represent the demand for money as the *sum* of L_1 and L_2 demand:

$$L \equiv L_1 + L_2, \text{ or, if } L_1 \equiv L_1(Y) \text{ and } L_2 \equiv L_2(i), \tag{1}$$
$$L \equiv L_1(Y) + L_2(i). \tag{2}$$

L is the total demand for money. It is the amount of money people *wish to hold* at various interest rates and income levels. The amount *actually held* depends upon how much money exists in the economy at any moment of time. In most advanced economies the latter is controlled by the monetary authorities. Hence we represent it as a given quantity, M.

The amount of money in existence may either exceed or fall short of the amount of money people wish to hold. Suppose $M > L$. Two choices are open to the public. It can reduce its excess monetary holdings by increasing its purchases of goods, in which event, of course, national income will rise. The rise in national income, in turn, will expand the transactions demand for money and thus work to reduce the excess supply of money. The second option open to holders of excess money balances is to increase the portion of their portfolios devoted to securities. Increased purchases of securities should raise their prices and lower interest rates. Lower interest rates, in turn, work to increase the amount of money demanded and reduce the excess supply of money. If $M < L$, the opposite adjustments should occur: the excess demand for money should be eliminated by a fall in national income and a rise in interest rates.

Equilibrium in the money market requires that $M = L$, that the amount of money people wish to hold equals the existing stock of money. The equation for identity (2) allows us to rewrite this condition as

$$M = L_1(Y) + L_2(i), \tag{3}$$

which makes it clear that the demand for money equilibrates with the supply through both income and interest rate adjustments.

If we also wish to recognize the possible interest rate effects upon the transactions demand for money, the latter can be written as $L_1 \equiv L_1$ (i, Y). In doing so, however, it would be superfluous to write an additional expression for the speculative demand for money, L_2, since the latter is a function of the interest rate. Hence, some writers now write the total demand for money as

$$L \equiv L(i, Y), \qquad (4)$$

thus eliminating the symbolic distinction between the two types of monetary demand. We shall not follow this practice here, since it is pedagogically convenient to retain the identity of the principal types of balances people wish to hold, even though there is some artificiality in the distinction.

Graphical Derivation of Money Market Equilibrium

Graph 10.3 describes the properties of money market equilibrium. All directions should be read as positive. Hence, as we travel from the zero origin, north, east, south, or west, the variable in question grows in value, always maintaining a positive sign. Quadrant IV describes the transactions, or L_1 demand for money. It is really Graph 10.1 with its ordinate pointed down. Quadrant II is Graph 10.2 with its abscissa

GRAPH 10.3

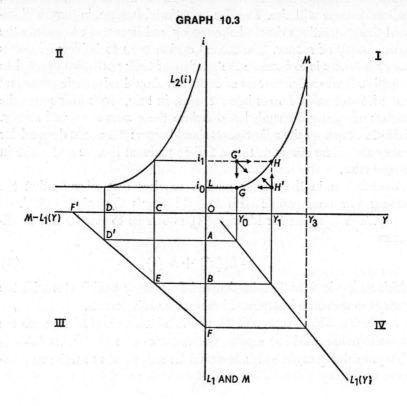

pointed west instead of east. It is still the speculative, or L_2 demand for money. Quadrants I and III are described below.

Assume national income to have settled at Y_0. According to the function $L_1(Y)$, people may wish to hold OA in transactions balances. Now, the money stock is presumed to be fixed by the monetary authorities. Hence if the stock exceeds the amount people wish to hold for transaction purposes a surplus will be available for use as speculative balances. According to equation (3), this would be M *minus* $L_1(Y_0)$. In the diagram, $L_1(Y_0)$ is OA. The total money stock is OF. Hence the amount available for speculative purposes is $OF - OA$, or AF. Plot OD equal to AF. OD is the money stock available for speculative uses when income is Y_0. Since AD' is equal to OD, D' is a point on FF' indicating division of the money stock between transactions and speculative balances.

Indeed, every point on FF' indicates a division of the money stock between the two uses. Try point E. If income is Y_1, transactions demand will be OB. Since the surplus of money over L_1 demand is BF, draw OC equal to BF. Since BE is the same length as OC, E is a point on FF' indicating a division of the money stock between L_1 and L_2 demands.

Point F indicates that the income level is such that the whole money stock is devoted to transactions demand, with none of it going to speculative uses. Point F', on the other hand, indicates a zero transactions demand and a complete absorption of money into speculative uses. F and F' are clearly extreme points, equal in distance from the origin.

Suppose in fact that income is at Y_0. Our diagram indicates that OD will be available for speculative purposes. Will the public hold that much? The answer depends on the interest rate. According to the $L_2(i)$ function in quadrant IV, the public will hold OD speculative balances if the rate of interest is i_0. Indeed, if the interest rate and the level of income accidentally settle at i_0 and Y_0, the money market will be in equilibrium, for then the demand for money, OA plus OD, will equal the supply of money, OF. That is

$$M = L_1(Y_0) + L_2(i_0),$$
$$(OF) = (OA) + (OD).$$

Point G in quadrant I represents the combination of interest and income—i_0 and Y_0—which make the demand and supply of money equal. Point H in the same quadrant, on the other hand, records a combination of i_1 and Y_1. This, too, is a combination which makes the demand for money to hold equal to its supply. Why so?

Assume that income is increased from Y_0 to Y_1. The transactions demand for money will now rise to OB, leaving OC $(= BF)$ left for use as speculative balances. The money market is now out of equilibrium, for, at an interest rate i_0, people will wish to hold OD speculative balances. OD exceeds OC, the available money for use as speculative balances. In other words, so long as the quantity of money remains at OF, and interest remains at i_0, an income level of Y_1 will promote an excess demand for money ($= DC$). People will attempt to acquire this money by selling off securities; hence, security prices must fall and the interest rate must rise. At an interest rate of i_1, the excess demand for money will disappear and the money market will be in equilibrium. Point H describes the new equilibrium combination of interest and income.

Every point on LM describes a combination of interest and income which promotes equilibrium in the money market. Given the supply of money, and given time for adjustment of demand and supply, both in the money market and in the commodity markets, interest and income should settle somewhere along the LM function. In describing LM, however, it is conventional to assume a given level of income for the purpose of finding the interest rate which equates the supply and demand for money. Hence LM can be called a "money market equilibrium curve." Given the stock of money, LM describes the interest rate which each level of income promotes.

If points on LM describe positions of money market equilibrium, other point in quadrant I must be points of disequilibrium, where the demand for money either exceeds or falls short of the supply of money. Try point H'. Here the interest rate is i_0 and the level of income is Y_1. Transactions demand for money is OB, leaving OC available for speculative purposes. At i_0, however, the demand for speculative balances is OD. Hence excess demand for money exists and, if we assume Y_1 to hold, the interest rate must rise. The upward pressure on the interest rate is indicated by the vertical arrow attached to H'. Acually, *for any point to the right of LM, the pressure on interest will be in an upward direction,* provided of course that the particular income level is assumed constant and the supply of money does not change. The reader ought to experiment with other combinations of interest and income to the right of LM in order to verify this assertion.

Similarly, *any point to the left of LM indicates an excess supply of money and a downward pressure on the interest rate.* This is illustrated by point G'. Here the transactions demand for money is OA. OD is available for speculative purposes, while OC is demanded for the same purpose. An excess supply of money, DC, therefore exists when the interest rate is i_1 and income is Y_0. The holders of the excess money stock will attempt to get rid of it by purchasing securities. This drives security prices up and the interest rate down. Hence, so long as Y_0 holds and the money supply remains fixed, i_1 is an unstable interest rate, tending to fall. Such will be true for any interest rate to the left of LM.

It must be evident to the careful reader that our description of the process of money market equilibration could have proceeded in a different way. We have adopted the convention of assuming a given level of income and watching the interest rate adjust to the point where the excess demand or supply for money is eliminated. A different procedure would have been to assume that the demand and supply for speculative balances was in equilibrium. In this event, our interest rate would be fixed and income would be the adjusting dependent variable. For example, suppose that the interest rate is i_1 and that people actually hold OC in speculative balances. This is but another way of saying that the interest rate is such that the proportion of money held in portfolios in relation to other assets is equal to the proportion which people actually wish to hold. But since the money supply is OF', people are holding CF' which may be used for transaction purposes. By construction, CF' equals OB. OB is the level of transactions balances people would hold if income were Y_1. Assume income to be only Y_0. It follows that an excess of AB in transactions balances exists. Hence, since the interest rate of i_1 promotes an equilibrium holding of money in relation to other portfolio assets, the excess quantity of money should be used to purchase goods. Increased purchases of goods will take place, driving income up until it reaches Y_1, at which point the demand for transactions balances equals the money available for use as transactions balances.

Income adjustment as a method for equating the demand and supply of money could be shown by an arrow extending horizontally from G', or any other point, in the direction of LM. In this way of looking at things, a point to the left of LM indicates an excess demand for goods. A point to the right would indicate an excess supply of goods, since transactions balances would fall short of the amount necessary to carry the level of income indicated by the point.

This discussion should make it evident that a point to the left of LM may represent either an excess demand for goods or an excess demand for securities, or both. This is because so long as $M > L_1(Y) + L_2(i)$, the excess supply of money can be utilized to purchase either goods or securities. Hence, instead of a point like G' moving either vertically or horizontally until it bumps into LM, the point should move in an intermediate direction, such as shown in the diagram. The same may be said of a point to the right of LM, since such a point can represent an excess demand for money which can be satisfied by both a reduction of goods purchases or a sale of securities.

However true the argument of the preceding paragraph, we can still use a simplifying assumption: the adjustment of income takes time—time for the excess demand for goods to express itself in depleted inventories, extra production, and increased employment. Security markets, on the other hand, are well organized and portfolio adjustments can take place swiftly. Hence, we should expect the interest rate to adjust more rapidly than income to any excess supply of money. For this reason, the principal movement from a point such as G' should be in the downward direction. In what follows, therefore, we shall be assuming that income moves slowly enough to allow people to be continually in possession of the transactions balances they wish to hold. Any surplus cash will be used to adjust portfolios in such a manner that the amount of money will also be the amount desired. Such an adjustment can only come through interest rate changes, which we shall assume to take place so rapidly that the combinations of income and interest will always be on the LM line. The reader should remember, however, that such an assumption is for convenience only.

Shape of the *LM* Function

The LM function will have a large or small slope, depending on the slopes of both the speculative demand function and the transactions demand function. If $L_2(i)$ in Graph 10.3 is steep, for example, LM will be steep. An $L_1(Y)$ function which inclines more toward the vertical than the graphed function will also steepen LM.

An extreme version of steepness of LM was implied by classical theory. Since classical economists denied all but the transactions demand for money, the speculative demand function in 10.3 would disappear. All existing money would then be used for transactions balances and a line, emanating from OF, would be drawn across $L_1(Y)$. The dotted vertical line stemming from Y_3 would then become the LM function. Such a vertical line means that any positive interest rate is compatible with the given level of income, a conclusion which describes the classical position.

Effects of Changes in the Demand for Money

If either the speculative or transactions demand function shifts, the LM function will also shift. Suppose, for example, that the "normal" range of interest rates increases. This implies that the $L_2(i)$ curve will shift up. Since we have not assumed a change in the transactions demand for money, the same amount of money will be available for speculative uses. Hence the interest rate should increase, regardless of the initial level of income. Higher interest, combined with the same initial level of income, will place the interest-income point above the previous point of *LM*. Since the same would be true for any income level, we have a new locus of points above the old *LM* curve. In effect, we have a new *LM* function.

An increase in the transactions demand for money would be indicated by a downward shift (in Graph 10.3) of the $L_2(Y)$ function. By tracing through the effects of the shift on the interest rate, the reader will see that the *LM* function is again shifted up. Hence, an increase in the demand for money, regardless of the source of the increase, will shift *LM* up. Conversely, *LM* will shift down with a fall in the demand for money.

Effects of Changes in Money Stock

So far we have worked with the assumption of a constant money stock. Suppose now that the money stock is increased. Our assumption that people are always holding the transaction balances they wish to hold means that the increased money stock becomes available to satisfy the speculative demand for money. But if people were previously satisfied with the speculative balances they held, they are now holding a surplus of such balances. In attempting to get rid of the excess balances, people will drive up bond prices and cause the interest rate to fall. This effect is shown in Graph 10.4, where an increase in the money stock to OF_1 from OF is indicated. If income holds at Y_1, the full increase in money is devoted to an increase in speculative balances, measured by CC'. This results in a fall in the interest rate to i_0 from i_1, the former equilibrium rate.

The fall in interest means that *LM* no longer describes the locus of equilibrium interest rates, for the new combination equilibrium interest rate and income is i_0 and Y_1: point H' rather than point H. Since the increase in the money stock would have lowered the equilibrium interest rate for any level of income, we have, in effect, a new curve of equilibrium in the money market—LM'.

The only exception to the above statement is the interest rate i_0. Since the $L_2(i)$ function is flat at that rate, indicating an infinite demand for money, an increase in the money stock will not decrease i.

As we have seen, there may be a rate such as i_0, indicating that the public will absorb the increase in speculative balances without the neces-

GRAPH 10.4

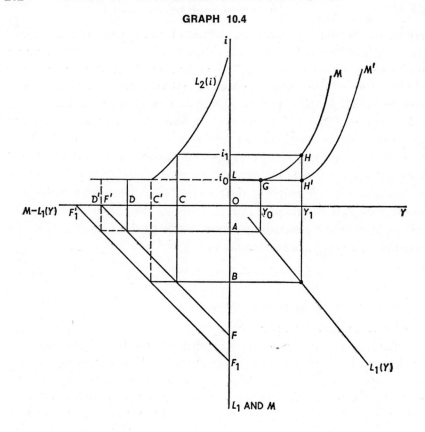

sity of being induced to do so through a drop in interest. If the latter is too low, the cost of switching into securities, or the belief on everyone's part that interest rates are going to rise, will cause the additional money to be hoarded without interest rate repercussions. If such a "liquidity trap" does exist, the increase in the money supply will extend the flat portion of the *LM* curve, since (for example) at some income levels above Y_0 interest rates will already have been lowered to i_0.

An increase in the money stock shifts *LM* down and to the right. Decreases in the money stock, on the other hand, shift the function up and to the left. The reader need only reverse the preceding argument to see why this is so.

Effects of Changes in the Price Level

If the prices of all goods and services doubled, people would wish to hold twice the number of dollars they held before the change in prices. The reason is that to effect the same volume of transactions in goods or services they would need twice the amount of money they needed before. The same proposition should hold for both precautionary and speculative balances, since both of these money demands are for the purpose of effecting future transactions in goods or services, whose prices will also have doubled if people expect the new price level to be maintained.

In equation (3) we did not explicitly consider the price level, since up to that point we were working with an assumption of constant prices. Now that we are considering price level variations, we must rewrite that equation as follows: Let M be the number of dollars made available by the authorities for people to hold. Let $P \cdot L$ be the number of dollars people wish to hold, where P is the price level and L is the demand for dollars of constant purchasing power. Since $L = L_1(Y) + L_2(i)$, we have the following variant of equation (3):

$$M = P \cdot L = P[L_1(Y) + L_2(i)], \text{ or} \tag{3a}$$

$$\frac{M}{P} = L_1(Y) + L_2(i). \tag{3b}$$

Equation (3b) says that the money market will be in equilibrium if the demand for *real* money balances equals the supply of real balances. The supply of real balances is the number of dollars made available by the authorities times the "purchasing power" of each dollar, defined as $1/P$. A rise in the price level lowers the purchasing power of each dollar; hence, it also lowers the supply of real balances. Conversely, a drop in prices raises the supply of real balances. Because of this property, whenever the price level varies, the effect is much like a change in the money supply in Graph 10.4. For example, an increase in real balances following a decline in the price level would show up in Graph 10.4 as a shift in the FF' curve to say $F_1F'_1$. This shift would, as in the diagram, cause a movement of the LM function to LM'. By similar analogy, a rise in the price level would shift the LM function to the left.

The economic reasoning behind the conclusion of the previous paragraph is relatively straightforward. Consider a decline in prices. Such a decline means that people can purchase the same number of goods and services with fewer dollars. If the price level change is expected to persist, people need fewer precautionary and speculative balances as well. Hence, dollars are "released" and they become available to spend upon other things. Graph 10.4 assumes that the released dollars go initially to purchase securities. The increased demand for securities drives the interest rate down until the speculative demand for money absorbs all of the released money. Opposite reasoning leads to the conclusion that the interest rate increases as a result of an increase in the price level.

Whether or not these interest rate changes resulting from price level variations will be permanent or temporary depends upon conditions in the markets for goods and services. Later in this chapter we shall consider this problem. Here, we only wish to establish that increases (or decreases) in the price level will, taken alone, have the effect of shifting the *LM* function to the left (or to the right).

Commodity Market Equilibrium: The *IS* Function

The *LM* function describes a locus of possible money market equilibria. Clearly, we cannot arbitrarily pick an interest rate-income combination and call it the equilibrium level of income and interest. In order to find a unique combination which we can identify as an equilibrium, we need the further information which can be provided only by the demand and supply for goods. For this we need only to summarize what we have learned in earlier chapters.

Our device for summarizing the commodity market information will be a four-quadrant diagram relating the level of interest to investment, saving, and income. As before, we shall assume that the supply of goods is highly elastic, so that changes in the demand for goods are paralleled by a similar increase in supply.

Consider Graph 10.5. Quadrant III shows an investment demand function relating the level of investment spending to the rate of interest. The only difference between this function and earlier ones is the direction of the ordinate and abscissa, which have been pointed south and west rather than north and east, as is usual. Quadrant IV shows the familiar relationship between investment, saving, and the level of income. Here, the ordinate points down instead of the usual up. The line in quadrant II is simply a 45 degree helping-line, showing the identity, $i \equiv i$. As we shall see, the *IS* function in quadrant I indicates a locus of alternative equilibria in the markets for goods and services.

Our present purpose is to derive the *IS* function, or the relationship between the interest rate and equilibrium levels of production. Start with any rate of interest, say i_0. The investment demand function in quadrant III tells us that businessmen will settle at a rate of investment spending of I_1; hence income must rise by enough to equate saving to that level of investment. The level of income which equates saving to I_1 is shown in quadrant IV to be Y_1. So long as the interest rate holds at i_0, and so long as the investment demand and saving functions do not

GRAPH 10.5

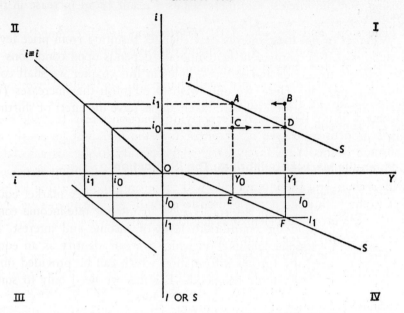

shift, the equilibrium will be maintained at Y_1. Moreover, since we have assumed that supply always rises to match demand, Y_1 also denotes an absence of either excess demand or supply of goods and services. Point D on the *IS* function denotes this equilibrium combination of interest and income for the commodity markets. Point A and every other point on *IS* is derived in a similar way.

Note that the derivation of *IS* proceeds from an arbitrarily assumed interest rate. Any disequilibrium must therefore be resolved through movements in income. Take, for instance, the combination of interest and income (i_0 and Y_0) at point C. A check of quadrant III will show that investment generated by i_0 is I_1, which is greater than the level of saving (Y_0E) generated by Y_0. National income is therefore below its equilibrium level and, through the familiar multiplier process, it should rise to Y_1. The direction of change is shown by the arrow at point C. Any point located to the left of *IS* indicates a level of income below the equilibrium level. Hence, any time such a point occurs it will move in the direction indicated by the arrow at point C.

The reverse will be true of all points to the right of *IS*. Point B, for example, reveals an interest rate (i_1) which causes investment to be I_0. But an income level of Y_1 produces Y_1F of saving, which is larger than

I_0. Hence national income must fall, as is indicated by the arrow at point B.[4]

The slope and position of the *IS* function are determined by the slopes and positions of the investment demand function and the saving function. A steep investment demand function means that any change in interest rates produces only small changes in the level of investment spending. Hence the multiplier has little to work with and the change in income will not be great. A steep saving function means that the marginal propensity to save is large (or that the marginal propensity to consume is small). A large marginal propensity to save is associated with a small multiplier. Any change in investment spending associated with a change in the interest rate will therefore produce a smaller rise in income with a large, as opposed to a small, propensity to save. The steeper the investment demand function and the saving function, then, the steeper will be the *IS* function.

The position of the *IS* function likewise depends on the investment and saving functions. If either or both shift away from the origin in Graph 10.5, the *IS* function will also shift away from the origin. The reasoning is as follows: a shift of the investment demand function away from the origin means that at each interest rate a higher level of investment spending is induced. Hence, if the saving function remains unchanged, a higher level of income will now be necessary to equate saving to the new level of investment. Since this would be true regardless of the initial interest rate we started with, the higher level of income would be associated with the same rate of interest. The *IS* function would now lie to the right of its former position. Similar reasoning would be applied to a rightward shift of the saving function, except that the rise in income would be induced by a fall in the rate of saving rather than an increase in investment spending.

The reader should experiment with various shapes and positions of both the investment demand function and the saving function to familiarize himself with the impact these changes might have upon the shape and position of the *IS* function.

---

[4] The points always move in a horizontal direction because of the arbitrary assumption of a constant interest rate. The classical analysis (Chapter 3) assumes that gaps between saving and investment lead to interest rate adjustments in the capital markets. Hence, if we combined the classical with Keynesian analysis, arrows from disequilibrium points would point up and down as well as right and left, indicating adjustments of both income and interest in response to disequilibrium in the commodity markets. In the present discussion, however, we are assuming that the interest rate reflects equilibrium in the money markets. Such an assumption means that points like B or C fall on an *LM* function (not shown in Graph 10.5).

Interdependency of Interest and Income

The *LM* functions of Graphs 10.3 and 10.4 tell us that the rate of interest is dependent upon the level of income. The *IS* function of Graph 10.5, on the other hand, shows that the level of income is dependent upon the rate of interest. We cannot, in other words, have either without the other. Interest and income are mutually determined and determining. They are interdependent.

To find the equilibrium level of income and interest we need a diagram such as Graph 10.6, in which the *IS* and *LM* functions are super-

GRAPH 10.6

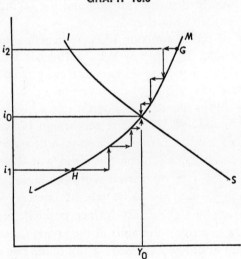

imposed upon each other. Equilibrium interest and income are indicated in the diagram at i_0 and Y_0.

There are several ways of showing why i_0 and Y_0 are equilibrium values. Consider the meaning of a point on the *LM* function. Any interest rate on the *LM* function implies that the money market is in equilibrium: that the amount of money demanded and supplied are the same at the indicated combination of interest and income. A point on the *IS* function means that the amount of goods and services demanded and supplied are the same; that saving neither exceeds nor falls short of investment. Hence, a point which falls on both the *IS* and the *LM* function indicates that equilibrium prevails in both the money market and the commodities markets. So long as the basic conditions of the economy remain unchanged, there is no reason to expect the interest rate and the income level to change from i_0 and Y_0.

Another way to see the nature of the equilibrium rate of interest and income is to consider interest rates both above and below i_0. If the interest rate is i_2, for example, the economy will find itself at point G. Point G is not a stable point because it is to the right of the IS function; hence a state of excess supply $(S > I)$ will exist in the markets for goods and services. National income should fall. As income falls, money is released from transactions balances and becomes available for the purchase of securities. This puts downward pressure on the interest rate. However, even if the money market does equilibrate at a lower interest rate, so long as the point on LM lies to the right of IS income will continue to fall and the interest rate will come under a downward pressure. The path of adjustment is indicated by the linked arrows starting at point G. Once the point lies on both LM and IS, the process will stop. This is at i_0 and Y_0.

The reasoning for interest rates below i_0 is symmetrical to that above. Point H, for example, shows i_1 to be an interest rate which brings the money market into equilibrium at the indicated level of national income. The latter, however, is not an equilibrium quantity, for it stands to the left of IS, indicating an excess demand for goods and services $(I > S)$. Hence national income should begin to rise, increasing the demand for transactions balances and setting up an excess demand for money. So long as a point on LM stands to the left of IS, the upward pressure on the demand for money will persist, and the interest rate will rise. Once the combination i_0 and Y_0 is reached, however, the excess demand for both goods and money will disappear and the economy will be in equilibrium.

Changes in Equilibrium Level of Income and Interest

The IS–LM diagram is useful because it provides us with a direct way of analyzing the impact upon the economy of a rather broad class of events which might occur. We need only decide whether the event strikes the money market, the market for goods and services, or both. Then, given certain presumptions about the general shapes of IS or LM, we can use the diagram to predict the probable direction of change of interest rates and/or national income.

Disturbances in the economy which affect the commodity markets directly, for example, are fluctuations in investment demand, changes in

government spending, shifts in the consumption function (either independently or from tax changes), and changes in net exports. Graph
10.7(a) shows that increases in any one of these items will shift the *IS*

GRAPH 10.7

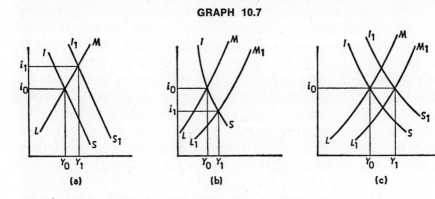

(a)   (b)   (c)

function to the right. If the supply and demand for money, in the meantime, remain unchanged, such a shift will raise both interest and income.

A disturbance, of course, may be directed solely to the money market. An increase in bank reserves, for example, should lead banks to expand the money supply. Under these conditions, a shift to the right of
the *LM* function, Graph 10.7(b), will cause an *expansion* of income
and a *fall* in the interest rate. Similar results would obtain from a fall
in the demand for money accompanied by an increase in the demand for
securities.

Graph 10.7(c) describes a simultaneous shift in both *LM* and *IS*.
Such a situation could arise, for example, from an increase in government spending financed by increases in the money supply, with banks
purchasing debt issued by the government. In the graph, the shift in *IS*
is matched by the shift in *LM*; hence, the interest rate remains constant
and income rises by more than it would if the increased government
spending were financed by sales of debt to the nonbank public. This
latter case, illustrated by Graph 10.7(a), would require a bidding up of
interest rates in order to entice the necessary money away from its
owners. Rising interest rates would reduce private investment spending
and hence offset somewhat the positive impact upon income of the increased government spending.

Changes in private spending will also have different effects on the interest rate and income, depending upon how these changes are financed.
If increases in business and/or consumer spending are financed by new

bank money, for example, the rightward shift of the *IS* function will be joined by a rightward shift of the *LM* function, just as in the case of increased government spending financed by bank purchased debt issues. Increases in private spending which are not financed by new bank money may also be directly financed by simultaneous reductions in the demand for either speculative balances or precautionary balances by those consumers and businessmen who have increased their demand for goods. Analytically, expenditures financed in this way can also be represented as a simultaneous shift to the right of both *IS* and *LM*. Finally, increases in private spending which are financed neither by an increase in the money supply nor by a decrease in the demand for money may be represented as in Graph 10.7(a). Consumers or businessmen will issue securities which, in order to entice holders of cash balances to part with their money, must bear higher interest rates than those prevailing before the increase in the demand for goods. This latter case is similar to the one in which an increase in government spending is financed by sales of securities to the nonbank sector of the economy.

Modification of the Multiplier

The theory of the multiplier presented in Chapters 4 and 5 must be modified in the light of materials presented in this chapter. The earlier discussion ignored money market conditions. Hence, changes in investment or government spending were simply multiplied by the multiplier in order to derive predicted changes in national income. No attention was paid to the way in which the changes in investment or government spending are financed. The conclusions of the previous section, however, show that the method of financing new expenditures makes considerable difference to the final result. An increase in investment or government spending financed by changes in the money stock produces a full multiplier effect, since no increases in interest rates intervene to choke off part of the increase in spending. When investment and government spending are partially or not at all financed by increases in the money stock, the expansion of national income may be accompanied by increasing interest rates. Hence part of the initial increases in investment or government spending are likely to be offset by declines in spending induced by rising interest rates. Under these conditions, the full multiplier effect is not to be expected.

There is one important case in which the method of finance does not matter to the multiplier. Suppose that the speculative demand for money has a highly elastic floor. This would produce a flat portion in the LM function, as with line i_0M_1 in Graph 10.7(c), if the latter is designated as the LM function. If the increase in government or investment spending shifts the IS function to I_1S_1 from its initial lower position, the full multiplier effect will operate, whether or not the increase in spending has been financed by new money.

This is obviously a special case. Nevertheless, it represents a possible condition in a severe depression. In times of high employment, however, the condition is not likely. Hence, we must conclude the modification of the multiplier analysis presented in this section is necessary for most situations. Predictions of changes in national income based upon predicted changes in investment and government spending must always take money market conditions into account.

Summary

In this chapter we have shown how the theory of interest, as a phenomenon of the money market, may be integrated into the theory of income, a phenomenon of the market for goods. We have argued that true equilibrium in the economy entails equilibrium in both markets. Moreover, since the rate of interest and the level of income affect both the demand for goods and the demand for money, general equilibrium implies an interdependency between interest and income, in the sense that there is only one interest rate and one level of income consistent with equilibrium in both the goods market and the money market. The $IS-LM$ apparatus was used to demonstrate this proposition.

The apparatus was also used to show how the method of financing income changes affects the multiplier. Under most conditions, it is necessary to look at changes in the supply and demand for money before a judgment can be made about the size of the impact of changes in government spending, taxes, investment spending, or in the propensity to consume.

ADDITIONAL READINGS

BAUMOL, W. J. "The Transactions Demand for Cash—An Inventory Theoretic Approach," Quarterly *Journal of Economics,* November, 1952. A seminal article on the transactions demand for money.

BRUNNER K. and MELTZER, A. H. "Predicting Velocity: Implications for Theory and Policy," *Journal of Finance,* May, 1963. An empirical "horserace" between various theories of the demand for money.

HICKS, J. R. "Mr. Keynes and the Classics," *Econometrica*, April, 1937. Reprinted "everywhere," most recently in H. R. WILLIAMS and J. O. HUFFNAGLE, eds., *Macroeconomic Theory: Selected Readings*. New York: Appleton-Century-Crofts, 1969. Original statement of *IS-LM* apparatus.

LAIDLER, D. *The Demand For Money: Theories and Evidence*. Scranton, Pa. International Textbook Co., 1969. A useful review of many of the topics in this chapter.

PATINKIN, D. *Money, Interest, and Prices*. 2d ed.; New York: Harper and Row, 1965. A modern classic dealing with a number of the issues raised in this and the next two chapters.

Chapter 11

CONTRASTS IN KEYNESIAN AND CLASSICAL THEORY: EMPLOYMENT

In Chapter 3 we developed the main content of classical macroeconomics. Recall that full employment was taken to be the norm of the classical system and that failure of the system to achieve full employment could be attributed to the inflexibility of money wages or interest rates. In this chapter we shall see how Keynesian theory explains the possibility of persistent unemployment. We shall then contrast Keynesian with classical explanations of the phenomena. After that, we shall take up certain amendments to the classical analysis made in recent years in order to rebut Keynesian explanations.

The Liquidity Trap

Many Keynesians seek to explain the persistence of unemployment in periods of depression by several routes. First, they believe peculiarities in the demand for money might prevent the proper functioning of the capital market. Second, they believe that the capital market itself, even in the absence of barriers in the money market, might not work properly. Third, they also have a special view of the functioning of the labor market. We shall take up these points in order.

Assume the labor market to function in the way the classical economists described it. This means that unemployment would ordinarily put enough pressure upon money wages to reduce them by enough to bring full employment into existence. As shown in Graph 11.1(a), wage and price flexibility would bring about a real wage of $(W/P)_0$ and an employment level of N_0. N_0 is a full-employment level because all the workers willing to work at the given real wage are employed. Full employment would bring about a level of output Y_0, as shown by the production function in Graph 11.1(b). Graph 11.1(d) is merely a helping diagram, which allows us to show the relation in Graph 11.1(c) of the full-employment level of output to the level of aggregate demand.

223

GRAPH 11.1

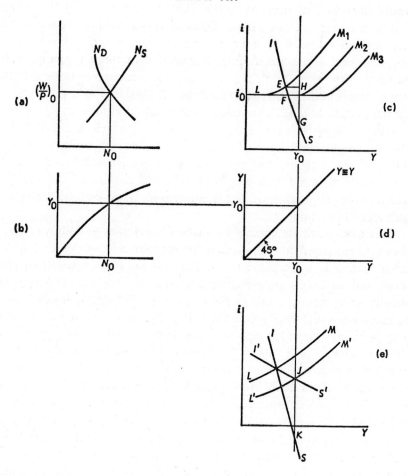

The crucial question at hand is whether the full-employment level of output will be matched by a high enough level of demand to maintain that level of output. If demand chronically falls short of this level, full employment cannot be maintained.

Chapter 10 was devoted to a description of the forces which operate in the money and commodity markets to produce equilibrium levels of expenditure and interest. The point where the *IS* and *LM* functions cross determines these levels. In Graph 11.1(c), for example, the intersection of *IS* with LM_1 determines an interest-income combination at point *E*. Recall that such an intersection implies a given stock of money and price level. A fall in prices or an increase in the quantity of money would shift the *LM* function to the right. In the case illustrated in the graph, however, the speculative demand function underlying the *LM* function has a floor at an interest rate of i_0, resulting from the liquidity trap discussed in the last chapter. Increases in the money supply, or reductions in the price level, therefore cannot reduce the interest rate below i_0. Shifts in the *LM* function will be accompanied by a stretching of the flat portion of the *LM* function, as with LM_2 and LM_3.

Point *E* shows a level of aggregate demand which is clearly below the full-employment level of output. Moreover, given the conditions shown in the diagram, full employment cannot be maintained, even if temporarily achieved. Full employment would require an *LM* function which crosses *IS* at point *G*. The liquidity trap, however, would preclude such an *LM* function.

This particular case implies a continuous deflation of both wages and prices. Consider an initial position for the economy at point *E*. If the labor market is in equilibrium, output will be at its full-employment level, and an excess supply of goods equal to *EH* will appear. This should set in motion a fall in the price level. If full employment is to be maintained, the wage level must fall in the same proportion as prices. The reduction in wages and prices, however, will release transaction balances and force a fall in the interest rate. So long as the released transaction balances are incorporated into securities, the price of the latter will rise and the interest rate will fall. However, if the money released by the fall in prices and wages is incorporated into idle balances, the interest rate will not fall. The case illustrated in Graph 11.1(c) assumes a stabilization of interest at i_0. At that rate, aggregate demand is still short of the full-employment level of output by an amount *FH*. Hence wages and prices will continue their downward course, unless businessmen reduce output to the level indicated at point *F*, or unless some force intervenes to lift the *IS* function (say increased consumption or investment demand) so that it intersects the vertical full-employment income line at i_0.

We shall discuss the forces which may automatically shift the *IS* function to the right later in the chapter. Here, however, it is important to describe the conditions resulting from a liquidity trap and flexible wage and price levels. So long as wage and price flexibility assure the maintenance of the real wage at $(W/P)_0$, businessmen will be induced to attempt a full-employment level of production. However, since aggregate demand in the model under discussion always falls short of aggregate supply, the full-employment level of production will go partly unsold. Hence businessmen will be forced periodically to cut back output in order to clean out their undesired accumulations of inventories. Once such inventories are reduced, however, there is nothing in this particular model which prevents them from attempting to raise production back to the full-employment level. Hence, the model implies a condition of continuous deflation with production fluctuating between its full-employment level and below. Moreover, under these conditions, expansion of the money supply will be useless, since any such increase will run off into hoards.

"Defects" in the Capital Market

Removal of the liquidity trap does not necessarily solve the unemployment problem. To illustrate, suppose that the whole *LM* function shifts to the right as either deflation takes place or the authorities increase the money stock. There may be no *positive* rate of interest which can induce enough spending to bring aggregate demand into equality with the full-employment level of production. Such a situation is illustrated in Graph 11.1(e), where the *IS* function intersects the full-employment vertical at point *K*. Point *K* requires a negative rate of interest in order to equate aggregate demand and supply. Such a rate of interest is impossible in a money using economy, since lenders would prefer to store their savings in money form at a zero rate of interest (with negligible storage costs) rather than pay borrowers for the privilege of lending to them, which is what a negative interest rate implies.

Evidently, this case requires a very steep *IS* function to be at all meaningful. Recall the forces which give shape to the *IS* function. First, there is the possibility of a steep investment demand function. Such an investment demand function could go at least part of the way in producing a steep *IS* function. Another force would be an interest-insensitive saving function. Such insensitivity was assumed by Keynes, and indeed is still assumed by most economists, since there is little empirical evidence to deny it. Finally, a low value for the expenditure multiplier would also contribute to a steep *IS* function. A high marginal propensity to save and/or a low marginal propensity to invest would reduce the impact of any increase in investment or consumption spending stimulated by changes in the interest rate.

All of the forces enumerated here *could* produce a steep *IS* function. It is an empirical question, of course, as to whether they *do* produce such a function. The importance of the question should, however, be underlined; for there are those who believe that the *IS* function is relatively flat, as with $I'S'$ in Graph 11.1(e). Such a function requires only slight deflation or monetary expansion to raise aggregate demand into equality with full-employment output. The steeper the IS function (i.e., the more dominant the above enumerated forces), the more of a burden will price flexibility and/or monetary expansion have in reviving the economy. The diagram in 11.1(e) illustrates an extreme form of this problem.

This particular case, incidentally, is labeled as one in which there are "defects" in the capital market for two reasons. The first is the assumed lack of response of saving to changes in the rate of interest, and the second is the assumed weak response of investment to interest changes. If cuts in the interest rate produce negligible increases in investment spending and only minor reductions in the rate of saving, the capital market, as certainly viewed by classical theorists, would be defective; for, it is fluctuations in the rate of interest upon which the classicals depended in order to maintain aggregate spending at a full-employment level.

Functioning of the Labor Market

Both of the cases—the liquidity trap and the "defective" capital market—were given in the context of a classical labor market, wherein both money wages and commodity prices were assumed to be completely flexible. As already indicated in Chapter 3, Keynes believed money wages to be relatively inflexible, in that institutional barriers such as trade unions would prevent a collapse of money wages in the face of unemployment. Following Keynes, we may assume that money wages are either perfectly inflexible, or at least less flexible than commodity prices. In this event, as we shall see, neither a liquidity trap nor special assumptions about the interest responsivness of investment and saving are needed to explain prolonged unemployment.

In Graph 11.2(c), assume that a decline in investment demand occurs. If the economy had initially been at full employment, aggregate demand would have equaled full-employment aggregate supply at point Z, where IS and LM cross the vertical line stemming from Y_0. The full-employment equilibrium real wage would have been W^*/P_0. The decline in investment spending, however, shifts the commodity equilibrium curve to $I'S'$. If prices are flexible downwards, the money market equilibrium curve will shift to $L'M'$ from LM. However, we are now assuming a sticky money wage rate. Hence the reduction in the

GRAPH 11.2

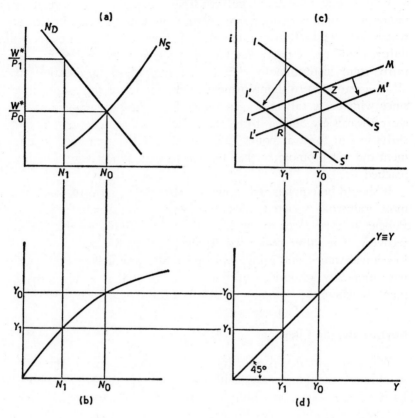

price level to P_1 raises the real wage rate to W^*/P_1. The higher real wage forces employers to contract their employment offers to N_1 from N_0, and production falls to Y_1.

What is the result as illustrated in Graph 11.2? First, aggregate demand is matched by the flow of production at point R. Second, because of the equality between demand and supply, the price level should stabilize at P_1. Hence, the real wage should rise no further. Unfortunately, the stabilization of prices will halt the rightward shift of the LM function as well, so that even if both LM and IS are "well-shaped," the full-employment point T, appropriate to the new IS function, cannot be reached. In other words, the economy will stabilize at a less-than-full-employment level of production. This is what Keynesians mean when they speak of an "underemployment equilibrium."

The underemployment equilibrium is clearly based upon sticky money wage rates. While we need not hold to this assumption, it is difficult to believe that modern wage standards, including government minimums and union bargained rates, would allow much flexibility in money wages. At best, such institutions would allow only limited over-all flexibility, made up of fairly flexible competitively determined wages and fairly rigid institutionally determined rates. Such a situation would allow a return to full employment in the model of the graphs in 11.2, since with every fall in wages below W^*, the production line would shift towards Y_0. Such a shift would allow further deflation and further shifts in LM towards point T. Eventually, if the continued unemployment did not promote further leftward shifts of IS, point T would be reached.

It should be emphasized, however, that under modern conditions in most industrial societies, such a recovery would take a long time. Policies to raise IS or to increase the money supply would give faster recovery. The latter policy would shift LM to the right, raise prices, lower real wages, and raise employment and production. Presumably, a wise monetary authority could so shift LM that it would cross IS at point T, where the economy is back to a full-employment level.

Keynes and the Classics

We have now discussed three conditions under which the economy would have considerable difficulty in attaining a full-employment state. Each of these cases—the liquidity trap, the "defective capital market," and wage rigidities—was discussed within the context of a Keynesian theoretical apparatus. The reader may recall the discussion in Chapter 3, wherein it was shown that the classical system could also be "rigged" to produce conditions of unemployment. Indeed, the rigging of the classical system performed in Chapter 3 was very similar to the situations developed in this chapter. It was shown there that a sticky interest rate, inelastic investment and saving schedules, intersecting at a negative interest rate, and an inflexible money wage rate could produce underemployment in the classical apparatus. Why, then, all the fuss and feathers about the "Keynesian Revolution"?

Among the principal contributions of Keynes' *General Theory* was the provisions of *explanations* for the rigidities which might afflict the adjustment mechanisms of the economy. The speculative demand for money, for example, was a brilliant and novel hypothesis which could provide an explanation of the downward inflexibility of interest rates. Again, the reformulation of the theory of labor supply, in which workers stipulate for money rather than real wage (as explained in Chapter 3), gave a reason for rigidity of the money wage rate. Finally, the rejection of an interest-sensitive saving function, gave a new perspective on the ability of the capital market to maintain full-employment aggregate demand at positive rates of interest. That we can now "rig" the classical system to obtain unemployment solutions is due to the fact that Keynes provided the hypotheses which made such rigging realistic.

It should also be noted that Keynesian and classical theory differ because the latter contains no multiplier. In a sense, this confirms our interpretation above that pre-Keynesian economists were not interested in using their model to explain persistent unemployment. An unemployment or income multiplier makes no sense in a classical labor market: the workings of such a market always guarantee full-employment equilibrium levels of production. Under such conditions, increases in expenditure merely change price levels, not employment and production. Keynes' argument that workers' behavior implies sticky money wages, however, leads to the possibility of underemployment equilibrium. Under such conditions, increases in aggregate demand can lead to the expansion of employment and output. Hence the environment for the working of a multiplier exists because of the special hypotheses made by Keynes.

Price Flexibility and Full Employment: Classical and Keynesian Views

Periods of depression and unemployment are often accompanied by assertions that labor is "pricing itself out of its market" and that the solution to unemployment problems is a general wage cut.

In the classical view, this argument centers upon the demand for labor. Unemployment is a symptom of an excessively high real wage. Hence, if real wages are reduced through cuts in the money wage, employment will expand. The increased level of output can always be sold because the interest rate mechanism guarantees that aggregate demand will increase by enough to match the increase in output. In other words, Say's Law guarantees that insufficiency of demand poses no barrier to the successful absorption of aggregate supply, whatever that supply might be. If wage cuts produce a full-employment level of output, it will be bought.

It is important to recall exactly why the classical economists believed that aggregate demand and supply would be equated. The increase in production and income which follows a cut in the real wage can flow into either consumption or saving. If income is allocated to saving it is the job of the capital market to see that excessive saving does not result in an excess supply of goods. For classical theory it is enough that the interest rate should respond to temporary surpluses of saving over investment. Such a surplus leads to a lowering of the interest rate, a reduction in saving (increase in consumption), and an increase in investment spending. The rate will continue to fall until surplus saving is eliminated, i.e., until aggregate demand rises by enough to match the new level of output.

The Keynesian view of the adjustment process is as follows: As in the classical system, money wage cuts leading to reductions in the real wage also expand employment and production. Again, the increase in saving is not matched by changes in investment spending; we have a surplus of saving. It is here, however, that the Keynesian analysis begins to differ. Since Keynes believed saving to be insensitive to the interest rate, any decline in the latter will stimulate investment, but not consumption. Hence, if the stimulus to investment is not much larger than it is under the classical system, aggregate demand will not rise by enough to absorb the full increase in production. Put another way, Keynes' denial of a significant interest-saving relationship meant that the investment demand schedule must either be more elastic than the classical schedule, or that the interest rate must fall by much more than it needs to in the classical system; otherwise, the increase in production will not be completely absorbed. As we have already seen, Keynes' liquidity trap and "defective capital market" hypotheses were designed to show how this latter might come about.

The "Keynes Effect"

Neither Keynes nor most classical economists believed that a general deflation of both wages and prices would have much direct effect upon the level of aggregate demand for final goods and services. Yet, we know that under a competitive economic system a deficiency of demand will lead to a cumulative deflation of prices. By assuming downward rigidity of money wages Keynes was able to argue that employment and output will fall rather than prices, particularly when either a liquidity trap or "defective capital market" exists. Hence he could have avoided the whole question of the relationship between aggregate demand and price level flexibility.

Keynes, nevertheless, did attempt an analysis of the effects of full wage-price flexibility upon aggregate demand. He proceeded by asking what effects a once-and-for-all decline in the price-wage level (assuming that all prices and wages move proportionately) would have upon the level of real expenditure. If the effect is neutral, he reasoned, no good can come from promoting a policy of deflation. If the effect is to increase real spending, more employment will ensue because output will have to rise in order to satisfy the additional demand for goods and services. If deflation reduces real spending, of course, it will have bad effects upon employment. Which of these three effects is most probable? Only an analysis of the spending of consumers, investors, and government can yield the answer.

The spending of investors is influenced by the marginal efficiency of capital, which underlies the investment demand schedule. A general reduction in wages and prices, with no further reductions (or increases) expected on the part of businessmen, should leave the marginal efficiency of capital unchanged. This is because prospective revenues, operating costs, and capital goods prices all fall together and to the same relative degree. An unchanged MEC means that real spending on the part of investors will not change, provided the interest rate remains the same.

Keynes thought that the main determinant of consumption spending is the level of disposable income. An overall decline in prices and wages, according to this analysis, will leave real consumption unchanged: since the lower prices of goods will be matched by a lower level of money income, consumers will be unable to increase their purchases.

Government spending acts much the same way. A cut in the prices and wages of the goods and labor services it buys will reduce its revenue needs. Assuming that taxes are reduced to the same degree as spending, the injections and leakages of government budgetary operations will leave the stream of real income and expenditure unchanged.

Since these three spending streams constitute all spending in a closed economy, Keynes believed that the *IS* function would remain unaffected by a general price and wage reduction. In an open economy, however, deflation would have a favorable effect upon net exports. A reduction in domestic prices encourages exports and discourages imports, especially if the reduction is not offset by increases in foreign tariffs and quotas or matched by price and wage declines abroad. This favorable effect is very important for countries such as Great Britain, which depends heavily upon net exports for its national income; but it is likely to have only a negligible effect upon income in the United States, where net exports are a small proportion of expenditure upon final output. If the I_1S_1 function of Graph 11.3(a) is that of the United States, therefore, we can say that an all-around proportionate decline in prices and wages will leave its position essentially unchanged, under the Keynesian analysis.

GRAPH 11.3

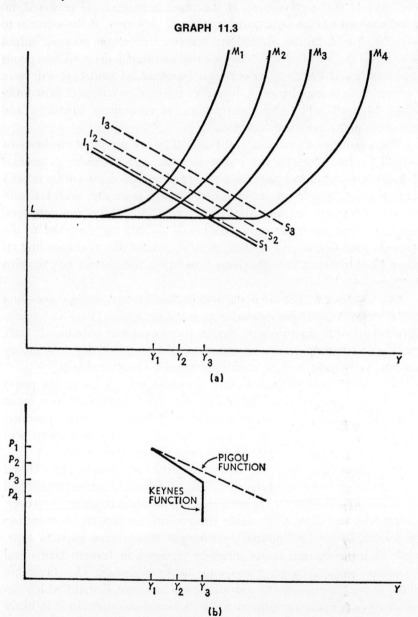

(a)

(b)

The same cannot be said for the *LM* function. The reduction in prices and wages reduces the need for transactions balances at all levels of real national income. The money so released now becomes available for use in the security markets, where bond prices will be driven up and interest ratio will be driven down. With lowered levels of commodity prices and wages, therefore, the *LM* function will shift to the right: except where the curve is horizontal, each level of real income will be associated with lower equilibrium levels of the interest rate. This is shown by the shift of the *LM* curve in Graph 11.3(a) from LM_1 to LM_2. LM_3 and LM_4 represent further declines in the price level.

Each shift in the money equilibrium curve brings a lower interest rate and a higher level of aggregate demand, even though the *IS* function has remained constant at I_1S_1. However, as LM shifts, the flat portion stretches out further to the right, indicating that more and more of the released transactions balances will flow into idle balances unless real income is greatly increased. Once the *IS* function cuts the *LM* function at the latter's floor, further cuts in the price level will have no influence upon the interest rate and national income. This is because additional releases of transactions balances will flow into idle balances rather than into the purchases of securities. Bonds will have become so high in price by this time that speculators, fearing a decline in capital values, will prefer to keep their assets in money form.

The reader will note that the Keynesian conclusion does not necessarily depend upon the existence of a liquidity trap. Even if no such trap exists, an interest-inelastic investment demand function would prevent a flexible interest rate from producing significant increases in aggregate demand.

The "Pigou Effect"

Keynes' reasoning leads to the proposition that price and wage reductions will increase national income and employment only so long as reductions in the interest rate can be counted upon to stimulate demand. After that point, however, further reductions in prices and wages will be of no avail, since income and employment will not be stimulated by any further increases in investment. Graph 11.3(b) shows that Y_3 is the highest level of demand compatible with a given stock of money and any price level. After prices fall below P_3, no further increases in income are possible along the "Keynesian function." If Y_3 is less-than-full-employment level of income, the only way to increase income up to a full-employment level is to shift the Keynesian function to the right. This can be done by pursuing policies that will shift the IS function to the right. In the absence of forces that will increase investment or decrease the propensity to save, government spending is the most obvious route to full employment; hence, Keynes' emphasis upon fiscal policy in his book.

Adherents to the classical line countered Keynes' arguments in an interesting way. Professor Pigou, in an article in 1943, and again in 1947,[1] argued that general deflation of prices and wages would shift the IS function to the right, and would continue to do so until a full-employment level of income is reached. As Graph 11.3(a) and (b) show, a rightward shift of IS will reinforce the rightward shift in LM, producing higher levels of demand than if IS remained the same. Further, even though IS might cross LM at a floor, rightward shifts of IS will still produce increases in income. Pigou's function relating income to the price level is denoted by the dotted line in Graph 11.3(b).

Why did Pigou think that IS would shift to the right as price and wage levels decline? His basic argument rested upon the assumption of a decrease in the average propensity to save as prices decline. This decrease comes about because households have accumulations of liquid assets—money and titles to debt—which increase in purchasing power as prices decline. As prices decline, the necessity to save out of current income becomes less and less because the real value of past savings, held in liquid or semiliquid form, rises. The result is a decline in the average propensity to save and a rightward shift of the IS function.

How good is the Pigovian argument? One line of criticism suggests that although a decline in prices is stimulating to holders of debt (creditors), it is depressing to holders of credit (debtors). And, since the amount of credit equals the amount of debt, will not the decline in the price level have a neutral effect upon the propensity to save? An answer to this argument may be made by pointing out that one kind of debt, namely money issued by the government, will not depress its issuer during a price decline. The reason why the government will not be depressed is obvious: it never has to redeem its money except with debt of the same kind. On net, therefore, an increase in the real value of money will stimulate spending and shift the IS function to the right.

But, the argument doesn't stop there. While a decline in prices in-

---

[1] A. C. Pigou, "The Classical Stationary State," *Economic Journal*, December, 1943; "Economic Progress in a Stable Environment," *Economica*, August, 1947, reprinted in Lloyd C. Mints (ed.), *Readings in Monetary Theory* (New York: Blakiston Co., Inc., 1951).

creases the real value of credit to the same degree that it increases the real value of debt, debtors may react more strongly to the increase in their burden than creditors will to their gain. Indeed, if, on balance, debtors tend to be poorer than creditors, the decline in prices will increase the inequality of wealth. The consequence of this will probably be a net reduction in the propensity to spend for the community (a leftward shift of the *IS* function), for the poor will be more motivated to decrease their spending than the rich will be to increase theirs. In addition, businesses with significant amounts of outstanding debt—e.g., corporations with large amounts of bonded debt in their capital structures—will have their liquidity impaired and their investment spending will no doubt fall.

On net, therefore, it is difficult to say whether the *IS* function would shift to the left or to the right with a general deflation. It is simply not known whether the increase in the value of liquid assets would stimulate spending more than the redistribution of wealth would discourage it.

The Pigou Effect and Reality

Pigou's answer to Keynes was, as he himself admitted, an academic exercise, "of some slight use perhaps for clarifying thought, but with very little chance of being posed on the chequer board of actual life." He thought that no government would allow money wage rates to rush down very far before establishing some legal minimum rates. Moreover, he may have had in mind actions by oligopolies and unions to prevent prices and wages from falling too far.

But these are surely not the only reasons why the exercise is "academic." One can imagine a government, swayed by the arguments of price flexibility enthusiasts, refusing to set minimum wage rates and mounting a heavy attack upon administered prices and wages with an antilabor, antitrust campaign. What really makes the Pigovian argument academic is the belief that prices and wages can be deflated substantially without inducing pessimism about future deflation. Pigou's argument depends upon the assumption that deflation can take place instantly, without inducing people to believe that further deflation will take place. Moreover, it assumes that the widespread bankruptcies which the deflation would produce would not induce pessimism. It is in this latter sense, therefore, that Pigou's argument is unrealistic. Because deflation takes time, and produces bankruptcies, pessimistic expectations would be produced. Once this happens, the policy of deflation would compound the difficulties of depression.

Conclusions of the Price-Flexibility Debate

The Keynesian attack upon the classical position that deflation produces beneficial effects upon income and employment was answered by Pigou in terms relevant to Keynes' mode of analysis. He pointed out that the value of money and money assets do increase during deflations. The implication of this fact for the Keynesian argument is a reduction in the propensity to save and a resultant increase in income and employment. Presumably, since the strength of the Pigou effect is proportional to the degree of deflation, there is always a price level low enough to stimulate a full-employment level of national income: low enough, even, under certain conditions, to offset the effects of a redistribution of wealth.

The result of the price-flexibility debate is curious. At one level, one can say that the classical school, as amended by Pigou, triumphed. But, even on purely theoretical grounds, the triumph was a conditional one; for certain distributions of wealth will throw the argument on the side of Keynes. On practical grounds, however, Keynes' instinct was correct. If the prescriptions implied by the Pigou adherents were ever put into practice (if, indeed, it would be possible), the dynamic effects of falling wages and prices upon expectations would result in a rapid decline in expenditure, especially on the part of business. Practical application of the Pigovian approach would compound the difficulties of depression, not alleviate them. Perhaps this is the real contribution of the debate. Impractical nostrums can not be effectively revealed except with strong theoretical arguments.

ADDITIONAL READINGS

LEKACHMAN, R. (ed.) *Keynes' General Theory. Reports of Three Decades.* New York: St. Martin's Press, 1964. An interesting collection of early and later reactions to Keynes' theories by a set of distinguished Keynesian and non-Keynesian economists.

KLEIN, L. R. *The Keynesian Revolution.* New York: The Macmillan Co., 1949. A good introduction to Keynes' evolution from a classical economist to a "Keynesian."

PATINKIN, D. *Money, Interest, and Prices,* 2d ed. New York: Harper & Row, 1965. An elaborate and important work which develops the implications of the Pigou effect (often called the real balance, or wealth effect) for both classical and Keynesian economics.

Chapter 12

NATIONAL INCOME AND THE PRICE LEVEL

In the last several chapters we concerned ourselves with problems and interpretations of the economy in a state of less-than-full employment. For this reason, we did not discuss in detail the factors underlying price level changes, except insofar as we took the presence of excess demand or excess supply to indicate conditions in which price levels tend to rise or fall. By implication, we also took absence of excess demand or supply to mean a condition of price level stability. In this chapter, we must investigate the meaning of such stability in more detail. In order to do so, we must first deal with the economy in a state of full employment. After that, we shall consider the relationship between the price level and the level of employment when the latter is less than "full."

Stability of the Price Level—The Case of Full Employment

Recall that in the classical system full employment of labor was maintained by flexible money wage rates. Hence, if we start with an economy in a state of full employment and vary the price level, the wage level must vary in the same direction and in the same degree as prices in order to maintain full employment. Let us assume that competition in the labor market produces such a result. Our problem at present is to ask whether there is a *unique* price level associated with the full-employment level of national income when both the supply and demand functions for money and the investment and saving functions are taken as given.

Point G in Grape 12.1 is on the IS function, the LM function, and the vertical output "supply" curve associated with full employment in the labor market. Because G is on all of these curves we know that there is no discrepancy between intended saving and investment and no excess demand for or supply of money. Moreover, the demand for goods equals

GRAPH 12.1

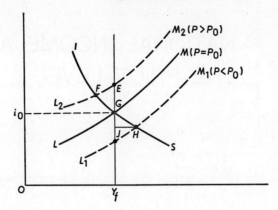

the amount being produced. Such would not be true if *IS* and *LM* inter-
sected to the left or right of the vertical full-employment supply function. In those cases, the economy would be producing too much or
too little.

Because point *G* indicates an equality between the aggregate demand
for and supply of goods, there should be some price level, P_0, connected
with it. How stable is that price level? If some omnipotent authority
were either to depress or to raise that level and then relax, would
prices snap back to P_0, or would they remain permanently depressed or
raised?

Consider first a reduction in the price level below P_0. Such a reduction, we have seen, would shift *LM* to the right, say to the dotted L_1M_1
function in Graph 12.1. The intersection of the new money market
equilibrium curve with *IS* is at *H*. Because *H* is on both the *IS* function
and L_1M_1, it might seem that both the commodity and the money markets are still in equilibrium. Actually, this is an illusion. The reduction
of the interest rate below Y_fG would, it is true, expand investment
spending. However, since real income cannot expand beyond OY_f, the
level of saving cannot increase. Point *H,* then, represents the level to
which real income *would* rise *if* the level of production could be increased. Since full employment prevents such an increase, it follows
that neither the new income level nor the rate of interest can be as
indicated at point *H.* Indeed, if we are to hold to our assumption in
Chapter 10 that the money market is always nearest to equilibrium, the
interest rate will be at Y_fJ, where L_1M_1 crosses the vertical supply function.

Point *J*, it should immediately be noted, is not an equilibrium point, for it stands below and to the left of the *IS* function. So long as this is true, the commodities market will be in a state of excess demand, and prices will rise. The rising price level will lift the *LM* function until it coincides with the old one and joins *IS* at point *G*, where there is equilibrium in the commodities market at price level P_0. It appears, therefore, that so long as basic conditions in the economy remain fixed, any price level below P_0 will be a temporary one.

Now consider a price level *higher* than P_0. The money market equilibrium curve will shift up to $L_2 M_2$. Again, it would seem that point *F*, where the new curve intersects the *IS* function, would be the new combination of income and interest. This too, however, would be an illusion. For if we suppose that the money wage rate increases in proportion with the price level, output will remain constant at OY_f, its full-employment level. Hence, although the rise in the interest rate reduces investment spending, the level of saving will not decrease. The economy will find its interest-income combination at a point close to *E* in the diagram. Point *E* is above the *IS* function, indicating an excess supply of commodities. Such a condition will lead to a drop in the price level. The reduction in prices will propel the money market equilibrium curve down and to the right, until it coincides with the old function at a price level of P_0. So long as basic conditions in the economy remain unchanged, any price level above P_0 will be a temporary one also. P_0, then, is the only price level which is not temporary and subject to change from the corrective forces in the commodities market. It is an *equilibrium price level*, not accidentally arrived at, not "just there." It is uniquely related to the full-employment level of output and the supply and demand functions for money implied in the money market equilibrium curve.

Pigou Effect and Price Level Stability

The last section proved that under conditions of full wage-price flexibility there would be some equilibrium price level consistent with full employment. It should now be noted that no use was made of the Pigou effect in establishing P_0. This may seem strange because fluctuations in the price level are bound to affect the real value of the money stock, M/P, if the nominal stock of money, M, is held constant. The argument of the last chapter should lead one to the conclusion that a fall in the price level below P_0, which automatically raises M/P, will shift the *IS* function in an upward direction. Hence the decrease in the demand for money occasioned by the fall in prices should be joined by an increase in the demand for commodities. On the same argument, a rise in the price level should both increase the demand for money and lower the demand for goods.

There is nothing about this argument which disturbs our conclusion in the last section. Indeed, the conclusion that P_0 is an equilibrium level of prices is fortified by the inclusion of Pigou's argument, since it means that there are now *two reasons* for the creation of an excess demand or supply of goods by a fall or rise of the price level. A fall in the price level decreases both the interest rate and the propensity to save. Hence an increase in investment is joined by an increase in consumption spending. By similar reasoning, a rise in the price level decreases both investment and consumption.

Although the inclusion of the Pigou effect helps the analysis, it is not necessary. Our full-employment and constant money stock assumptions have already allowed us to arrive at a determinate price level. To see this, consider the following equations:

$$Y_f = I(Y_f, i) + C(Y_f, i) , \tag{1}$$

$$\frac{M}{P} = L_1(Y_f) + L_2(i) . \tag{2}$$

Equation (1) tells us that full-employment output, Y_f, equals the demand for investment goods plus the demand for consumption goods. Investment demand, $I(Y_f, i)$, and consumption demand, $C(Y_f, i)$, are both functions of income and the interest rate for generality. Note, however, that the interest rate is the only variable in equation (1). Hence equation (1) can determine an equilibrium interest rate by itself.

Can we be certain that the interest rate determined in equation (1) is consistent with equilibrium in the money market? Equation (2) shows the equilibrium condition for the money market. Real balances, M/P, must equal the demand for these balances. The latter is made up of the transactions demand, $L_1(Y_f)$, plus the speculative demand, $L_2(i)$ for money. The interest rate which equates the demand for money with its supply must be the same as that which equates the demand and supply for goods. If that rate is i_0, then it is clear from equation (2) that the price level must also have a given value. In Graph 12.1 we have assumed that value to be P_0. If the price level had any other value, the money market would require the interest rate to be different than i_0 in order to stay in equilibrium. A different value for the rate of interest would then throw the commodity market, equation (1), out of equilibrium. It follows, then, that there is only one combination of prices and interest, P_0 and i_0, which will give us general equilibrium.

As a footnote to this argument, we should recognize the relation between the model in equations (1) and (2) and the classical model in Chapter 3. They are actually the same model: for equation (1) sets the interest rate at i_0 and is, in fact, nothing more than the equilibrium relationship $S(i) = I(i)$ (see Chapter 3). Putting i_0 into equation (2) means that the money market has no other job than that of determining the equilibrium price level, P_0. Hence, equation (2) in this system does precisely the same job as the equation of exchange in the classical theory.

This latter conclusion is reinforced by considering a doubling of the quantity of money. Note that the equilibrium rate of interest is unaffected by such a change, since the money stock does not appear in equation (1). Equation (2), however, is thrown out of equilibrium, for its left-hand side is now $2(M/P)$, while the right-hand side is unchanged. For equation (2) to regain its balance, the price level has no choice but to double. This is exactly the same solution the equation of exchange would have given.

Price Level Stability, the Keynesian Case

Once we enter the Keynesian world of employment and output variability, the mechanism affecting the price level changes. We have already hinted at the process in the last chapter, but it is well to detail the argument here. Graph 12.2 repeats the basic diagrams in Graph 11.2. The money wage rate is now fixed (Keynes) and the equilibrium output is at an underemployment level. The price level is P_0, and the money and commodity markets are in equilibrium at an interest rate indicated at point G.

Now, apply the same test as before: let the price level wander below P_0 to P_1. Will it now return to P_0, or will it stay below?

The fall in prices below P_0 shifts the LM function to L_1M_1. In contrast to the full-employment case earlier in the chapter, however, the wage rate does not fall; hence, there is an automatic increase in real wages to W^*/P_1. The increase in real wages will lead employers to reduce their work force to ON_1, and national product will fall to OY_1. The result of these movements is to place the economy at point K in Graph 12.2(c). Point K is below the IS function, where excess demand

GRAPH 12.2

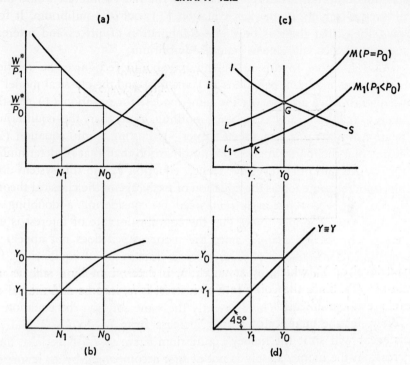

for commodities exists. The excess demand should drive prices up to P_0, in which case the economy is back where it started.

A similar experiment will show that a price level higher than P_0 will force the economy to adjust in a manner which returns production to Y_0 and prices to P_0. Hence, we must conclude that P_0 is an equilibrium price level. In this case, however, it is a sticky wage rate, not a fixed, full-employment level of income, which produces such stability. If workers stipulate for a different average money wage, the price level will alter, as will the level of production.

Money, Employment, Interest, and Prices

In sharp contrast to the full-employment, flexible money wage model, the Keynesian "sticky wage" model gives the quantity of money an important role in determining the rate of interest and real income, as well as the price level. Consider, for example, the state of the economy as depicted by Graph 12.3. Initial real income is set at an underemploy-

GRAPH 12.3

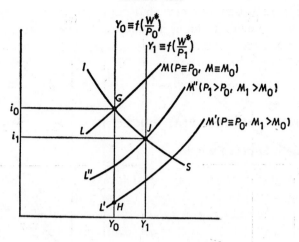

ment level of Y_0 which, by assumption, is determined by a real wage rate W^*/P_0. Since the going rate of interest is i_0, income and the price level are at equilibrium.

Now, let the quantity of money increase from M_0 to M_1. Initially, this event will shift the money equilibrium curve to $L'M'$ because the increase in the money supply is not at first accompanied by an increase in production or income, and none of the new money is needed for transactions purposes. A temporary equilibrium is therefore established at point H. Point H, however, lies below the IS function, indicating excess demand for goods. The excess demand for goods will drive the price level above P_0, lifting the LM function back toward its old position. In the meantime, however, the rising price level is depressing the real wage, making it profitable for employers to take on additional workers. The increased employment will be followed by an increase in production. The excess demand for goods generated by the initial increase in the money supply will therefore be reduced by two forces: the rise in the price level and the increase in production. This second force, however, will prevent prices from increasing in proportion to the increase in the quantity of money. In addition, the interest rate will not return to its former level. Real balances will have been permanently increased, and part of these real balances will have been absorbed permanently into speculative balances through a reduction in the interest rate.

The mechanism described above shows that income and interest, as well as the price level, will be permanently changed by the injection of money. Graph 12.3 shows the new equilibrium position for the economy to be at point J, where income is Y_1 interest is i_1, and the price level is P_1. Had we used the classical assumption of flexible money wages, the economy would have returned to Y_0 and i_0, with a price level double its level at P_0.

PRODUCTIVITY, WAGES, AND PRICES

The Aggregate Supply Function, I

The classical full-employment model makes the price level fully dependent upon the level of demand in the economy. Increases in demand, either independent of or resulting from increases in the quantity of money, are translated into changes in the price level, without moderating influences from the production side of the economy. The Keynesian model, however, does permit increases in production to take place. It would therefore appear that increases in the price level under the Keynesian system must result from the interaction of both supply and demand forces. In this section we shall focus upon the conditions of supply in the economy in order to demonstrate this proposition.

We wish to construct an aggregate supply function, relating alternative levels of aggregate production to alternative price levels for commodities. Recall that we are dealing with an economy in which it is assumed that firms act as if they are perfect competitors, adjusting output so that price equals the marginal cost of production, i.e., so that

$$P = MC, \tag{3}$$

where MC is marginal cost. We are also dealing with all firms taken together, as if they were a single integrated firm, producing a single finished good.

The principal, if not the only, variable input in such a heroic model is labor, and the cost per unit of labor is W^*, or the average money wage, assumed to be fixed in Keynesian theory. Marginal cost is defined as the added variable cost resulting from an additional unit of production. It is therefore proper to define marginal cost as the product of the additional cost per added unit of labor (W^*) and the labor required per unit of additional output $(\Delta N/\Delta Y)$. Hence equation (3) can be restated as

$$P = W^* \left(\frac{\Delta N}{\Delta Y} \right). \tag{4}$$

$\Delta N/\Delta Y$ is nothing more than the reciprocal of the marginal product of labor, MPN. The equilibrium condition in equation (4) can therefore be defined as the ratio of the fixed money wage to the marginal product of labor,

$$P = W^*/MPN, \tag{5}$$

or as the equality of the real wage and the marginal product of labor,

$$MPN = W^*/P, \tag{6}$$

a result we used in describing the demand for labor in Chapter 3.

Equation (5) demonstrates some important relationships between the price level, productivity, and money wages. A rise in the price level should lead employers to expand production, because such a rise increases the profitability of additional output. The increase in production, however, may be accompanied by a reduction in the marginal productivity of labor. Indeed, assuming a given level of money wages, it is the fall in productivity of additional labor which ultimately limits the expansion of production. For, as equation (5) shows, once the ratio of the money wage to the marginal product of labor reaches equality with the new price level, further increases in production and employment will cease.

Equation (5) and, especially, equation (6) illustrate another point. If increases in the price level are matched by proportionate increases in money wages, employers will have no incentive to increase output. Hence, the level of employment will also remain unchanged. Proportionate increases in money wages and prices, recall, are to be expected once the point of full employment has been reached in the economy.

The argument of the last two paragraphs leads to the following description of the aggregate supply function: For employment levels below full employment, output and prices should be positively related. After full employment, this relationship should cease to exist, since further increase in the price level will be unaccompanied by change in the level of production.

Graph 12.4 gives a geometrical description of the aggregate supply function in quadrant I. The other quadrants give the information necessary to derive the function. As with the other diagrams of this type earlier in the book, each quadrant contains only positive values of the variables in question. Quadrant IV contains an aggregate production function which, for lower levels of production, shows a constant relationship between marginal changes in labor input and aggregate out-

GRAPH 12.4

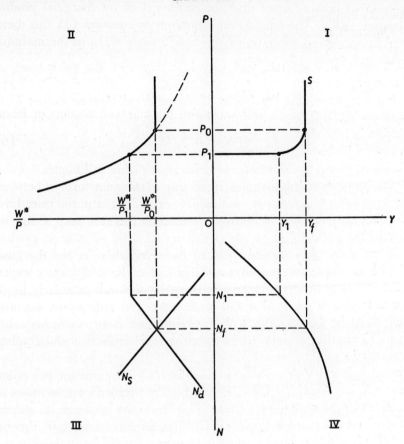

put. After output Y_1, however, diminishing returns are supposed to set in. The shape of this aggregate production function is a nod in the direction of the many empirical studies which seem to show that American industry operates under conditions of constant cost for large stretches of below capacity output.

Quadrant III describes the labor market. The demand curve for labor, N_d, reflects the shape of the production function, since the slope of the latter is the marginal product of labor. The diagram assumes the marginal product of labor to be constant for employment levels up to N_1; thereafter, the marginal product declines with further increases in employment. A classical labor supply function, N_s, is drawn in for reference. If the labor market operated according to classical ideas, employment would persistently approximate N_f and the aggregate supply function in quadrant I would be a vertical line, stemming from point Y_f in the diagram.

Quadrant II shows the relationship between the price level and the real wage rate, when a fixed money wage is assumed. For a money wage W^*, the real wage rate will vary inversely with the price level, as shown by the curve.

Suppose now that the forces of demand call for an output level equal to Y_1. It is apparent from the diagram that such a level of production is consistent with an employment level of N_1. N_1 employment, in turn, will be offered by employers if the real wage is W^*/P_1; and the latter, of course, assumes a price level of P_1. Actually, so far as employers are concerned, they will be willing to offer any level of employment up to N_1 at a real wage of W^*/P_1, provided that they can sell the resulting output. Such is the consequence of the assumed production function.

If real demand increases beyond Y_1, however, a rise in the price level will be required; for employers will not offer the additional employment necessary to increase production unless the real wage is reduced. For example, to purchase a full-employment level of output, the real wage must be depressed to W^*/P_0. Hence, a rise in production from Y_1 to Y_f requires an increase in the price level from P_1 to P_0. Further increases in production can only be had if the real wage can be depressed below W^*/P_0. But, since N_f is a full-employment point, increases in the price level above P_0 will be accompanied by proportionate increases in the money wage rate. This is shown by the vertical line imposed on the curve in quadrant II. The real wage cannot fall below W^*/P_0; hence the dotted portion of the curve cannot be attained.

The aggregate supply function in quadrant I follows the verbal description offered above, with the exception of the flat portion for output levels below Y_1. It is relevant now to ask how stable the function is. There are two forces which fix the general position of the curve: the money wage rate and the position of the production function. An increase in the money wage rate, say through collective bargaining, will shift the curve in quadrant II up and to the left, carrying with it the aggregate supply function in quadrant I. An upward shift in the production function (rightward in quadrant IV), on the other hand, will shift the aggregate supply function to the right, particularly since such an increase in productivity will be accompanied by an increase in the demand for labor, or a shift of the N_d function to the left in quadrant III. The reader can readily verify that such an occurrence will both lower the flat portion of the aggregate supply function in quadrant I and will move its vertical portion to the right.

The Aggregate Supply Function, II

The formal presentation of the derivation of aggregate supply given is a first approximation. Actually, the supply function is a dynamic animal, reflecting a large variety of factors which operate either individually or severally at various stages of business activity. Nevertheless, the lesson given by the formal theory is that, in the last analysis, conditions of productivity and wages are among the ultimate determinants of the price and output levels.

Suppose that, after a period of slump, the economy begins to move to higher levels of output. Whether the increase in production and employment takes place without significant price changes depends upon a number of factors. In the American economy, production is generally highly flexible: large ranges of production are possible without significant variations in unit costs. With unit costs more or less constant (or, in other terms, with the marginal physical productivity of labor more or less constant) as output increases, little pressure is placed upon the price level. That is, little pressure originates from the basic conditions of productivity.

But there is still the possibility of bottlenecks. Not all industries can expand at the same rate. Some are in more advantageous positions to hire labor and will, on this account, be able to increase output more rapidly. Firms coming out of the depression with sizable inventories of raw and semifinished materials are in a position to boost production more rapidly than those with reduced inventories. Before adequate and skilled labor can be found, and before adequate inventories can be built up, the whole economy will begin to feel the pressure. Increases in the production of automobiles and other steel-using products may have to await an expanded supply of metal, which in turn may have to wait upon the coal and metal mines, which often take considerable time to expand production. Such disproportionalities are especially a problem after a prolonged depression, when inventories have sunk to low levels and skilled workers in the labor force have declined, through retirement, atrophy of skills, and a reduced number of new apprentices. The experience in the United States going into World War II is a good illustration of the importance of the bottlenecks in producing price increases. Prolonged depression before the war had produced serious shortages of both skilled workers and raw materials. Before such shortages were overcome, significant increases in prices resulted in many areas.

Once these bottlenecks are overcome, however, there is no reason to suppose that the resulting increases in prices will be permanent, except, of course, as money wage rates of skilled workers have been pushed up in the process—these wage increases are likely to be permanent because of the ability of these people to maintain higher wages through their unions.

Indeed, the bargaining position of labor as a whole improves as unemployment declines. Both skilled and unskilled workers find themselves in sellers' markets and, if they are sufficiently well organized, they may press their advantageous positions upon employers. Although the relative bargaining positions of employers and unions are significant in wage determination, employers in oligopolies and monopolies are not likely to press their positions too hard. Rising demand puts them in a position to pass wage increases to consumers by increasing prices, and there is ground for the suspicion that the increase in prices in such industries is often in excess of the rise in wage costs.

An increase in money wage rates may not mean an increase in real wages for all workers. The possibility that price rises in administered-price industries may exceed wage increases stemming from union pressure is supplemented by the fact that not all workers are organized. This means that even though some workers may be able to increase money wages faster than the price level, others will fall behind. With substantial amounts of unemployment, the unorganized sector of the labor force is still likely to feel the pinch of rising prices without being able to do anything about them in the way of increased money wages. Only when employment reaches an advanced stage, with employers competing heavily for their services, will they be able to extract significant wage increases from business.

While pressures upon the price level from bottlenecks and the labor force are significant, the basic cost functions of firms in the economy may be constant enough to prevent a substantial eruption of the price level. Moreover, if the recovery is sparked primarily by an investment boom, another force may be operating to offset the upward pressures upon the price level—increases in labor productivity.

Increases in labor productivity are a normal accompaniment of economic recovery based upon an upswing of capital formation. During the lull in activity represented by depression, businessmen are not actively adding to their capital equipment. Indeed, prolonged slumps such as occurred in the 1930's normally produce *negative* net investment: retirement of old equipment without replacement. In addition, there is the continuing stream of invention which goes on but which does not, because of the low state of confidence, result in applications in the form of new investment. These events set the stage for significant increases in productivity during the upswing. Depreciated equipment is replaced with new and efficient machinery. Technological change, often requiring new and special equipment, takes place rapidly. It is a standard observation that such happenings typically produce increases in labor productivity during recovery which substantially exceed the average annual increases taking place over long periods of time. In terms of the analysis of the aggregate supply function, then, recovery is often accompanied by a displacement down and to the right of the schedule in quadrant I of Graph 12.4.

The notion of *efficiency wages* is useful in analyzing the net impact of wage and productivity changes on the price level. The right-hand side of equation (5) may be labeled as such. From the equation it is obvious that the efficiency wage varies directly with money wages and inversely with the marginal physical product of labor. If increases in money wages dominate during a business recovery (that is, if new capital equipment and improvements in technology do not increase the marginal productivity of labor sufficiently) the efficiency wage will rise, putting upward pressure upon the price level. On the other hand, it is equally possible for wage increases to be offset by increases in productivity, especially in the early stages of the recovery period. The resulting fall in the efficiency wage may even be sufficient to offset the inflationary effects of bottlenecks, if the latter are not too serious.

As recovery progresses, certain strains begin to develop, and these are reflected in the shape and position of the aggregate supply schedule. Production in most industries begins to reach the point of full capacity, and this in turn is reflected by a leveling-off of the economy's production function, as shown in quadrant IV of Graph 12.4. Labor is becoming fairly scarce and employers are motivated to offer higher money wages, even to the unorganized, in an attempt to keep the workers they have and to secure more. Productivity increases begin to taper off. The net result of these factors is a sharp rise in the efficiency wage.

The dynamics of aggregate supply are fully illustrated by the happenings in the economy as it approaches full employment. As shown in Graph 12.5, the initial phase of the function is likely to be fairly flat, as wage and productivity changes tend to offset one another. At some point, which might be designated as the full-employment level of output (Y_f), the supply function will turn quite inelastic. Actually, the supply function (S_1S) represented in the diagram is a dynamic creature, reflecting the shifts in both directions imposed by wage and productivity changes. The inelastic portion of S_1S reflects the fact that the off-

GRAPH 12.5

Dynamics of Aggregate Supply

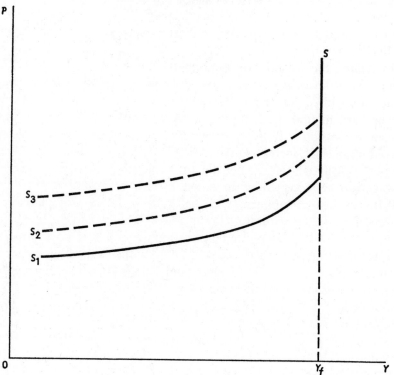

sets, at full employment, to rising prices no longer exist in sufficient strength to prevent prices from rising rapidly. The result is a sharp upward shift of the function, as attempts by employers to expand employment result in nothing but wage increases. This is shown by the series of partial supply functions stacked up at the full-employment point.

Downward rigidity of the price level, when recession sets in, is a phenomenon often observed. Graph 12.5 helps to explain it. Suppose that the boom results in a rise in money wages such that the final aggregate supply function is S_3S. If the new level of money wages is one from which labor will not retreat, then, as aggregate demand falls from its cyclical high, most of the impact of the decline will be upon output, and prices will fall only very slowly. On the other hand, if labor is willing to retreat from the high attained by money wage rates, the decline in demand will be accompanied by a downward shift of the aggregate supply function, and prices will decline more rapidly. In this case, however, we cannot be sure that the fall in output will be cushioned by the drop in prices. As noted in the previous chapter, the dynamic influence of deflation of wages and prices may act to accelerate the decline in aggregate demand.

In reality, the second case is normally not the operative one. The money wage level has considerable downward rigidity. Unions resist wage cuts with fierce determination. The reason why they do should not be hard to find. Each wage cut means that the time of the next bargaining session with the employer will be spent mainly in restoring the old wage level. Increases beyond that level may be difficult to obtain. Unions, as well as firms, do not like to "spoil" their markets. But, even if wage cuts are accepted by the union, there is no assurance that there will be any less unemployment in the industry. In the first place, employers may not be willing to lower prices. This would be especially true in the so-called administered-price industries where prices are administered by the firms themselves and not by the competitive forces of the marketplace. In the second place, and unions know this, unemployment is not something that individual firms can typically control, stemming as it does from the broader forces in the economy. In the face of a general recession or depression, the wage bargain in an individual firm or industry appears as only a minor influence upon the number of available jobs.

It appears, therefore, that S_1S in Graph 12.5 is not a "reversible" function. While it is appropriate to an expansionary situation, when contraction comes wage and price rigidities will conspire to cause the downward movement to take place along the highest supply function attained during the boom: e.g., S_3. We do not mean to suggest, however, that S_3 will continue to be the appropriate function, regardless of the depth and duration of the slump. Eventually, if the depression is severe enough, wage and price cuts will probably take place. In this event, the supply function will shift downward, say to S_2 (or even S_1). Recovery, when it occurs, will then take a path indicated by S_1S, or some similar function.

SUMMARY AND CONCLUSIONS

The theory of the price level discussed in this chapter may seem strange to those who habitually think in terms of the traditional quantity theory of money. Rather than stressing the direct linkage of changes in the money supply with changes in the price level, the indirect connections between money, aggregate demand, and output have been emphasized. An increase in money will normally expand aggregate demand, but not necessarily and certainly in no fixed proportion to the change in the money stock. The rise in aggregate demand, on the other hand, will not necessarily produce price level changes. If unemployed resources exist, the increased spending is likely to stimulate more output than price expansion, subject, of course, to the possibility of bottlenecks. As full employment is approached, however, marginal costs begin to rise sharply as a result of declining marginal productivity. By this time, too, new capital formation and innovations are drying up, and, together with money wage increases, these forces are asserting themselves upon efficiency wages and the price level. At some point, further increases in aggregate demand will spend themselves fully upon increases in the price level.

A "Contraquantity Theory of Money?"

The analysis of changes in the price level presented here is often called a "contraquantity theory of money." The reason for this label is that emphasis is seemingly put upon variations in output and costs as the ultimate determinant of prices. This is only partially correct. It is true that, within the theory, increases in output can cause prices to increase as a result of declining marginal productivity. Moreover, if the higher level of output and prices are to be sustained, an increased use of existing money for transaction purposes must accompany the expansion. If this does not happen, the quantity of money as a whole must increase, and this can happen if producers borrow from commercial banks in order to sustain the larger volume of business. In this sense, it is correct to speak of a contraquantity theory, because increases in the money supply or its rate of use are seen as results of rising output and prices, not as causes.

Nevertheless, the criticism does not fit too well. It is within the province of the present theory to speak of money as an independent variable, acting upon prices and output, as well as the reverse. The great merit of the approach is that it integrates both supply and demand elements into a theory which explains the forces operating on both the level of output and the level of prices. This the simple quantity theory of money did not and, within the framework of its approach, could not do. Its emphasis was upon the demand side of the price determination problem, and it said little about the link between aggregate demand and the level of output.

ADDITIONAL READINGS

ACKLEY, GARDINER.   *Macroeconomic Theory.* New York: Macmillan Co., 1961.

PATINKIN, DON.   *Money, Interest, and Prices.* 2nd ed. New York: Harper and Row, 1965.

DILLARD, DUDLEY.   *The Economics of John Maynard Keynes.* Englewood Cliffs, N.J.: Prentice-Hall, Inc., 1948.

KEYNES, J. M.   *General Theory of Employment, Interest, and Money.* New York: Harcourt & Brace, 1936.

HANSEN, ALVIN H.   *A Guide to Keynes.* New York: McGraw-Hill Book Co., Inc., 1953.

————.   *Monetary Theory and Fiscal Policy.* New York: McGraw-Hill Book Co., Inc., 1949, chap. 9.

Chapter **INFLATION**
13

Since 1939 there have been four major waves of inflation and one minor wave. During World War II consumer prices rose
by 30 percent over their 1939 level, despite sharp increases in taxes and
price controls imposed by the federal government. When controls were
lifted after the war, an even more rapid inflation occurred, carrying the
consumer price index to a level in 1948 some 34 percent over its reading
in 1945. Inflationary forces subsided in the recession of 1948–49, but
with the outbreak of the Korean War in June of 1950 inflation was
renewed. From mid-1950 to mid-1951, the consumer price index rose
by 8 percent. A mild inflationary movement accompanied the capital
goods boom of the mid-1950's. From 1956 to 1958 prices rose at about
a 3 percent annual rate. This bout of inflation was disturbing to a number of investigators because it continued after the boom had peaked in
the fall of 1957. The last wave of inflation is one which started in
1965 and which, at the present writing (August, 1969), is still continuing, much to the pain of the author and everyone else.

WHAT IS INFLATION?

Economists are not agreed upon a definition of inflation.[1] Most of
the competing definitions will not do by themselves. A popular approach, for example, is to identify inflation with an increase in the
money supply, on the supposition that the price level will rise. But, this
is to confuse cause with possible effect. An increase in money may not increase aggregate demand, and, even if it does, a rise in prices will not
necessarily ensue. Moreover, it is possible to conceive a situation in
which prices rise without an increase in the money supply, as when, for
example, the demand for money to hold declines.

---

[1] A comprehensive review of inflation theory may be found in Bronfenbrenner and
Holzman, "A Survey of Inflation Theory," *American Economic Review*, September, 1963.

Actually, there is no completely satisfactory definition of inflation. A commonly accepted one, in accord with professional usage today, is that inflation is "an upward movement of price levels."[2] Yet, this is not too satisfactory. Wartime experience has taught us that we may have all the conditions necessary for inflation, and some of its results, without an upward movement in price levels. Price control and rationing systems may prevent the movement from taking place. Economists have dubbed this situation "repressed inflation."

Is an upward movement of price levels enough to warrant the name of inflation? In most cases it is. However, even here there are pitfalls. Suppose that the upward movement is of a once-and-for-all variety, caused by a sudden increase in import prices of a number of essential raw materials. Is this inflation? Should Congress immediately mobilize itself to produce a set of anti-inflationary controls? Obviously not; such a program would carry serious depressionary implications under the postulated conditions. Or take the case of a temporary upward movement, followed by a decline in the price level. This does not seem to qualify as inflation either. In the normal workings of the economy, fluctuations of the price level are everyday occurrences. Temporary increases in prices are not things that policy makers or economists worry about very much.

Then what *is* inflation? The thing that most people have in mind, and this includes most politicians and professional economists, is a *continuing,* and perhaps *progressive,* upward movement in price levels. It is the continuous and progressive aspects of the upward price movements which finally insinuate themselves upon the consciousness of the public and create a demand for solutions. We shall therefore accept Hart's definition of inflation, with the proviso that upward price movements must not be temporary or of the once-and-for-all variety. But, in accepting the amended definition, we should hasten to admit the possibility of repressed inflation, whereby government controls prevent upward movements in prices which would take place in the absence of such controls.

Sources of Inflation

Simply defining inflation as continuous and perhaps progressive increases in the price level really does not get us very far in understanding the phenomenon. To do this, we must probe into the forces which produce the upward movements. This is not easy; for inflation can arise from a multitude of circumstances, and once in existence it can lead a

---

[2] A. G. Hart, *Money, Debt, and Economic Activity* (2nd ed.; Englewood Cliffs, N.J.: Prentice-Hall, Inc., 1953), p. 256.

life of its own, even after the original forces have spent themselves. The task of identifying the determinants of continuous upward movements of price levels is therefore a double one. First, the economic environment giving rise to increasing prices must be identified. Second, the poss'' 'lity of independent mechanisms, which take hold and extend the price level movements beyond those implicit in the initial forces, must be investigated. In real life, all of these causes may be intermingled: one cause may be the effect of another and may itself induce a third cause, or work back upon the initial one. The reader is therefore warned that the theoretical explanations of this chapter cannot be directly applied to the study of an economy undergoing inflation. Indeed, sometimes it is impossible, despite a wealth of data, to determine accurately cause and effect in the real world.

"DEMAND-PULL" INFLATION

Our study of national income determination has already given us a good start in investigating the forces that may produce rising prices. We know, for example, that when intended investment, government spending, and net exports exceed intended saving and taxes national income tends to rise. That is to say, when aggregate demand rises, whether national income rises in real terms, or simply in money terms—i.e., through upward movements in the price level—depends upon aggregate supply. If the gap between the "injections" and "leakages" occurs in the stage where the aggregate supply function is flat, the price level will not rise, and the increase in national income will be an increase in aggregate output. However, if the gap occurs at a level of output where further increases in production can be gained only at the expense of rising costs, pressure upon the price level will be the result.

This is the simplest case of inflation. If aggregate spending is rising continuously as a result of a continuous gap between spending injections and leakages from the income stream, a continuous increase in the price level will be the result. Indeed, if the increases in spending do not increase productivity, as with investment which induces a downward shift of the aggregate supply function, the upward movements of prices may become progressive. This is because of the progressive steepening of the aggregate supply function which occurs as the economy nears full-capacity levels of output.

Inflation produced by continuing increases in aggregate demand is appropriately called "demand-pull" inflation. As the reader is well aware, the increases in aggregate demand may result from a number of sources—increased investment demand, stemming either from a rise in the marginal efficiency of capital or a cheapening of credit; sudden upward shifts in the propensity to consume; increases in government spending on final output; increased transfer payments or tax reductions; or a boom in exports which raises net exports on a continuing basis. Actually, in the United States it is rising investment and government spending which have provided the source of many inflationary movements of the past.

Inflation as a Monetary Phenomenon

There is a school of economists, led by Professor Milton Friedman,[3] which argues that inflation is essentially a monetary phenomenon, in the sense that it is almost always started and sustained by excessive increases in the quantity of money. The Keynesian approach to inflation analysis, as expressed in the preceding section, stresses changes in particular types of expenditure streams as the originating causes of inflation. It does not deny that money is important. Indeed, it is clear from the general model of the last three chapters that monetary expansion can be an important inflationary force. Nevertheless, it is probably true that many economists of the Keynesian persuasion have either underplayed monetary changes as an initiating cause of inflation, or have looked upon changes in the money supply as being an effect rather than a cause of the increases in aggregate demand which provoke rising price levels. That is, even though they probably would agree that inflation cannot proceed very far without monetary expansion, they do argue that government deficits, increases in investment spending, either or both of which almost always accompany inflation, are the original causes and that the reason the money supply expands is because the deficits and investments are financed by newly created bank money. We shall review this argument in the last chapter of this book, since it involves some rather important general issues in macroeconomics. In the meantime, we proceed with another approach to the problem of inflation.

---

[3] See, for example, Friedman's book of essays, *Dollars and Deficits* (Englewood Cliffs, N.J.: Prentice-Hall, Inc., 1968), especially Part One.

Another Meaning for Demand-Pull—the Swedish Approach

Analysis of inflation with the Keynesian approach starts with the gap between injections into the spending stream and leakages out of it. That is, the possibility that $I + G > S + T$ is first investigated, and then statements about the aggregate supply function are made. Swedish writers have complained that this method concentrates attention solely upon the markets for *final goods and services* and ignores the conditions in the *factor markets* that the inequality may imply.[4] The Swedes argue that when the inequality produces inflationary pressures, excess demand is implied in both the markets for final goods and in factor markets. To see this argument in its simpler terms, we shall, in what follows, abstract from the influence of government and foreign trade and speak only of a simple economy, where consumption and investment spending are the only sources of aggregate demand.

Since expansion of national income in the simple economy occurs when intended investment exceeds intended saving, the analysis begins with this inequality, breaking it down in terms of other magnitudes of the income accounts. (It should be noted, however, that all of the magnitudes in the analysis refer to their *ex ante* meanings, that is, from the standpoint of the expected magnitudes at the beginning of a period.)

Investment — Saving ≡ Investment — (Total income — Consumption).

But,

$$\text{Investment} \equiv \text{Value of production} - \text{Sales}$$
$$\equiv \text{Purchases of factors} + \text{Income of capitalists} - \text{Sales}$$

The first identity in the light of the last one becomes:

Investment — Saving ≡ Purchases of factors + Income of capitalists — Sales — Total income + Consumption.

≡ Purchases of factors — (Total income — Income of capitalists) + Consumption — Sales.

≡ Purchases of factors — Income of factors + Consumption — Sales.

---

[4] See Bent Hansen, *A Study in the Theory of Inflation* (London: Allen and Unwin, Ltd., 1951), chap. i for a discussion of the material presented in this section.

$$\equiv \text{(Demand for factors — Supply of factors)} + \text{(Demand for goods — Supply of goods)}.[5]$$

The last identity reveals a double condition for income equilibrium. If the gap between investment and saving is to be zero, so must each of the gaps between the demand and supply for factors and the demand and supply for goods.[6] However, our interest at the moment is not equilibrium, but disequilibrium: to be more exact, *inflationary* disequilibrium. To see this situation more clearly, let us translate the above last identity into a slightly different form:

$$\text{Investment — Saving} \equiv \text{Goods gap} + \text{Factor gap}$$
$$\equiv (\Sigma p_i q_{di} - \Sigma p_i q_{si}) + (\Sigma w_j n_{dj} - \Sigma w_j n_{sj}) ,$$

where the p_i's refer to the prices of individual goods, the q_{di}'s and q_{si}'s to the individual demand and supply of these goods at their prevailing prices, the w_j's to individual wage rates, and the n_{dj}'s and n_{sj}'s to the demand and supply of labor at each of the given wage rates. (Since rent and interest are fixed contractually, they are not included in the analysis.)

This new translation allows us a clearer picture of the forces involved in demand-pull inflation. In the first place, it becomes quite obvious that inflationary pressure can originate in the factor market, while in the goods markets, equilibrium in the composite sense (not *every* good need be priced at equilibrium) prevails. This means that although the demand for national product may be balanced with supply at very high levels, the demand for labor implied by this level of output may be such as to exceed the supply of labor forthcoming in the various submarkets at going wage levels. The result will be a rise in wages, before a rise in the price level (which will come about from the rise in costs).

A case quite close to the above situation is probably more realistic. Suppose that excess demand exists in both the composite goods and the composite labor markets. If the excess demand for goods continuously exceeds that for labor, the price level is likely to move up more rapidly than the wage level. But if the inflationary gap for labor is continuously

---

[5] By "sales" is meant sales of final goods, and by "capitalists" is meant recipients of noncontractual income as opposed to the recipients of factor incomes who sell their services at prices fixed at the beginning of the period. The analysis is drawn almost *verbatim* from William J. Baumol, *Economic Dynamics* (New York: Macmillan Co., 1951), p. 135.

[6] It is not enough merely to have a positive (negative) factor gap exactly offset by a negative (positive) goods gap. For example, a positive goods gap coexisting with a negative factor gap indicates an expansionary situation because business will have to disinvest in inventories in order to satisfy the excess demand.

greater than the gap existing for goods, the wage level will increase more than the price level.

Finally, there is the possibility of full employment (equilibrium in the labor market) and excess demand in the commodity market. In this event, prices will rise, but wage rates will tend to remain stable. (Unless, of course, the reduction in real wages implied by rising prices causes workers to demand pay increases. We shall treat this possibility in a later section.)

The various possibilities for demand-pull inflation are spelled out in rough terms in Graphs 13.1(a) and 13.1(b). These graphs indicate the

GRAPH 13.1

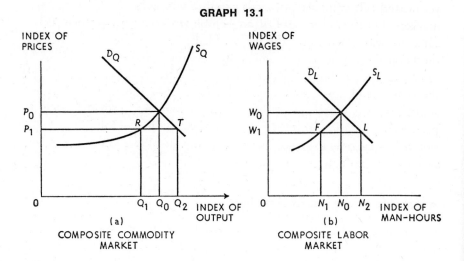

(a) COMPOSITE COMMODITY MARKET

(b) COMPOSITE LABOR MARKET

supply and demand conditions in the composite commodity markets and composite labor markets, respectively.[7] An absence of inflationary pressure is indicated by an index of prices of OP_0 and an index of wages settled at OW_0. However, if the price or wage index, or both, are below their equilibrium levels, inflationary pressure exists. The pressure is measured by $OP_1TQ_2 - OP_1RQ_1 \ (= \Sigma p_i q_{di} - \Sigma p_i q_{si})$ in the commodity market and by $OW_1LN_2 - OW_1FN_1 \ (= \Sigma w_j n_{dj} - \Sigma w_j n_{sj})$ in the labor market. Each of these measures may be called the "monetary pressure of inflation"[8] in the respective markets.

---

[7] No precision should be attached to these supply and demand functions. The argument in the text deliberately skirts the knotty problem of aggregation. Needless to say, it also assumes competitive conditions in both sets of markets.

[8] Bent Hansen, *op. cit.,* p. 7.

When the monetary pressure of inflation in the commodity markets exceeds the pressure in the labor markets, prices should move more rapidly than wages; vice versa when the pressure in labor markets exceeds that of the commodity markets. Increases in these pressures can come about through a further widening of the gap between investment and saving. In this event, both demand functions are likely to move to the right and up, putting the new equilibrium level of prices and wages above OP_0 and OW_0. When this occurs, the greatest added pressure will be put upon the set of markets having the least elastic composite supply function. If full capacity of the existing stock of capital equipment is neared or reached by the shift in demand, while the labor force has not yet neared full employment, most pressure will occur in the commodity markets. On the other hand, if full employment is reached before full capacity, wages will have the most added pressure. The later stages of the boom in industrial economies, such as the United States, are likely to be characterized by the latter situation. Underdeveloped countries, on the other hand, are often characterized by labor surpluses and capital shortages. It is therefore not surprising to find that growing monetary pressure of inflation in these countries typically first results in an eruption of prices, only to be followed after considerable additional pressure by increases in money wage rates.

A Warning on the Use of Statistics

An insight into the difficulties confronted by empirical studies of inflation is provided by the model presented above. Suppose that an episode of inflation is approached by an investigator with the hypothesis that rising wage rates, propelled by union pressures, are the cause of rising prices. In order to test this hypothesis, it seems reasonable to look at the relative movements of prices and wage rates for confirmation of the hypothesis. If prices are increasing less rapidly than wage rates, this may seem like good evidence in favor of the hypothesis. Is it? Not necessarily. As we have seen, the monetary pressure of inflation, stemming from excess demand, may be greater in the labor than in the commodity markets. And, if the elasticity of commodity supply is greater than the elasticity of labor supply, wage rates will, unless *held down* by union-management contracts, rise more rapidly than commodity prices.

If a comparison between wage and price movements is not sufficient to test the hypothesis, what of a comparison between price movements and *efficiency* wages? This is better: presumably, if wages are rising faster than productivity and the resulting efficiency wages are growing faster than the price level, the cause is not excess demand for labor; for employers' profits, on the margin, are falling. But, unfortunately, this is not enough either. Suppose that prior to the increase in wage rates the price level had risen, or that an increase in productivity had taken place. Either of these events would provoke an increase in the demand for labor. If the increase in demand occurs at or near full employment, the relatively low elasticity of labor supply may cause wages to move up very rapidly, perhaps rapidly enough to push the efficiency wage up faster than the price level. Of course, this situation cannot continue. Once employers realize that the rise in efficiency wages exceeds the amount necessary for maximum profits, they will begin to lay off the surplus labor they have hired. Indeed, this provides us with the clue we need. If we find efficiency wages continuing to rise along with prices, while unemployment is developing, this is good evidence that some force outside of the demand-pull mechanism is causing inflation; this force can easily be trade-union pressure.

Repressed Inflation

When monetary pressure of inflation causes prices and wages to rise, *open inflation* is said to exist. But prices and wages need not rise in the face of excess demand; government agencies may be put to work to keep the inflationary forces from realizing themselves in open inflation. This is what the government did during World War II. The tremendous expansion of government spending, not offset by taxes, promoted an expansion of employment and output. When full employment was reached, inflationary pressures of very large magnitudes were exerted in almost every industry and labor market. The government used price and wage controls to prevent open inflation from developing on a serious scale. In terms of Graphs 13.1(a) and (b), this meant that the regulated price and wage levels, say OP_1 and OW_1, were kept below the equilibrium levels, OP_0 and OW_0. The result was a very large accumulation of liquid assets in the hands of consumers and businessmen. Since these liquid assets could have been used to buy goods and labor, above the officially established maximum prices, a rationing system, especially in commodities, was established. The rationing system required that coupons, in addition to money, be exchanged for goods. The rationing authorities issued the coupons, and this gave them the ability to control spending in relation to the available supply of commodities. In essence, the coupons became the effective money supply, since the goods for which they were exchanged fell considerably short of the goods the cash assets of the public could buy. As might be expected, some people were able to evade the system and to buy in illegal "black markets," where prices were considerably higher.

Demand-Pull Inflation and the Interest Rate

Excess demand for goods and factors implies an excess supply of money in the hands of spenders. To see this, the device may be adopted of considering each offer to sell a commodity (factor) at a given price as equivalent to a demand for money, and each offer to buy a commodity (factor) at a given price an equivalent supply of money. It is apparent that when we sum the supply and demand for each commodity and factor and find that excess demand exists in the composite markets, the other side of the coin is an excess supply of money.

Will the excess supply of money result in open inflation? Putting aside the possibility of price control, it is evident that it probably will. However, if we frame our problem to include the market for securities, it is also evident that the interest mechanism is operating along with the direct inflationary pressures in the commodity and factor markets. There are several possibilities. If part of the excess supply of money spills into the security markets, the prices of securities will rise and interest rates will fall, providing an additional stimulus to the demand for commodities and factors, especially in the investment-goods industries. In this case, however, the expansion of demand for goods is likely to drain money out of the securities markets and reverse the movement of interest rates. Unless the stock of money is increased by the authorities, this upward movement of interest will provide some deterrent to additional inflationary pressures.

Indeed, it is probable that this deterrent will be operative from the beginning. Excess demand in the commodity and factor markets typically means that buyers want to turn liquid assets of *all* types into goods and services. Since securities are one type of liquid asset, they, along with money, will be in excess supply.[9] As a result, security prices will tend to fall from the beginning, putting upward pressure on interest rates. If the authorities maintain strict control upon the monetary stock, continued monetary pressure of inflation will produce a rapid rise in interest, providing a possible ultimate upward limit to the rise in prices.

---

[9] Because high investment demand implies additional bond sales, excess bond supplies will increase.

"COST-PUSH" INFLATION

In his study of inflation, Bent Hansen makes a distinction between "induced" and "spontaneous" increases in prices.[10] By "induced" increases in prices he means the result of monetary pressures of inflation, or, in our terms, "demand-pull inflation." Any inflation other than that induced by excess demand may be called "spontaneous." It is easy to think of many possible sources of spontaneous inflation. For some countries, a rise in the level of import prices is sufficient to produce a rise in the price level, especially when imports are important relative to domestic production, both in terms of final output and the extent to which they enter into it as raw and semifinished materials. Another source might be "administered prices," that is, the prices of goods in heavily concentrated industries which are set by the dictates of businessmen rather than by the forces of the market. If prices in a sufficient number of key industries are advanced by "price administrators," a general rise in the price level can be precipitated. Finally, there are the wage increases which may be forced by strong trade unions. Of all the sources of spontaneous inflation, this is the most important. Indeed, it is this sort of pressure which has been dubbed "cost-push inflation" by many observers in recent years.

The Cost-Push Mechanism

Any analysis of cost-push inflation must start with the assumption of a strong labor movement, able to push wages up faster than productivity: that is, able to push up the average efficiency wage. This assumption does not mean that one big union for the country as a whole is required. Certain industries, such as steel and autos, typically set the pattern for wage increases in other unionized industries. Nevertheless, the assumption does require that a substantial portion of the labor force is (*a*) unionized and (*b*) able to push through increases in efficiency wages.

Another assumption, implicit in the notion of cost-push inflation, is that employers will pass increases in wage costs on to consumers in the form of higher prices. The ability of employers to do this will vary with the industry involved. The administered-price industries may pass the full increase in unit costs on to buyers, especially if the wage in-

---

10 Bent Hansen, *op. cit.*, pp. 14–18.

crease affects the industry as a whole. In the more competitive industries, the same may not be possible, especially if the wage increases are confined to only a few firms. For these firms, a rise in prices would mean a substantial loss in business to competitors. Of course, if the wage increase affects the whole industry, the industry price is likely to rise; but, it is the more competitive industries in the United States that typically do not bargain on an industry-wide basis.

Whatever type of industry it is that we consider, a rise in wage costs which precipitates an increase in prices is likely to cause the industry to lose business to industries not faced with union-pressured increases in costs. The nonunionized industries, faced with an increase in demand, will be in a position to advance their prices. They will do this if their supply schedules are inelastic. But, if they are faced with significant excess capacity, they will probably expand output rather than prices. In either case, the demand for labor in these industries will expand, perhaps putting additional pressure upon money wage rates. In this way, the upward pressure upon price levels started in the heavily unionized industries can become generalized throughout the economy.

Can a cost-push inflation continue indefinitely? This is an "iffy" question; it can be answered only by making further assumptions. Clearly, much depends upon the attitude of the monetary authorities. Suppose they adopt the policy of preventing further increases in the monetary stock. In this event, the increases in the money level of national income, induced by the price and wage increases, must be financed out of nontransaction money balances. As money flows out of the security markets into the transactions sphere, the rate of interest will tend to rise. Investment spending will be further discouraged by a shift in the income distribution in favor of workers and against profit receivers, especially if wage costs are rising more rapidly than prices. Emphasizing this shift will be the differential effects of the income tax. Both profits and wages will be increasing in absolute terms; but, since profit receivers are typically in higher income brackets, they will be subjected to higher marginal rates of taxation than will wage earners. It is difficult to say whether the increase in consumption spending induced by the shift of income to wage earners will be enough to offset the discouragement to investment.

At this point, a further assumption is needed. Are unions willing to sacrifice employment for continued higher wages? If they are, the inflation can continue (albeit, at a somewhat reduced pace. The unemployed workers will compete with employed workers in the nonunionized industries, tending to depress wages in them). It is by no means clear that unions are willing or able to do this. Even if the leadership is not concerned with unemployment, the unemployed membership is likely to put pressure upon it to reduce wage demands in favor of more jobs. Furthermore, the bargaining position of management is likely to stiffen considerably, especially if profits are falling in either absolute or relative terms. These pressures, in combination with public opinion, are likely to put a damper upon additional wage increases.

Suppose we now assume that the authorities allow the stock of money to expand at a rate which is sufficient to allow prices to rise in proportion to the increase in wage costs. In this event, except for the redistribution of income stemming from the tax effect, profits will not fall relative to other functional shares in national income. The increase in money will also tend to keep the interest rate from rising, as money in the speculative markets will not be needed for transaction purposes. The maintenance of profit's share of national income and the continuation of relatively low interest rates should prevent unemployment from developing.

But, even if the share of national income going to profit receivers is remaining more or less constant, the share going to labor will probably rise. This rise comes about because recipients of fixed income (in the form of interest and pensions) rarely have the bargaining power necessary to maintain *their* relative share of income. In addition to these are the people who receive rental income, which is usually based upon relatively long-term contracts. As prices rise and the money income of these groups remains more or less constant, their share in the national income will decline in favor of the labor force.

If inflation in the home country is proceeding more rapidly than in other countries, an additional temporary benefit may be reaped by the labor force from increasingly favorable terms of trade. Prices, in terms of the home currency, of foreign goods will enter into domestic production and living costs at a level lower than domestically produced goods.[11] This will allow the real wage of labor to rise without entailing a loss of profits to employers. While this effect is not particularly important in the United States, it is of extreme importance in countries heavily engaged in foreign trade.[12]

The beneficial effects upon labor's share of national income may not

---

[11] However, ultimately, the increase in prices may cause the demand for exports to decline and create some unemployment.

[12] See F. A. Lutz, "Cost- and Demand-Induced Inflation," *Banca Nazionale Del Lavoro Quarterly Review* (Rome: March, 1958), pp. 7–12 for a fuller discussion of these matters.

continue. In the first place, bond holders may recognize the loss of purchasing power their claims are undergoing and either shift their funds into stocks or other assets which preserve the real value of their capital. The shift from bonds may cause a rise in interest rates sufficient to check business investment. In the second place, the benefit from foreign trade cannot last forever. It involves a balance of payments deficit which sooner or later must be resolved by devaluation, by price stabilization, or by unemployment. It must be emphasized, however, that each of these checks may take some time to appear. In the meantime, the inflation can proceed, and labor can experience a substantial increase in its share of national income.

To summarize: cost-push inflation with tight money has ultimate limits, especially if trade-unions are concerned with unemployment. A liberal monetary policy, however, can prolong cost-push inflation and prevent unemployment from developing for some time. In the latter case, labor's share of national income can rise, although there are probably limits. Since the rise takes place mainly at the expense of fixed-income receivers, profits share of national income need not fall at all.

The Phillips Curve

The theory of the aggregate supply function discussed in the last chapter indicates a possible inverse relationship between the level of unemployment and the price level. When the economy is operating at less-than-full-employment levels, it is likely to be characterized by a number of industries with excess supplies of labor, even though other industries may find themselves with excess demands for labor at current wage rates. If the Keynesian presumption about the supply curve of labor is correct, such a state in the economy is not likely to produce falling average money wage rates, for money wages in excess demand industries will be rising, and in industries with excess labor supplies, wages will be more or less stable. The strength of average money wage movements, of course, will vary with the degree of unemployment; the larger the degree of unemployment the fewer will be the markets in which labor is in excess demand, and vice versa. Moreover, the bargaining strength of unions is probably inversely related to the degree of unemployment, so that general contract increases in money wages are probably smaller in periods of widespread unemployment.

This reasoning suggests the following relationship: an increase in the rate of change in money wages when unemployment falls, and an increase in the general price level when money wages increase more rapidly than productivity. What is the evidence?

A number of recent studies[13] both in the United States and elsewhere have indicated that a relationship between changes in money wage rates and the level of unemployment probably does exist, particularly when variables such as profit rates and the rate of change in unemployment are added to the level of unemployment to explain money wage rate changes. Changes in the rate of unemployment give employers a way to judge future hardening or softening of the labor market and hence may influence them to grant larger or smaller wage increases in order to maintain competitive positions in the labor market. In addition, if profits are high when unemployment is shrinking, employers will feel more relaxed about granting wage increases, while low profits will harden their positions, even if unemployment is decreasing. Both the Phillips and the Bowen and Berry studies (footnote 13) find a significant connection between rates of change in money wages and rates of change in unemployment. Otto Eckstein and Thomas Wilson[14] have found that the addition of a profit variable to the unemployment rate improves considerably the explanation of postwar money wage movements in American manufacturing.

The implications of these various studies can be displayed on a diagram (Graph 13.2) which the profession calls the "Phillips Curve," after the first investigator in this field. Suppose that in the United States it would take roughly 8–10 percent unemployment to stabilize money wages, as a study by Paul Samuelson and Robert Solow may suggest.[15] With productivity increasing at a rate of 3 percent a year, the efficiency wage actually would be falling. The fall in efficiency wages would, in turn, lead to a decline in the price level at a rate of about 3 percent a year. If aggregate demand rises by enough to reduce unemployment to (say) 5.5 percent, wages might begin to rise at a rate of 3 percent a year, which would stabilize both the efficiency wage and the price level. Finally, a reduction of unemployment below 5.5 percent would lead to

---

[13] The first was A. W. Phillips' "The Relationship Between Unemployment and the Rate of Change in Money Wages in the United Kingdom, 1861–1957," *Economica,* November, 1958. Since then, similar studies with Canadian and U.S. data have been conducted. For a bibliography as well as a study with U.S. data, see W. G. Bowen and R. A. Berry, "Unemployment and Movements of the Money Wage Level," *Review of Economics and Statistics,* May, 1963.

[14] Eckstein and Wilson, "Determination of Money Wages in American Industry," *Quarterly Journal of Economics,* August, 1962.

[15] Samuelson and Solow, "Analytical Aspects of Anti-Inflation Policy," *American Economic Review,* May, 1960, p. 187. This figure is highly tentative, as the authors recognize.

GRAPH 13.2

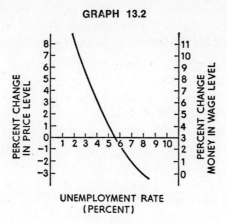

UNEMPLOYMENT RATE
(PERCENT)

positive rates of increase in both efficiency wages and the price level, the latter two items accelerating the closer unemployment approximates to some irreducible "frictional" level. If a Phillips curve exists, therefore, there may be some level of unemployment which just stabilizes the price level. Below this critical level, reductions in unemployment will be bought with inflation.

The analysis of the last paragraph is extremely "iffy." In the first place, the curve of Graph 13.2 is only illustrative. We have no certain knowledge of a Phillips curve, or at any rate of a *stable* Phillips curve. Secondly, the analysis assumes a constant rate of increase in man-hour productivity. Actually, the evidence of other studies indicates an acceleration of productivity increases during periods of expanding output. This would tend to moderate increases in efficiency wages and prices during periods of falling unemployment. Finally, the rate of increase in wages might be considerably accelerated if unemployment were reduced rapidly or if the reduction in unemployment were accompanied by rapid increases in profits. The whole curve, in other words, might shift to the right under certain conditions. Whether this would be translated into rapid inflation would depend upon how rapidly productivity was increasing at the time.[16]

---

[16] Phillips curve studies represent attempts by economists to discover critical unemployment levels below which further reductions in unemployment will lead to inflation. Furthermore, the theory underlying many of the studies seems to be that inflation is essentially a wage-, or cost-push phenomenon. Disputes over the whole Phillips curve idea continue to rage in the professional literature. Indeed, the literature has become so large that one must become a specialist in order to keep up with the debate. This author can do no more at this point than to refer the interested reader to some of the main studies. In this connection see the useful and simple presentation by R. W. Spencer, "The Relation Be-

Schultze's Theory of Inflation

"Cost-push" and "demand-pull" may be misleading labels to apply to inflationary forces, particularly since they may be taken by the unwary as mutually exclusive explanations of inflation during particular periods. The Phillips curve analysis should dispell this interpretation, for it shows that both sets of forces may be operating at the same time unemployment is decreasing. On the other hand, it is distinctly possible that neither concept is appropriate to describe inflationary forces, in that the latter may not stem from broad cost or demand changes, but rather from structural shifts in the economy. Such a possibility is described by a theory developed by Charles L. Schultze.[17]

Schultze's theory was developed in an effort to explain the changes in the price level during 1955–57, a period characterized by boom in business investment but declining sales in automobiles and housing. Money demand in this period grew at an average rate of 5 percent, but real growth was only about 1.5 percent, implying an average increase for the price level of 3.5 percent. Prices in many industries rose more rapidly than unit wage costs.

The period, therefore, was a strange one, and Schultze chose an explanation in which *neither* demand-pull nor cost-push play the dominant role. His theory may be summarized as follows:

1. In the American economy prices and wages are much more sensitive to increases in demand than to decreases. As a consequence, a rapid shift in the composition of demand will lead to a general rise in prices, even without an excessive growth in the over-all level of demand or an autonomous upward push of ages. Prices rise in those sectors of the economy where demands are growing rapidly, and decline by smaller amounts, or not at all, in sectors where demands are falling.

2. When the composition of demand changes rapidly, prices of semifabricated materials and components tend to rise, on the average, since price advances among raw materials in heavy demand are not balanced by price decreases for materials in excess supply. Wage rate gains in most industries tend to equal or almost equal those granted in rapidly expanding industries. As a consequence, even those industries faced by sagging demand for their products

---

tween Prices and Employment: Two Views," Federal Reserve Bank of St. Louis *Review,* March, 1969. The "two views" can be further pursued in George L. Perry, *Unemployment, Money Wage Rates, and Inflation* (Cambridge: The M.I.T. Press, 1966), and Milton Friedman, "The Role of Monetary Policy," *American Economic Review,* March, 1968.

[17] *Recent Inflation in the United States,* Joint Economic Committee of Congress (86th Cong., 1st Sess.), September, 1959.

experience a rise in cost. This intensifies the general price rise, since at least some of the higher costs are passed on in prices.

3. The resulting inflation can be explained in neither terms of an over-all excess of money demand nor an autonomous upward push of wages. Rather, it originates in excess demands in particular sectors and is spread to the rest of the economy by the cost mechanism. It is characteristic of the resource allocation process in an economy with rigidities in its price structure. It is impossible to analyze such an inflation by looking only at aggregate data.[18]

Schultze therefore avoided the standard explanations of inflation. It should be recognized, however, that inflation such as he described can continue only so long as general monetary conditions permit. A restrictive monetary policy will eventually cause excess demand to disappear in the expanding sectors of the economy. Unfortunately, however, such a policy punishes the weak as well as the strong sectors, hence it may be more restrictive than it would be if inflation were characterized by over-all excess demand in the economy.

SELF-GENERATING INFLATION

We have been speaking of inflation which results from demand and cost pressures of various sorts. Continuous pressure from these variables will typically result in a continuous upward movement of the price level. However, it is also possible for inflation to continue after the pressures are removed. The continued rise in the price level may become a function of itself: in a manner of speaking, inflation can lead a life of its own. The mechanisms by which "self-generating" inflation can come about will be the subject of this section.

There are two mechanisms which are most relevant: the *wage-price spiral* and the *velocity mechanism*. It is important to stress that these mechanisms need not operate independently of one another or without the "pressure" inflations discussed earlier in the chapter. Indeed, any actual inflationary situation is likely to be a compound of all types of inflation, including both the self-generating and the pressure varieties. Analytical convenience is the only motive for discussing them separately.

The Wage-Price Spiral

"Wage-price spiral" is a term applied to an inflationary process which proceeds by way of mutual reinforcement of wages and prices. These spirals can be provoked in a number of ways: unions can set

---

[18] *Ibid.*, pp. 1–2.

them off by negotiating wage rates that raise wage costs to a point where profits are reduced below a level considered normal by entrepreneurs. As a result, businessmen will presumably raise prices in order to reestablish the desired level of profits. The rise in prices, in turn, can set off a new round of wage increases, as unions press to regain the real content of the previous wage increase. But, the increase in wages will again provoke an increase in prices, and then wages, and so on. Evidently, so long as employers and workers only temporarily gain a level of earnings which they regard as normal, the process can continue for quite some time.

A rise in wages need not be the only initial pressure. Suppose, because of excess demand in a number of markets, the price level begins to rise. As it rises, real wage rates begin to fall and workers demand wage increases in order to regain their lost positions. Employers might take this occasion to raise prices again, which, if labor is still unsatisfied, will provoke another round of wage increases, and so on.

Internal pressures need not be the only source of initial provocation. In some countries, a rise in import prices may be the devil of the piece, causing an initial fall in real wages. The point is, whatever initially instigates the process, the wage-price spiral can continue even after the initial pressure is removed.

But, how long will the spiral last and how high will the price level rise before it is stopped? The spiral represents a struggle between labor and business for inconsistent shares of national income. So long as these inconsistent demands exist, and so long as labor and management have the power to raise wages and prices in order to satisfy their demands, the spiral will continue. This does not necessarily mean that the process will have an infinite duration. Both labor and business may be able to get what they want by extracting it from groups in the economy which do not have bargaining power—from *rentiers* and pensioners. The increases in prices and wages will ultimately reduce the relative income shares of these groups in favor of the shares going into wages and profits.

Whether the ultimate increase in prices and wages required to satisfy labor and management are very large, or relatively small, depends upon the relative importance of the groups without bargaining power and the relative size of the demands of the conflicting groups. Suppose that at the beginning of the process labor demands 70 percent of national income and management demands 20 percent, while the nonbargaining groups receive 20 percent. Prices and wages will have to double in order to satisfy the bargaining groups. In the meantime, *rentiers* and pensioners will have their share cut to 10 percent of national income. On the other hand, if labor and business cut their desired shares to 68 and 17 percent respectively, they could be satisfied by a 33⅓ percent increase in the price level.

If the initial share going to pensioners and *rentiers* is larger, the increases in the price level necessary to satisfy workers and entrepreneurs will be greater also. Suppose that the nonbargaining groups have 25 percent of national income to begin with. A demand by workers and businessmen for 90 percent of the national product will cause prices to rise to *two and one-half times their original level*, rather than the "mere" doubling which took place when we assumed that the nonbargaining groups had 20 percent of the national product to begin with.[19]

It is not to be supposed that all management and labor groups in the economy actually have the power to get what they want. In actuality, only a limited segment of the labor force and a limited number of firms have the monopoly power to always achieve what they want. The majority of workers are unorganized and, even in industry, where unions have achieved greater memberships, the bargaining power of labor is somewhat limited by what employers are willing and able to grant to workers. Employers who are unable to pass wage increases on to the public in the form of higher prices will resist wage increases more resolutely than employers who have control over prices. On the other hand, any significant increase in monopoly, either in the labor or product market, obviously increases the dangers inherent in the wage-price inflation mechanism.

---

[19] To see these relationships between the desired shares of labor and business, the *actual* initial shares going to *rentiers* and pensioners, and the price level, consider the following argument. Let R be the combined relative share of the national product *desired* by business and labor. Let r be the initial share of the product going to the nonbargaining groups. It follows that *rentiers* and pensioners will initially get rY_1 of the original level of income, Y_1. Throughout the inflationary process, the nonbargainers will not be able to change this absolute amount. However, once prices have risen by enough to bring the relative share of national income to the level desired by workers and management, the absolute share going to nonbargainers will be $(1 - R)Y_2$, where Y_2 is the new level of national income achieved by the rise in the price level. (Real output is assumed to be constant.) In other words,

$$(1 - R)Y_2 = rY_1,$$

when workers and employers have achieved their desired share of national income. The absolute share going to the nonbargainers, $(1 - R)Y_2$, is the same as their initial absolute share, rY_1; but, their relative share is now $(1 - R)$. The above equation boils down to

$$\frac{Y_2}{Y_1} = \frac{r}{1 - R}.$$

From this second equation it can be seen that the magnitude of Y_2 in comparison to Y_1 depends directly upon r and R.

It is not generally recognized that pensioners and *rentiers,* as a class, have power to produce inflation. These people are usually designated the victims rather than the culprits of the inflationary process. Nevertheless, our discussion of the conditions underlying the price-wage spiral indicates that these groups have considerable power. Let us suppose that labor and management are satisfied with their shares of the national product. At the same time, however, let us postulate an increase in the share going to *rentiers* and pensioners. This can come about either through an increase in the number of retired people or through an increase in the average income going to these groups. (In the United States, both of these effects have been operating in recent years: the aged have increased in proportion to the rest of the population and Social Security and private pensions have been increasing both in terms of the numbers of people receiving them and in terms of the average payment per pensioner.) However it comes about, the increase in the share of income going to pensioners will reduce the share going to both workers and employers. If the reduced share of wage and profit income is regarded as unsatisfactory by the affected groups, a wage-price spiral may be set off by the attempts of workers and employers to regain their lost positions. If the forces which produced the increased share of income going to pensioners and *rentiers* continue to operate, the spiral may continue for a considerable period of time.

Before leaving the topic of wage-price spirals, it must be repeated that monetary conditions must be favorable for its continuation. The supply of money and credit must be elastic enough to allow the economy to finance the higher levels of money income which attend the continued advance in wages and prices. If the money supply does not advance rapidly enough, idle and speculative balances will have to be drawn into the transactions sphere. This can produce a rise in interest rates which, if continued, will ultimately discourage investment activity and produce a fall in income and employment. As discussed before, this may be sufficient to moderate the demands of workers and employers and bring a halt to the increases in wages and prices.

The Velocity Mechanism

Many of the very severe inflations of the past have been initiated by large increases in the quantity of money generated by government deficits. These inflations have also been fed by a self-generating velocity mechanism: the tendency of price increases to perpetuate themselves by provoking people to speed up their spending by reducing their holdings of money. Carried to its extreme, such a mechanism is at least theoretically capable of continuing the inflation long after the injections of new money cease.

Imagine a situation in which the government increases the quantity of money by a very large amount as a result of a rise in deficit spending; but, let this be a once-and-for-all increase in money, with the budget being balanced in the next period. Also, let there be full employment. Will this sequence of acts lead to a self-generating, velocity-induced inflation? Begin with the initial effects of the deficit. The increase in government spending generates a direct increase in the demand for goods; but, since the government returns to a balanced budget in the next period, this inflationary force is temporary. The increase in the money supply, however, has more enduring effects, since it lowers interest rates and stimulates a rise in investment spending. The increase in money also initially increases the amount of real wealth held in monetary form in the portfolios of the public. (The reason is that prices have not yet risen, hence the amount of real balances—M/P—held by the public has increased.) This increase in real wealth, according to the Pigou effect, should directly stimulate the demand for goods and services by consumers. In short, by various routes, the increase in the money supply leads to a state of excess demand for goods and services in the economy.

Since the state of excess demand exists in the context of full employment, prices and wages begin to rise. According to the theory of the last few chapters, the rise in prices and wages should eventually cease, since the very fact that they are rising sets in motion forces which lead to their eventual cessation. One force is a rise in interest rates, which comes about because people require more money to carry out expenditures at higher price levels and they get this money by shifting out of securities into money. A second force is a reduction in real monetary balances. Even though these balances had been initially increased by the injections of new money, the rise in the price level operates to bring them back to their initial level. As real balances fall the Pigou effect pulls down the demand for goods and services.

Can anything happen to prevent the eventual stabilization of prices? Not if we retain our present assumptions. However, it may not be realistic to do so. Rising prices can easily lead people to the belief that prices in the future are bound to rise even further. If such a belief becomes widespread, it can lead to a general movement away from money into goods—in the jargon, a substantial reduction in the demand for money. A fall in the demand for money in favor of an increased demand for goods should set in motion further increases in the price level and prevent the stabilizing influences discussed above from achieving their task. Moreover, if this secondary spurt in prices leads people to expect a further increase in the rate of inflation, another reduction in the demand for money and another spurt of prices is a distinct possibility. One can even conceive of a fourth, fifth, sixth, etc. round of price level spurts operating in the same manner. If this should happen, a genuine, self-generating inflationary spiral will be the result.

How important is this self-generating mechanism as an explanation of the inflationary process? Theoretically, the mechanism is capable of carrying the price level far beyond the point implied by some initial increase in the quantity of money. Nevertheless, there are reasons to doubt that it is easy to set off such a mechanism. An inflation must be fairly virulent and prolonged before it convinces most people that it has a future. The theory, of course, requires that most people be so convinced, since it depends upon a general flight from cash in order to sustain the self-generating mechanism. In addition, this flight from cash must work against the stabilizing forces discussed earlier. Studies that have been made of some of the world's worst inflations have found such cash flights, but they have also found that once the money spigot is turned off the cash flights taper off and eventually cease. The reason for this behavior seems to be that rising interest rates and the operation of the Pigou effect (via a reduction in M/P as prices rise) eventually reduce the excess demand for goods and services, slow the rate of increase in prices, and break down the widespread belief in future inflation. Once inflationary expectations cease to influence the behavior of people, the flight from money ceases and inflation is at an end.[20]

ADDITIONAL READINGS

BRONFENBRENNER, M. and HOLZMAN, F. D. "Survey of Inflation Theory, *American Economic Review,* September, 1963.

BALL, R. J. *Inflation and the Theory of Money.* London: Allen and Unwin, 1964. A first-rate survey of the problem, with some original contributions by the author.

---

[20] See the most interesting study by Phillip Cagan, "The Monetary Dynamics of Hyperinflation," Milton Friedman (ed.), *Studies in the Quantity Theory of Money* (Chicago: University of Chicago Press, 1956). Cagan's study covered seven cases of extreme hyperinflation and is probably the most sophisticated study of this phenomenon to date.

BROWN, A. J. *The Great Inflation, 1939–1951.* London: Oxford University Press, 1955. A fine survey of worldwide inflationary problems of this period. Also, much originality in the treatment of the problem.

PERRY, G. L. *Unemployment, Money Wage Rates, and Inflation.* Cambridge: Mass. M.I.T. Press, 1966. An important study of the Phillips curve in the U.S.

U.S. CONGRESS. *The Relation of Prices to Economic Stability and Growth.* Joint Economic Committee, 85th Congress, 2d Sess. U.S. Government Printing Office, Washington, D.C.: March 31, 1958. An important collection of papers on the problem of inflation in the U.S.

————. *Study of Employment, Growth, and Price Levels.* "Hearings" (10 volumes), "Study Papers" (23 separate ones), and a final "Report" (January 26, 1960). Sponsored by the Joint Economic Committee of Congress during 1959–60, this is a massive study of the past and prospective performance of the U.S. economy, including a large amount of material on the problem of inflation. This study is likely to be a standard reference work for many years.

Chapter 14 : THE HIGH THEME OF ECONOMIC PROGRESS

The problem of economic growth, the "high theme of economic progress," has agitated professional economists throughout the history of the discipline. Adam Smith, David Ricardo, John Stuart Mill, Thomas Malthus, Karl Marx, Alfred Marshall, Joseph Schumpeter, J. M. Keynes, and the other great figures of the literature either made growth the central problem of their work or felt compelled to relate their work to it. Whether explicit or not, concern with the problem of progress probably lurks in the minds of most economists, whatever may be the other general problem at hand. We shall do well to be explicit here. Much of the analysis of this book has direct relevance to the theme of economic growth, and although we cannot exhaust the topic—an impossible task—we must spend some time with it.

Meaning of Economic Growth

We shall define economic growth quite simply as sustained growth of full-employment real national income. We use full-employment income because national income can grow from one year to the next simply from putting unused productive potential to work, even though the potential itself may not be growing. We use the growth of national income as a measure because there is no other obvious single measure to use.

We may wish to indicate that growth is accompanied by improved economic welfare for the people of a country, in which case we would add the proviso that growth of national income must exceed the growth in population. In doing so, however, we must recognize that we are asking two questions: What makes national income grow? and, What makes it grow faster than population?

The use of per capita real income growth as a measure of welfare improvement for society is a gross oversimplification. An increase in per capita production of final goods and services may be accompanied by changes in income distribution which leave some people worse off even while making others better off. In this event, the best our measure can tell us is that *potential welfare* has improved, since it may be possible in principle to force those who have gained to compensate those who have lost and still leave the former better off than they were before.

Another difficulty is that real income is measured by using the prices of some arbitrary base year to value the output of a series of years. These prices may correctly reflect the valuations placed upon the goods by people in the base year, but they may be bad value indicators for the goods produced in other years. Suppose, for example, that in the base year people value a marginal unit of good A at $10 and a marginal unit of good B at $7. Now let the production of good A increase by one unit and the production of good B decrease by one unit. Using the prices in the base year, national income will have increased by $3. Does this mean that potential welfare has increased? Not necessarily. People's valuation of the two goods may have changed radically, particularly since they are now available in different relative quantities. Good A, having increased in amount relative to good B, will presumably now be valued at less than $10, while good B, being in shorter supply, may well be valued at more than the base price of $7. Suppose, for example, that after its production has been increased good A is valued at $7, while the relatively smaller amount of good B is valued at $10. If we now use this second set of values to compare the change in potential welfare resulting from a unit gain in A and a unit loss in B we shall find that there has been a $3 *loss* of potential welfare.

When such situations arise, the best we can do is to accept their ambiguity, since there is no clear-cut way of deciding upon the proper prices to use in our constant dollar estimate of national income. We hasten to add, however, that the situations need not always arise; for, if constant dollar output increases with both sets of prices, we may be sure that potential welfare has increased, even though we may not be able to ascertain exactly how much it has increased.[1]

A final difficulty involves comparisons over time. Real per capita production today may be twice what it was 30 or 40 years ago, yet both the composition of production and the people consuming it have changed drastically. To say that a different group of people consuming a different

---

[1] See Tibor Scitovsky, *Welfare and Competition* (Homewood, Ill.: Richard D. Irwin, Inc., 1951), pp. 70–81, for a further discussion of the welfare implications of national income estimates.

aggregate of goods is better off, simply because per capita real income is higher, is a dubious statement. Nevertheless, if such a measure is supplemented by other data showing increased health, more food intake, and more leisure, etc., it would be hard to deny that potential economic welfare has increased. It must be recognized, however, that such a view implies a certain constancy in human nature, or tastes, over time.

Standard growth theory most often avoids these philosophically important questions. Instead of asking whether potential welfare has changed, it concentrates upon production itself, leaving aside the more difficult questions of the meaning of it all. Economists typically confine themselves to the following three interrelated questions:

a) What are the forces underlying the growth of production potential?

b) What are the conditions necessary to insure that production potential is fully utilized over time?

c) Will a departure from full utilization in a capitalist society be followed by a return to full utilization? That is, how *stable* is the growth path in a capitalist society?

The Growth of Output Potential

We must rely upon the concept of the production function in order to discuss the forces underlying the growth of output potential. In order to apply the concept to the economy as a whole, we shall assume, as we did in Chapter 3, that the business sector acts as a single, purely competitive firm, producing a single output with inputs of homogeneous capital and labor. Since we are discussing output potential, we shall also assume the existing labor force and capital stock to be fully employed at all times. These assumptions are not realistic, of course, but they do allow us to treat the growth problem unhampered by such things as the index number problem.

The level of potential output is affected by three factors—the quantity of labor in use, the quantity of capital in use, and the technical efficiency of the productive process. Technical efficiency is related to the quality of capital and labor in use as well as the effectiveness with which they are combined in the production process.

Let each of these three factors be represented as influencing the *growth* of potential output. However, to simplify our discussion, let us also assume that (*a*) capital and labor are substitutes for one another, but not perfect substitutes; (*b*) that equiproportionate increases in both inputs lead to equiproportionate increases in output;[2] and (c) that technical change operates independently of increases in both capital and labor. Assumption (c) is least acceptable of all, since it is quite obvious that new technology or better quality factors of production are normally introduced with the employment of additional quantities of the inputs, especially capital. Assumption (c) is tantamount to assuming that the whole character of the production process and the quality of inputs are altered every time technical change occurs. While this is not true, it is convenient for the present to pretend that it is, since our argument is thereby simplified.

Consider, now, equation (1):

$$G_y = \alpha G_n + \beta G_k + T .\qquad(1)$$

G_y represents the *annual percentage rate of growth in potential output*. G_n and G_k represent percentage rates of growth for labor and capital. If technical change, T, were nonexistent, G_y would equal the weighted sum of G_n and G_k, where the weights of G_n and G_y are α and β, respectively.

To see what such a weighted sum means, let us decompose (1). Assuming $T = 0$,

$$G_y \equiv \frac{\Delta Y}{Y} = \alpha \left(\frac{\Delta N}{N}\right) + \beta \left(\frac{\Delta K}{K}\right).\qquad(2)$$

Now suppose that the capital stock is not growing: that $\Delta K/K$ is zero. Equation (2) then reads

$$\frac{\Delta Y}{Y} = \alpha \left(\frac{\Delta N}{N}\right), \text{ or}\qquad(3)$$

$$\alpha = \frac{\Delta Y}{Y} \bigg/ \frac{\Delta N}{N} = \frac{\Delta Y}{\Delta N}\cdot\frac{N}{Y}.\qquad(4)$$

Equation (4) shows that α represents two concepts. The first is the elasticity of potential output with respect to labor input: that is, the percentage change in output per unit percent change in labor input.

The second concept represented by α is the share of output going to labor in a competitive system. This is shown by the extreme right-hand expression in (4). $\Delta Y/\Delta N$ is the marginal product of labor. In a competitive labor market, we have shown in Chapter 3 that the real wage

---

[2] Technically, we are assuming the production function to be homogeneous of degree 1.

rate, W/P, equals the marginal product of labor; i.e., that $\Delta Y/\Delta N$ $= W/P$. Substituting W/P for $\Delta Y/\Delta N$ in (4) we have

$$\alpha = \frac{W \cdot N}{P \cdot Y} = \frac{\text{wage income}}{\text{total income}} = \text{labor's relative share of income.} \quad (5)$$

The weight for $\Delta K/K$ in (2) yields similar concepts: β is both the output elasticity of capital and capital's share of total income.

Since both capital and labor absorb the whole of income, it is evident that $\alpha + \beta = 1$. Such a result is consistent with our other assumption that equiproportionate increases in both inputs will produce the same proportionate increase in output. For example, let $\alpha = .75$ and $\beta = .25$ and apply to equation (2) a 3 percent increase in both capital and labor:

$$G_y = \alpha \left(\frac{\Delta N}{N}\right) + \beta \left(\frac{\Delta K}{K}\right),$$

$$G_y = .75 \times 3 + .25 \times 3 = 3.$$

(If we had added a positive value of T, say 2 percent, to the weighted sum of inputs in the above calculation, G_y would have been 5 percent.)

Maintenance of Growth of Output Potential

Both classical and modern economists have persistently worried about the ability of a capitalistic society to maintain a growth of per capita production: a continued improvement in potential welfare, if you like. To see what this concern is based upon, consider (6), which is (1) with G_n subtracted from each side.

$$G_y - G_n = (\alpha - 1)G_n + \beta G_k + T. \quad (6)$$

$G_y - G_n$ gives us the annual average percentage change in output per unit of labor input. If labor input grows at the same rate as population, $G_y - G_n$ also tells us the rate at which per capita income is changing.

Now a G_y of (say) 3 percent, and a G_n of (say) 1.5 percent, would produce a 1.5 percent rate of increase in per capita income. If technical change is negligible, per capita income growth would depend solely upon a very rapid rate of increase in capital relative to labor—upon *capital deepening,* to use the language of the classicals. For suppose $T = 0$: Using α and β of .75 and .25, as in our earlier example, a 1.5 percent annual growth in per capita income would require a 7.5 percent rate of increase in capital, a value five times the size of G_n!

Without sufficient technical change, then, the burden upon capital formation would be heavy and the capital stock would have to increase rapidly relative to the labor force. In a relative sense, capital would be substituted for labor and, because these inputs are not perfect substitutes, we would expect the productivity of capital to fall. This is shown by equation (7), where $T = 0$ and G_k is subtracted from each side of (1):

$$G_y - G_k = \alpha G_n + (\beta - 1) G_k. \tag{7}$$

$G_y - G_k$ is the percentage rate of change of output per unit of capital. If $\beta = .25$ and $\alpha = .75$, then, a G_k of 7.5 percent combined with a G_n of 1.5 percent would cause the productivity of capital to *fall* at a 4.5 percent annual rate. The fall in productivity would be accompanied by a reduction in the rate of return on capital.

Unless sufficient improvements in technical efficiency accompany growth, then, growth of per capita production is likely to be purchased at the expense of a falling profit rate. For a time, such a situation might be endured: So long as the return to capital is fairly high, it may be possible to compensate capitalists and savers with enough to maintain a fairly rapid rate of investment. But whether or not such a situation can be endured indefinitely is a different matter. Much depends upon the society's willingness to offer its savings at low rates of return.

The predicament is illustrated in Graph 14.1, which depicts full-employment saving and investment schedules. A fall in output per unit

GRAPH 14.1

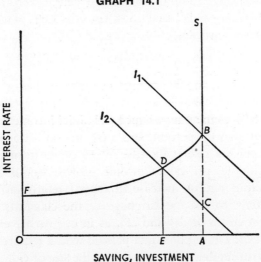

INTEREST RATE

SAVING, INVESTMENT

of capital would be reflected in a fall in the marginal efficiency of capital and in investment demand, as shown in the figure by the shift of the investment schedule from I_1, to I_2. Under Keynesian assumptions, of course, saving is not sensitive to the interest rate, hence the rate of full-employment investment and saving would not be reduced by the fall in productivity and the rate of return on capital. In the diagram, AS is our Keynesian saving function, and the decline of the investment demand function (and interest rate to AC from AB) does not impair the full-employment rate of capital formation, OA.

A classical, interest-sensitive saving function, FS in the figure, would produce a reduction in the rate of capital formation. Note that the same drop in investment demand reduces the interest rate to ED and the rate of capital formation to OE.

In the last analysis, then, continued satisfactory growth in the capital stock depends upon (a) the rate of fall in the productivity of capital, and (b) the sensitivity of business and household savers to such a fall.

For any given rate of technical advance, the rate of growth in per capita full-employment production will depend upon the rate of increase in capital compared to that of labor input. But the faster capital grows relative to labor, the faster will be the reduction in capital productivity and the return on capital. If savers are sensitive to the fall in return, they will act to slow the increase in capital. If savers continue to provide funds in the face of falling returns, the rate of capital formation will continue. It is pessimism over this latter point which has produced doubts among some theorists about the continuation in the long run of capital expansion and growth in per capita output.

Clearly, a hero is needed to save the system from stagnation. What the hero must do is maintain per capita output growth above zero by preventing a substantial fall in capital productivity over time. Such a hero, of course, is technological change.

Technological Change as an Offset to Diminishing Returns

Economists have always been fascinated with the ability of improvements in technical efficiency to offset the tendency to stagnation implied by the diminishing returns resulting from a rising capital-labor ratio. Since 1889, for example, the growth of physical capital in the U.S. private economy has exceeded the rate of growth in man-hour input by about $1\frac{1}{2}$ percent. During the same period, capital productivity actually doubled. This is a dramatic demonstration of the power of technology, since if improvements in technical efficiency had not intervened, the productivity of capital would have fallen to about one-half its level in 1889.[3]

Using the growth equation developed above, we can easily calculate just how much technical change is needed to prevent the productivity of capital from falling, hence inviting long-run stagnation: Capital productivity will not fall if $G_y - G_k$ *is at least zero*. Hence, adding T to equation (7) and setting it equal to or greater than zero we find:

$$G_y - G_k = \alpha G_n + (\beta - 1) G_k + T \geqq 0, \text{ or,}$$
$$\text{since } (\beta - 1) = -\alpha, \tag{8}$$
$$T \geqq (G_k - G_n)\alpha. \tag{9}$$

Equation (9) gives us the *minimum* requirement for technical change if inputs and outputs are to expand in the economy without a fall in capital productivity. Applying this equation to the U.S. private economy since 1889, as we did above, we find that T would have had to be at least 1.125 percent per year in order to prevent capital productivity from falling. As things turned out, of course, the productivity of capital doubled and T was some 2.3 percent per year.[4]

The Sources of Growth: Capital Formation?

Let us be clear about what the previous calculations mean. Gross private product in the United States grew at an average annual rate of about 3.6 percent during the period 1889 to 1960. We have reckoned T to have been 2.3 percent per year. Since neither 1889 nor 1960 represented full-employment years, we cannot say that *potential* production

---

[3] The data in this paragraph, from which we have calculated the rate of change in the capital labor ratio $(G_k - G_n)$, are from John Kendrick, *Productivity Trends in the United States* (Princeton University Press, for the National Bureau of Economic Research, 1961), Appendix A. The 50 percent hypothetical fall in capital productivity (without technical change) is estimated as follows: Assume a fairly realistic α of .75 (also from Kendrick); β is therefore .25. Now from equation (7),

$$G_y - G_k = \alpha G_n + (\beta - 1) G_k + T$$
$$= .75\, G_n - .75\, G_k + 0$$
$$= .75\, (G_n - G_k) = .75\, (-1.5) = -1.125.$$

The 1.125 percent annual average reduction in capital productivity (during the period 1889–1960), if it had occurred, would have reduced the level of capital productivity by about one half (as calculated from a compound interest table).

[4] $\alpha G_n + (\beta - 1) G_k + T = G_y - G_k$, or
$$T = (G_y - G_k) - \alpha G_n - (\beta - 1) G_k, \text{ or}$$
$$T = (G_y - G_k) + \alpha (G_k - G_n)$$
$$= 1.125 + .75\ (1.5) = 2.25, \text{ or } 2.3 \text{ rounded.}$$

See footnote 3 for the source of the data.

grew at a 3.6 percent annual average rate. Nevertheless, we should not be far from the true figure.

More importantly, however, we cannot say much in detail as to *why* production grew at a 3.6 percent rate. Two and three-tenths percentage points or *two thirds of the average annual growth rate in output during the years 1889 to 1960 is accounted for by technical change. Only one third of the increase can be explained by increases in the quantities of the factors of production as normally understood—physical capital and labor.*

Either we have left something out of account or we must inquire more searchingly into the concept of technical change. Before we do so, however, we must discuss the meaning of our findings for the traditional and strategic role accorded capital formation by both classical and Keynesian economists.

As we have strongly hinted, economists have long believed that net saving and investment, or capital formation, is crucial to growth. We have now demonstrated that, in a quantitative sense at least, capital growth contributes far less than does technical change. We can demonstrate this more forcibly, perhaps, by rewriting equation (1) as follows: ΔK is net investment; we know that ΔK can be expressed as equal to the saving portion of national income, sY, where s is the average propensity to save and Y is national income:

$$\Delta K = sY . \tag{10}$$

Hence,
$$\frac{\Delta K}{K} \equiv G_k = s\left(\frac{Y}{K}\right) . \tag{11}$$

Y/K is the average productivity of capital, or in more common professional parlance, the inverse of the *capital output* ratio, v. Therefore, (11) reads,

$$\frac{\Delta K}{K} \equiv G_k = \frac{s}{v} . \tag{11a}$$

We can now modify (1) as follows:

$$G_y = \alpha G_n + \beta \frac{s}{v} + T . \tag{12}$$

Equation (12) may be used to assess the quantitative contribution which saving makes to the growth of potential production. For every percentage point of the rate of saving, s, the rate of growth in output potential is β/ν. If $\nu = 2\frac{1}{2}$,[5] and $\beta = .25$, each unit change in s would add one tenth of 1 percent to the rate of output growth, G_y; a net saving rate of 8 percent of national income would add only eight tenths of 1 percent to G_y. Eight percent is, roughly, what the United States has averaged since 1948 in net saving as a percentage of national income. Real national income during 1948–60 grew at a rate of 3.3 percent a year. Hence, even a prodigious effort at raising the propensity to save, say a doubling to 16 percent, would have directly increased G_y by only .8 percentage points, or by only one fourth.

The reason current saving contributes so little directly to output growth is that, even though it may be drastically increased, it will have only a small impact upon growth of the whole capital stock. Kendrick and Sato, for example, estimated the 1960 private capital stock at 521.4 billion *1929* dollars. Saving was 6.64 percent of real private income, or 13.4 billion *1929* dollars. If saving had been miraculously doubled (to 13 percent), the rate of increase in the capital stock would have been 5 percent a year in 1960 instead of $2\frac{1}{2}$ percent. Given a β of .25, potential G_y would have been directly raised by only six tenths of a percentage point.

Understandably, economists in recent years have looked with increasing doubt upon tax and other programs which are designed to increase the rate of growth in output potential by raising the rate of saving.[6] This is a considerable change in view from the past, since capital formation per se has traditionally been stressed by economists as the means by which output growth can be increased.

Investment and Technological Change

As the direct contribution of saving and investment has been downgraded, a "new view," linking investment and technological change, has sought to give investment new significance.[7]

The new view of investment concedes that net investment does not directly contribute as much to the growth rate of potential output as does

---

[5] J. Kendrick and Kyuzo Sato, "Factor Prices, Productivity, and Growth," *American Economic Review,* December, 1963, p. 999, have estimated ν in 1948 and 1960 to be 2.6–2.7. The data in the rest of this section are from the same article.

[6] Note that we are not discussing programs to raise *actual* output. That is a matter of raising both the demand for output as well as the level of potential output.

[7] Robert Solow has been instrumental in broadcasting this view: "Investment and Technical Progress," *Mathematical Methods in the Social Sciences* (Stanford, 1960). See also E. Phelps, "The New View of Investment," *Quarterly Journal of Economics,* November, 1962.

growth of the labor supply and, especially, technological change. It does stress, however, that capital goods are the vehicles by which the new technology is introduced and that investment is therefore crucial to the process of growth.

We must approach this argument with some care, since a distinction between replacement investment and net investment is crucial to an understanding of it. Replacement investment can indeed embody a significant amount of technology; the case for net investment as an important carrier is less secure.

The essentials of the argument may be simply presented as follows: Suppose, for illustrative purposes, the average life expectancy for capital is 20 years, and that punctually every year the 20-year-old capital is ushered out by new capital. If the capital stock loses its efficiency evenly over time (a bad assumption probably, but not crucial) both its average age and efficiency should stay the same. A replacement rate of 5 percent of the stock will occur annually if there is no net investment.

Now let a $3\frac{1}{2}$ percent uniform rate of improvement in the quality of capital, reflecting invention and innovation, take place. If such a rate is compounded annually, an interest table will show that the replacement capital in any period will be *twice* as productive as capital put in place in period $t - 20$, which is being retired. A rate of improvement which is higher or lower than $3\frac{1}{2}$ percent will, of course, make replacement investment more or less than twice as efficient as the 20-year-old capital being replaced.

Now, if present capital is twice as efficient today as an equal amount put in place 20 years ago, we may be allowed to say that it is equivalent to twice the amount of 20-year-old capital. For example, if desk calculators now are twice as good as a 20-year-old adding machine, for the same cost we may get two 20-year-old adding machines.[8] Assuming no difference in life expectancy of capital of the two types, this device allows us to isolate the impact of replacement investment on the current rate of output: A replacement rate of 5 percent per year with doubly efficient capital is equivalent to a 10 percent rate of gross investment: 5 percent for replacement plus an additional 5 percent of "net investment." The 5 percent "net investment" of course is the equivalent of the 100 percent increase in efficiency of the new over the retired capital.

The effect of modernization upon output growth may be measured by multiplying the extra 5 percent derived above by β. If β is .25, then

---

[8] This calculation assumes that the market will value the two machines of vintage $t - 20$ the same as one new machine vintage. Since capital is valued by its expected profitability, such an assumption seems warranted.

the effect of modernization in our example is to contribute 1.25 percentage points ($.25 \times 5$) to the growth rate of potential output. As our example implies, no net investment of the usual kind (i.e., that which actually increases the stock of capital) is needed for output growth, since modernization alone, along with a positive G_n, will keep potential output growing.

More importantly, however, such a calculation helps to reduce our area of ignorance about growth, since it reduces the value of T in the growth equation (interpreting T to be the technical change *not* embodied in new equipment). For, suppose our $3\frac{1}{2}$ percent assumed improvement rate for capital is correct (we don't really know the true rate). Combining this assumption with our data for 1889–1960 and with an assumed life for capital of 16 years, we would rewrite our estimates of the sources of growth as

$$G_y = \alpha G_n + \beta G_k + \beta G_k' + T$$
$$3.6 = .75 \times 1 + .25 \times 2\frac{1}{2} + .25 \times 4.69 + T$$
$$T = 1.1 .$$

where G_k' is the effective increase in net capital due to modernization.[9]

It must be stressed that the above is only a hypothetical calculation. The improvement rate of $3\frac{1}{2}$ percent is a pure guess. Nevertheless, the example here does seem to show at least one way in which our measure of ignorance, T, may be reduced with proper information. Modernization of capital may be a prime source of growth.

Can *net investment* also be a significant carrier of technical change? To answer this, consider the position of increments to the capital stock vis-à-vis new technology. No special or peculiar part of that technology can be assigned to additional stocks of capital. Indeed, both replacement investment and net investment have access to the same new capital goods. The reason replacements give such a boost to productivity is that they incorporate all of the improvements between the time the replaced capital stock was first put in place and the time of its actual retirement. It is in getting rid of the old as much as in introducing the new that replacement investment improves productivity.

By contrast, net investment improves the over-all productivity of the capital stock by increasing the proportion in that stock of recently pro-

---

[9] E. F. Denison, *The Sources of Economic Growth* (New York: CED, 1962), p. 235 estimated the 1929 average life of U.S. capital at 15.8 years. G_k' is estimated as follows: a 16-year life for capital implies an annual replacement of 6.25 percent of the capital stock. A $3\frac{1}{2}$ percent improvement rate raises the efficiency of capital by about three fourths during a 16-year period. G_k' is therefore three fourths of 6.25, or 4.69.

duced capital goods. The effect of increasing this proportion of newly produced capital goods is to lower the average age of the whole stock. This reduction in age allows an earlier capture of the improvements in technology.

For example, assume that net investment is sufficient after 10 years to lower the average age of the capital stock by one year. This means that in 10 years the economy will be working with the technology that it would, in the absence of net investment, have to wait for the 11th year to acquire.

Now, if we assume, as before, an average 3½ percent improvement rate in the efficiency of new capital goods, the effect after 10 years of net investment will have been to raise the over-all efficiency of new capital by 3½ percent. As before, we can speak of such an improvement in efficiency as if it were more net investment: in this case, 3½ percent more, spread over 10 years, or an average of .35 percent per year.

We can add the .35 percent extra "net investment," G_k'', to the direct effect of new investment itself. If we then multiply this figure by β (= .25, again) we can, as before, estimate the contribution made to the rate of growth: $.25 \times .35 = .09$. Hence T, our measure of ignorance, is not much lowered:

$$G_y = \alpha G_n + \beta G_k + \beta G_k' + \beta G_k'' + T$$
$$3.6 = (.75 \times 1) + (.25 \times 2.50) + (.25 \times 4.69) + (.25 \times .35) + T$$
$$T = 1.0 \ .$$

The embodiment of new technology in net investment, then, is not likely to raise the growth rate very much. Indeed, unless net investment continues to lower the average age of the capital stock, additional minor improvements will not be forthcoming, since the technology-embodiment effect of net investment works only through the accelerated capture of new improvements. For such an acceleration to occur, the age of the stock of capital must fall.[10]

Other Sources of Economic Growth

The argument in the preceding section was directed to reducing the area of ignorance now prevailing as to the sources of growth of potential output. Our ignorance is measured by the size of T relative to G_y, and, even though we know that capital modernization reduces our measure of

---

[10] In actual fact, the average age of the capital stock in the United States has changed very little since 1929 and, indeed, seems to be very hard to change. See E. F. Denison, "The Unimportance of the Embodied Question," *American Economic Review*, March, 1964, p. 91. Denison estimates a change from 1929 to 1961 of between .3 and 1.0 years in the average age of business plant and equipment.

ignorance, we actually do not know by how much. To know this we must also know the actual rate of improvement in the quality of capital goods and the rate at which the very best of new technology is actually captured by businessmen in their investment programs. Industries vary considerably in the degree to which the best of new knowledge and equipment is actually utilized. Moreover, since progress is uneven both within and between industries, it is possible to get increases in productivity merely from a shift of resources to the more efficient firms and away from the laggards. Such an improvement has little to do with the over-all annual rate of improvement in the quality of capital goods.

Serious efforts to understand the sources of growth of potential output are now under way in many areas. One strategy is to see if some important factor has been overlooked. Theodore Schultz[11] and others have been arguing for the inclusion of educational expenditure as an investment, since they view the skill and knowledge stemming from education and embodied in labor as akin to the stock of capital goods. Schultz estimates that the stock of education in the labor force grew by $8\frac{1}{2}$ times from 1900 to 1956, whereas tangible capital increased by $4\frac{1}{2}$ times. This is a 4 percent rate of growth as opposed to a $2\frac{3}{4}$ percent rate. Schultz argues that this growth in educational investment accounts for between three tenths and one half of T, the unexplained residual in the growth rate of potential output during 1929–56. That growth rate was about 3 percent, with T equal to about 2 percentage points.

E. F. Denison has attempted further to reduce the residual by developing a whole series of quantitative estimates of the contributions of improved vigor of the labor force resulting from better health and shorter workweeks, changes in the sex composition of the labor force, shifts in resources from agriculture to other industries, reductions in waste, economies of scale, etc.: all in addition to items such as investment in education. Interesting as Denison's work may be, we shall not further report on it here. The student, however, should read his fascinating study[12] for the full flavor of his approach.

Utilization of the Growth in Potential Output

The growth rate of potential output is set by the rate of change of a fully employed labor force and a fully utilized capital stock, plus whatever contribution technical change may make. The actual growth in

---

[11] See Schultz's essay, "Investment in Human Capital," *American Economic Review*, March, 1961.

[12] *The Sources of Growth, op. cit.*

production, however, depends upon how fast demand is growing. A growth of demand which consistently falls short of the growth in potential output will induce deflation and unemployment. A growth in demand which exceeds the growth of potential output will be inflationary. It is important, therefore, to discover the conditions under which demand may be expected to grow by enough to match the growth of potential output.

We shall approach this problem from two points of view; the classical and Keynesian. The classical system, it will be recalled, is characterized by competitive labor and product markets. Hence any discrepancy between demand and supply in either the labor or the commodities market should be resolved by price fluctuations.

The relevance of the classical assumptions may be seen by referring to Graphs 14.2(a)–(d), which are adapted from similar diagrams in Chapter 11. Let Y_0 be a temporary full-employment position (N_0) for national output. This output will be absorbed, as shown in 14.2(c),

GRAPH 14.2

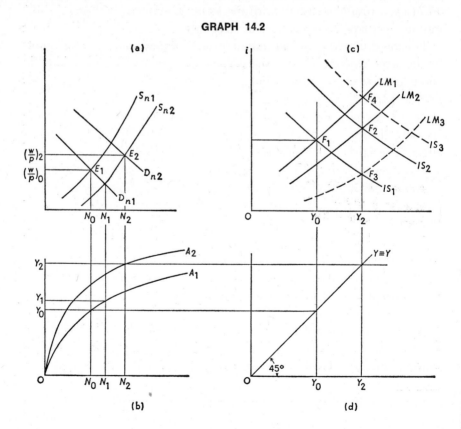

because both the money market and the goods markets are in equilibrium at an interest rate of Y_0F_1.

The seeds of growth are being planted even as income, potential and actual, is reached. The labor force is in the process of expansion—shifting labor supply to S_{n2} from S_{n1}—and the net and replacement investment of the period, plus the improvements in "unembodied" technology, are pushing the production function to OA_2 from OA_1. The shift of the production function raises the employers' demand for labor to D_{n2} from D_{n1}. The result of these forces is to push potential production to Y_2 from Y_0.

Parenthetically, it is interesting to note the components of the shift from Y_0 to Y_2. Y_0 to Y_1 [14.2(b)] would occur simply from an increase in labor supply [along D_{n1} in Graph 14.2(a)] and a movement along the production function OA_1 to the coordinate of ON_1 and OY_1. The rest of the change, from Y_1 to Y_2, comes from the shift in the demand for labor and the production function to D_{n2} and OA_2, respectively. Note that a higher real wage $(W/P)_2$ is indicated in Graph 14.2(a), a result consistent with the assumed improvement in technology and, perhaps, increased capital-labor ratio.

For the enlarged potential output to be absorbed, demand must grow by the same amount in the same period: *IS, LM,* or both must shift by enough to clear the money and goods markets somewhere along the vertical Y_2F_4 in Graph 14.2(c).

Now, this is a familiar problem. We saw in Chapter 11 that the classical theory requires the operation of something like the Pigou effect. The latter will come into operation once an excess supply gap appears. Such a gap would be represented by the horizontal distance between point F_1 and the vertical Y_2F_4. This deflationary gap would press prices and wages down and push *IS* and *LM* in the direction of IS_2 and LM_2 from their initial positions of IS_1 and LM_1. If the shift is accomplished in the same period and employers attempt to produce the new potential output, a new temporary equilibrium will be had at, say, F_2. The equilibrium will be temporary, of course, because the labor force, capital stock, and level of technology will still be changing, pushing potential output beyond Y_2.

We have already learned that the Pigou effect is a weak reed upon which to support the maintenance of full employment. We have an additional reason now for arguing this; for, as we have seen, prices and wages must fall at a rate which allows a continuous matching of supply and demand. If prices and wages fall too slowly, as they are likely to in most modern economies, demand will not grow fast enough to maintain full-employment equilibrium, even if the Pigou effect is powerful.

Indeed, if the lag in wages and prices is more than one period (as it is likely to be in economies characterized by business and labor monopoly) then something else must take the place of deflation in order to maintain full employment.

Monetary Problems of Growth

There are only two (possibly joint) alternatives to price flexibility. One is monetary expansion, sufficient to shift *LM*, say to LM_3, and another is some force which shifts *IS* far enough to the right (say to IS_3). We shall discuss these possibilities in order.

"Monetary expansion" must be understood in a general sense. *LM* can shift because of a fall in the demand for money or an increase in its supply. The question at hand is whether there is anything inherent in the growth process which promotes either of these two forces.

Consider first the demand for money. We know that economic growth is accomplished by an accumulation of both tangible, or physical, assets and financial assets. The very process of net and replacement investment leads to the creation of paper claims on physical capital. These paper claims include equities and debt instruments of various sorts. Some of these instruments are bonds issued by firms and placed directly with savers. Bonds and other debt instruments are also held by financial institutions, which buy them with money acquired from claims they issue upon themselves to savers in the form of bank deposits, saving and loan shares, etc.

As wealth grows the demand for the whole variety of wealth forms will also grow. Far from shifting the *LM* curve to the right, this growth in money demand (which is distinct from transactions demand) will shift the *LM* function to the left. In the context of inflexible prices and money wage rates, and in the absence of an expanding money supply, such a leftward shift in *LM* would continue, resulting in rising interest rates and retardation of the growth rate of aggregate demand.

Is there anything other than rising interest rates which will prevent this "perverse" shift in the demand for money? If the financial evolution of advanced countries is any indication, there is such a force: the creation of money substitutes. If instruments of debt closely resembling money can be created, the expansion in the demand for money itself can be slowed. Indeed, John Gurley and Edward Shaw[13] have argued that the creation of money substitutes is one of the major features of the evolution of nonbank financial intermediaries. By offering the public assets which perform the store-of-value function of money and which are highly liquid, such institutions can bid for and lend to firms the money which the public might otherwise refuse to relinquish.

Important as this process of money-substitute creation may be, there is no assurance that such financial evolution can completely fill the needs of an expanding economy. In the absence of price flexibility and money creation, the *LM* curve can hardly be expected to drift rightwards at a pace sufficient to keep aggregate demand supply equal at full-employment levels.

Under modern conditions, growth of the money supply is controlled by the monetary authorities, principally central banks. The rate at which central banks allow monetary expansion to proceed depends upon their views as to the impact of those increases upon employment, growth, and price levels. In recent years, the U.S. central banking authority, the Federal Reserve System, has also worried about the impact of its policies upon the U.S. balance of payments.

The judgments of the monetary authorities are influenced both by the priorities they place upon their goals and the degree to which they believe their actions in controlling the money supply will allow the economy to approximate the desired objectives. If high priorities are placed upon price stability and a favorable balance of payments, for example, the authorities may feel impelled to restrict monetary growth below the level necessary to maintain a full-employment growth of demand. This would be particularly true if the authorities believe that monetary growth will have a large impact upon demand. A high priority on full employment and upon growth, or underestimate of the responsiveness of demand to monetary growth, may lead the authorities to allow an inflationary growth in the money stock; that is, a growth which would push the *IS–LM* intersection to the right of the vertical potential output line in Graph 14.2(c).

So far as monetary growth is concerned, then, nothing in the growth process itself automatically induces such growth. It is the response of the authorities to the evolving situation which determines the pace of monetary growth. The response may or may not be adequate to the maintenance of full-employment growth of actual output.

---

[13] *Money in a Theory of Finance* (Washington, D.C.: Brookings Institution, 1960).

Automatic Shifts in the Demand for Goods

If monetary expansion fails to keep demand growing fast enough, is there anything inherent in the growth process itself which will shift the *IS* curve to the right by enough to prevent an excess supply of goods from emerging? There are three possibilities of this sort: (*a*) changes in government spending or taxing; (*b*) shifts in the propensity to consume; and (*c*) shifts in investment spending.

An automatic expansion of government spending, or tax reduction, with each increase in potential output would be difficult to imagine. To be sure, there is a tendency for government spending to grow along with increases in population and income, if for no other reason than to maintain per capita government services. Nevertheless, taxes may also be expected to increase. Hence, unless government is expected to run a continuous deficit, continuous increases in government spending are not by themselves likely to provide enough increases in demand to keep pace with the growth in potential output.[14]

Automatic shifts in consumer spending, on the other hand, can be expected. We argued earlier that the long-run marginal propensity to consume is larger than the short-run marginal propensity to consume. This is due to the gradual drift upwards of the consumption function, which, it will be recalled, seems to have imparted a constancy to the long-run average and marginal propensities to consume and save.

This upward drift of the consumption function can be interpreted on Graph 14.2(c) as a drift rightward of *IS,* reflecting the continuous upward shift in the consumption function. Indeed, this drift implies a *connection* between the vertical potential output line and the *IS* function. This connection may be seen by imagining that entrepreneurs actually produce the output indicated at, say, Y_2. The income created by this productive activity will be distributed to the various recipients. Since this income exceeds that of the previous full-employment level, the past peak of per capita income, the short-run consumption function shifts upwards, moving *IS* to the right.

Since the long-run propensity to consume appears to be less than unity, the shift of *IS* will not be sufficient, by itself, to fill the gap between potential and actual production. Hence, unless price flexibility, fiscal policy, or monetary expansion assures a further expansion in

---

[14] A balanced budget increase in government spending, recall, has small multiplier effects.

aggregate demand, the gap must be filled by an increase in net investment.

Net investment may rise *autonomously,* that is because entrepreneurs are seeking to apply innovations which the stream of technical change is allowing or which their forecasts of the future profitability of capital may provide. Moreover, the expanding population may stimulate investment in housing and other capital. A good deal of investment, however, may be *induced* by the growth of income itself, via the *acceleration principle.*

In Chapter 9 we stated the acceleration principle as the relationship between the *growth* of production and the *level* of investment. The principle was stated in a rather rigid form, with a constant capital-output ratio being assumed. Here we refer simply to the general notion that expansions in production are likely to require and induce investment spending.

Yet, even stating this rather loose relationship does cause some difficulties of interpretation, particularly as to timing. If income growth is continuous and businessmen expect each and every increase in income to be permanent, then investment spending may rise continuously also, particularly if businessmen respond to growth instantaneously. If expectations and business investment responses are imperfect, however, increases in investment spending may force an overshooting of aggregate demand growth, or leave it short of expansion in potential output. The possibilities are, perhaps, best illustrated by a rather rigid form of the acceleration principle, combined with the multiplier, in what has come to be called the *Harrod-Domar Theory of Growth.*

The Domar Model[15]

Consider a rigid relationship between the level of production and the capital stock, *where v is a technologically fixed capital-output ratio,* and *t* indicates the period in question.

$$K_t = vY_t. \tag{13}$$

So long as Y_t remains constant, there is no need for net investment. But suppose net investment does occur, so that $K_{t+1} > K_t$. $K_{t+1} - K_t = \Delta K_t$ is net investment (I_t); hence, it follows that output potential is raised by $\Delta K_t/v$, or

---

[15] See Domar, "Expansion and Employment," *American Economic Review,* March, 1947.

$$\frac{\Delta K_t}{v} \equiv \frac{I_t}{v} = \Delta Y_t, \tag{14}$$

where I_t and ΔY_t refer to investment and the increase in output potential during the period.

Now, if output potential is to be fully utilized, aggregate demand must rise. This is necessary because consumption and investment spending in period t were enough to sustain Y_t, not $Y_t + \Delta Y_t$ ($\equiv Y_{t+1}$). If we assume that Y_t is a full-employment income level, then only a fixed proportion of ΔY_t will be purchased by consumers (since the long-run marginal propensity to consume is constant and less than unity). The rest must be purchased by an increase in investment spending (we are abstracting from government spending here). As our earlier simple multiplier model indicates, the change in demand can be stated as

$$\Delta Y_t = \frac{\Delta I_t}{s}, \tag{15}$$

where s is the marginal propensity to save and ΔI_t is $I_{t+1} - I_t$.

Equations (14) and (15) can be set equal, giving the equilibrium condition for maintaining full capacity growth of production and demand.

$$\frac{I_t}{v} = \frac{\Delta I_t}{s}, \text{ or}$$

$$\frac{\Delta I_t}{I_t} = \frac{s}{v}. \tag{16}$$

The meaning of equation (16) should be made clear. A saving rate (s) of .09, or 9 percent of national income, and a constant capital-output ratio (v) of 3 would give a 3 percent rate of growth in investment spending as the growth required to mtaintain equality between demand and supply. *The reason such a rate would be required is that investment performs a dual role: it creates productive capacity and it forms part of aggregate demand.* Barring major shifts in consumption spending habits (or in government spending), investment must increase if the capacity it has earlier created is to be fully utilized.

A growth rate of investment of 3 percent per year would also result in a 3 percent rate of growth in output: Since s is a constant, then

$$\frac{I}{s} = Y, \tag{17}$$

and dividing (15) by (17) we get

$$\frac{\Delta I}{I} = \frac{\Delta Y}{Y}.$$ (18)

Substituting (18) into (16) we find that

$$\frac{\Delta Y}{Y} = \frac{s}{v} = \frac{.09}{3} = .03.$$ (19)

Equation (19) merely restates our growth condition for demand in aggregate terms, rather than that of investment alone. Note that both conditions show a *geometric* rate of growth in demand as a requirement for continuous utilization of capacity.

Graphs 14.3(a) and 14.3(b) give a geometrical interpretation of this theory. In Graph 14.3(a) the capital output ratio is depicted by the slope of *OA*. Each point on the line gives the amount of capital required

GRAPH 14.3

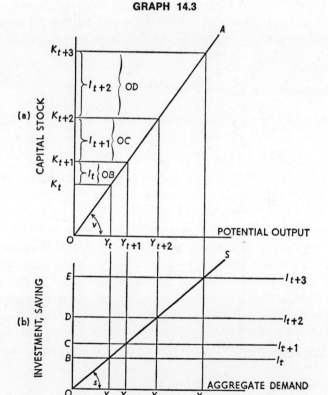

to produce the given level of output. Hence output Y_t requires K_t, Y_{t+1} requires K_{t+1}, etc. Investment in period t (I_t) raises the capital stock to K_{t+1}, and investment in $t+1$ (I_{t+1}) raises the stock to K_{t+2}, etc.

Investment also generates demand. Hence, given the saving function, OS in Graph 14.3(b), I_t will generate a demand equal to potential production, Y_t. Now, given the capital-output ratio, v, the new capital stock, K_{t+1}, will generate a potential production level of Y_{t+1}. If investment in $t+1$ were to stay at its level in t $(= OB)$, demand would not grow and excess capacity equal to $Y_{t+1} - Y_t$ would appear. Indeed, investment spending must rise to OC to insure full utilization of productive capacity. But if OC is investment in $t+1$, capacity will grow to Y_{t+2}, requiring a further increase in investment to OD, and so on.

The graphs clearly show that both investment and aggregate demand must grow by an increasing absolute amount. The rate of increase, of course, is governed by v, the slope of the capital-output function, and s, the slope of the saving function. As we have already seen, the ratio of s to v gives the required percentage rate of change in investment and aggregate demand. Note also that this rate of growth must be sufficient to maintain a continuous equality between saving and investment.

Harrod's Model

The theory of required investment growth given above is in the spirit of E. V. Domar, an early contributor to the modern theory of growth. The theory speaks only of requirements; it does not detail a theory which guarantees that such a growth will actually occur. In order to do so, one must argue that the growth rate itself actually stimulates proper investment responses from businessmen. Such a theory, a variant of the acceleration principle, has been proposed by Sir Roy Harrod.[16]

Harrod's basic point is that successful growth is likely to set up expectations which may lead to further growth. Take the growth from Y_t to Y_{t+1}. If Y_t is an income level which has produced full capacity production, then businessmen will have successfully increased their rate of investment spending in the past, at a rate equal to s/v. Indeed, the very fact that they have increased their spending has made prior investments successful. Nothing now should deter them from duplicating

---

[16] *Towards a Dynamic Economics* (London: Macmillan, 1949).

their feat and increasing their rate of spending again. This means that potential output Y_{t+1} will be fulfilled, leading to expectations of further increases in sales and hence further inducements to increase in planned investment, and so on.

On this theory, s/v is a sort of equilibrium rate of growth which is not only required, but if experienced by businessmen will lead them to expand spending at the same percentage rate in the future. Harrod calls this rate the *warranted rate of growth*, i.e., that rate of income growth which will just keep businessmen happy to continue doing the same thing in the future. Symbolizing this warranted rate as G_w, and inserting it into equation (19) we have:

$$G_w = \frac{s}{v}. \tag{20}$$

Now, as Graphs 14.3(a) and (b) show, the warranted rate of growth is also that rate which equates saving and investment.[17] This means that neither excess demand nor excess supply of goods is developing.

From a classical point of view, potential output can grow either because of an increase in capital or because an expanding labor force and technology are allowing it to grow. Harrod recognizes this in what he calls the *natural growth* rate, G_{nat}. G_{nat} is the limit at which the economy can grow, as determined by the growth of the labor force and the advance of technology. Using Harrod's assumed constancy in the capital-output ratio and our earlier "neoclassical" production function [equation (1)]:

$$G_y = aG_n + \beta G_k + T,$$

or since $G_y = G_k$, as per the assumption of a constant capital-output ratio,

$$G_y = G_{nat} = G_n + \frac{T}{a}. \tag{21}$$

---

[17] An algebraic proof:

$$G_w = \frac{\Delta Y}{Y} = \frac{s}{v}, \text{ or}$$
$$v \Delta Y = sY = S,$$
$$\frac{\Delta K}{\Delta Y} \cdot \Delta Y = I = S.$$

Hence, if G_n is 1 percent, $\alpha = .75$, and T, technical change, is 2 percent, then G_{nat} would be 3.7 percent a year.[18]

Secular Stagnation and Exhilaration

Given constancy in the capital-output ratio, the economy can grow no faster than the natural rate, G_{nat}. What happens if the warranted rate, G_w, exceeds the natural rate? According to Harrod, $G_w > G_{nat}$ means a condition of secular stagnation, for capital expansion will continually produce excess capacity. This can be proved by letting G_{nat} equal the actual rate of growth in national income $\Delta Y/Y$:

$$G_w = \frac{s}{v} > \frac{\Delta Y}{Y} \text{ . Since } s = \frac{S}{Y}, \tag{22}$$

$$\frac{S}{Y} > \left(\frac{\Delta Y}{Y}\right) v, \tag{23}$$

$$S > \Delta Y \cdot \frac{\Delta K}{\Delta Y}, \text{ or} \tag{24}$$

$$S > I. \tag{25}$$

Result (25) shows that $G_w > G_{nat}$ leads to a condition of chronic oversaving in relation to investment. This result may seem a bit strange, for so long as actual growth and G_{nat} are the same, unemployment will not occur. The point is that *capital* will not be fully employed: employers are expanding it at a rate which is faster than the labor force growth and laborsaving technological change will permit.

Persistent failure to utilize capacity might lead businessmen to slow or even cease their expansion of capital. The result, of course, would be economic depression and, unless some force intervenes to save the economy, the depression might continue indefinitely. But even if some force does intervene (e.g., a sudden increase in autonomous invest-

---

[18] Note that the warranted rate of growth assumes a constant capital-output ratio. If the capital labor ratio is also constant $(G_k = G_n)$ then equation (1) will show T to be zero. It follows that any positive T implies a rising capital-labor ratio $(G_k > G_n)$, meaning that labor is becoming scarce relative to capital. Ordinary production theory argues that such a condition should lead to a fall in the marginal product of capital relative to that of labor, unless technological change should assume a laborsaving bias. Such a bias would, by reducing the relative rate of increase in the demand for labor, offset the tendency for relative labor scarcity to increase. The result would be stability in the relative marginal products of capital and labor, even with a rising capital-labor ratio.

ment), if G_w again rises above G_{nat}, the economy will be slated for another depression.

If $G_w > G_{nat}$ produces secular stagnation, $G_w < G_{nat}$ will produce the opposite, what Harrod has labeled "secular exhilaration." For $G_w < G_{nat}$ means that businessmen can continue to expand capacity without running into labor shortages. Population growth and labor-saving innovations will assure continuing abundance of labor. With labor abundant and relatively cheap, employers in some industries might seek to expand investment beyond the warranted rate. Hence the actual growth rate ($\Delta Y/Y$) may exceed G_w, even though it might still fall below G_{nat}. In this event

$$G_w = \frac{s}{\nu} < \frac{\Delta Y}{Y}, \tag{26}$$

$$\frac{s}{Y} < \left(\frac{\Delta Y}{Y}\right)\nu, \tag{27}$$

$$S < \Delta Y \cdot \frac{\Delta K}{\Delta Y}, \tag{28}$$

$$S < I. \tag{29}$$

Result (29) indicates a continuous lag of production behind demand. So long as this persists, employers will go on being happy, the economy will be buoyant, perhaps inflationary, and investment will continue to accelerate.

The Razor's Edge

Harrod's warranted or equilibrium rate of growth is a path which, once left, is difficult to come back to. There is nothing inherent in Harrod's model to cause such a return. To be sure, the situation is not all black. Not all investment is induced by the accelerator. Some is "autonomous," undertaken in order to take advantage of changes in technology, changes in the interest rate, changes in population, etc. Moreover, if "secular stagnation" sets in the authorities may shift to monetary ease which, together with some decline in price and wage levels, may stimulate aggregate demand.

Nevertheless, Harrod's conclusions *are* disturbing. Unless some of these "ad hoc" events take place, a condition of $G_w > G_{nat}$ would cause a condition of chronic slack. $G_w < G_{nat}$ would lead to chronic inflation amidst growing unemployment.

Hence, the question naturally arises: can we put something into the Harrodian model which will cause gaps between G_w and G_{nat} to close?

Adjustments in *v* and *s*

When discrepancies between the natural and warranted rates of growth exist and threaten to produce either secular stagnation or exhilaration, it is possible to have changes in the capital-output ratio and/or the saving ratio which tend to close the gap between G_w and G_{nat}. Indeed, there is reason to believe that discrepancies will *call forth* such adjustments.

Take first the case of exhilaration, where G_{nat} stands above G_w. This situation is characterized by a relative abundance of labor, a high capital-output ratio, and an insufficient level of aggregate saving in every period. The relative abundance of labor should operate to lower the price of labor relative to that of capital. This will encourage substitutions of labor for capital at given levels of output and lower capital-output ratio. Such substitutions will take place in two ways. First, throughout the economy labor-using techniques will be encouraged. Second, the cost to consumers of labor-intensive goods and services should fall relative to those which are capital intensive. This should lead to an increase in the production of labor-intensive, as opposed to capital-intensive, products. As a result, the over-all average capital-output ratio in the economy should fall.

A second effect of the fall in the price of labor relative to that of capital might be a shift in the distribution of income away from labor. Such a shift depends upon the degree of substitutability of labor for capital. If it is small, then labor's share will fall if wages decline relative to profits. If it is large, labor's share will rise.[19]

If labor's share of income does fall, the saving rate in the economy might rise, because labors' propensity to save is smaller than that of businessmen. If labor's share rises, of course, the saving rate for the economy might fall.

---

[19] Students familiar with the theory of production will note that "degree of substitutability of labor for capital" refers to the "elasticity of substitution of labor for capital." If this elasticity is below unity, a 1 percent decline in the price of labor relative to that of capital will cause a decline in labor's share. Vice versa if the elasticity is greater than unity.

Kendrick, *op. cit.,* believes the elasticity of substitution in the United States is less than unity.

Two forces, then, might combine to raise G_w when $G_w < G_{nat}$. The first is a fall in v and the second is a (possible) rise in s. It might be noted, parenthetically, that G_{nat} might also be affected, since a persistence of labor surplus in this case could lead to a slowing of labor force growth, G_n.

Secular stagnation—$G_w > G_{nat}$—might be accompanied by opposite adjustments in v and s. Since Harrodian stagnation implies labor shortages relative to the capital stock, laborsaving technological change is insufficient to overcome these shortages. Hence the price of labor should rise relative to that of capital, inducing a rise in the capital-output ratio. A fall in the saving rate might accompany the rise in v, particularly if the increase in the relative price of labor causes labor's share of income to rise. Such a rise, of course, would lead to a decrease in s, the over-all propensity to save in the economy. At the same time, the persistent labor shortages might lead to an increase in G_n, tending to raise G_{nat}.

It is important to emphasize that the adjustments spoken of above may not be complete enough to actually close the gap between G_w and G_{nat}, except for short periods of time. There is no mechanism, for example, which will guarantee enough substitution of labor for capital to raise G_w (through lowering v) into line with G_{nat} during a period characterized by secular exhilaration. The appropriate mechanisms for this would be sufficient price flexibility of both labor and capital goods and intensified application of capital-saving technology, neither of which may be forthcoming.

In the short run, however, the adjustments may be overly complete, in the sense that the gap $G_w > G_{nat}$ may be converted into the gap $G_{nat} > G_w$, and vice versa. In other words, the adjustment may operate to switch temporarily stagnation to exhilaration and exhilaration to stagnation. Such a result can easily stem from a short-run marginal propensity to save which is greater than the long-run propensity. Exhilaration, for example, implies that $\Delta I/I > s/v$. The rapid growth of income may be sufficient to raise the short-run s by enough to switch the inequality to $\Delta I/I < s/v$. The result, of course, would be deflationary, and the fall in income may pull investment, the left side of the inequality, down also. But the fall in income will probably also result in a decline in the short-run s, and if a sufficient substratum of autonomous investment exists, the contraction may soon be reversed and the inequality $\Delta I/I > s/v$ may again assert itself. Adjustments in s, therefore, can lead to a state of secular exhilaration with short-lived relapses into mild depression. Secular stagnation will probably lead to opposite conditions—long and deep depressions with temporary revivals.

Obstacles to Steady Growth

The warranted rate of growth proceeds along a rather precarious growth path. Indeed, the path is cluttered with potential obstacles standing in the way of continuous growth. In the first place, as will be remembered, the warranted growth rate is that rate which keeps businessmen satisfied enough to continue increasing their investment outlays in a way which will just keep the economy growing at the appropriate rate. Of course, this does not imply that all businessmen are kept satisfied by gains. It does imply, however, that those suffering losses and reducing their investment outlays will just be counterbalanced by entrepreneurs experiencing gain. One wonders if losses can be neutral, if the dismal expectations induced by setbacks can be confined to unlucky firms and not be transmitted to more fortunate ones. The theory presupposes the compartmentalizing of expectations in the economy, but during periods of stagnation (or exhilaration) pessimism (or optimism) hardly seems likely to be confined to particular groups of entrepreneurs. Indeed, if the gap between G_{nat} and G_w produces stagnation (exhilaration), the contagion of bad (good) times would probably lead businessmen to expect worse (better) results in the future than those of the immediate past. The spread of such expectations would throw the economy off the equilibrium path of growth into deeper stagnation (or more rapid inflation).

An additional potential obstacle to growth might appear in the money and capital markets. Continued growth of real output implies the necessity of an increasing money supply. If money does not increase at an appropriate rate, the drain upon the financial markets resulting from the growing size of transaction balances will put upward pressure upon interest rates. Rising interest rates will tend to dampen enthusiasm for additional capital projects and lower the rate of investment. This cannot help but push the economy off the equilibrium path of growth. The only way out of this, short of increasing the money supply, is for prices and wages to fall along with the growth in income. This will have the multiple effect of raising the real level of cash, of leaving the marginal efficiency of capital unimpaired, and, if the Pigou effect is operative, of lowering the propensity to save (thereby decreasing s/v). However, effective price flexibility depends upon competitive product and labor markets. If "price-administering" industries and labor unions refuse to let prices and wages fall, the money supply must increase in order to prevent an excessive rise in the interest rate.[20]

The problem of creating opportunities for and actually generating a continuous and increasing flow of *autonomous investment* poses one of the main secular, or long-run, potential obstacles to steady growth. Autonomous investment is important because it makes possible adjustments to excessive or deficient growth in the labor force, the economizing of scarce raw materials, and application of advances in technology and invention. In short, without a proper flow of autonomous investment, the growth of the economy would grind to a stop through a fall in the output-capital ratio.

But autonomous investment does not necessarily proceed at a pace, and with a composition, which will guarantee steady progress. It depends upon the willingness and ability of the business community to apply appropriate innovations; and this is notwithstanding the necessary existence of the appropriate technology. Despite the inventiveness of engineers and scientists, there may be compelling economic reasons which prevent the application of the most up-to-date developments. For one thing, a new process or superior equipment may be too expensive to install and may require too long a period for recovery of the investment. The old equipment may not be obsolete enough to make economical its replacement with the new. Furthermore, even given the economy of the new methods and equipment, an individual firm may have to wait upon actions of other firms, and even the government, before changes can be made. This is because new technology often requires the development and manufacture of specialized equipment, the training of proper personnel, the development of new sources of power and raw materials, and, perhaps, the unbottling of unexercised patent rights. The difficulties connected with the industrial application of atomic power indicate, perhaps too dramatically, the problems faced by innovators.

To be sure, the problems of innovation are somewhat less serious in industrially advanced countries than they are in the backward areas of the world. The latter do not have reservoirs of trained workers and managers, advanced machine-tool industries, well-developed power resources, and, what is probably most important, broad enough markets to support capital-intensive mass-production industries. On the other

---

[20] Moreover, falling prices would probably generate pessimism among businessmen, even though falling costs are keeping real profits unimpaired. In such circumstances, it is hard to believe that the warranted rate of growth in investment could be maintained.

hand, being backward does have the advantage of putting a country in the position of starting with the most advanced technology appropriate to local conditions. The burden of obsolete methods and equipment need not be borne during the growth process. As a result, autonomous investment may have considerable scope.

A variety of institutional impediments may also block the growth of autonomous investment. Mention has already been made of the obstacles provided by the patent system. Patents may be issued to firms which do not care to exercise them but wish only to prevent other firms from applying the new inventions. Patents may be used as a device for forcing firms to accept a whole array of outmoded equipment in the interest of getting the patented item. Patentees may also refuse to grant licenses to other firms, thus preventing a broad application of the new technology.

An important item on the list of institutional blockages is monopoly. Whether in the form of a single firm or an oligopoly, monopolistic market structures can result in considerable delay in the application of new technology. Monopolies typically operate with excess capacity, and the inducement of new technology must be fairly large to encourage its application. Oligopolistic firms must first consult the impact on competitors before launching upon a project which will seriously injure their relative market positions. To some extent, of course, monopoly may yield more rapid innovation, because higher profits make research and innovation somewhat easier. It is hard to say, however, whether this advantage offsets the disadvantages progress meets under imperfect competition.

If a proper rate of autonomous investment and technical change do not offset them, deficient population growth and increasing scarcity of raw materials may substantially reduce the output-capital ratio as successive applications of new investment meet diminishing marginal returns. Most growth models simply postulate a given population growth and compare it with the rate of growth in capital and income. If the rate of growth in population (and labor) falls below that of capital, other things being equal, the models predict a fall in the marginal productivity of capital and the rate of growth. A rate of growth of population which exceeds that of capital will enhance the economy's growth rate. It may be more realistic to make population a variable which, in addition to capital, is also dependent upon the economy's growth rate. A more rapid rate of growth in income should result in rising wages and, perhaps, in increasing desire on the part of workers to raise larger families. Moreover, larger incomes make possible better medical care and should induce a fall in the death rate. By similar reasoning, a slowing of the rate of increase in income may lead to a fall-off of population.

If the induced changes in population growth are directly proportional to changes in the rate of income growth, they will tend to offset the decline in the marginal productivity of capital occasioned by initial disparities in the growth of capital and population. However, a large measure of caution must qualify this conclusion. It is not at all necessary that workers exercise higher incomes in the form of larger families. They also have the option of higher levels of consumption. Moreover, as income growth takes place, society may choose not to take further increases, taking instead increased leisure. This effect may offset some of the increase in the labor force resulting from rising population. The laws governing the growth of population and the labor force are not yet known with sufficient accuracy to permit confident forecasts.

Generally speaking, increasing raw material scarcities have been offset by technical change in the more advanced countries. This has been accomplished by importation, by finding natural substitutes, and by synthesizing others. At present, raw material scarcity does not appear to be a major obstacle to growth in the industrialized countries of the world. However, it does plague the efforts of many underdeveloped countries which have severe resource deficiencies and few means of importing or synthesizing them.

SUMMARY

In this chapter we explored three principal questions: (*a*) what determines the growth in potential output? (*b*) What are the conditions necessary to assure that production potenial is fully utilized over time? (*c*) How stable is the growth path over time?

The first question was approached with the concept of the production function. This concept allowed us to assess the role of capital and labor force growth and the part played by technical change. We concluded that technical change explains the major part of growth in potential output in the United States. Investment—particularly replacement investment—is important to the growth of potential output mainly because it is the carrier of new technology. Recent studies have also placed new emphasis upon education and other factors in the growth process.

The continuous utilization of expanding potential output is a complicated problem, involving appropriate adjustments in the supply and demand for money, price level movements, and continuing expansion of consumption and investment demand. There is some reason to believe that both consumption and investment demand expand automatically with output growth. However, as Harrod's model in particular shows, continuous equilibrium between actual and potential output is difficult to maintain over time.

ADDITIONAL READINGS

DOMAR, E. D. "Expansion and Employment," *American Economic Review,* March, 1947. Reprinted in H. R. WILLIAMS and J. D. HUFFNAGLE, *Macroeconomic Theory: Selected Readings.* New York: Appleton-Century-Crofts, 1969. An early post-Keynesian classic in growth theory.

FELLNER, W. *Trends and Cycles in Economic Activity.* New York: Henry Holt, 1956. Useful discussion of problems of economic growth, with particular attention given to stability of growth paths.

HARROD, R. *Towards a Dynamic Economics.* London: The Macmillan Co., 1948, Lecture 3. Harrod's contribution, along with Domar's, set the stage for postwar development of theory of growth.

HICKS, J. R. *Capital and Growth.* New York and Oxford: Oxford University Press, 1965. Hick's widely read survey of and contribution to growth theory.

KALDOR, N. and MIRLEES, J. A. "A New Model of Economic Growth," *Review of Economic Studies,* June, 1962. Reprinted in Williams and Huffnagle, *op. cit.* A widely discussed growth model incorporating a "technical progress function" and obsolescence.

SCHUMPETER, JOSEPH. *The Theory of Economic Development.* Cambridge: Harvard University Press, 1934. An exciting and influential book on how technological change and entrepreneurial innovation affect growth and fluctuations in a capitalist society.

SOLOW, R. M. "A Contribution to the Theory of Economic Growth," *Quarterly Journal of Economics,* February, 1966. (Reprinted in Williams and Huffnagle, *op. cit.*) An influential statement of growth theory in neoclassical terms.

TOBIN, J. "A Dynamic Aggregative Model," *Journal of Political Economy,* April, 1955. (Reprinted in Williams and Huffnagle, *op. cit.*) An early attempt to introduce money into growth models.

Chapter 15

AGGREGATE THEORY AND PUBLIC POLICY

The macroeconomic models discussed in the last several chapters purport to describe how the economy works. In those models there is considerable scope for government to have an impact upon the economy. Through fiscal policy—public spending and taxing—and monetary policy—manipulation of the money supply—government officials can attempt to intervene in the workings of the economy with the purpose of achieving certain goals or targets. The theory of economic policy is designed to grapple with the manner and purpose of policy. The theory of policy makes use of the macroeconomic theory, but macroeconomic theory is not designed to tell officials exactly what their goals *ought* to be: that is a problem for welfare economics, a subject we briefly commented upon in Chapter 1. In this and the next chapter we shall not go beyond our earlier discussion of welfare economics. We shall, instead, provide a general discussion of the various targets of economic policy and the means by which government may achieve them.

The Theory of Economic Policy[1]

In a sense, the theory of economic policy turns macroeconomic theory around. Recall that the model developed in earlier chapters puts variables like real income, employment, prices, the interest rate, and consumption into the class of dependent or endogenous variables. As such, these items are determined partly by exogenous forces, such as expectations, and partly by variables controlled by the government. In the latter class fall government expenditure and tax policies and monetary policies. Policy variables are in most macroeconomic models. The theory of

---

[1] The following discussion is in the spirit of the approach of Jan Tinbergen, *Economic Policy: Principles and Design* (Amsterdam: North Holland Publishing Co., 1956). See, also, Bent Hansen, *The Economic Theory of Fiscal Policy* (Cambridge: Harvard University Press, 1958), Part I.

economic policy turns this scheme around. For example, instead of asking what the level of real income will be under assumed values for the various policy instruments, the theory postulates a target for real income and asks what the values of the policy instruments must be in order to achieve that target. The policy variables, in other words, become the dependent variables of the model, while some or all of the other variables become the independent variables.

By posing the question of policy in this way, economists have come up with some useful propositions. The first proposition is that the number of policy instruments used must at least equal the number of independent targets sought by policy makers. The second proposition is that when there are multiple targets, there must be coordination between the agencies responsible for the use of the various instruments.

A simple example illustrates both of these propositions. Macroeconomic theory teaches us that real income and the price level can both fall under the influence of monetary and fiscal policy. Formalize this knowledge in equations (1) and (2), where G refers to government spending and M refers to the money supply:

$$Y = a + bG + cM \tag{1}$$
$$P = d + eG + fM \tag{2}$$

In (1) and (2) we have two equations in *four* variables; hence, even if the equations are independent we cannot find unique solutions for the variables unless we reduce the number of variables to two. In our previous discussions we treated G and M as being given by government policy and sought the solutions for P and Y. In the present discussion, we reverse the process by assuming the policy makers have a good notion of what they want the values of Y and P to be; hence, Y and P take on given (or target) values, and solutions are sought for G and M (the policy instruments).

In order to achieve both of their targets, the authorities must use both of their policy instruments. That is what the equations require. If the authorities wish to add more targets, they must add more instruments. For example, suppose they wish to control the rate of interest. Their knowledge of the economic system may yield them the following equation respecting the impact of government spending and the money supply on the interest rate:

$$i = h + kG - qM \tag{3}$$

If i becomes a target, the equation system becomes (* indicates "target"):

$$Y^* = a + bG + cM \tag{1}$$
$$P^* = d + eG + fM \tag{2}$$
$$i^* = h + kG - qM \tag{3}$$

This is a system with three equations and only two unknowns. It cannot be solved unless we add another unknown (or instrument). To do so, we consult our economic knowledge and conclude that taxes, T, can be used as an additional instrument. Adding the effect of taxes to the system we get:

$$Y^* = a + bG + cM - jT \tag{4}$$
$$P^* = b + eG + fM - mT \tag{5}$$
$$i^* = h + kG - qM - nT . \tag{6}$$

If a fourth target is added, a fourth instrument must be added. The general rule, therefore, should be evident: There must be at least the same number of policy instruments as there are policy targets.

The proposition that there must be the same number of instruments as there are targets is, of course, too simple for adequate policymaking. It may be that some of the targets are not amenable to manipulation by policy instruments. For example, if the economy is already at full employment, manipulation of G, M, and T cannot help the authorities to achieve a real income target greater than the current level. Presumably, it is possible to use other policy instruments to raise income above its full-employment level—forced labor, for example; but this requires the use of instruments which go beyond those usually discussed in macroeconomic theory.

A related problem is potential conflict amongst policy goals. Earlier we discussed the concept of the Phillips curve. The Phillips curve tells us that there is a conflict between stable prices and the level of employment: Reduce unemployment and the economy will experience a rise in prices. Reduce unemployment further and the increase in prices will accelerate. Attempts to circumvent this conflict have forced authorities to go outside the policy instruments embedded in most macroeconomic models. The Kennedy and Johnson administrations, for example, tried to establish a set of "wage-price guidelines" in order to prevent prices from rising as a result of the inflationary forces unleashed by the applications of strong doses of expansionary monetary and fiscal policies during their administrations. Price and wage controls during World War II and the Korean War are other examples of such attempts.

The second proposition—that there must be coordination between agencies responsible for policy—follows directly from the equation system presented above. It is clear that in most cases no single target is related to only one policy instrument. If the fiscal authorities strive for a particular level of GNP, the monetary authorities must not allow fluctuations in the money supply which will conflict with the tax or expenditure policies designed to achieve the target. Otherwise, the economy may find itself entangled in a set of fluctuations induced by the government. One can imagine such a situation arising as follows. Suppose the fiscal authorities (Congress or the Administration) attempt to achieve a target GNP of $900 billion, but that the monetary authorities believe that the price level connected with this level of GNP is unacceptable. In pursuit of its target, Congress cuts taxes. As GNP rises, the price level also rises. The rise in prices leads the Federal Reserve System to reduce the money supply. The reduction in the money supply either prevents GNP from increasing to $900 billion or causes it to fall back. In response, taxes are again reduced and GNP is again stimulated, along with the price level, which causes the Fed to again reduce the money and hence GNP, and so on.

It is not true, therefore, that our economic policies can be conducted on the premise that each agency is responsible for a different policy target. To be sure, policy instruments are generally in the hands of different agencies,[2] but it does not follow from this that the different agencies are free to pursue independently separate policy targets. Common agreement on a set of targets is necessary; otherwise, the agencies can easily work at cross-purposes.

The two policy propositions derived above are not enough to equip policy makers to do their work. They need considerable knowledge about the way in which policy targets and policy instruments interact. This means that they must be able to specify a model of the economy which contains the appropriate interactions. In addition, they must undertake empirical studies which allow them to "fit" the model to the economy. The empirical studies are necessary because policy makers must have an idea of the *degree* of interaction to expect between the variables in the model. It is not enough to know, for example, that a tax cut will stimulate consumption and, through the multiplier, national income. It is also important to know the *degree* to which consumption is affected by a cut in taxes and the *degree* to which income is affected by an increase in consumption. Similar knowledge is also required for judg-

---

[2] This is not completely correct. Monetary powers are mainly in the hands of the Federal Reserve System, but the U.S. Treasury also has power to affect the money supply if it so chooses.

ing the potential impact of changes in other policy instruments upon consumption and income, especially since these other instruments will generally be in use along with taxes to help achieve other policy targets. The point is that *each* instrument will affect *all* targets; hence, an optimal mix of instruments cannot be achieved without a knowledge of the potential quantitative impact of each instrument on all targets.[3]

We are far from being able to conduct an efficient program of economic policy in the sense discussed in this section. Economists both in and out of government are currently engaged in a number of studies of the structure of the economy and the relation of policy instruments to policy targets. Many of these studies are highly detailed and highly sophisticated econometric exercises. There is still much disagreement as to exactly how the various policy instruments affect the various aspects of economic activity. It would take us too far afield to launch into a discussion of these studies. In the final chapter we shall comment upon some of the controversies arising from recent findings. In the meantime, we use the balance of this chapter to comment upon four important targets or goals of aggregative policy: full employment, stable prices, economic growth, and the balance of payments. In the next chapter we shall concentrate upon some of the major instruments of policy.

The Meaning of Full Employment

Full employment has been variously defined by different writers. In the final analysis, however, policy makers are free to adopt whatever definition they wish, so long as the implications of the definition are understood and accepted. A committee for the United Nations, for example, in a 1949 report defined full employment "as a situation in which employment cannot be increased by an increase in effective de-

---

[3] A simple example will help explain this paragraph. Let Y^* and P^* be the policy targets to be achieved through manipulation of G and M:

$$Y^* = bG + cM$$
$$P^* = eG + fM .$$

An optimal mix of G and M is derived from the solution of these two equations:

$$G = \frac{fY^* - cP^*}{bf - ec}$$

$$M = \frac{bP^* - eY^*}{bf - ec} .$$

The policy makers know Y^* and P^* because they are targets. But they cannot set G and M at appropriate levels without quantitative information about b, c, e, and f.

mand."[4] Presumably, the committee was thinking in terms of the point on the aggregate supply function at which the curve turns completely inelastic. After this point, further increases in aggregate demand will evoke price increases without any increases in output.

For some writers, R. A. Gordon, for example,[5] this definition goes too far, because it implies an acceptance of inflation as a price for stimulating increases in employment. (Before the aggregate supply function turns completely inelastic, marginal costs typically rise with the increase in output and employment.) Nevertheless, we cannot quibble with the definition so long as inflation is accepted as a cost to be borne in achieving the defined level of full employment.[6] Those who do not like inflation would probably define full employment to be that point at which a further increase in effective demand and employment would induce increases in the price level. Actually, this is not full employment, but "stable prices employment." It indicates a policy of *high* employment levels, with stable prices as a twin objective. In terms of the U.N. definition, the cost of this policy is some unemployment.

Full employment is often defined from the standpoint of the desires of the labor force. Thus, a committee of the American Economic Association in 1950 defined full employment to mean

that qualified people who seek jobs at prevailing wage rates can find them in productive activities without considerable delay. It means full-time jobs for people who want to work full time. It does not mean that people like housewives and students are under pressure to take jobs when they do not want jobs, or that workers are under pressure to put in undesired overtime. It does not mean that unemployment is ever zero. People are unemployed for a time while changing jobs. Full employment is the absence of mass unemployment.[7]

This definition deserves some comment. First, it obviously does not state that full employment exists when all of those who *can* work *are* working. The reason for this is clear. Only those who want to work should be considered part of the labor force in a capitalist economy. This is probably considerably less than the size of a labor force in noncapitalist authoritarian societies: slavery and other forced labor can greatly

---

4 United Nations, *National and International Measures for Full Employment*, p. 13.

5 *Business Fluctuations* (2nd ed.; New York: Harper & Bros., 1961), pp. 545–46.

6 The experts who framed the U.N. report were aware of the cost and recommended policies to modify it. See Arthur Smithies' "Comment" on Professor Viner's attack on the U.N. report in William D. Grampp and Emanuel T. Weiler (eds.), *Economic Policy* (Homewood, Ill.: Richard D. Irwin, Inc., 1953), pp. 93–97. Smithies was a member of the U.N. committee that framed the report.

7 "The Problem of Economic Instability," *American Economic Review*, Vol. XL (September, 1950), p. 506.

expand the size of the working population. Indeed, in these countries it is possible to expand employment considerably without forcing a rise in the price level.

The definition does not imply, however, that labor under capitalism is absolutely free. Workers must be qualified and must not seek work at wage rates in excess of those which are prevailing in the jobs in which work is sought. Workers who do not abide by these conditions are excluded, by definition, from the labor force. In essence, the committee is saying that a capitalist society cannot be expected to employ workers on workers' terms if those terms conflict with the ones which are prevalent in the market. On the other hand, if workers are willing to accept the terms laid down in the labor market and they do not find employment, they will be counted as unemployed. Thus, the engineer who cannot find work at the prevailing salary in his specialty will be counted as unemployed, even though he may have been forced to accept a low-wage job as a common laborer.

There is some point to singling out those workers who are employed in less productive occupations than their training and skills suit them for. To a degree they are unemployed: aggregate output in the economy is lessened because of the nonrealization of their potential contribution. There is also some point to stipulating that qualified workers who seek work at prevailing wage rates should be able to find jobs without considerable delay. When they cannot, this indicates that the demand for their services is insufficient to give them the employment they seek. The definition therefore implies that unemployment can be eliminated by policies which result in an increase in aggregate demand.

Keynes has been criticized for adopting a definition of unemployment similar to that implied in the AEA committee's statement. He maintained that workers were involuntarily unemployed when they could not find work at going wage rates. Keynes' critics maintained that such unemployment can be eliminated if workers agree to accept lower wage rates. If they do not, they are not involuntarily unemployed, but are out of work of their own choice.

Keynes' answer to this kind of criticism is contained in Chapter 2 of the *General Theory*. The classical theory, he argued, assumes that labor can lower its *real* wage by accepting lower *money* wages. He pointed out that this assumption may not be, and probably in general is not, correct. What may be true of an individual worker is not necessarily true for the whole of labor. A general reduction in money wages increases employment only if it induces expansion in aggregate demand. As he pointed out in his subsequent analysis (which we have explored above), an expansion in aggregate demand induced by wage cuts depends upon the repercussions of the cuts on interest rates and spending. The extent and certainty of these indirect effects are by no means clear. It was this uncertainty that Keynes had in mind when he asserted: "There may exist no expedient by which labour as a whole can reduce its *real* wage to a given figure by making revised *money* wage bargains with the entrepreneurs."[8]

Actually, from the standpoint of acceptable economic policy, Keynes' definition of involuntary unemployment is more useful. The practices of industry, the preferences of workers, and the insistence of trade unions generally keep wage rates fairly rigid during periods of unemployment. A government which proceeded to conquer unemployment with forced wage cuts would soon be out of office. For practical purposes, therefore, unemployment at prevailing wage rates is the most useful concept for policy makers.

Since the Keynesian and AEA committee definitions suggest that involuntary unemployment may be cured by increasing aggregate demand, other kinds of unemployment are still possible, even though the economy is at "full employment." One of these varieties is *frictional unemployment*. Frictionally unemployed workers are those who are in the process of changing jobs (because of choice or because their particular employers are forced to lay them off), those who are unemployed because of sickness, and those who are temporarily out of work due to seasonal factors. This kind of unemployment always exists and there is little that general economic policy can do to eliminate it. Indeed, if ordinary monetary policies were used to reduce frictional unemployment, inflation, with very little added employment, would probably result. Actually, so long as the frictionally unemployed can go back to work without unreasonable delay, as the AEA committee suggests, it does not represent a serious national economic problem.

A different breed of unemployment is *technological unemployment* —workers displaced by machinery or by new processes. It is this kind of unemployment which Karl Marx argued would result in a growing army of unemployed in capitalist societies. Technological unemployment can be wiped out only if aggregate demand and output increase rapidly, or if industries which are relatively labor intensive expand rapidly. Classical economists used to argue that the reduction in wage rates resulting from the competition of the unemployed with the employed plus the increase in productivity resulting from the technological innovation would lower prices and increase the amount of goods and

---

[8] Keynes, *General Theory*, p. 13.

services sold. Actually, if the elasticity of aggregate demand with respect to reductions in the price level is less than unitary, the reemployment of the technologically unemployed will be relatively less than the decrease in prices. Moreover, if forces keeping wages from falling are present, the mechanism will not operate at all. From our discussions of the Pigou effect and the effect of trade-union policies, these results are definite possibilities. Should they happen, the only way to put the technologically unemployed back to work is by using fiscal and monetary policy to increase aggregate demand.

A third kind of unemployment not traceable to a fall in aggregate demand is *disguised unemployment*. Disguised unemployment exists in many of the labor-surplus underdeveloped countries. It can be detected by removing the suspected worker from his "employment." If the result is an increase in output (signifying that his marginal physical product is negative), or no decrease in output (zero marginal productivity), it may be said that the worker was nominally employed, but that, since his work was not economically significant, he was in a state of disguised unemployment. There is some dispute as to the prevalence of disguised unemployment. Many writers argue that, given the level of technique and organization for production, the industries in which disguised unemployment is said to exist would suffer from a loss of labor.

In recent years the concept of *structural unemployment* has become popular. Writers who use the term are not always clear about what they mean. However, most seem to be referring to unemployment resulting from "defects" in the labor market which prevent the unemployed from either finding or acquiring jobs. The list of these defects includes geographical and occupational immobilities, sex, race, health, and age barriers, and imperfect knowledge of job opportunities.

The concept of structural unemployment includes the notion that there exists in some markets excess demand for workers: a surplus of jobs waiting for workers who, if they were of the right age, sex, race, geography, training, etc., could have those jobs. Those who use the concept of structural unemployment usually admit its kinship to the concept of frictional unemployment, particularly for those thrown out of work because of automation or other causes. Structural unemployment in some ways may be thought of as substantial and long-term frictional unemployment.

It should not be supposed that the various kinds of unemployment are unrelated. Aside from the strong family resemblance between frictional and structural unemployment, there is also the connection between technological unemployment and the structural type. Technical change which throws people out of work is the initiator of unemployment. Structural factors may prevent reemployment of the people thrown out of work. Again, *disguised unemployment* may be due to the inability of workers to find alternative employment.

Much of the confusion over definitions of unemployment can be eliminated if it is recognized that unemployment has two principal aspects: that which might cause workers to initially lose their jobs and that which might prevent them from acquiring new ones. Deficient demand or rapid technological change may cause job losses, while structural factors and deficient aggregate demand may prevent them from being reemployed. In this context, disguised unemployment simply represents a form of existing labor use which might be eliminated with, say, a removal of structural barriers.

It is also helpful to recognize a possible positive correlation between structural unemployment and unemployment resulting from deficient aggregate demand. The barriers which exist between the unemployed and the jobs they need may be thought of as cost barriers. For example, geographical immobility is a compound of the cost of leaving an area —e.g., selling a home in a depressed area—and the cost of transporting and resettling a worker and his dependents in a new area. In addition, of course, there are the psychic costs of moving to a new environment.

Moving the worker to a new location is a matter of reducing the relocation costs, making wages attractive enough to overcome the costs, or accepting the costs as a public or business burden rather than as a burden on the worker and his family. The first alternative is difficult to achieve, since relocation costs change very slowly. Shifting the cost burden to the public is a proposal often made by people who have studied the retraining and relocation programs of Sweden. Making wages more attractive can be accomplished either by subsidizing the employer or by increasing employers' demand for labor. Finally, employers will accept costs of increasing mobility only if they find it profitable to do so.

It is in the last two alternatives that the connection between removing geographical structural unemployment and raising aggregate demand exists. An increase in aggregate demand will lead to an increase in the demand for labor. With sufficient profit incentives employers will be motivated to raise wages and even help pay part of the relocation costs of workers—e.g., through subsidizing the transport of household goods and family.

It should be apparent that the same principle applies to other types of structural unemployment. High potential profits encourage employers to accept retraining costs, to accept women, oldsters, and even invalids into the labor force. The same conditions lead employers to advertise job vacanices more widely and to hire labor recruiters to scout the country for appropriate workers. Finally, employers may be induced to change their methods of production to accommodate different types of workers.

Those who have studied the rapid expansion of employment during World War II will readily appreciate these remarks. Unemployment, which was chronic through the preceding decade, fell from some 10 percent of the labor force in 1941 to about 1 percent in 1944. Gross national product, meanwhile, rose extraordinarily fast: from $125 billion to $211 billion. In the process, people were rapidly retrained, shifted to defense centers, and were employed seemingly regardless of sex, age, or race.

To be sure, eliminating structural unemployment by increasing aggregate demand may be quite inflationary. Whether society is willing to accept this cost is a matter for society to determine through its political processes. Nevertheless, it is useful to know of the relationship between structural unemployment and unemployment induced by deficient demand. If structural factors are the source of substantial unemployment, society can choose to eliminate such unemployment by accepting the costs of reducing them or by pumping up aggregate demand.[9]

Stable Prices

The AEA committee defines the goal of price stability as follows: "Price-level stability means the absence of any marked trend or sharp, short-term movements in the general level of prices."[10] Marked upward and downward trends and heavy short-term fluctuations in the *price level* are to be avoided. This does not mean that *individual prices* should not change; such changes are necessary if the price mechanism is to perform its allocating function.

The committee's preference for stable prices was based upon the belief that sharp declines in the price level are likely to be accompanied by serious unemployment and that rising prices hurt those whose income

---

[9] For a good discussion of the relationship between unemployment due to structural factors and that due to deficient demand, see the *Economic Report of the President*, January, 1964 (Washington, D.C.: U.S. Government Printing Office), pp. 166–90. This is a reprint of a statement of the Council of Economic Advisors before the Senate Committee on Labor and Public Welfare, October, 1963.

[10] "The Problem of Economic Instability," *op. cit.*, p. 506.

does not rise as rapidly as the rise in living costs. In addition, inflation is to be condemned because it "sharpens conflicts of economic interest and impairs the group consensus necessary for solving national problems."

There are additional arguments for making stable prices the goal of economic policy. Professor Lloyd Mints, for example, believed that a policy which succeeds in stabilizing an appropriate price index will also stabilize employment and production. His argument was that sharp declines in the price level signify depression and that policies which bring back the old price level will also stimulate aggregate demand and employment. Inflation, on the other hand, indicates overfull employment and can be taken care of without danger of precipitating extensive unemployment, which the policy will automatically prevent. Mints' proposal, somewhat oversimplified here, will not begin to work unless prices are flexible and sensitive to changes in demand and cost-push is not a serious force underlying inflation. If prices are not flexible, a recession will bring significant reductions in income and employment, even though prices remain fairly stable. Moreover, if prices are rising because of cost increases, stabilization of the price level will result in a reduction of employment.[11]

In his book *Banking Policy and the Price Level,* the influential English economist, D. H. Robertson,[12] eschewed short-term price stability and recommended instead that "appropriate" fluctuations be allowed. His view was based upon the idea that periodic upward surges in the price level are necessarily associated with capital booms and that, since these booms are necessary to economic growth in capitalist societies, they should not be inhibited by restrictive economic policies. Robertson's approach would probably result in a long-term rise in the price level, because it is difficult to imagine modern authorities allowing "appropriate" *declines* in the price level. As Robertson himself was aware, such declines have an excellent chance of turning into major depressions, a situation which is much more difficult to handle than inappropriate increases in the price level.

A distinction is often made between short-run and long-run price stability; but it is a nice but crucial question whether long- and short-run price movements can be discussed separately. If the trend is dependent

---

[11] Mints' arguments are presented in his book, *Monetary Policy for a Competitive Society* (New York: McGraw-Hill Book Co., Inc., 1950).

[12] D. H. Robertson, *Banking Policy and the Price Level* (Reprint of 1932 ed.; New York: Augustus M. Kelley, Inc., 1949).

upon the nature of the short-run fluctuations, then long-term policy is intimately bound up with policy for the short run. This is Robertson's point. On the other hand, if the trend movement of the price level is independent of short-run fluctuations, a separate long-term policy is conceivable.

Those who believe that a separate long-term policy is possible fall into three categories—those who recommend gently rising prices, those who believe in constant prices, and those who think the price level should drift down. The first group bases its argument upon the need to provide favorable incentives for businessmen and a liberal credit environment for new investment. The third group thinks that falling prices should be geared to increases in productivity so that the public at large, as well as entrepreneurs, may enjoy the benefits. The second group believes in price stability, mainly because of the evils that may be connected with the two other positions. They argue that gently rising prices, especially if the public is aware of them as a policy objective, are impossible. Soon the public will begin to anticipate the rise and act in ways to accelerate it. The end result will be galloping inflation. Falling prices, presumably would have the opposite effect. If the public *expects* prices to fall, it will hold back its spending in anticipation of the lower prices. This will cause prices to fall faster than planned, lead the public to hold back again, and accelerate the speed of price declines even more. The only sane policy, therefore, is one directed toward price stability; this goal will not lead the public to act in ways which accelerate price movements either way. As a matter of fact, governments rarely have the luxury of being able to establish a long-term price level policy. The struggles with short-term fluctuations are so great and so complicated that trend price movements bear little or no relation to a conscious long-run policy.

Economic Growth

Economic growth is wanted both for its own sake and because it is necessary in a capitalist society to have growth in order to maintain stability of production and employment. Presumably, the higher the rate of growth the better we like it, especially if the proceeds of growth are shared by most participants in the economy. Unfortunately, we cannot always have the rate of growth we desire. It was pointed out in Chapter 14 that there exists at any point in time a potential rate of growth, imposed by the existing rate of growth in population and changes in technology. General monetary and fiscal policies cannot push the actual rate of growth in the economy much beyond the natural growth rate. If the actual rate of growth is pressing hard against the potential rate, however, policies designed to raise the potential rate of growth are possible. These include the stimulation of technical change (via research, tax subsidies, social investments, improved educational facilities, etc.) and, perhaps, encouragement of population growth and programs designed to utilize more effectively the labor force.

A policy of growth cannot stand by itself. In the first place, since growth requires saving it also requires the sacrifice of present consumption. An increase in the rate of growth can take place with additional personal saving, but it normally entails more business saving as well. The extra business saving may not be available without changes in the corporate share of national income, the average dividend paid to stockholders, the tax structure, or the organization of capital markets.

Equally important, a policy of growth cannot stand isolated from stabilization policy. If the policy forces growth at too rapid a pace, inflation may result. On the other hand, a too-modest objective may lead the economy down the path of depression. Indeed, it is probably not far from the truth to say that a policy of growth must come after stabilization needs are taken care of; unless this is done, economic instability will negate the effect of any given long-term policy.

The Balance of Payments

Until recent years authorities in the the United States could pursue domestic goals without regard to the impact of their policies on the external accounts of the country. During the 1930's and World War II, the United States built up an enormous gold hoard. By 1948 the hoard exceeded $24 billion. The strength of the dollar was further enhanced by the fact that it became the world's most important medium of exchange. This meant that foreign countries used the dollar to buy goods from one another as well as to acquire gold or goods from the United States. Thus the latter could run deficits with the rest of the world without much fear that all the surplus dollars earned by foreigners would be used to buy U.S. owned gold.

This system gave considerable flexibility to U.S. authorities in the pursuit of domestic goals. For expansionary policies producing inordinate increases in imports, either because of domestic inflation or because of income-induced purchases of foreign goods, could be sustained without resulting in serious consequences for the United States' gold reserve.

This pleasant state of affairs gradually deteriorated in the 1950's, during which time the United States experienced a balance of payments deficit in most years. The deficits during 1958–63 were particularly heavy. The deficits were accompanied by a substantial gold outflow. Foreigners, stuffed with dollars, cashed them in for gold. By the end of 1963, U.S. gold holdings had dropped to $15.5 billion. Continuation of the problem has brought these holdings down to $10.5 billion in December of 1968.

The decline of the gold stock has been paralleled by a rise in importance of favorable international balances as a policy goal. Indeed, there are those who might now give this goal priority over the triumvirate of growth, full employment, and price stability. But whether this be desirable or not, there is little question that concern over the balance of payments reduces considerably the flexibility of monetary and fiscal authorities in the pursuit of their three principle goals. Domestic events such as tax cuts, increases in government or private spending, increases in the money supply, and lower interest rates all have negative impacts upon the balance of payments. The liberality of expansionary acts by authorities is considerably reduced when they must keep worried eyes upon the balance of payments.

Importance of Other Goals

If emphasis in this chapter has been placed upon the stability of prices, employment, and production, and upon economic growth, it is only because these goals are attainable with the application of the tools of aggregate economics. The discussion should not lead to the proposition that these are the only, or even the most important, objectives of economic policy. The list of other goals would include national security, more (or less?) income equality, elimination of monopoly, better conservation of our national resources, tax equity, etc. At times, these other objectives conflict with the goals of stability and growth. While it is not the economist's place to establish priorities, it is his function to point out the conflicts in policy both to the public and the responsible authorities.

It is not always easy to stay within this assigned role. The economist may point out to legislators that a given goal may be achieved in any number of ways. It is only natural for the legislator to ask which way is best. How is the economist going to reply? He can assume an Olympian attitude; he can abstain from answering on the ground that his value judgments must not enter into his advice. But this would in many instances leave the legislator in his quandary. The temptation is therefore great to give legislators one of two judgments—one based upon what the economist himself judges to be best, or one that he thinks will fit the values of the legislators best. While most economists try to limit their advice to technical matters, all too often situations develop in which they are giving philosophical as well as technical information, sometimes consciously and sometimes unconsciously.

A common complaint from laymen is that economists give conflicting advice, that for every economist one can find a separate opinion. To a large extent this is true; but the sources of disagreement in economics are rarely recognized. Disagreement can result over facts, over logic, or over value judgments. When economists disagree over facts or logic, the conflict is not too serious and can often be resolved. But, when disagreement exists over values, the chance for reconciliation is usually quite small. This might not be too much of a danger if the conflict over values is recognized for what it is. Unfortunately, this does not always happen. Violent disagreement over the proper route to certain goals often occurs because the routes also lead to other goals. Thus one analyst may recommend general monetary or fiscal controls as cure for inflation because he believes in minimizing government interference in the economy, while another may recommend direct price and wage controls because he believes in a wider scope for state participation in economic affairs. When this sort of disagreement occurs, when economists do not specify the philosophical basis for their disagreements, the public has every right to be disgusted. But economics is neither an exact nor complete social science. It is therefore rather boorish to carp at economists who cannot give unanimous and scientifically correct answers to questions of logic and fact which are not yet resolved.

ADDITIONAL READINGS

BOULDING, K. E. *Principles of Economic Policy.* Englewood Cliffs, N.J.: Prentice-Hall, 1958.

HANSEN, A. H. *Economic Issues of the Sixties.* New York: McGraw-Hill, 1960.

HANSEN, B. *The Economic Theory of Fiscal Policy.* Cambridge: Harvard University Press, 1958.

KLEIN, L. and BODKIN, R. G. "Empirical Aspects of the Tradeoffs Among Three Goals: High Level Employment, Price Stability, and Economic Growth," Commission on Money and Credit, *Inflation, Growth, and Employment.* Englewood Cliffs, N.J.: Prentice-Hall, 1964.

MUSGRAVE, L. A. *The Theory of Public Finance.* New York: McGraw-Hill, 1959, Part Four.

SMITHIES, A. and BUTTERS, J. K.   *Readings in Fiscal Policy.* Homewood, Ill.: Richard D. Irwin, Inc., 1955, chaps. 27, 28. AEA report and a critique by Arthur Smithies.

TINBERGEN, J.   *Economic Policy: Principles and Design.* Amsterdam: North Holland Publishing Co., 1956.

Chapter 16 | THE BURDEN OF STABILIZATION

Since fluctuations in aggregate demand cause departures from economic stability, the goal of stabilization can usually be tackled with policies designed to stabilize the flow of spending. Long-term objectives, when they can be considered in isolation, must generally be treated with a different set of policies. In this chapter we are concerned primarily with stabilization policy.

THE NATURE OF STABILIZATION POLICY

On its face, the problem confronting policy makers seems quite simple. Depression and inflation ordinarily boil down to situations in which $C + I + G + (X - M) \neq GNP$ (or, which is saying the same thing, $I + G + X \neq S + T + M$). It follows that measures to eradicate or minimize price level and employment instability should operate upon one or a number of the income and employment determining expenditure flows.

Unfortunately, a number of further questions arise. Which expenditure flows should be operated upon in any given situation? Should policy result in direct or indirect manipulations? Should policy give officials discretionary powers, or should stabilizers be "built-in" the economy so that they work automatically? Is a single set of policies appropriate to all states of economic instability, or are different policies appropriate to different situations? If a variety of policies are needed to treat a variety of situations, how are the appropriate policies indicated? Finally, is it more desirable to use the tools of fiscal policy or monetary policy?

MONETARY POLICY

Prior to World War II, monetary policy was the orthodox means for controlling excessive fluctuations in the general level of economic activity. This does not mean that fiscal policy was never used: the New Deal used budgetary manipulations to a great extent during the Great Depression. It is still true, however, that the use of fiscal policy was not a reputable way to combat depression, mainly because it implied budgetary deficits.

The great expansion of aggregate demand and employment resulting from the huge wartime deficits of the federal government, and the realization that public debt is different than private debt, convinced many people of the power and appropriateness of fiscal policy. Moreover monetary policy during the Great Depression had not worked well. The result was that in the postwar period monetary policy fell into disrepute and fiscal policy became *the* way to stabilize the economy. While the pendulum has not swung completely back, monetary policy has had a considerable revival in recent years.

How Monetary Policy Works

Monetary policy works by indirection. Whatever particular method is used, the purpose of such policy is to control or influence the level of spending in the economy. In the main, the authorities seek to accomplish their ends by affecting the availability and cost of credit. Since this is done by exerting influence over the volume of cash reserves upon which commercial banks base their lending, monetary policy also influences the quantity of money. When reserves and the supply of money are restricted, interest rates tend to rise and banks and other lenders ration more carefully the loans they make. Rising interest rates make business firms and households more reluctant to borrow. Because they induce lower interest rates and less credit rationing, increases in reserves and the money supply should have the opposite effect upon borrowers.

The Federal Reserve System is the primary agency administering monetary policy. Through its open market operations in government securities, through its rediscount policies, and through its control over commercial bank reserve requirements, the Fed has a high degree of control over the money supply. Nevertheless, monetary policy also emanates from other sources. The Treasury, for example, can reduce the money supply by accumulating a surplus of tax receipts over expenditures and depositing the surplus with the Federal Reserve. This drains money out of the hands of the public and the reserves of the banking system. Again, by changing the interest rates at which federal obligations are offered to the money and capital markets, or even through open market operations, the Treasury can influence the whole structure of interest rates in those markets.

In addition to the Treasury, there is the host of federal lending agencies—the Federal Housing Administration, the Veterans Administration, the Small Business Administration, the Federal National Mortgage Association, the Federal Land Banks, etc.—which, through the amount and terms of the credit they grant, make a substantial impact on money and capital markets. Indeed, at times both the Treasury and these lending institutions have engaged in operations the monetary impact of which have been directly opposite to the objectives of Federal Reserve policy.

Monetary policy is not limited to control over the supply of money alone. The Federal Reserve System has control over credit margins available for purchases in the stock market. During and after World War II, the Federal Reserve had additional controls over consumer credit (as to size of down payment and duration of the loan contract), and in 1950 the Board of Governors issued Regulation X, restricting the credit available for residential construction. These "selective" controls over consumer and real estate credit no longer exist, but they can presumably be added to the armory of present Federal Reserve weapons if the occasion for their use again arises.

Virtues of Monetary Policy

All economic policies have their limits: they all work somewhat imperfectly in terms of their own objectives, and, if pressed too hard, they may frustrate achievement of other objectives. But, bearing this in mind, what does monetary policy have to recommend for itself?

Monetary policy in capitalist societies is traditionally administered by central banks such as the Federal Reserve System. While other agencies of government can and do exercise monetary controls, traditional thinking in central bank literature has emphasized the need for a separation between the monetary authority and the regular agencies of government. Because of this philosophy, the Federal Reserve System was organized as a separate agency, partly owned by private banks, and directly responsible only to Congress. There are several reasons for this curious arrangement. A long history of money mismanagement by governments convinced many thinkers that government cannot be trusted to exercise restraint in monetary matters. Any pressing budgetary need, they argued, immediately sends officials to the printing presses: it is much easier to print money than to extract taxes or loans from the public. Taking away government's power to create money forces it to budget its outlays within its taxing and borrowing powers.

Separation of bank and state also served a basic ideological objective. Central banking philosophers have traditionally adhered to the idea of laissez-faire, to the rule that the government should generally abstain from interfering with the workings of the economy. Since money is a basic part of the economic mechanism, it was only natural to believe that the government should abstain from tinkering with the money-making engine. This responsibility should lie solely with the banking system.

Governments have rarely heeded this advice. Money is simply too important not to be an object or tool of general economic policy. Nevertheless, the same spirit still pervades the management of our monetary affairs. The Federal Reserve System still dominates the administration of monetary policy, notwithstanding the close and continuous attention Congress pays to that administration. The Federal Reserve makes up its own mind about what to do in a given situation, and only later, if at all, answers to Congress. This is not to say that the Fed has unlimited power. It is unrealistic to believe that it would go its own way against the determined will of the majority of Congress, the Administration, and the public. Nevertheless, when opposition opinion is not strong or crystallized, the System does have considerable independent discretion.

The relative independence of the monetary authority is a strong recommendation for monetary policy to those who believe in laissez-faire. Consistent with this belief is that, even when exercised on the behalf of government, monetary policies to combat depression and inflation represent a minimal interference of the state in economic affairs. A general tightening of credit, which results from a restrictive monetary policy, involves no direct involvement by the government in the economy. Rather than government officials denying individual transactions or dictating their terms, the market itself does the job by adjusting to the change in conditions. Thus, instead of a bureaucrat from some agency vetoing a loan, some banking official, mindful of the low state of his bank's liquidity, does the job. This is believed to be all to the good, because bankers are believed better equipped to judge the worthiness, or unworthiness, of any given loan applicant. In other words, the market is deemed a better allocator of credit than is the government, primarily because it responds to the motivations of profit and loss, which is not true of a government official.

Another argument for monetary policy is its flexibility. Generally speaking, it takes little time and machinery to turn from a policy of restraint to one of ease, and vice versa. No act of Congress, with its innumerable delays in hearings and debates, its required for a change in policy. Once the need is apparent, the Federal Reserve can institute the needed action without delay. If mistakes are made, they can readily be corrected by some new action, again without delay.

Criticisms of Monetary Policy

The power of monetary policy is derived from the impact which monetary instruments have upon the total level of spending. Restriction of the money supply should reduce spending by forcing banks to reduce lending and by discouraging consumers and business from borrowing. Actions resulting in an increase in the money supply should encourage lending and borrowing. When a tight or easy monetary policy does not have the desired effect, the instruments of policy may be considered defective.

Great power is usually attributed to monetary control when the objective is the prevention of inflation. Under full-employment boom conditions, when prices are tending to rise, a refusal by the central bank to allow significant increases in bank reserves should cause interest rates to rise and investment spending to fall. This in turn should moderate the rise in aggregate demand and reduce the pressure upon the price level.

In recent years, the effectiveness of monetary policy in controlling inflation has ᵇeen questioned. If the primary force underlying inflationary pressure stems from the cost side, restrictive monetary policies will suppress inflation only at the expense of considerable unemployment. But, even if inflation arises from excess demand, some writers still question the effectiveness of central bank instruments:

The initial impact of tight money is upon the value of assets: the rise in interest rates reduces capital values. Keynesians have tended to emphasize the influence of income changes upon spending and to ignore or minimize the effects of changes in the value of assets. Whether this emphasis is grounded in fact or predilection, it has led to a belief that government tax and expenditure policies are more potent than monetary policy because of their more immediate impact upon spending. Recent theorizing, however, has shifted its attention to the additional influence upon spending exerted by assets. A fall in capital values reduces the ratio of assets to income; asset holders will attempt to build the ratio back to the desired level by reducing expenditures and increasing their stocks of liquid assets. A rise in capital values, following an easing of monetary conditions, will presumably produce the opposite effects—a rise in expenditure and a reduction in liquid assets. Such considerations have led one writer to state: "There can be no *general inferiority* of monetary to fiscal controls on the grounds of a supposedly *general inferiority* of assets to income as the basis of economic decisions."[1]

Rising interest rates are supposed to discourage investment and to encourage saving; both of these results reduce inflationary pressure. In earlier chapters we have already raised doubts about this mechanism. Except for long-term fixed investment, interest rate movements may play a secondary role in influencing investment spending, and little positive correlation has been found between saving and interest.

Nevertheless, the effect of tight money upon *lenders* has in recent years been emphasized. Banks and other financial institutions hold large quantities of government and other securities. Rising interest rates cause the value of these assets to fall. If financial institutions do not want to realize these losses, they will retain their securities rather than sell them. Financial capital is in this way "locked-in" in the form of securities, and it is unavailable for lending.

Actually, "locking-in" may not be too effective. Better alternative uses of funds, fear of further rises in interest rates, and (for commercial banks) ability to charge capital losses against taxes seem to militate against the phenomenon. Recent studies have indicated that it is not very significant.[2]

Far from tightening the position of lenders, extensive holding of securities may give the economy a way of avoiding the impact of a tight money policy. If reserves are not available from the "Fed" to finance attractive loans, banks can sell part of their portfolios to insurance companies, corporations, and state and local governments having idle balances. The latter institutions, looking at the higher reward for parting with liquidity (the higher interest rates), will more readily part with such funds. The released funds can be used for loan expansion by banks. (In terms of monetary theory, velocity will increase because idle funds have been transferred to active use.) The ability of financial institutions to utilize more intensively the existing money supply may offset a good deal of the credit rationing which might have to be done if these institutions did not have such large stocks of securities.

---

[1] Howard S. Ellis, "Limitations of Monetary Policy," *United States Monetary Policy,* American Assembly (New York: Columbia University, 1958), p. 151. Ellis points out that changes in taxes, by changing the net income of assets, also affect capital values.

[2] See John Kareken, "Post-Accord Monetary Development in the United States," Banca Nazionale del Lavoro (Rome), *Quarterly Review,* September, 1957, pp. 344–45, and Warren L. Smith, "On the Effectiveness of Monetary Policy," *American Economic Review,* September, 1956, pp. 589–93.

Frequently heard is the charge that the Federal Reserve cannot directly reach through its policies the actions of a large number of financial intermediaries whose lending resources are independent of Federal Reserve controls. Such intermediaries—life insurance companies, saving and loan associations, pension and investment funds—can, it is argued, act in ways which directly oppose Federal Reserve policy. They can, for example, expand loans during a period of general credit tightening, and there is no way the monetary authority can force them to conform.

The charge is true in form, but it may be somewhat overdrawn. A general tightening of credit affects all institutions in the economy. While it is true that the Federal Reserve cannot directly influence the lending abilities of the financial intermediaries, its power to make credit tight all around does have considerable impact upon them. Intermediaries depend upon the general capital market for their resources.

Recent writings of Milton Friedman and other monetarists have stressed the power of money and monetary policy. Great uncertainty still attaches to the *channels* through which money works its effects upon the economy. Nevertheless, an increasing number of economists are convinced that money is far more important than money Keynesians have been willing to admit. The next chapter is devoted to a summary of this debate.

Some critics have attacked the assumption of flexibility in monetary policy.[3] While they recognize that it takes much less time to put monetary policy into operation than it does fiscal policy, they aver that it takes much longer for monetary measures to take hold. Fiscal policy, on the other hand, "has a direct and powerful impact upon the income stream, whereas monetary policy's first impact is on the asset structure and only through its effects on this structure does it indirectly and with some delay affect the income stream."[4]

We have already argued an agnostic position with respect to the superiority of income—as opposed to asset—effects upon spending. Nevertheless, it is interesting to further observe that, if the operational lag of monetary measures is too long, business fluctuations may be aggravated rather than moderated. By the time a tight money policy takes hold, the economy may be in the midst of a recession, and a depression-oriented easy money policy may find its impact in the midst of a boom.

This possibility has been particularly stressed by Milton Friedman, an important critic of current monetary policy practices. In an extensive

---

[3] Smith, *op. cit.,* pp. 605–6.

[4] Smith, *op. cit.,* p. 606.

study of the behavior of the U.S. money supply over the last 80 years, Friedman concluded that a long and variable lag exists between peaks and troughs in the rate of change in the money stock and peaks and troughs in general business activity. For peaks he found that increases in the money stock slowed, on the average, 16 months before the peak of economic activity was reached. For troughs, he found that monetary changes preceded the upturns in business activity by an average of 12 months. He also found wide variability in timing, so that there is no way to base a reliable forecast of business changes upon monetary changes.

Friedman's findings are highly controversial, but they do raise serious questions about the effectiveness of monetary policy.[5]

Heavy use of monetary policy leads to instability in financial markets. Not only are capital values subjected to strong and somewhat arbitrary pressures, speculative excesses based upon outguessing the authorities may also characterize the money and capital markets.[6] The resulting fluctuations in security prices may run over into a general fluctuation in economic activity. Thus a too rapidly declining securities market may spread its psychology to the economy as a whole.

Defenders of monetary policy admit this defect; but, as they point out, it is not possible to stabilize everything. Excessive concern with stability of financial markets might lead to instability of employment and prices. Of course, instability of financial markets in addition to instability of prices and employment is the worst of all worlds. The monetary authorities must therefore closely watch the situation, being prepared to stabilize security prices should they promise to lead to a general decline in economic activity.

FISCAL POLICY

It is only in the last 25 to 30 years that the idea of using the government's financial and budgetary operations to stabilize the economy has been widely accepted. Resistance to the idea has come from groups objecting to "interference" by government in the economy and from

---

[5] Friedman's views are expressed in a number of places. See, for example, "The Lag in Effect of Monetary Policy," *Journal of Political Economy,* October, 1961. See also the critique of J. M. Culbertson in "Friedman on the Lag in Effect of Monetary Policy," *Journal of Political Economy,* December, 1960, and his reply to Friedman in the October, 1961, issue of the same journal. For an up-to-date review of the literature, see T. Mayer, *Monetary Policy in the U.S.* (New York: Random House, 1968), chap. 6. Mayer gives an excellent bibliography in this chapter.

[6] For example, the 1957–58 experience as described in the *Federal Reserve Bulletin,* August, 1959, pp. 860–69.

those who believe that monetary policy is more effective. Actually, the government has little choice under modern circumstances; its receipts from and payments to the public bulk so large relative to all transactions in the economy that it cannot help having an important impact on the rest of the economy. Whether one believes in fiscal policy or not, the government must have one. Even if it is not consciously exercising stabilization policy, the government is having an enormous influence upon the economy: even no policy is a policy.

Functional Finance versus Sound Finance

Since, for good or for evil, government fiancial and budgetary operations are bound to affect the level of economic activity, most economists today argue that the government must see to it that its operations do not result in general economic instability. A majority of economists would probably argue that one of the main rules of fiscal operations should be the prevention of depression and inflation. This is the rule of *functional finance.*

Acceptance of functional finance means that "sound finance," or balanced budgets, cannot be the rule guiding fiscal operations. Functional finance and sound finance are conflicting fiscal policies. Functional finance means that the government is willing to run a budgetary deficit during depressions and a budgetary surplus during booms. Sound finance means the government must reduce its expenditures (or increase tax rates) during periods of depression (when tax revenues are falling), and raise its expenditures (or reduce tax rates) during periods of prosperity or inflation (when tax revenues are rising). Sound finance therefore means added economic instability in the interest of maintaining budgetary stability. Functional finance sacrifices budgetary stability for economic stability.

The Instruments of Functional Finance[7]

The instruments of functional finance include six items which exhaust the means by which fiscal policy can be exercised. In its financial and budgetary operations the government can either:

1. Buy or sell,
2. Give or take (tax),
3. Lend or borrow.

---

[7] Abba P. Lerner in the *Economics of Control* (New York: Macmillan Co., 1944), developed many of these notions.

An increase in the first item in each of the three pairs of acts tends to expand national income and employment. A decrease in each of the first items tends to lower income and employment. As for the second item in each pair, an increase tends to lower national income and a decrease tends to raise it.

Increased government spending raises national income both directly and indirectly. The rise in spending elicits an initial increase in production. The income, earned by the public from the increase in production, may then be used to make additional expenditures, eliciting more production and income (the multiplier-accelerator effect). An increase in government "giving" (transfer payments) expands disposable income and lets consumers spend more. An increase in government lending increases the supply of loanable funds and operates to lower interest rates or to reduce credit rationing. This, in turn, should encourage investors and consumers to borrow and spend more. By having an opposite effect upon spending, a decrease in government buying, giving, and lending will tend to reduce national income and employment.

Regarding the second item in each of the pairs of acts: an increase in each will be deflationary. An increase in government sales (e.g., of surplus goods) tends to lower income and employment, because it siphons off purchases from private producers. Private producers, in turn, must reduce production and income payments in order to avoid building up excess inventories.[8] An increase in taxes takes purchasing power out of the hands of the public and prevents them from spending what has been taxed away. Government borrowing reduces loanable funds available to private borrowers and leads to increases in interest rates and credit rationing. To the extent the tighter credit conditions discourage private spending, inflationary forces are restrained.

It is important to treat each fiscal act independently. There is no necessary linkage between any pair of them. The government does not necessarily tax and spend, borrow and spend, tax and give, etc., simultaneously. Indeed, there is a school of fiscal philosophy which argues that taxation exists only to prevent inflation and possibly to act as a device for social control (e.g., discouraging liquor consumption by heavy excises, redistributing income through a progressive income tax, etc.). The logic of this argument is that the (federal) government can create all the money it needs in order to support its spending, giving, and lending programs. If it did this, however, the competition of gov-

---

[8] Sales of newly produced government manufactures, however, are not deflationary. They may be treated as part of GNP. In any case, sales of surpluses are not important fiscal acts in the U.S.; they are mentioned in the text for completeness only.

ernment spending with private spending would be inflationary. To prevent this competition, the government takes (taxes) money away from people so that it may spend without forcing the price level to rise. The importance of this argument is that each individual fiscal act must be thought of in terms of its individual impact upon the economy. Taxing is simply taxing, not taxing-and-spending. Borrowing is simply borrowing, not borrowing-and-spending. Taxing and borrowing each have a deflationary impact upon the economy; spending, by itself, has an expansionary effect.

Who Administers Fiscal Policy?

It is easy to argue that the government should apply functional finance, but it is less easy to argue that the political machinery of the United States is well designed for the job. Fiscal policy is divided between Congress and the Administration. Congress sets tax rates, appropriates money for government agencies, and holds hearings at which administration officials must defend their actions. Under the Employment Act of 1946 the President must annually present to Congress the *Economic Report of the President,* prepared by his Council of Economic Advisors, in which he reviews the past and expected state of the economy and presents his program for the near future. Under the law, it is the responsibility of the President to coordinate the activities of the Executive Branch "to maintain employment, production, and purchasing power," that is, to stabilize the economy. After the *Report* is issued, the Joint Economic Committee, a Senate-House standing committee with its own staff of experts, studies the President's analysis and program and issues its own report, together with a published record of its hearings.

The President can choose to act according to his own program or accept the (inevitable) amendments made by the Joint Economic Committee. In either event, building upon the taxes, appropriations, and borrowing capacity given him by Congress, the President has great fiscal powers. Congress can only appropriate money. It cannot determine the rate at which it is spent. The latter responsibility lies with the President or, perhaps more realistically, with the various administrative agencies within the Executive Branch. Some of these agencies, the armed services for example, have enormous unspent sums of money at their disposal. This ability to determine the timing of expenditures gives functional finance a great deal of flexibility. The rate of use of unexpended appropriations can be stepped up during periods of slump and slowed during periods of prosperity.

The flexibility of Administration fiscal powers should not be over-emphasized. The congressionally imposed ceiling upon the national debt may prevent the Administration from increasing its spending (and budgetary deficit) by enough to counteract a serious decline in income and employment. To be sure, Congress, on these occasions, typically increases the height of the ceiling; but, this is only a recognition of the limits of the President's fiscal powers.[9]

There is also the problem of time lags. Even though a decision might be made to increase or decrease spending, considerable time may pass before the change in spending actually takes place. Projects must be planned, contracts must be let, and contractors must recruit a work force and organize production. Much old spending cannot be immediately reduced. Contracts made in the past must be honored, and uncompleted projects, desirable in themselves, must be finished. Add to these difficulties the inability of the President to change tax rates, and a picture of Administration omnipotence in the field of fiscal policy becomes somewhat overdrawn. But, just as we should not overestimate the fiscal powers of the President, neither should we underestimate them. Even with the restrictions, he has a great deal of latitude.

Limitations of Functional Finance

As already indicated, a serious limitation of functional finance is the division of government fiscal powers between Congress and the Administration and within the Administration itself. This division leads to incoherence and inflexibility in policy. (Unfortunately, the same thing exists, though in a modified form, with monetary policy. Here there is a three-way split in responsibility between Congress, the Administration, and the Federal Reserve System.) Add to this the further complication of 50 different states and thousands of different local governmental units, all of which follow, in some degree, independent programs. It is no wonder that at times "the government" is found operating an ineffective and inconsistent stabilization program. Although it may be admirably designed to maintain democracy, the American political system is hardly a perfect instrument for the rational pursuit of given economic ends.

But, even granted the ponderousness of the political machinery, and even granted the problem of time lags mentioned earlier, are there other

---

[9] The President has another alternative which he may exercise. Rather than ask Congress for an increase in the debt ceiling, he can borrow money indirectly from the public through one of the specialized agencies (e.g., the Commodity Credit Corporation).

limitations? Probably the main one is the imperfect state of the art of forecasting. Coupled with the inflexibility of the fiscal machinery, this poses a most serious threat to effective use of functional finance. Bad forecasts lead to bad use of fiscal instruments. The situation is doubly serious if the misuse of the instruments cannot be reversed immediately once the mistaken forecast is discovered. This difficulty has led to the idea of building into the fiscal system stabilization devices which, without human intervention, will operate correctly in a stabilizing direction. Similar proposals exist for monetary instruments. The debate over these proposals and their merits relative to discretionary monetary and fiscal policy has continued over a number of years. In the next section we shall comment upon that debate.

RULES VERSUS AUTHORITIES IN MONETARY AND FISCAL POLICY

The modern debate of "Automatic versus Discretionary Controls" has an older version in the form of "Rules versus Authorities." The older title suggests some of the origin of the debate: it was concerned with whether Congress, through the establishment of definite, intelligible, and inflexible rules, should seek to regulate economic fluctuations, or whether rule making should be delegated to some authority—e.g., the Administration, the Federal Reserve—charged with the responsibility of economic stabilization. A number of writers,[10] found this latter system intolerable and inconsistent with laissez-faire. As a consequence, they proposed a set of rules which they thought would lead to stable economic conditions, but which would not seriously violate the free enterprise system they believed in. These proposals were mainly concerned with money management, and we shall begin our discussion of automatic controls by referring to them. We shall then discuss some rules designed in more recent years to stabilize automatically the general level of economic activity. Afterwards, we shall attempt to assess the debate.

100 Percent Money

Probably one of the most drastic proposals ever issuing from the ranks of professional economists was the plan put forth by a small band of able conservative thinkers, in which it was proposed to eliminate the

---

[10] Notably, Henry C. Simons. See his *Economic Policy for a Free Society* (Chicago: University of Chicago Press, 1948).

power of banks to create money. In brief, the main points of the plan were:

1. Outright federal ownership of the Federal Reserve banks.
2. Annulment of all existing bank charters, and enactment of new federal legislation providing for complete separation between different classes of corporations, of deposit and lending functions of existing deposit banks.
3. Legislation requiring a 100 percent reserve against all deposit (checking and saving) liabilities, reserves to be held with the Federal Reserve banks.
4. Provision during the transition period for gradual displacement of private bank credit as circulating medium by credit of the Federal Reserve banks.
5. Displacement by notes and deposits of the Reserve banks of all other forms of currency in circulation, thus giving us a completely homogeneous circulating medium.
6. Prescription in legislation of an explicit simple rule of monetary policy, and establishment of an appointive administrative body, charged with carrying out the prescribed rule, and vested with no discretionary powers as regards fundamental policy.
7. Abolition of reserve requirements against notes and deposits of Reserve banks, and broad grants of powers to the administrative body for performance of its function.[11]

The main point of the plan was to put control of the money supply completely in the hands of the government in order to give it the power to form some impersonal and automatic rule by which monetary affairs would be arranged. Without this power, the private banking system, with its independent ability to multiply and contract the money and credit supply, would continue to frustrate public policy.

Monetary Rules

What are some of the possible rules which Congress might establish once the government's power over the money supply becomes complete? One rule, the stabilization of some price index, was discussed in the last chapter. It was pointed out there that, even assuming an appropriate price index can be found, inflexibility of prices and wages would make such a policy difficult to operate, especially if employment stabilization is another objective of the policy.

Another rule might be simply to fix the quantity of money at a given level and hold it there, regardless of fluctuations in income and output. This proposal has some merit as a stabilization device. During boom periods, when the demand for money is growing, the interest rate would

---

[11] *Ibid.*, pp. 62–63, paraphrased and quoted.

be pushed up, increases in investment and other spending would be slowed, and inflationary movements resulting from demand-pull factors would be restrained. Contractions in income and employment would also be slowed because as income falls the demand for money falls. This, together with a fixed supply of money, would quickly bring interest rates down from their boom levels, and investment and other spending would be encouraged. Unfortunately, this proposal would not do as a long-term monetary policy. Economic growth implies a long-run increase in the demand for money. A fixed supply of money in relation to a long-term growth in the demand for it would result in a rising level of interest rates. Such a situation is not conducive to growth, unless the unlikely happens and the marginal efficiency of capital also increases at the same or higher rate as the rise in interest. Failing this, interest rates must be kept down, and this will happen only if prices and wages fall by enough to allow the *real* supply of money to grow. The price and wage rigidities characterizing the modern economy would not allow this sort of thing.

A third rule which meets the long-term growth requirements of the economy is to allow the money supply to grow every year by some fixed amount. This device would result in some automatic stabilization, especially if the growth in money is made proportional to the trend growth in income and output. During booms, when income is growing faster than the trend rate, the demand for money also grows faster than its trend rate. Since the rule says that the money supply should grow only according to a fixed trend rate, regardless of boom or bust, it would become relatively scarce. Interest rates would rise and the boom would be moderated. During slumps, the short-term fall in the demand for money, combined with the continued increase in the money supply, would depress interest rates, loosen credit, and slow down the fall in spending.

The proposal to institute a fixed and automatic annual increase in the stock of money has been endorsed by two distinguished monetary theorists, Milton Friedman[12] and Edward S. Shaw.[13] These theorists argue for the rule on the ground that discretionary monetary policy in the past has been destabilizing rather than stabilizing, mainly because of bad management, incorrect priorities in goals, political pressures, and

---

[12] Friedman, *A Program for Monetary Stability* (New York: Fordham University Press, 1960).

[13] Shaw, "Money Supply and Stable Economic Growth," *United States Monetary Policy* (New York: Columbia University, 1958). See also the discussion of the doctrine by Richard Selden, "Stable Monetary Growth," *In Search of a Monetary Constitution,* Leland D. Yeager (ed.) (Cambridge: Harvard University Press, 1962).

the lags between the application of policies and their resulting effects. While they admit that the automatic rule would not lead to perfect stabilization, they argue that it would lead to better stabilization than now exists.

Critics argue that the Friedman-Shaw rule is too rigid, and that no automatic rule can accommodate all contingencies. Needless to say, the monetary authorities are particularly unimpressed with the proposal. Nevertheless, the idea of an automatic rule continues to intrigue monetary theorists, some of whom feel that the days of discretionary control of the money stock are numbered.[14]

Automatic Fiscal Stabilizers

The federal budget does have certain "built-in," or automatic, features which operate to counteract fluctuations in economic activity. Thus, increases and decreases in national income are slowed by rising and falling taxes, not because Congress passes new tax legislation on each occasion, but because the existing tax rates dampen fluctuations in disposable personal income. Further dampening occurs because unemployment insurance contributions rise relative to payments in periods of prosperity and fall relatively during times of recession. These and other "built-in" features (e.g., farm price supports) of the budget provide an excellent first line of defense against inflation and depression, but by their nature they cannot suppress strong inflationary forces nor overcome substantial declines in the aggregate level of spending. They were not designed for these purposes and they must be either improved or supplemented in order to counter strong fluctuations in economic activity.

The CED Budget Proposal

In two documents, the Committee for Economic Development, a private nonprofit organization of businessmen devoted to the study of economic policy questions, has outlined a budgetary program which they believe would improve the "built-in" stabilizers.[15] The program pro-

---

[14] Selden, *op. cit.,* p. 355. ". . . the chances seem very good that the successor to monetary discretion will be stable monetary growth."

[15] *Taxes and the Budget,* November, 1947; and *Monetary and Fiscal Policy for Greater Economic Stability,* December, 1948. Milton Friedman published a similar proposal in 1948 in "A Monetary and Fiscal Framework for Economic Stability," *American Economic Review,* June, 1968.

ceeds upon the assumption that Congress must first decide upon the scale of expenditures required to meet social needs; but, after having done this, tax rates must be set so as to balance the budget at 93 percent of full employment, and to provide a surplus of $3 billion when employment is "full" (when 96 percent of the labor force is employed). When employment falls below 93 percent, a budgetary deficit would develop, continuing until the 93 percent level is again reached. The tax rates should be preset and left alone throughout the business cycle, unless some major policy change necessitates a revision. The revision, however, should allow the retention of the basic features of the program. The program, generating surpluses during booms and deficits during slumps, would dampen business fluctuations and make a major contribution to economic stability.

Formula Flexibility

The CED did not present its program as a comprehensive proposal for combating inflation and depression. It recognized the need for supplementary monetary and fiscal policies, especially if the forces creating instability are particularly strong. In the main, however, the CED preferred supplementary monetary policies of the discretionary type. While others might accept the basic CED position, they might recommend further steps in instances where economic fluctuations are strong.

Many of these additional proposals utilize the principle of *formula flexibility,* a combination of automatic and discretionary principles. The general idea is that the government must watch certain indexes of economic activity, and be prepared automatically to institute some stabilization program if the indexes reach a certain point. Thus, if the CED budget were the main stabilization device, and if employment dipped below 93 percent of the labor force, the President might do nothing. However, at some specified level of employment, say 90 percent of the labor force, Congress might require the President to increase the rate of unemployment compensation, reduce income tax rates, proceed with a program of prearranged public works, etc. Additional flexibility might be required if employment falls below, say, 85 percent of the labor force. Another variant of this approach, involving somewhat more discretionary power, is to give the President standby controls which he is authorized, but not required, to use on certain occasions (such as when unemployment reaches a given level). In the past, Congress has been reluctant to give this much discretion to the Executive, primarily because it is reluctant to give up any of its power over the purse strings. There is also the belief, held by many members of Congress, that matters involving such wide discretionary powers are as much Congress' business, perhaps more, as they are of the Administration. To many Congressmen, the President is no more capable of exercising proper discretion in anticyclical matters than is Congress. Be that as it may, formula flexibility, provides a fruitful area to explore possible bases for compromise between the disputants in the debate over rules versus authorities.

The "Mix" of Monetary and Fiscal Policy

Whether monetary policy or fiscal policy should be emphasized as a stabilization device is partly a matter of technical effectiveness and partly a matter of ideology. We have already discussed the conditions under which successful monetary and fiscal policies may be pursued.[16] Let us therefore now discuss some of the ideological issues.

Graph 16.1 will aid the discussion.[17] Assume that technical conditions allow either pure monetary policy, pure fiscal policy, or some mix of the two to be used to bring the economy from point A to a level of full

GRAPH 16.1

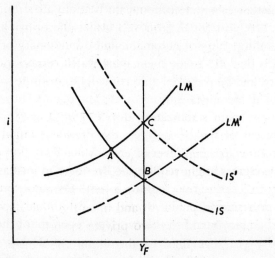

---

[16] Chapter 11.

[17] The following is based upon Franco Modigliani's discussion in "The Monetary Mechanism and Its Interaction with Real Phenomena," *Review of Economics and Statistics,* Supplement: February, 1963, pp. 93–97.

employment (anywhere on vertical Y_FC). Pure monetary policy would shift LM to LM', and bring the interest rate down to Y_FB. Pure fiscal policy would shift IS to IS' and would raise the interest rate to Y_FC. A mix of monetary and fiscal policy would obviously result in an interest rate between the other two.

Aside from different interest rate effects, each of the full-employment positions can also be distinguished with respect to the division of output between the government, consumers, and business (private capital formation):

a) If fiscal policy takes the form of an increase in government expenditure, without a change in tax structure and without a change in the demand for or supply of money, position C will result. If private consumption is only marginally affected by changes in the interest rate, the increase to full-employment income by use of government experditures will have about the same effect upon consumption as would the use of monetary policy alone. However, the division of output between government and business is affected, because the higher interest rate at C would choke off some business investment, causing resources to flow to the government.

b) If position C results from a consumers' tax cut, government spending constant, then, relative to position B, there will be a shift of resources to consumers, away from businessmen, whose spending would be curtailed by the higher interest rate.

c) Finally, a tax cut for business might stimulate some additional investment spending; however, some reduction in investment spending relative to B is likely to occur because of the higher interest rate at C. This should promote a relative shift of resources to consumers, if government spending remains fixed.

A "mix" of monetary and fiscal policies would produce allocations of goods between the public and private sector and allocations within the private sector which are intermediate to those indicated above. If we assume, as we have, that *any* mix would achieve the full-employment goal, the only valid bases for choosing a particular mix lie in the effects of this mix upon economic growth and upon the division of goods between the public sector and the two private sectors. If pure public expenditure policy is to be emphasized, then it must be because it is believed (*a*) that public consumption in the form of more government services is desirable relative to private consumption and investment, or (*b*) that public capital formation (spending on public projects) is better for economic growth than is private capital formation. Tax cuts for consumers may retard economic growth, since resources are shifted away from investment. While tax cuts for business may stimulate some investment, the maximum stimulus to investment would come from monetary policy.

We should emphasize here that the above analysis is not a plea for fiscal policy as against monetary policy, or vice versa. To point up the implications of the "mix" is one thing, to argue about which mix is ideologically most acceptable is quite another. On this we made no comment, except to say that the technical or even practical efficacy of both approaches are also important. If monetary policy cannot be used to achieve full employment, it does little to argue that it is best for economic growth. If Congress will not accept the increase in public debt which may ensue from a tax cut or expenditure increases, it does no good to deny monetary authorities full use of their tools.[18]

DIAGNOSIS AND PRESCRIPTION

The great merit of the automatic stabilizers is that they go into operation without human intervention; no prediction or evaluation of the state of business affairs is needed before appropriate adjustments in the money markets and the government's budget begin. If the automatic stabilizers are combined with pure- or semidiscretionary devices, however, Congress and the Administration need guideposts which can only be provided by a properly interpreted set of data.

Professor Robert A. Gordon has suggested a useful set of categories for policy formation.[19] He argued that policy must recognize three types of cyclical contractions: (1) the "pure" minor recession; (2) the hybrid downturn; and (3) the major cycle proper. To understand these categories it is first necessary to examine Gordon's concept of the "stock of investment opportunities."

The *stock* of investment opportunities at any moment may be defined as the difference between the existing capital stock and that which businessmen would

---

[18] A footnote on the relation between the balance of payments problem and the correct policy mix is in order. It is often argued that capital outflows are encouraged by domestic interest rates which are low relative to those abroad. If this be true, and if the balance of payments problem is considered severe, then it might be wise to weight the policy mix in favor of fiscal policy, since this would have the effect of raising domestic interest rates. If it is also desired to do least damage to domestic growth, then fiscal policy might itself be weighted in favor of either increasing public capital outlays or improving business investment incentives.

[19] "Types of Depressions and Programs to Combat Them," *Policies to Combat Depression*, National Bureau of Economic Research (Princeton, N.Y.: Princeton University Press, 1956), pp. 7–21.

find it most profitable to have if they were well informed regarding all relevant cost and demand relationships and the forces making for long-run growth in the economy. Thus we may speak of an "appropriate" level *and composition* of the capital stock, and we may look upon all investment (not based on mistaken expectations) as an attempt to modify the existing capital stock in the direction of what is appropriate.[20]

In Gordon's view, minor contractions in business activity will remain moderate so long as the basic stock of investment opportunities remains large. Thus, his first category, that of "pure" minor recessions, is a situation in which no drastic discretionary policy is needed, for the situation will correct itself, especially with the aid of the automatic stabilizers.

Hybrid contractions are sharper than minor recessions, but are still relatively short in duration. They occur, Gordon says, for either of two reasons. First, once a contraction begins, the deterioration in short-term expectations may affect long-term expectations and result in a decline in fixed capital formation, even though the stock of investment opportunities remains large. Second, the end of a strong boom may induce shortages of both money or real capital, causing a temporary decline in the stock of investment opportunities. The contraction, however, brings its own reversal; for the reduction of excess inventories, the leveling of capital goods and other prices, lower interest rates, and the greater availability of money restore the stock of investment opportunities.

The hybrid contraction clearly requires more than automatic stabilization. Policies involving deficit financing, special tax relief, and vigorous use of existing monetary instruments, to flood the system with liquidity and bring down interest rates, are called for. The requirements of the situation demand some use of discretion, as well as "automaticity." Government actions must be designed to restore confidence promptly and to clear away the barriers preventing the exploitation of investment opportunities. The built-in stabilizers, though well designed to cushion the fall in income and employment, are in themselves inadequate to the whole task of restoring long-term investment activity.

The major cycle proper comes after a long period of high-level capital formation which results in a depletion of the stock of investment opportunities. "When a depression develops for this reason, the forces making for revival that gradually emerge from the contraction will not be enough in themselves to restore the stock of investment opportunities. The severity of the depression will depend particularly on how much overbuilding went on during the preceding boom, on the strength of the

---

[20] *Ibid.,* p. 9 (emphasis in original).

forces making for further growth which open up new investment opportunities, and on the nature of the financial maladjustments resulting
from earlier speculative excesses."[21] Gordon believes there is no way the
government can *prevent* a major contraction; however, he does believe
there are a large number of policies it can pursue to bring revival. Policies applicable to hybrid contractions are, of course, appropriate to the
major cycle; but, such measures must be applied on a broader scale. Yet,
this is not enough. Since the depression is caused by depletion of the
major part of the stock of investment opportunities, government programs to restore the stock are necessary. A number of possibilities present themselves: special tax incentives to stimulate research and modernization in industry; public expenditures in areas creating external
economies and incentives to private industry (e.g., investments in atomic
facilities, roads, harbor improvements, slum clearances, etc.) ; financial
assistance to firms in difficulties; and technical aid to firms in order to
accelerate reductions in costs and improvements in products.

It is precisely these types of measures which economic conservatives
fear the most. The special government programs needed to combat the
major cycle almost inevitably bring with them considerable government
intervention into business affairs. Whether this intervention is worth the
beneficial effects upon the level of economic activity is a question only
the public, through Congress, can decide. Gordon's analysis is neutral
with respect to such questions.

If Gordon's analysis is correct, the task of formulating proper anti-
depression policies is both delicate and complicated. Diagnosis and
prescription are almost inseparable. The massive programs appropriate
to major cycles are both unnecessary and dangerous during minor recessions and hybrid contractions: they would serve mainly to create
severe inflationary pressures once recovery begins. On the other hand,
built-in and formula flexibility serve only to moderate the impact of
major depressions. Full recovery should not be expected until the stock
of investment opportunities is replenished by business itself or with
government help. The economic analysis required for proper diagnosis
and prescription goes far beyond the simple estimation of aggregate
demand. The economy must be subjected to a constant and searching
scrutiny, so that the stock of investment opportunities may be assessed.
This is not an easy task. Economic science still has no sure-fire methods
by which a proper assessment can be made. "Art," as well as science,

---

21 *Ibid.,* pp. 11–12.

must be called upon for the study of the business cycle and the connected policy questions. Let us hope this will be less true in the future.

ADDITIONAL READINGS

KAUFMAN, G. B. "Current Issues in Monetary Economics and Policy," *The Bulletin* (New York University Graduate School of Business Administration, Institute of Finance), No. 57, May, 1969. A very useful up-to-date survey, with an excellent bibliography.

MAYER, T. *Monetary Policy in the United States.* New York: Random House, 1968. Another good survey, somewhat lengthier than Kaufman's.

SMITH, W. and TEIGEN, R. *Readings in Money, National Income, and Stabilization Policy.* Homewood, Ill.: Richard D. Irwin, Inc., 1965. An excellent collection of readings. For stabilization policies see chap. 4.

SMITHIES, A. and BUTTERS, J. K. *Readings in Fiscal Policy.* Homewood, Ill.: Richard D. Irwin, Inc., 1955. Another good collection of articles.

Chapter 17

RECENT CONTROVERSIES:
THE MONETARISTS V.
THE "NEW ECONOMISTS"

In 1964, the U.S. Congress engineered a major tax cut the purpose of which was to bring the economy up to a full-employment level and to stimulate the economic growth of the country. The tax cut entailed a large increase in the government's deficit. The action, proposed by the Kennedy Administration and carried out in the first months of the Johnson Administration, was a major triumph for the Keynesian inspired "New Economics." Congress had been pursuaded that a deliberately created federal deficit should be used to stimulate the economy. After almost 30 years, the lessons of the *General Theory* had finally filtered through to enough people in power to convince them that a major experiment in fiscal policy should be undertaken. Indeed, the economy's performance after the tax cut seemed to justify the experiment. As predicted by the proponents of the action, in the year following the tax cut real gross national product rose by over $30 billion. With the rise of GNP the reputation of the economics profession in general and the "New Economists" in particular also rose.

Unfortunately, events of the years since the tax cut have to some extent tarnished the reputation of the New Economists. These have been years in which inflation rather than unemployment has been the main problem, and the economy does not seem to have been as responsive to fiscal policy as it was in 1964. At this writing the U.S. economy is caught up in a serious inflation. In July 1968, Congress, at the urging of the Johnson Administration, introduced a major tax increase in the form of a 10 percent surcharge on income taxes. At the same time, federal government expenditures were pruned to prevent large increases. The net result of these fiscal actions was a $25 billion swing toward surplus in the federal government's budget (national income basis). The expectation of most economists at the time of the tax surcharge legislation was that inflationary pressures would be eased in the first part of 1969. These expectations have proven to be wrong and, as a result, the Federal Reserve System, which in the latter half of 1968 had been pursuing a relatively relaxed policy in the belief that the tax surcharge would work, has switched to a policy of tight money in the hope that it can do what fiscal policy does not seem to have been able to do—reduce the inflationary pressures which continue to plague the economy.

The inability of fiscal policy to handle inflationary pressures comes as no surprise to a school of monetary economists who have taken up the doctrines of Professor Milton Friedman of the University of Chicago. For years Friedman has conducted a major research effort designed in part to show that the Keynesian framework is insufficient to understand the forces affecting the level of aggregate money income. He has accused Keynesians of underplaying the role of money and overplaying the role of investment and fiscal variables in the determination of national income. Indeed, it is his position that almost all of the major and many of the minor fluctuations in national income and employment over the last 100 years have their roots in monetary disturbances. In reference to the recent experience with fiscal policy, he has argued that the apparent success of the 1964 tax cut was due to a simultaneous liberalization of monetary policy. The apparent failure of the 1968 tax surcharge, in Friedman's view, can be traced to the liberal monetary policy pursued by the Federal Reserve in the last half of 1968 (when the money stock grew at an annual rate of over 6 percent per month). The Fed has since switched to a policy of severe restraint (from June, 1969 to date—August, 1969—the money stock has grown very little) and Friedman is now predicting an end to inflationary pressures by the end of 1969 or early in 1970.[1] Indeed, he is arguing that the Fed has overreacted to the inflation problem and that unless it eases up a bit, the chances are that tight monetary policies are going to cause a recession. By the time this paragraph is in print, the reader will know whether or not this particular prediction is correct. In the meantime, it is important to review Friedman's argument and the evidence which he and others have accumulated in its favor.

Friedman's Theoretical Views

Friedman has expressed his theoretical views in many of his voluminous writings. It would require a more extended treatment than is possible here to capture all of the subtleties and nuances of his ap-

---

[1] See Friedman's column in *Newsweek*, August 18, 1969. Friedman writes a regular column for *Newsweek* in which he has expressed many of the views attributed to him in this paragraph. Several of these are reprinted in his *Dollars and Deficits* (Englewood Cliffs, N.J.: Prentice-Hall, 1968).

proach, but fortunately the main outline is available in a famous essay he published in 1956, entitled "The Quantity Theory of Money—A Restatement."[2] In that essay Friedman made the following points:

1. The quantity of money "matters" in the sense that "any interpretation of short term movements in economic activity is likely to be seriously at fault if it neglects monetary changes and repercussions and if it leaves unexplained why people are willing to hold the particular nominal quantity of money in existence." (p. 3)

2. The reasons why people are willing to hold money are embodied in Friedman's theory of the demand for money: "The analysis of the demand for money on the part of the ultimate wealth-owning units in the society can be made formally identical with that of the demand for a consumption service . . . [it] depends upon three major sets of factors: (*a*) the total wealth to be held in various forms—the analogue of the budget restraint; (*b*) the price of and return on this form of wealth and alternative forms; and (*c*) the tastes and preferences of the wealth owning units." (p. 4)

3. Money is only one of a variety of the forms of wealth that can be held. Wealth holders attempt to apportion their assets between money and other wealth forms in such a way as to maximize the utility they derive from wealth services. In doing so, they must pay attention to the restrictions—i.e., the prices of and returns on various wealth forms—which affect the possibility of converting one form of wealth into another. "As usual, this implies that he [the ultimate wealth-owning unit] will seek an apportionment of his wealth such that the rate at which he *can* substitute one form of wealth for another is equal to the rate at which he is just willing to do so." (p. 5)

4. This formulation leads to a statement of the demand for nominal money balances of the following form (p. 10):

$$M_d = f(P, r_b, r_e, \frac{1}{P}\frac{dP}{dt}; w, Y; u),$$

Where P is the general price level, r_b and r_e are rates of return on bonds and equities, $(1/P)(dP/dt)$ is the (expected) percent rate of change in prices (or the price level appreciation expected on physical assets and equities), w is the ratio of nonhuman to human wealth, Y is money income broadly defined in its "permanent" sense, and u is an index representing tastes and preferences. Actually, this demand function is a bit narrower than Friedman's fuller statement, which includes terms expressing wealth-owners' estimates of potential capital gains and losses upon bonds and equities; nevertheless, the above equation suffices to show the basic approach. Friedman argues that the demand for nominal balances—M_d—is positively affected by the price level,

[2] In M. Friedman, ed., *Studies in the Quantity Theory of Money* (Chicago: University of Chicago Press, 1956), pp. 3–21.

negatively affected by the rates of return on equity and bonds, negatively affected by the rate of expected price increase, and positively related to the level of income. (He is not clear about the effects of w upon the demand for money.)

This formulation is similar to that of Keynes in that it includes the interest rate as an argument in the demand function. Nevertheless, it is also more general than that of Keynes since it takes into account more substitution possibilities—i.e., equities and physical assets. Friedman avoids the Keynesian distinction between a transaction demand and a speculative demand for money, arguing that since a dollar simultaneously serves a variety of purposes and that it makes no sense to create separate money balances for separate purposes. It should also be noticed that income in the Keynesian sense of measured current income is not included as an argument of Friedman's function.

5. This summary does not do justice to Friedman's rich treatment of the demand for money; nevertheless, it suffices to impart its essential flavor. For our purposes, the next thing to note is that Friedman regards the demand for money *function* to be very stable. Also, the factors bottled up in his variable u, or "tastes and preferences," are more than they seem: they include a whole variety of technical conditions of production and exchange affecting business practices, and these practices, in turn, are thought by Friedman to be the result of economizing activities on the part of firms and consumers. As a result, short-run changes in u are not to be expected, except under unusual circumstances.

6. According to Friedman, the factors affecting the demand for money can and should be sharply differentiated from the factors affecting its supply. The latter, to a large extent, emerges from the behavior of the banking system. The banking system expands and contracts the money supply by issuing deposits in exchange for securities issued to it by the public. To be sure, interest rates have something to do with this process, but Friedman (in many articles) has expressed the belief that the monetary authorities, through their control of the monetary base (reserves and currency) have essential control over the money supply; hence, the money supply is an independent variable in the economic system.

7. Friedman believes that fluctuations in the supply of money are the main reason for fluctuations in aggregate money income. He believes this because he believes the demand for money to be very stable and that as a result increases or decreases in the supply of money will not be absorbed by shifts in the demand for money. But what about interest rates? Friedman admits that if the amount of money demanded increases or decreases sharply as a result of relatively minor interest rate changes, his theory of money cannot be converted into a theory of money income. The reason is that an interest sensitive demand for money function implies that temporary surpluses or shortages of money will be absorbed by or taken out of wealth portfolios without much effect upon the demand for goods. In a study of the demand for money published in

1959,[3] Friedman argued that interest rates have a negligible influence upon the amount of money demanded. This being the case he also argues that changes in the supply of money are the principle reason for changes in the level of aggregate money income.

Friedman vs. Keynesians

How do Friedman's conclusions differ from those of Keynesians? In some ways, this is a difficult question to answer, since the supply and demand for money are also important ingredients of the Keynesian approach to the determination of aggregate income. Nevertheless, there does seem to be an important difference between the two schools when it comes to applying the theory to the interpretation of events. A recent case in point is an article by Arthur Okun, the last chairman of President Johnson's Council of Economic Advisors and a prominent Keynesian economist. The article, entitled "Measuring the Impact of the 1964 Tax Reduction,"[4] makes use of the theory of the multiplier to show how the tax cut worked its way through the economy to produce a $36 billion increase in GNP. It is a sophisticated exercise, yet it almost totally ignores the role of money in the process. Okun notes this, but goes on to argue that although monetary policy during the period in which the multiplier was working itself out was favorable, it had no crucial role to play: "monetary policies made a major contribution to the advance, but that contribution can be appropriately viewed as permissive rather than causal. The monetary authorities supplied a good sound set of tires for the economy to roll on, but they did not contribute the engine. That came from fiscal policies."[5] This kind of statement would be impossible for a quantity theorist, at least of Friedman's persuasion, to make. The reason is that quantity theorists do not trust analyses which seek to explain fluctuations in aggregate income by appealing to Keynesian multiplier theory. They do not trust such analyses because they do not believe in a stable consumption function (hence a stable multiplier) and they do not believe in the independence of the various components of aggregate expenditure.

To see the importance of this last point, let us conduct a fiscal experiment. Assume that the government's budget is initially balanced and

---

[3] Friedman, "The Demand for Money: Some Theoretical and Empirical Results," *Journal of Political Economy*, August, 1959.

[4] Okun, "Measuring the Impact of the 1964 Tax Reduction," In *Perspectives on Economic Growth*, edited by Walter W. Heller (New York: Vintage Books, 1968).

[5] *Ibid.,* p. 44.

that in order to combat unemployment government increases its spending without increasing taxes. Will the increase in government spending, via the multiplier, generate an increase in money income for the economy? The answer, according to Friedman, depends upon (*a*) the nature of the increase in government spending, and (*b*) the way in which the increased deficit is financed.[6]

There are many things government can buy with its increased outlays. All of them, however, do not necessarily add to total spending in the economy. If government directs its expenditure to things the public is already buying for itself, the public, in turn, might find itself with an opportunity to indulge in some extra saving. For example, if the object of the new government expenditures is a school lunch program, parents might decide to put all or part of the income so released into saving. A believer in the consumption function, of course, would argue that the school lunch program really increases disposable family income and that only part of the government's outlay's will be offset by increased household saving. This may or may not be true;[7] but, in any event, the example shows that it is distinctly possible for at least part of the increased government spending to be offset by a reduction in private spending. Theory is not much of a guide here because the emergence of such an offset depends upon the nature of the increased government outlays. This is shown by another example: Suppose that the object of increased government spending is a new public power project. Such a project might compete with the investment plans of a private power utility or might relieve the necessity of a large number of firms to provide their own power generating facilities. In either event, the government's investment might be completely or partially offset by private investment spending. Friedman argues that the only way to assure that the increase in government spending will not be offset is by having the government spend money on things which are "utterly useless." This is an overstatement, since things like national defense are hardly useless; but, it is hard to deny that Friedman has a point.

Friedman's second point is equally important. We have already seen (Chapter 10) that the impact of the increase in the government's outlays depends upon the way in which the deficit is financed. In our experiment, the government's deficit must be financed with an issue of securi-

---

[6] The following discussion is based upon Friedman's *Capitalism and Freedom* (Chicago: University of Chicago Press, 1962), chap. 5.

[7] If it is, we would certainly have to reformulate much of the theory of the consumption function. This theory does not take into account the effect upon real household income generated by government services.

ties which, to be sold, competes in the capital and money markets with private securities. Such competition generally means that interest rates will rise. If the demand for money is highly sensitive to interest rates, the government will have an easy time marketing its debt, since part of it will be bought by people who are willing to exchange money holdings for securities; interest rates, as a result, will not have to rise very far and private investment spending will not be much discouraged. Suppose, however, that the demand for money is highly insensitive to interest rates. In that case, interest rates might have to increase sharply in order to induce people to exchange their money holdings for the new government securities. The sharp increases in interest rates, in turn, might cause a decline in investment spending severe enough to offset the increase in government spending. Many Keynesians would deny that interest rates can have that much effect upon investment spending; nevertheless, this is still an open question and recent research does not deny that there is at least *some* sensitivity of investment spending to interest rates. The main point is that unless one makes extreme assumptions about the shapes of the demand for money function or the marginal efficiency of capital schedule, at least part of the increase in government spending will be offset by decreases in private spending. How much of an offset there will be is largely an empirical matter and cannot be decided on a priori theoretical grounds.

The quantity theorist not only believes that the demand for money is stable; he also believes it to be relatively insensitive to interest rate changes. (The older quantity theory denied any interest sensitivity.) He therefore denies that fiscal policy can work in the absence of a complementary monetary policy. Indeed, he would probably argue that in most instances it is really monetary policy that matters. This is almost opposite to the frequent complaint of Friedman that to Keynesians "money does not matter." This charge is, of course, not true. But one cannot help agree with Friedman and his followers that the so-called New Economists frequently forget how important money is, even in their own theoretical system. This is especially true when it comes to applying that system to practical affairs.

It should be clear that the dispute between the modern quantity theorists and the Keynesians cannot be solved logically. Both approaches represent empirical hypotheses about the way in which people in the economy behave. The best way to resolve the issues involved is to appeal to the facts of life. Unfortunately, such an appeal is not a simple thing. The natural sciences resolve issues of theory by performing controlled critical experiments designed to refute one or more competing hypotheses. Economists try to do the same thing, but in the nature of things it is rarely possible for them to perform controlled experiments. In their place, they must use statistical techniques to filter out the lessons provided by Nature's "experiments." Nature's experiments, needless to say, are never controlled. Nevertheless, they are still worth studying to see what light they shed upon theoretical issues. Friedman and his followers have made a number of such studies, and it is worth our while to look at the results.

Friedman's Empirical Studies

The empirical work of Friedman and his co-workers has been reported in a number of different studies. Here we review only the major findings. Together with Anna Schwartz and under the auspices of the National Bureau of Economic Research, Friedman has for a number of years been conducting numerous studies of the role of money in the U.S. economy. Some of the results of these studies have been reported in the monumental book, *A Monetary History of the United States, 1867–1960.*[8] Another important report is in an article, again coauthored by Anna Schwartz, entitled "Money and Business Cycles."[9] Finally, one of Friedman's most controversial studies is summarized in a report for the Commission on Money and Credit, entitled: "The Relative Stability of Monetary Velocity and the Investment Multiplier in the United States, 1897–1958."[10]

The following summarizes what Friedman and his co-workers have found:[11]

"1. *The rate of change in the quantity of money* (percent growth or decline per year) is closely correlated with the rate of change in (*a*) nominal income, (*b*) real income, and (*c*) prices. The correlation is higher for nominal income than for either prices or output separately. [It] holds both for cyclical movements and for periods longer than the usual business cycle. It holds for any of a number of definitions of the quantity of money. Both the closeness of the correlation and the functional relation between money and the other magnitudes appear to have remained the same over the past century." (*Dollars and Deficits*, p. 127)

---

[8] Friedman and Schwartz, *A Monetary History of the United States, 1867–1960* (Princeton: Princeton University Press for the National Bureau of Economic Research, 1963).

[9] Friedman and Schwartz, "Money and Business Cycles," *Review of Economics and Statistics,* Supplement, February, 1963.

[10] Commission on Money and Credit, *Stabilization Policies* (Englewood Cliffs, N.J.: Prentice-Hall, 1963).

[11] Part of what follows is from a summary by Friedman of his own findings in *Dollars and Deficits, op. cit.,* chap. 4.

"2. *Instability in the rate of change in the quantity of money* is highly correlated with instability in the rate of change in nominal income. . . . This is a particular manifestation of the relations summarized in point 1." (pp. 133–34.)

"3. Over cyclical periods, peaks and troughs in the rate of change in money tend to precede in time the dates designated by the National Bureau of Economic Research as cyclical peaks and troughs and also, though by a much smaller margin, peaks and troughs in the rate of change in nominal income." (p. 134)

"4. *Direction of influence in cyclical periods.* As for secular periods, there are influences running from money to business and from business to money. A number of pieces of evidence combine to suggest that the influences running from money to business are highly important in all cyclical fluctuations and dominant in major ones." (p. 134)

"5. *Interest rates.* . . . [A]s an empirical matter, there is a much looser relation between either the level of interest rates or their rates of change, on the one hand, and rates of change in nominal income, output, and prices, on the other, than between the rate of change in the quantity of money and these same magnitudes. . . . Whether or not interest rates are regarded as the primary channel through which monetary effects occur [the Keynesian position], they are a less accurate and stable indicator of the pressure being exerted by monetary magnitudes than is the rate of change in the quantity of money." (pp. 134, 136).

"6. *Supply of Money.* Over long periods, the major factor accounting, in an arithmetic sense, for changes in the quantity of money has been changes in the quantity of high-powered money [reserves plus currency and coin in the hands of the public, mainly controlled by the Federal Reserve System and, to a lesser extent, by the U.S. Treasury.]" (pp. 137–38). Friedman admits that variations in banks' reserve deposit ratios and in the public's desired currency deposit ratio have had important cyclical influences upon the quantity of money, but he still concludes that "variations in the monetary base [high-powered money] are far more important." (*Ibid.*) He also argues that the *control* over the quantity of money is mainly in the hands of the Federal Reserve system, in short periods; hence the Fed can "if it wishes, determine the rate of change of the quantity of money within fairly narrow limits and with relatively short lags." (*Ibid.*)

So it is that Friedman finds support for his argument that "money matters." Indeed, he also believes that the facts support his theoretical position that fluctuations in nominal income are far more closely connected with variations in the money supply than with variations in government spending and taxing or variations in investment spending by business. He put this belief to direct test in the article (mentioned above) that he coauthored with David Meiselman. In that article, Friedman and Meiselman ran a "horse race" between a simple version of the Keynesian approach and the quantity theory approach. They tried to find out whether or not variations in "autonomous expenditures," defined as the government deficit plus net private investment expenditures, had a higher correlation with variations in money income (over the years 1897–1958) than did variations in the money supply. Statistical considerations forced them to substitute money consumption for money income. The results, in their own words were:[12]

strikingly one-sided. Except for the early years of the Great Depression, money (defined as currency plus commercial bank deposits) is more closely related to consumption than is autonomous expenditures. . . . This is so both for nominal values, which is to say, when no adjustment is made for price change, and for "real" values, which is to say, when the variables are adjusted for price change. It is true for absolute values and for year-to-year or quarter-to-quarter changes. Such correlation as there is between autonomous expenditures and consumption is in the main a disguised reflection of the common effect of money on both.

So far as these data go, the widespread belief that the investment multiplier is stabler than the monetary velocity is an invalid generalization from the experience of three or four years [the early years of the Great Depression]. It holds for neither later nor earlier years.

One implication of the results is that the critical variable for monetary policy is the stock of money, not interest rates or investment expenditures.

Friedman's empirical results and the implications he draws from them have not gone unchallenged. Keynesians have denied that their approach ignores money as an important variable affecting the level of income. As we have seen, however, Keynesians have also tended to attribute less importance to money than to autonomous expenditures. They have therefore been somewhat surprised at Friedman's "one-sided" results and have attempted to refute his conclusions with arguments and studies of their own. One major complaint of the Keynesians is that Friedman consistently misinterprets the direction of causation between money and income (or "business"). As is well known, most of the money supply in the United States consists of bank deposits generated by variations in bank lending; and bank lending, in turn, is based upon reserves which expand and contract with (1) nonbank public deposits and withdrawals of currency, (2) bank borrowings from the Federal Reserve System, (3) inflows and outflows of money from abroad, and (4) purchases and sales of securities by the Federal Reserve System. Items (1) through (3) impart an endogenous element to the money supply, in the sense that when business activity expands both national income and interest rates tend to rise. This, in turn, encourages an expansion of bank reserves via items (1)–(3). In addition, by lending to each other, banks can make a more effective use of the

---

[12] Friedman and Meiselman, *op. cit.*, p. 166.

stock of reserves available to the whole banking system. Finally, business expansion encourages banks to keep fewer excess reserves. Studies have shown that a definite endogenous element in the money stock exists,[13] and Friedman himself admits to its existence. However, he denies that it is important enough to affect his conclusions. Nevertheless, this is still an unsettled issue.[14]

The Friedman-Meiselman conclusion that the velocity of money is more stable than the investment multiplier has also come under attack. In their study, Friedman and Meiselman used somewhat special definitions of autonomous expenditures and money. We cannot go into these rather technical issues, but suffice it to say here that other studies, covering the same period of time and using different definitions of money and, especially, autonomous expenditures, have come up with somewhat different conclusions.[15] The authors of these studies do not deny that money is important, but, contrary to Friedman and Meiselman, when using different definitions of money and autonomous expenditures they do not find money to be the most important determinant of the level of money income. In the words of De Prano and Mayer,

. . . one can conclude . . . that both autonomous expenditures and money are of very roughly equal importance. Due to specification errors in the models, as well as errors in the basic national income data, we do not want to attach much significance to the relatively minor differences between correlation coefficients of the autonomous-expenditures equations and the money equation. Moreover, even if one of the two simple models should turn out to be somewhat superior to the other one, a small degree of superiority would not allow one to say which of the two more complex, and hence more relevant, models would be superior. FM were able to generalize about complex models only because one of their two simple models performed vastly better than the other. But no vast difference divides the models in our test.[16]

---

13 See, for example, Patrick Hendershott, *The Neutralized Money Stock* (Homewood, Ill.: Richard D. Irwin, Inc., 1968).

14 Some recent research, however, seems to lean to the Friedman position. See R. G. Davis, "Does Money Matter? A Look at Some Recent Evidence," Federal Reserve Bank of New York, *Monthly Review*, June, 1969, and L. C. Andersen, "Additional Evidence on the Reverse-Causation Argument," Federal Reserve Bank of St. Louis, *Review*, August, 1969.

15 See "Velocity and the Investment Multiplier," by A. Ando and F. Modigliani; "Autonomous Expenditures and Money," by M. De Prano and T. Mayer; "Reply" by Friedman and Meiselman; the "Rejoinders" by the above authors to Friedman and Meiselman, all in the *American Economic Review*, September, 1965. Also see Donald D. Hester, "Keynes and the Quantity Theory: A Comment on the Friedman-Meiselman CMC Paper," Reply to Donald Hester, and Hester's "Rejoinder," *Review of Economics and Statistics*, November, 1964.

16 De Prano and Mayer, *op. cit.*, p. 746.

As additional evidence for their view, De Prano and Mayer point to the fact that econometric models based upon the Keynesian view compete quite well with quantity theory-type models in making forecasts of changes in the level of money income. This and other evidence has led many economists of the Keynesian school to reject Friedman's "money only" approach in favor of an "intermediate" or modified approach in which neither money nor autonomous expenditures is stressed to the exclusion of the other.

The Federal Reserve Bank of St. Louis Test of Monetary vs. Fiscal Policy

The latest round in the Monetarist–New Economist debate has been stimulated by an interesting study published in November, 1968, by two Federal Reserve Bank of St. Louis economists, Leonall C. Andersen and Jerry L. Jordan.[17] Andersen and Jordan, who are members of the monetarist school, set out to test the relative importance of monetary and fiscal actions in economic stabilization. As with the Friedman-Meiselman study, their procedure was relatively simple. Nevertheless, their results are equally provocative and controversial. Before discussing the results, however, it is necessary to examine their procedure.

In order to make their test, Andersen and Jordan experimented with various equations in which changes in money GNP were made a function of current and previous fiscal and monetary actions. Expressed in general notation, their test equation was

$$\Delta GNP_t = f(\Delta M_t, \ldots, \Delta M_{t-3}; \Delta E_t, \ldots, \Delta E_{t-3}; \Delta R_t, \ldots, \Delta R_{t-3}) \ .$$

In this equation ΔM represents monetary actions, ΔE represents government expenditure actions, and ΔR represents tax actions. The t subscripts represent the relevant time periods, measured in quarters.

Andersen and Jordan wanted to find whether or not "the response of economic activity to fiscal actions relative to monetary actions is (I) greater, (II) more predictable, and (III) faster. In order to make this test, they had to give empirical content to ΔM, ΔE, and ΔR. This is not as easy as one might expect, since their test required them to specify these variables in a way which would make them independent of each other and independent of ΔGNP. As in most studies of this sort, Andersen and Jordan were not completely successful; nevertheless, they were

---

[17] Andersen and Jordan, "Monetary and Fiscal Actions: A Test of Their Relative Importance in Economic Stabilization," Federal Reserve Bank of St. Louis *Review,* November, 1968.

very careful in their procedures and their results must be taken seriously.[18] As with the Friedman-Meiselman study, the conclusions were surprisingly one-sided:

This [study] tested the propositions that the response of economic activity to fiscal actions is (I) larger, (II) more predictable, and (III) faster. *The results of the test were not consistent with any of these propositions.* Consequently, either the commonly used measures of fiscal influence do not correctly indicate the degree and direction of such influence, or there was no measurable net fiscal influence on total spending in the test period [first quarter 1952 to second quarter 1968].

The test results are consistent with an alternative set of propositions. *The response of economic activity to monetary actions compared with that of fiscal action is (I') larger, (II') more predictable, and (III') faster.* It should be remembered that these alternative propositions have not been proven true, but this is always the case in scientific testing of hypothesized relationships. Nevertheless, it is asserted here that these alternative propositions are appropriate for the conduct of stabilization policy until evidence is presented proving one or more of them false.[19]

The Andersen-Jordan study has generated some vigorous criticism. Frank de Leeuw and John Kalchbrenner, for example, have attacked the assumption that either the money supply or the monetary base is an exogenous variable, free of any dependency upon economic conditions. This criticism has been rebutted by Andersen and Jordan,[20] but because of the complexity of the institutional arrangements by which both the monetary base and the money supply are generated, a convincing answer to the criticism is not possible.[21] Another criticism by Davis, cited earlier,

---

[18] For ΔM, Andersen and Jordan experimented with two variables: changes in the monetary base and, on the assumption that the authorities can control it, the money stock (defined as currency and coin plus privately held demand deposits). ΔE and ΔR were measured by high-employment expenditures and high-employment receipts. Since both government expenditures and revenues fluctuate to some extent in response to fluctuations in GNP, one cannot measure fiscal and monetary actions by simply recording their changes. This has led economists to devise measures of expenditures and receipts which do not reflect endogenous elements. The standard for such measures is a "high-employment" level of GNP (3 or 4 percent unemployment). Expenditures and receipts for this GNP level are assumed to be free of endogenous elements; hence changes in high-employment expenditures and receipts are assumed to be reflections of deliberate expenditure and tax decisions. Jordan and Andersen, by the way, also used a combination of ΔE and ΔR—changes in the high employment surplus or deficit—in their study.

[19] Andersen and Jordan, *op. cit.,* p. 22; (emphasis supplied).

[20] See the exchange between these economists in the Federal Reserve Bank of St. Louis *Review,* April, 1969.

[21] On this point, see the article by Davis, *op. cit.,* p. 125. It might also be noted, however, that some of Davis' experiments and those of Andersen in his August 1969 article in the St. Louis *Review* support the assumption of the Andersen-Jordan study that causation runs mainly from money to GNP rather than the other way around.

is more penetrating. After examining the performance of the Andersen-Jordan equation separately for the first half (1952–60) and second half (1961–68, 2nd quarter) of the test period, he concluded that the equation did not perform well for the first half and that most of the explanatory power of the study seems to have been derived from the equation's performance in the second half. Nevertheless, Davis was not prepared to throw out the conclusions of the study:

> On balance, it would seem fair to say that the St. Louis equation has not been devastated by the critical scrutiny to which it has been subjected. On the other hand, I think it is equally obvious that some distinctly troublesome questions exist regarding the equation. The equation's merits do not seem to me sufficient to compel by themselves our acceptance of the world it portrays.[22]

How Does Money Affect the Economy?

Apart from statistical difficulties associated with studies such as those of Friedman and Meiselman and Andersen and Jordan, the major reason why many economists have not accepted the conclusions is that the monetarists have not yet provided a convincing theory as to why the money stock and its variations should have such a strong and swift impact upon the economy. The St. Louis equation says that an increase in the money supply of $1 billion will, at the end of two quarters, increase GNP by $3.5 billion, about half of its ultimate influence. And this influence does not, in the framework of the Andersen-Jordan study, depend upon the manner in which the money stock is created. A $1 billion increase by means of newly printed bills handed over to the public will have the same effect in the study as an increase generated by an open market operation of the Federal Reserve system. Now, these are two entirely different situations, since the first technique involves a direct creation of new monetary wealth for public, whereas the latter involves an exchange of securities for money with the Federal Reserve (which increases bank reserves) and an exchange by the public of securities for money created by the commercial banking system. An open market operation, therefore, does not increase the *net* wealth of the community, hence it cannot rely upon the wealth (Pigou) effect to have an impact upon the economy. To be sure, open market operations affect interest rates and the *distribution* of wealth; nevertheless, many economists doubt that these effects are strong enough to have the strong and quick-acting effects implied by the St. Louis study.

---

[22] Davis, *op. cit.,* p. 129.

Monetarists do not seem to have such doubts. Indeed, they explain their results by arguing that monetary policy works its way through the economy by affecting a wide range of interest rates and asset prices. An increase in money, they argue, throws asset portfolios out of equilibrium, leading people to exchange surplus money for all sorts of new assets, not just bonds or other financial assets. Hence, in getting rid of excess balances people may purchase investment goods, housing, consumer durables, etc. As the new money is exchanged for assets by one group of persons, it falls into the hands of another group which, in turn, disposes of its excess money supplies by purchasing a broad range of other assets. As the new money is exchanged from one set of holders to another, therefore, the prices of a large spectrum of financial and real asset prices are bid up. If, as interest rates fall and existing real asset prices rise, it becomes profitable to buy newly produced assets, production in the economy will also be stimulated. Hence, depending on the state of employment in the economy, injections of new money will stimulate increases in nominal or real GNP, or both.[23]

Keynesians do not necessarily dispute this description of the process by which injections of new money affect the economy. They generally deny, however, that the effects are likely to be as strong, as swift, and, especially as reliable as the monetarist's believe them to be. Keynesians do not, in other words, have faith in the existence of a stable and interest-insensitive aggregate demand for money, upon which the monetarist position depends.

Keynesians also do not like the vagueness of the monetarists' model of the interaction between money and the economy. In their empirical work, monetarists have depended upon rather simple single equation models in which money and other economic variables are assumed to affect money income. Keynesians, in contrast, often build large models containing large numbers of detailed equations designed to explain variations in different types of consumption, investment, and government spending. These models sometimes also contain blocks of equations designed to explain interest rates, prices, and wages. A recent model, built jointly by economists of the Federal Reserve System and the Massachusetts Institute of Technology,[24] has an important block of equations designed to describe the behavior of the financial sector.

---

[23] See Friedman and Meiselman, *op. cit.*, pp. 217–22 for a more complete description of the monetarist view of the process described in this paragraph.

[24] F. de Leeuw and E. Gramlich, "The Federal Reserve–M.I.T. Econometric Model," *Federal Reserve Bulletin*, January, 1968. Also, by the same authors, "The Channels of Monetary Policy," *Federal Reserve Bulletin*, June, 1969.

These models, it is claimed, are superior to those of the monetarists because they give insights into the structure of relationships involved in the transmission of monetary influences to the real economy (The Fed–M.I.T. model does show that money is important, but not as quick acting and powerful as suggested by the St. Louis study). At the heart of the Keynesian counter-critique, therefore, is the belief that it takes a theory to overthrow a theory, and the monetarists, as yet, have not come up with a theory capable of overthrowing the Keynesian system.

Final Comment

Macroeconomic theory is at an important and exciting stage of its existence. Old ideas are being challenged and new ones are being put forth with increasing vigor. In addition, economists are now equipped with scientific tools which enable them to put ideas to test very rapidly. Rapid evolution in thought and practice is the inevitable consequence of this kind of situation. The reader should not despair over the lack of agreement in macroeconomic theory. Disagreement is normal in a healthy science. Moreover, when it is realized that macroeconomics sets out rather audaciously to explain the behavior of the *whole* economy, one should not be surprised that there are gaps in our knowledge. No one knows if these gaps will ever be closed; but, if this writer knows his profession, it won't be for lack of trying.

ADDITIONAL READINGS

The footnotes in this chapter will lead the reader deep into the relevant literature. In addition, he will enjoy reading a debate between Friedman and Walter W. Heller, former chairman of President Kennedy's Council of Economic Advisors:

M. FRIEDMAN and W. W. HELLER. *Monetary vs. Fiscal Policy: A Dialogue.* New York: W. W. Norton & Co., 1969.

AUTHOR INDEX

369

SUBJECT INDEX

*This book has been set in 12 point Garamond
Intertype, leaded 1 point, and 10 point Garamond Intertype, leaded 2 points. Chapter numbers and titles are in 18 point Helvetica. The
size of the type page is 27 by 46 picas.*